I went to a bento shop for eight years straight on days I was working on a manuscript, and now it's closed. A food crisis looms. The katsu-and-rice combo at a wholesale cost has been lost. With this dark development, the era descends into chaos... This is *World Trigger*, volume 21.

—**Daisuke Ashihara, 2019**

Daisuke Ashihara began his manga career at the age of 27 when his manga *Room 303* won second place in the 75th Tezuka Awards. His first series, *Super Dog Rilienthal*, began serialization in *Weekly Shonen Jump* in 2009. *World Trigger* is his second serialized work in *Weekly Shonen Jump*. He is also the author of several shorter works, including the one-shots *Super Dog Rilienthal*, *Trigger Keeper* and *Elite Agent Jin*.

TRIGGER

WORLD TRIGGER VOL. 21
SHONEN JUMP Manga Edition

STORY AND ART BY DAISUKE ASHIHARA

Translation/Caleb Cook
Touch-Up Art & Lettering/Annaliese "Ace" Christman
Design/Julian [JR] Robinson
Editor/Marlene First

Printed in the U.S.A.

Published by VIZ Media, LLC
P.O. Box 77010
San Francisco, CA 94107

10 9 8 7 6 5 4 3 2 1
First printing, November 2020

viz.com

PARENTAL ADVISORY
WORLD TRIGGER is rated T for Teen and
is recommended for ages 13 and up. This
volume contains fantasy violence.

SHONEN JUMP
shonenjump.com

21

DAISUKE ASHIHARA

WORLD TRIGGER

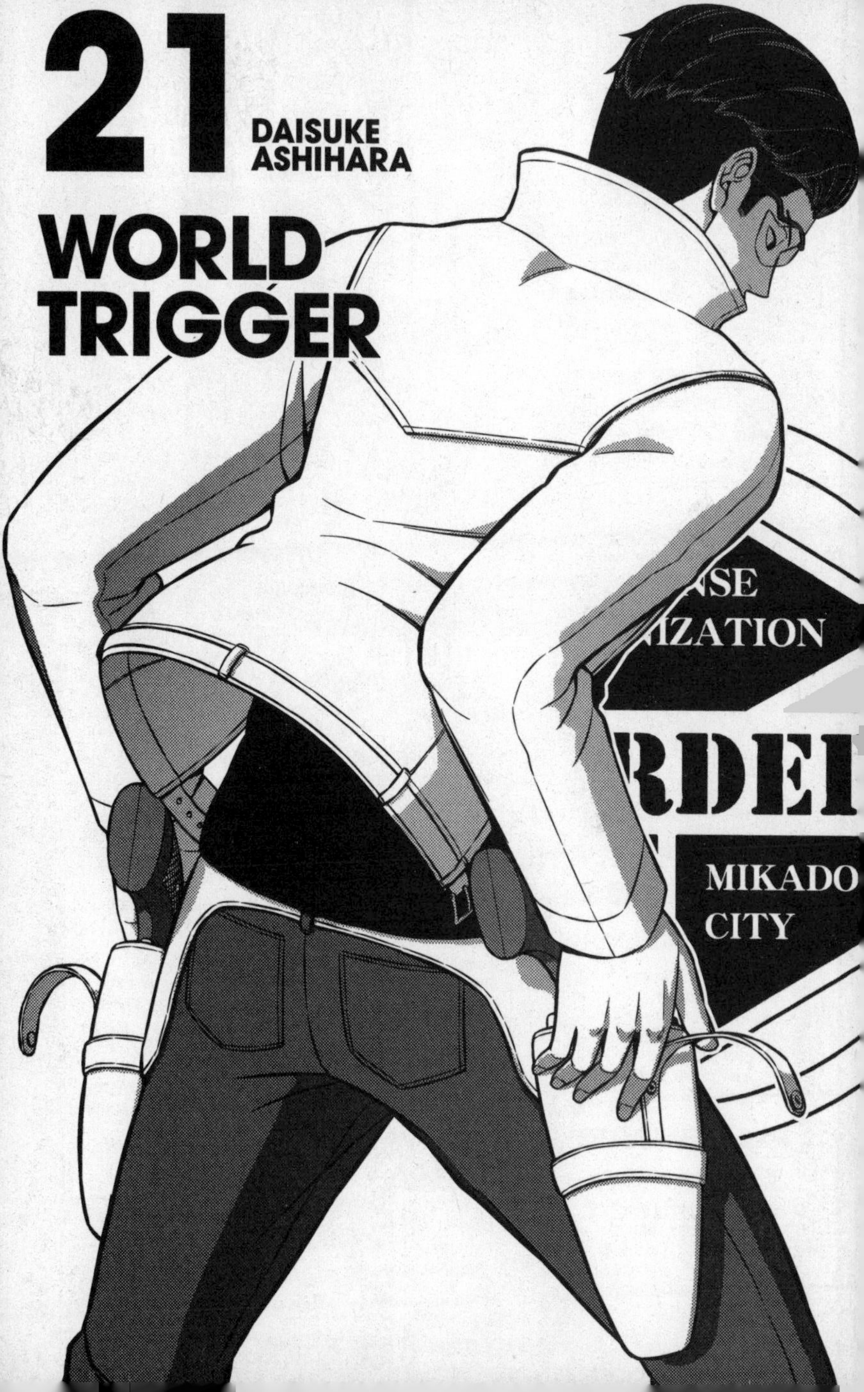
MIKADO
CITY

WORLD TRIGGER DATA BASE

BORDER

An agency founded to protect the city's peace from Neighbors.

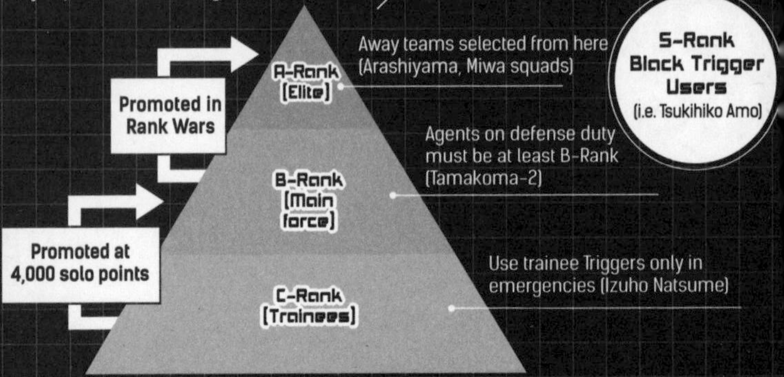

Away teams selected from here (Arashiyama, Miwa squads)
A-Rank (Elite)
Promoted in Rank Wars
S-Rank Black Trigger Users (i.e. Tsukihiko Amo)
Agents on defense duty must be at least B-Rank (Tamakoma-2)
B-Rank (Main force)
Promoted at 4,000 solo points
Use trainee Triggers only in emergencies (Izuho Natsume)
C-Rank (Trainees)

TRIGGER

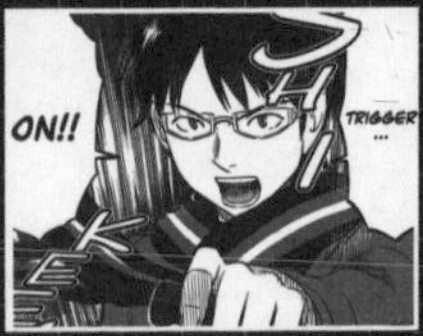

ON!!
TRIGGER...

A technology created by Neighbors to manipulate Trion. Used mainly as weapons, Triggers come in various types.

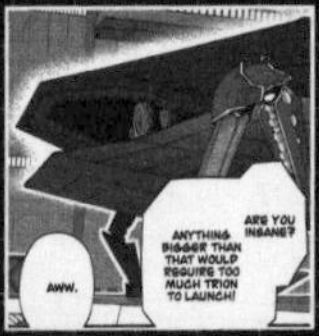

ARE YOU INSANE?
ANYTHING BIGGER THAN THAT WOULD REQUIRE TOO MUCH TRION TO LAUNCH!
AWW.

◀ A
miss
ships
also
run
Trion

POSITIONS

Border classifies them into three groups: Attacker, Gunner and Sniper.

Attacker

Close-range attacks. Weapons include: close-range Scorpions that are good for surprise attacks, the balanced Kogetsu sword, and the defense-heavy Raygust.

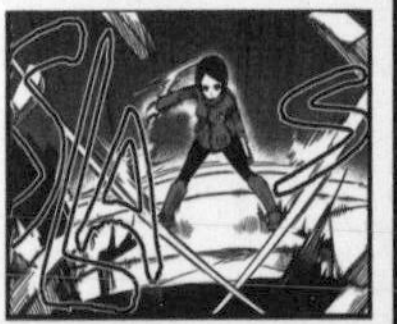

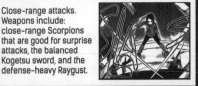

Gunner

Shoots from mid-range. There are several types of bullets, including multipurpose Asteroids, twisting Vipers, exploding Meteors, and tracking Hounds. People who don't use gun-shaped Triggers are called Shooters.

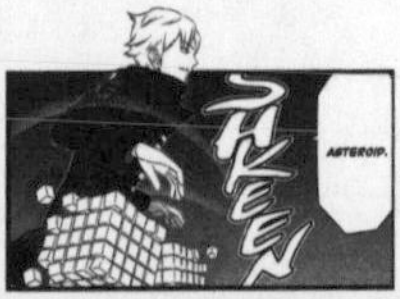

ASTEROID.
SHKEEN

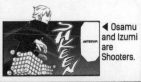

◀ Osamu and Izumi are Shooters.

Sniper

Fires from a long distance. There are three sniping rifles: the well-balanced Egret, the light and easy Lightning, and the powerful but unwieldy Ibis.

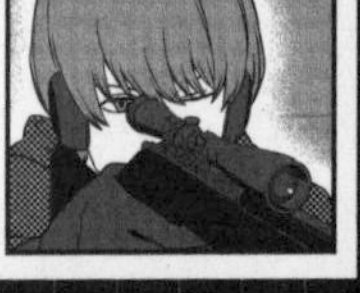

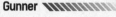

Operator

Supports combatants by relaying information such as enemy positions and abilities.

RANK WARS

Practice matches between Border agents. Promotions in Border are based on good results in the Rank Wars and defense duty achievements.

B-Rank agents are split into top, middle, and bottom groups. Three to four teams fight in a melee battle. Defeating an opposing squad member earns you one point and surviving to the end nets two points. Top teams from the previous season get a bonus.

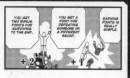

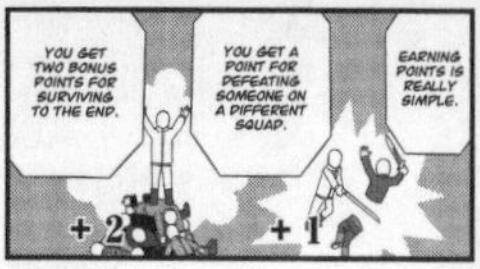
EARNING POINTS IS REALLY SIMPLE.
YOU GET A POINT FOR DEFEATING SOMEONE ON A DIFFERENT SQUAD.
YOU GET TWO BONUS POINTS FOR SURVIVING TO THE END.
+2
+1

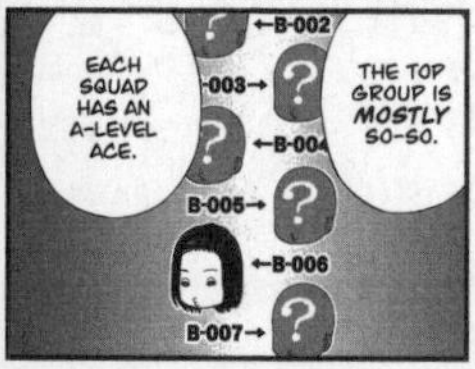
THE TOP GROUP IS MOSTLY SO-SO.
EACH SQUAD HAS AN A-LEVEL ACE.
←B-002
-003→
←B-004
B-005→
←B-006
B-007→

B-Rank middle groups have set strategies. Top groups all have an A-Rank level ace.

The lowest-ranked team in each match gets to pick the stage.

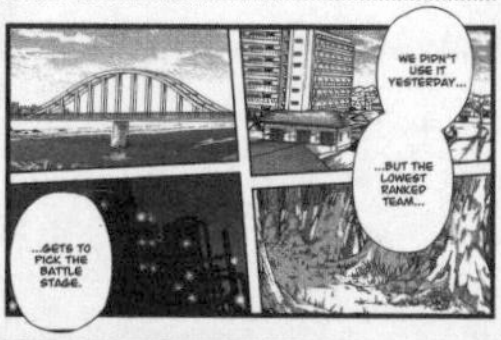
WE DIDN'T USE IT YESTERDAY...
...BUT THE LOWEST RANKED TEAM...
...GETS TO PICK THE BATTLE STAGE.

A-Rank

Top two B-Rank squads get to challenge A-Rank.

B-Rank

Agents ▶ (B-Rank and above) can't fight trainees (C-Rank) for points.

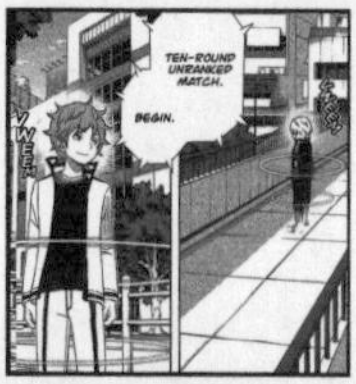
TEN-ROUND UNRANKED MATCH.
BEGIN.

C-Rank Wars are fought through solo matches. Beating someone with more points than you gets you a lot of points. On the other hand, beating someone with fewer points doesn't get you as many.

C-Rank

STORY

About four years ago, a Gate connecting to another dimension opened in Mikado City, leading to the appearance of invaders called Neighbors. After the establishment of the Border Defence Agency, people were able to return to their normal lives.

Osamu Mikumo is a junior high student who meets Yuma Kuga, a Neighbor. Yuma is targeted for capture by Border, but Tamakoma branch agent Yuichi Jin steps in to help. He convinces Yuma to join Border instead, then gives his Black Trigger to HQ in exchange for Yuma's enlistment. Now Osamu, Yuma and Osamu's friend Chika work toward making A-Rank together.

Aftokrator, the largest military nation in the Neighborhood, begins another large-scale invasion!! Border succeeds in driving them back, but over 30 C-Rank trainees are kidnapped in the process. Border implements more plans for away missions to retrieve the missing Agents.

Osamu's squad, Tamakoma-2, enters the Rank Wars for a chance to be chosen for away missions. In order to be chosen, Osamu and his squad must reach No. 2 or higher in B-rank. Osamu's new strategy leads his squad to victory in the fifth and sixth rounds. of the rank wars, Hyuse joins Tamakoma-2 and performs well the seventh round,, leading Tamakoma-2 to No. 3 in B-rank. All that remains is round eight. In the next strategy meeting, Hyuse wonders if Chika really can shoot people...

WORLD TRIGGER CHARACTERS

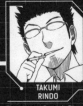

TAMAKOMA BRANCH

Understanding toward Neighbors. Considered divergent from Border's main philosophy.

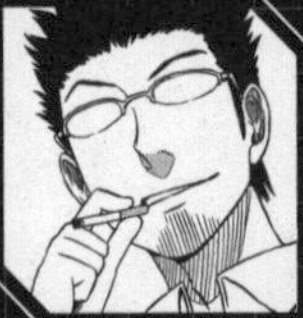

TAKUMI RINDO

Tamakoma Branch Director.

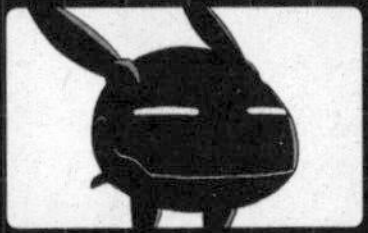

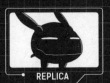

REPLICA

Yuma's chaperone. Missing after recent invasion.

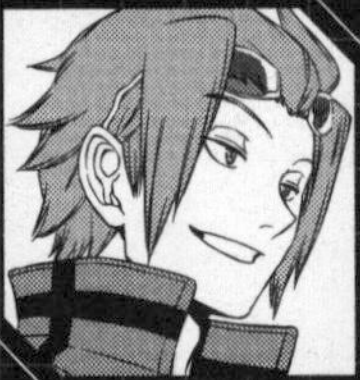

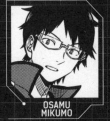

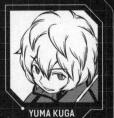

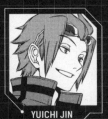

YUICHI JIN

Former S-Rank Black Trigger user. His Side Effect lets him see the future.

TAMAKOMA-2

Tamakoma's B-Rank squad, aiming to get promoted to A-Rank.

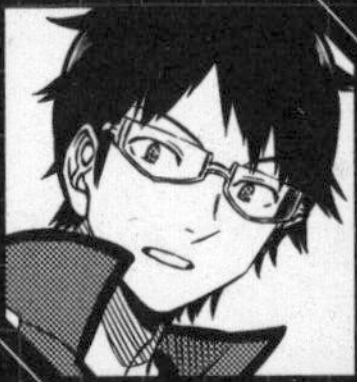

OSAMU MIKUMO

Ninth-grader who's compelled to help those in trouble. Captain of Tamakoma-2 (Mikumo squad).

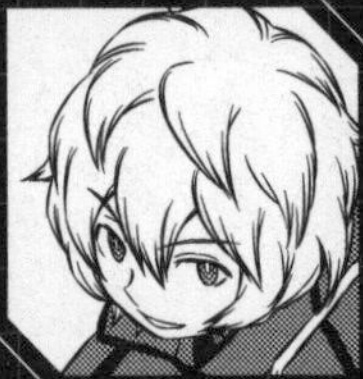

YUMA KUGA

A Neighbor who carries a Black Trigger.

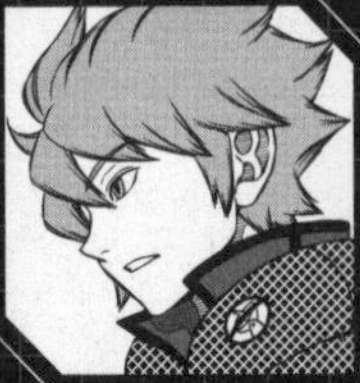

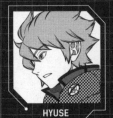

HYUSE

A Neighbor from Aftokrator captured during the large-scale invasion.

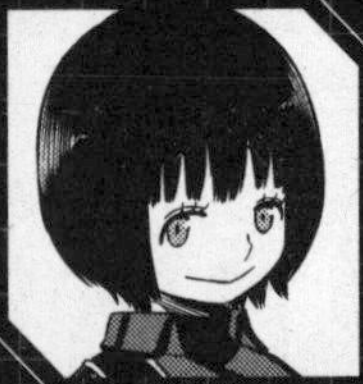

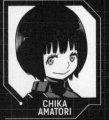

CHIKA AMATORI

Osamu's childhood friend. She has high Trion levels.

TAMAKOMA-1

Tamakoma's A-Rank squad.

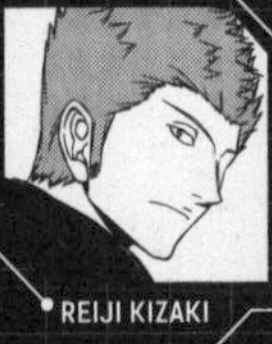

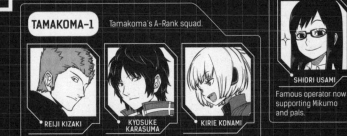

REIJI KIZAKI

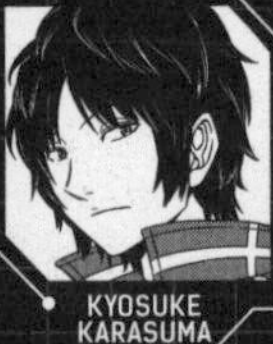

KYOSUKE KARASUMA

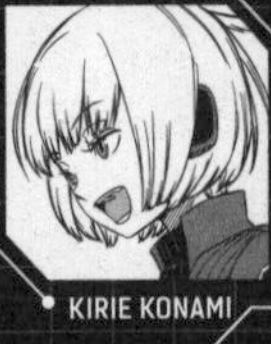

KIRIE KONAMI

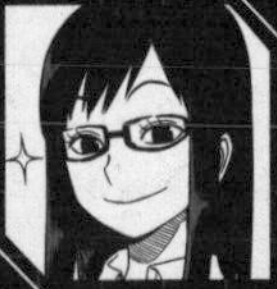

SHIORI USAMI

Famous operator now supporting Mikumo and pals.

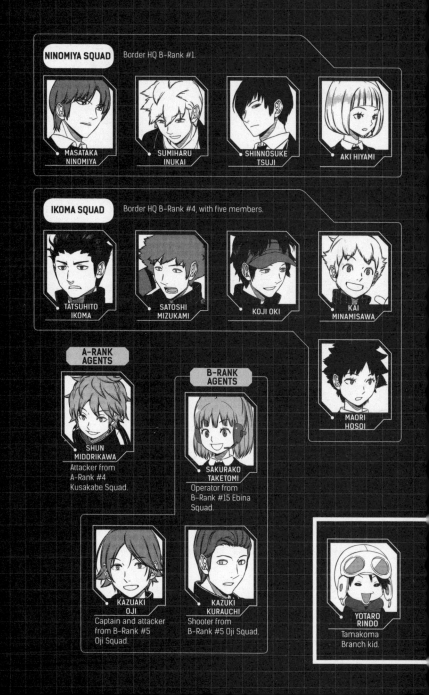

NINOMIYA SQUAD

Border HQ B-Rank #1.

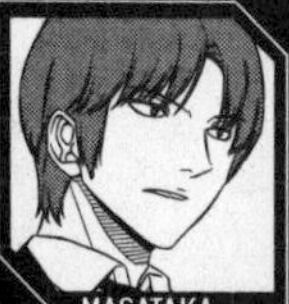
MASATAKA NINOMIYA

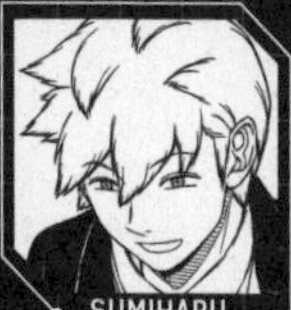
SUMIHARU INUKAI

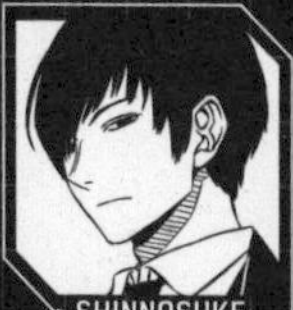
SHINNOSUKE TSUJI

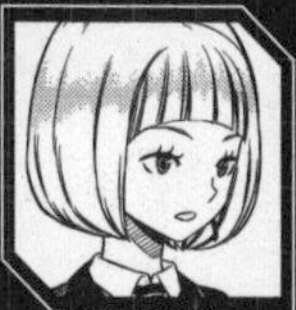
AKI HIYAMI

IKOMA SQUAD

Border HQ B-Rank #4, with five members.

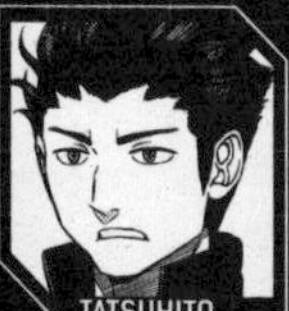
TATSUHITO IKOMA

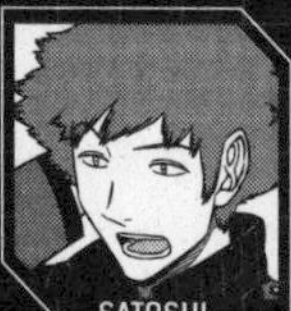
SATOSHI MIZUKAMI

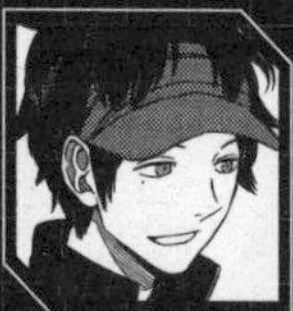
KOJI OKI

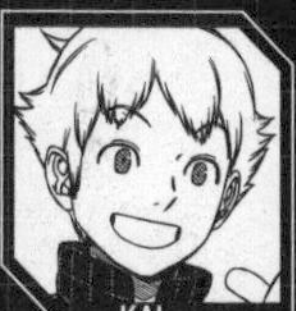
KAI MINAMISAWA

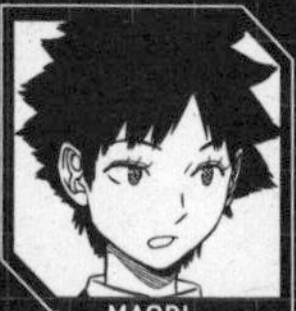
MAORI HOSOI

A-RANK AGENTS

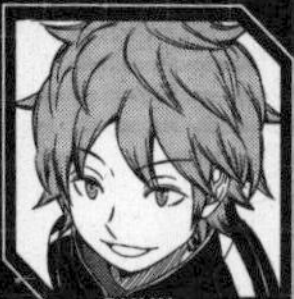
SHUN MIDORIKAWA

Attacker from A-Rank #4 Kusakabe Squad.

B-RANK AGENTS

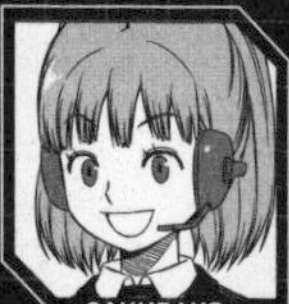
SAKURAKO TAKETOMI

Operator from B-Rank #15 Ebina Squad.

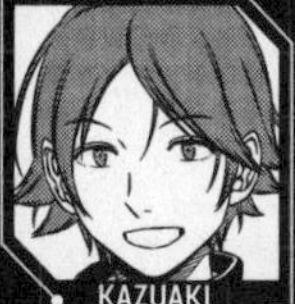
KAZUAKI OJI

Captain and attacker from B-Rank #5 Oji Squad.

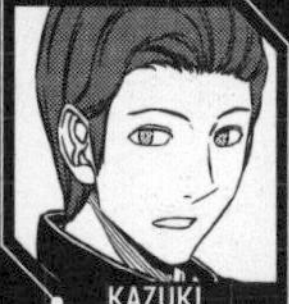
KAZUKI KURAUCHI

Shooter from B-Rank #5 Oji Squad.

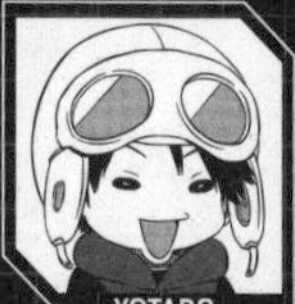
YOTARO RINDO

Tamakoma Branch kid.

WORLD TRIGGER
CONTENTS

2

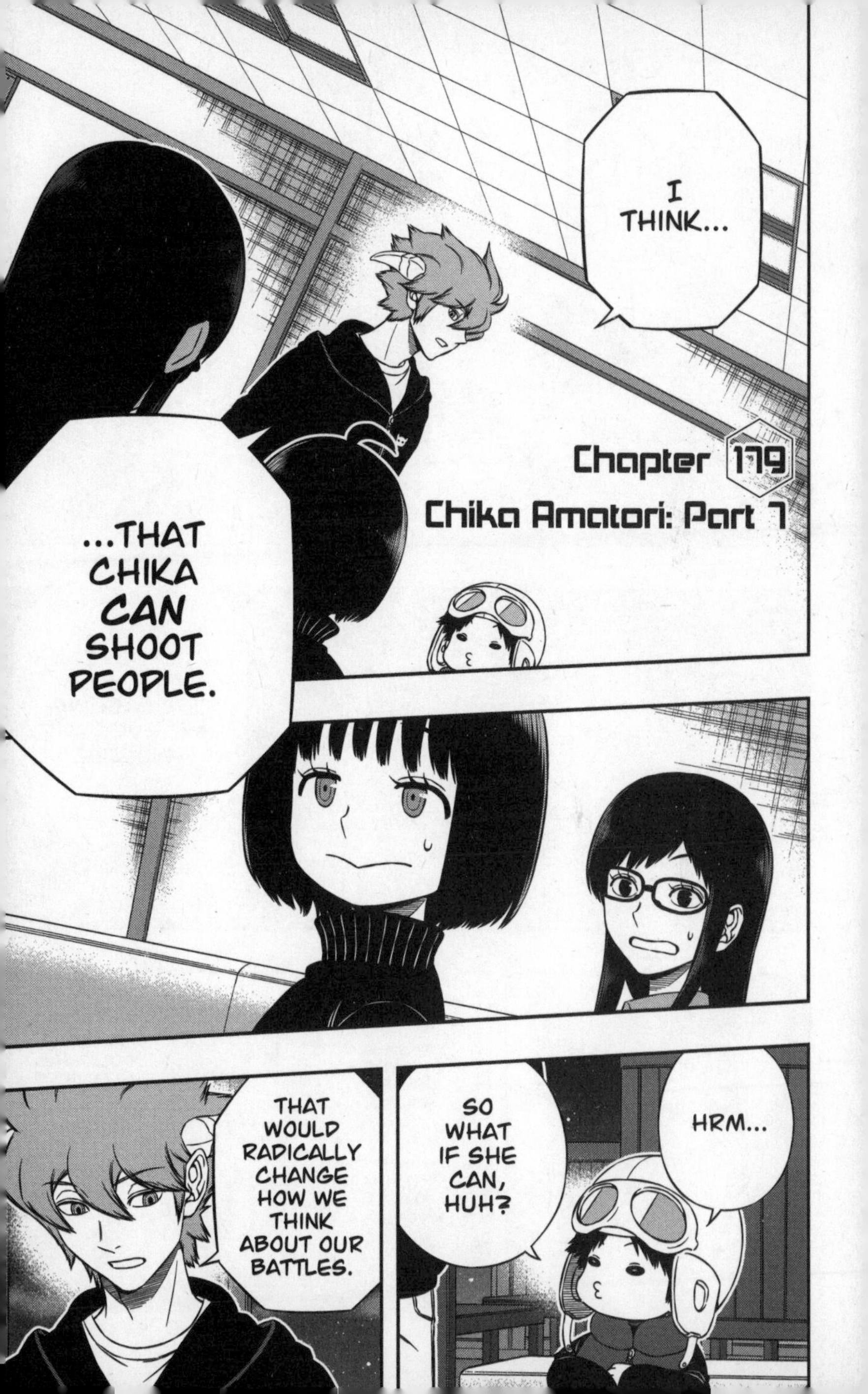
I THINK...
Chapter 179
Chika Amatori: Part 7
...THAT CHIKA CAN SHOOT PEOPLE.
HRM...
SO WHAT IF SHE CAN, HUH?
THAT WOULD RADICALLY CHANGE HOW WE THINK ABOUT OUR BATTLES.

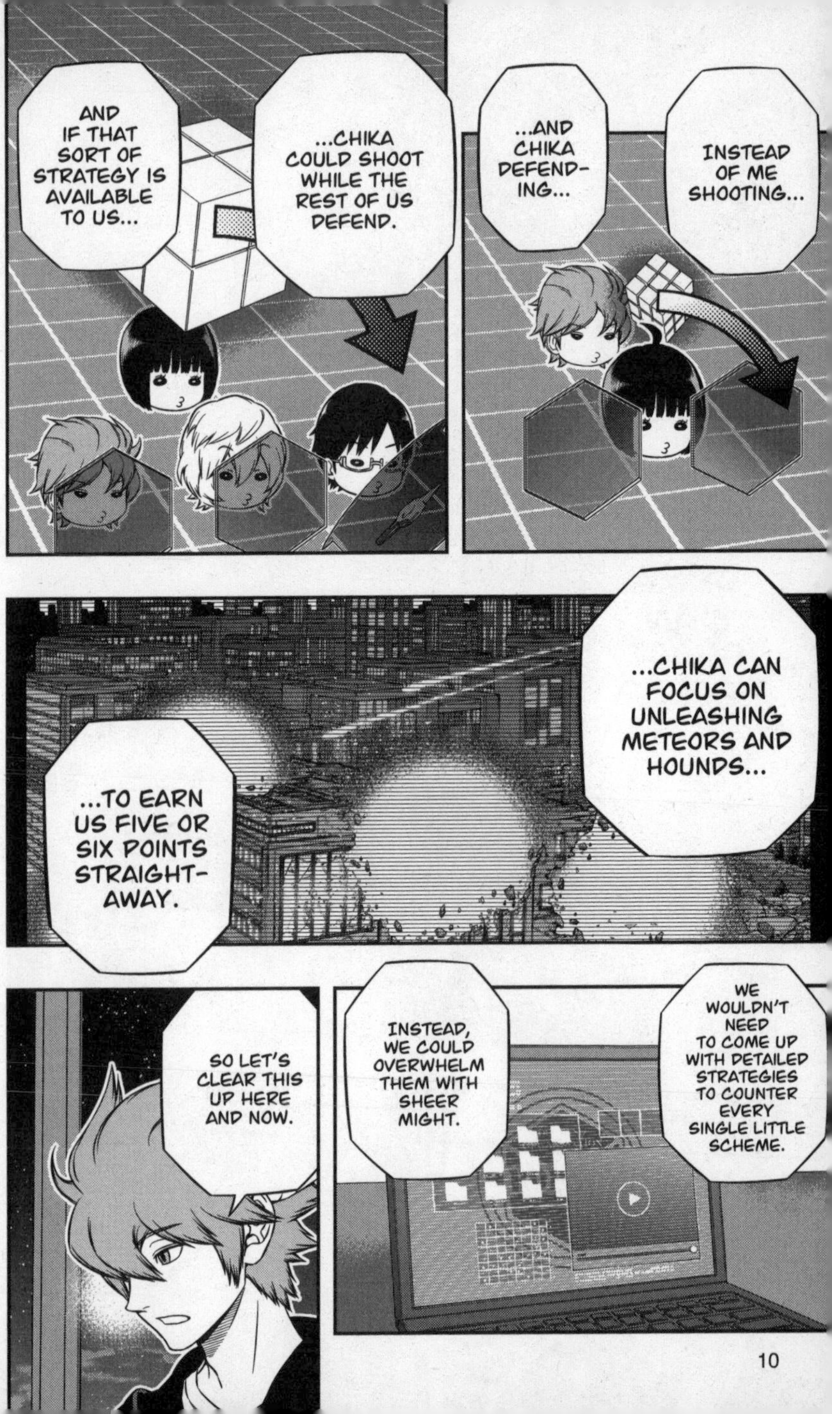
INSTEAD OF ME SHOOTING...
...AND CHIKA DEFENDING...
...CHIKA COULD SHOOT WHILE THE REST OF US DEFEND.
AND IF THAT SORT OF STRATEGY IS AVAILABLE TO US...
...CHIKA CAN FOCUS ON UNLEASHING METEORS AND HOUNDS...
...TO EARN US FIVE OR SIX POINTS STRAIGHT-AWAY.
WE WOULDN'T NEED TO COME UP WITH DETAILED STRATEGIES TO COUNTER EVERY SINGLE LITTLE SCHEME.
INSTEAD, WE COULD OVERWHELM THEM WITH SHEER MIGHT.
SO LET'S CLEAR THIS UP HERE AND NOW.

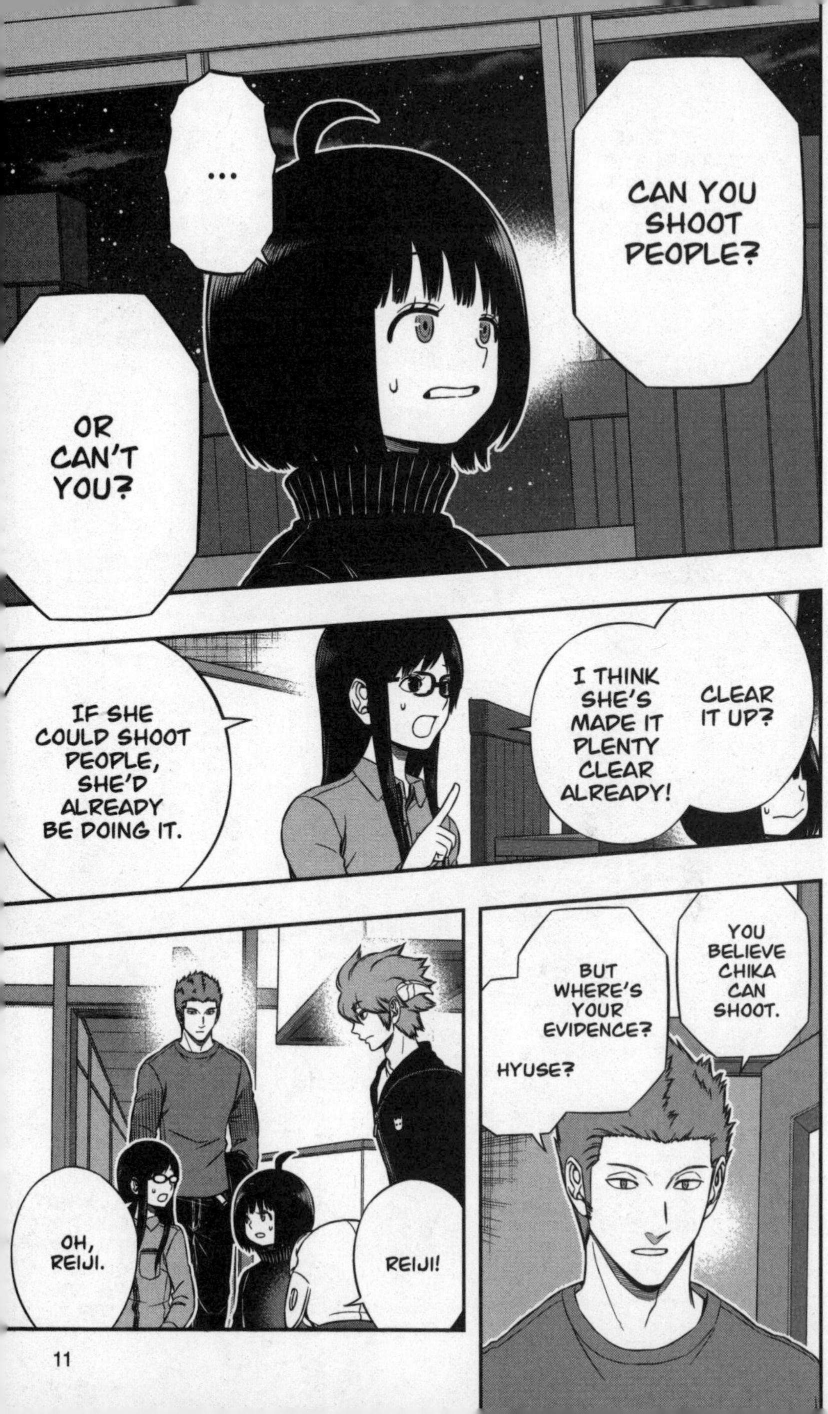

CAN YOU SHOOT PEOPLE?
...
OR CAN'T YOU?
CLEAR IT UP?
I THINK SHE'S MADE IT PLENTY CLEAR ALREADY!
IF SHE COULD SHOOT PEOPLE, SHE'D ALREADY BE DOING IT.
YOU BELIEVE CHIKA CAN SHOOT.
BUT WHERE'S YOUR EVIDENCE?
HYUSE?
REIJI!
OH, REIJI.

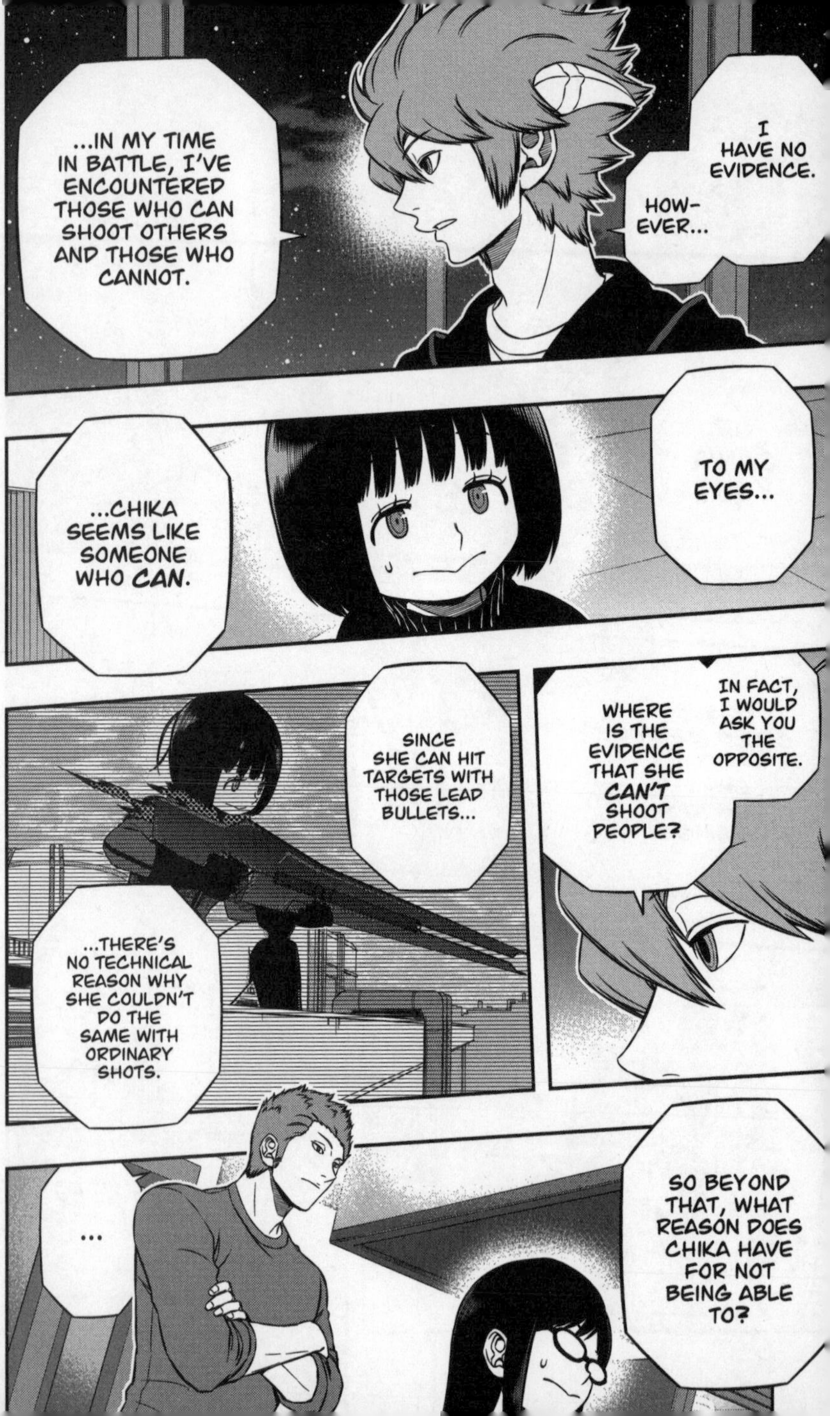
I HAVE NO EVIDENCE.
HOW-EVER...
...IN MY TIME IN BATTLE, I'VE ENCOUNTERED THOSE WHO CAN SHOOT OTHERS AND THOSE WHO CANNOT.
TO MY EYES...
...CHIKA SEEMS LIKE SOMEONE WHO **CAN**.
IN FACT, I WOULD ASK YOU THE OPPOSITE.
WHERE IS THE EVIDENCE THAT SHE **CAN'T** SHOOT PEOPLE?
SINCE SHE CAN HIT TARGETS WITH THOSE LEAD BULLETS...
...THERE'S NO TECHNICAL REASON WHY SHE COULDN'T DO THE SAME WITH ORDINARY SHOTS.
SO BEYOND THAT, WHAT REASON DOES CHIKA HAVE FOR NOT BEING ABLE TO?
...

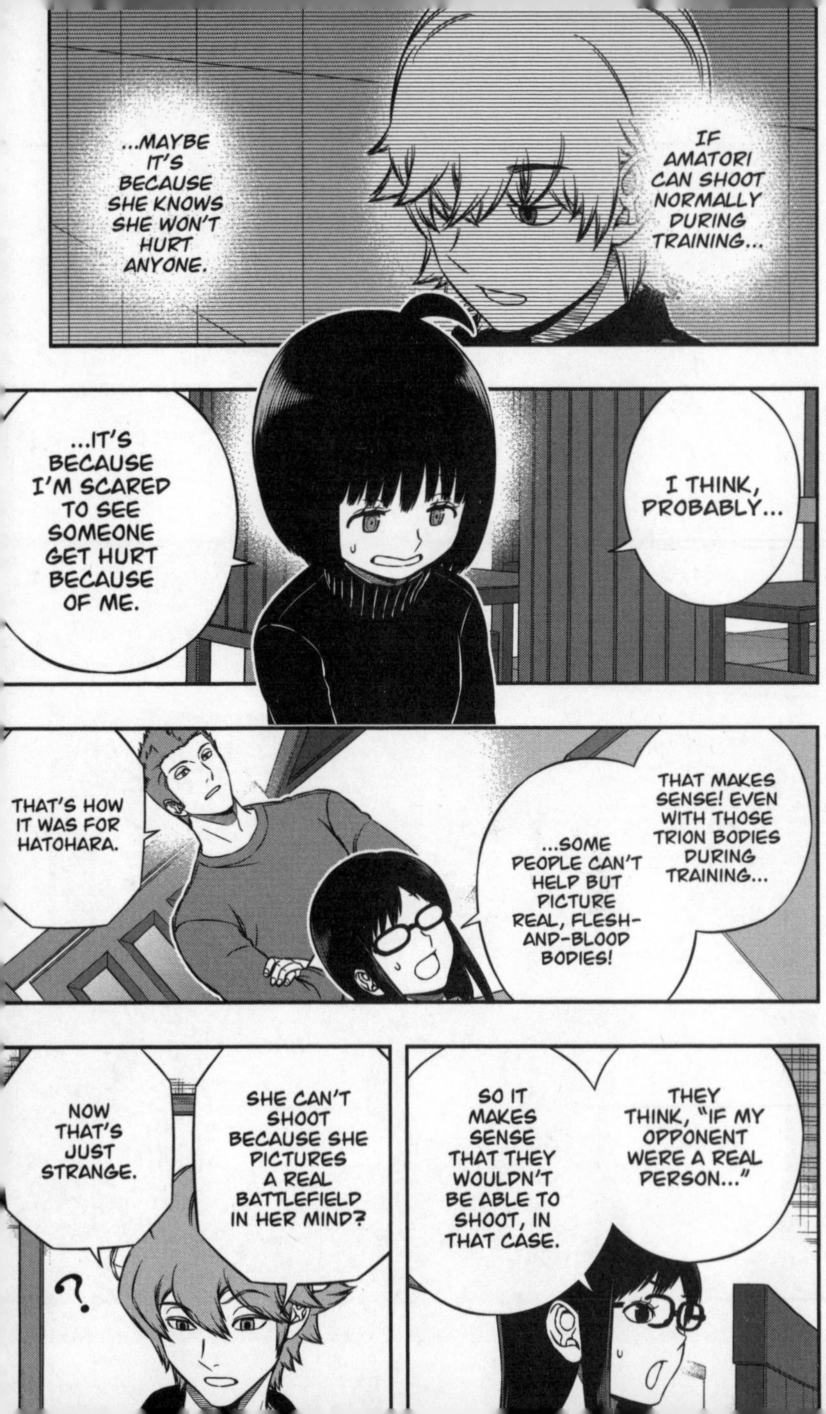
IF AMATORI CAN SHOOT NORMALLY DURING TRAINING...
...MAYBE IT'S BECAUSE SHE KNOWS SHE WON'T HURT ANYONE.
I THINK, PROBABLY...
...IT'S BECAUSE I'M SCARED TO SEE SOMEONE GET HURT BECAUSE OF ME.
THAT MAKES SENSE! EVEN WITH THOSE TRION BODIES DURING TRAINING...
...SOME PEOPLE CAN'T HELP BUT PICTURE REAL, FLESH-AND-BLOOD BODIES!
THAT'S HOW IT WAS FOR HATOHARA.
THEY THINK, "IF MY OPPONENT WERE A REAL PERSON..."
SO IT MAKES SENSE THAT THEY WOULDN'T BE ABLE TO SHOOT, IN THAT CASE.
SHE CAN'T SHOOT BECAUSE SHE PICTURES A REAL BATTLEFIELD IN HER MIND?
NOW THAT'S JUST STRANGE.
?

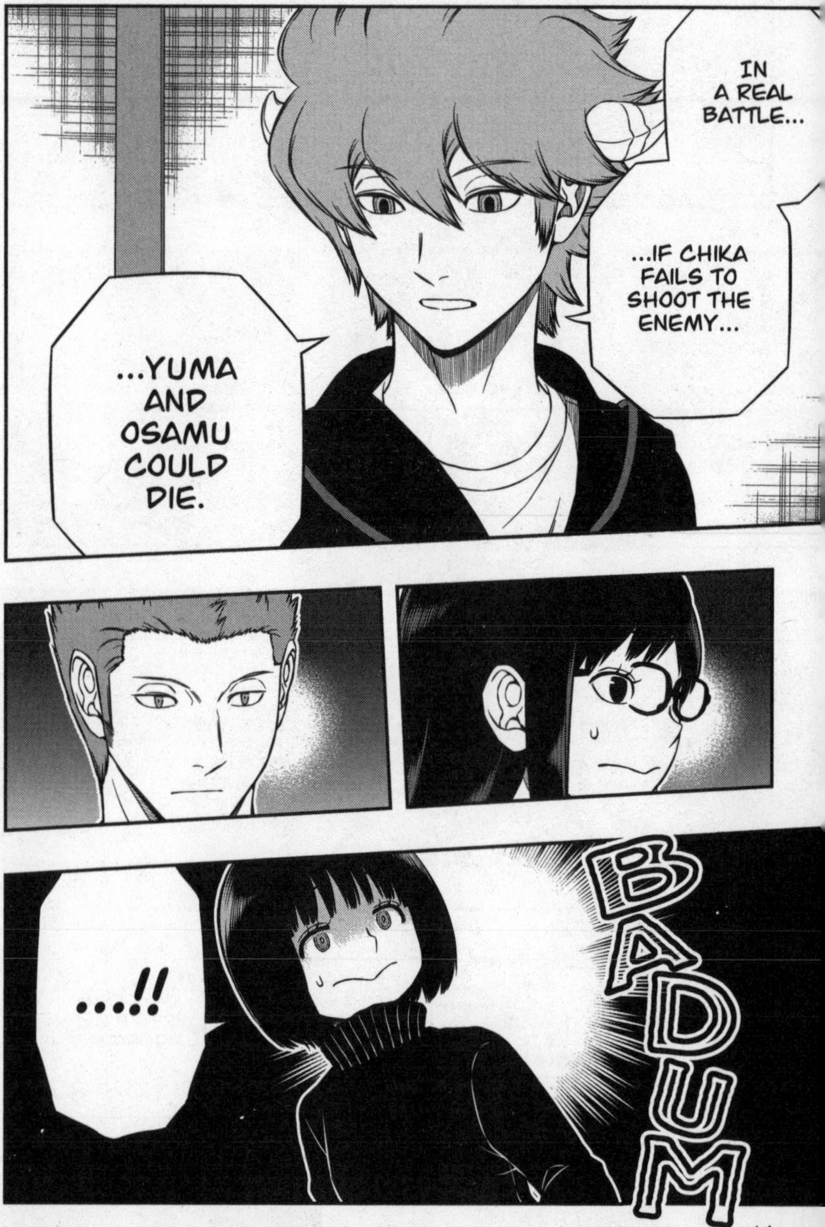
IN A REAL BATTLE...
...IF CHIKA FAILS TO SHOOT THE ENEMY...
...YUMA AND OSAMU COULD DIE.
BADUM
...!!

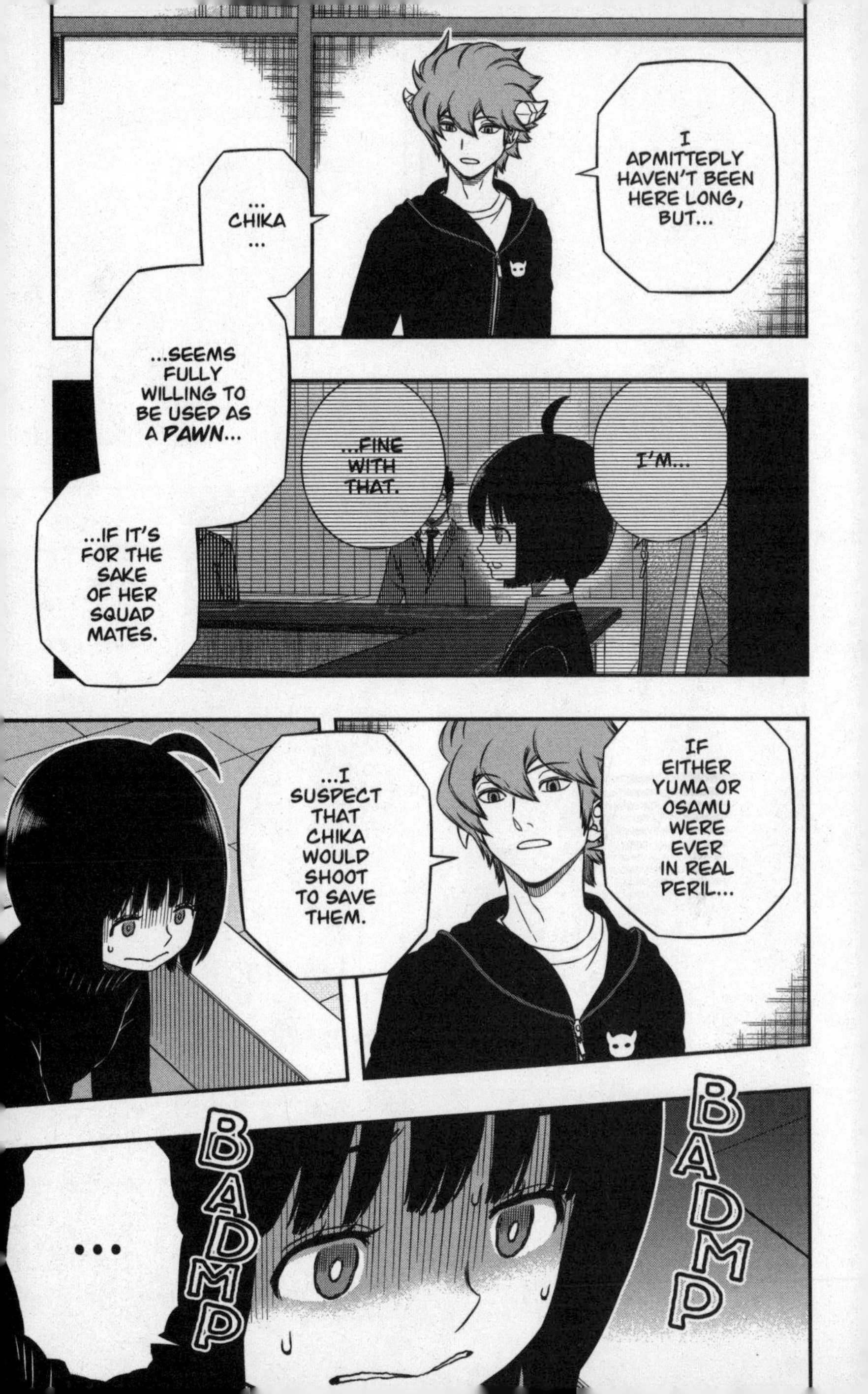
I ADMITTEDLY HAVEN'T BEEN HERE LONG, BUT...
... CHIKA ...
...SEEMS FULLY WILLING TO BE USED AS A PAWN...
I'M...
...FINE WITH THAT.
...IF IT'S FOR THE SAKE OF HER SQUAD MATES.
IF EITHER YUMA OR OSAMU WERE EVER IN REAL PERIL...
...I SUSPECT THAT CHIKA WOULD SHOOT TO SAVE THEM.
BADMP
BADMP
...

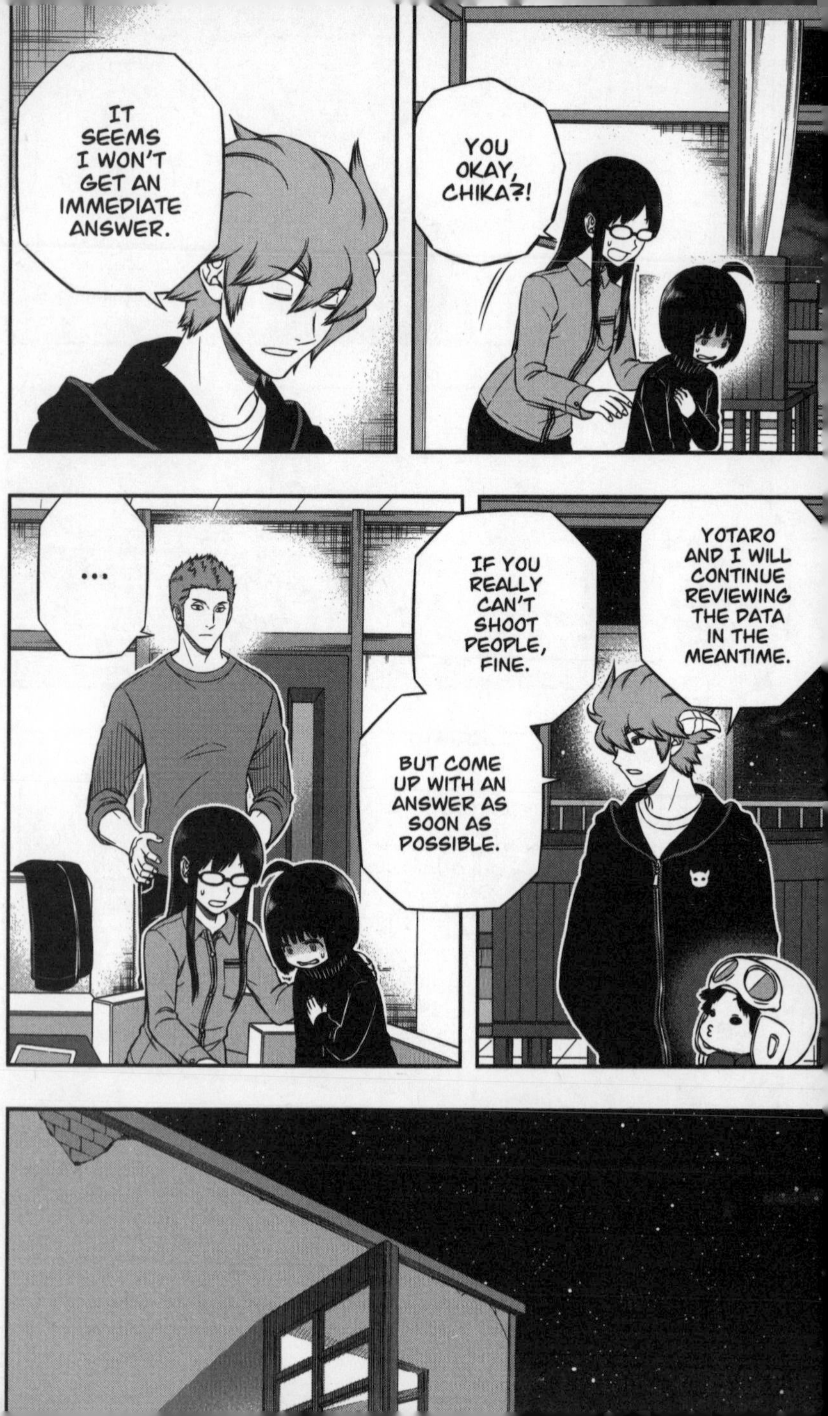
YOU OKAY, CHIKA?!
IT SEEMS I WON'T GET AN IMMEDIATE ANSWER.
YOTARO AND I WILL CONTINUE REVIEWING THE DATA IN THE MEANTIME.
IF YOU REALLY CAN'T SHOOT PEOPLE, FINE.
BUT COME UP WITH AN ANSWER AS SOON AS POSSIBLE.
...

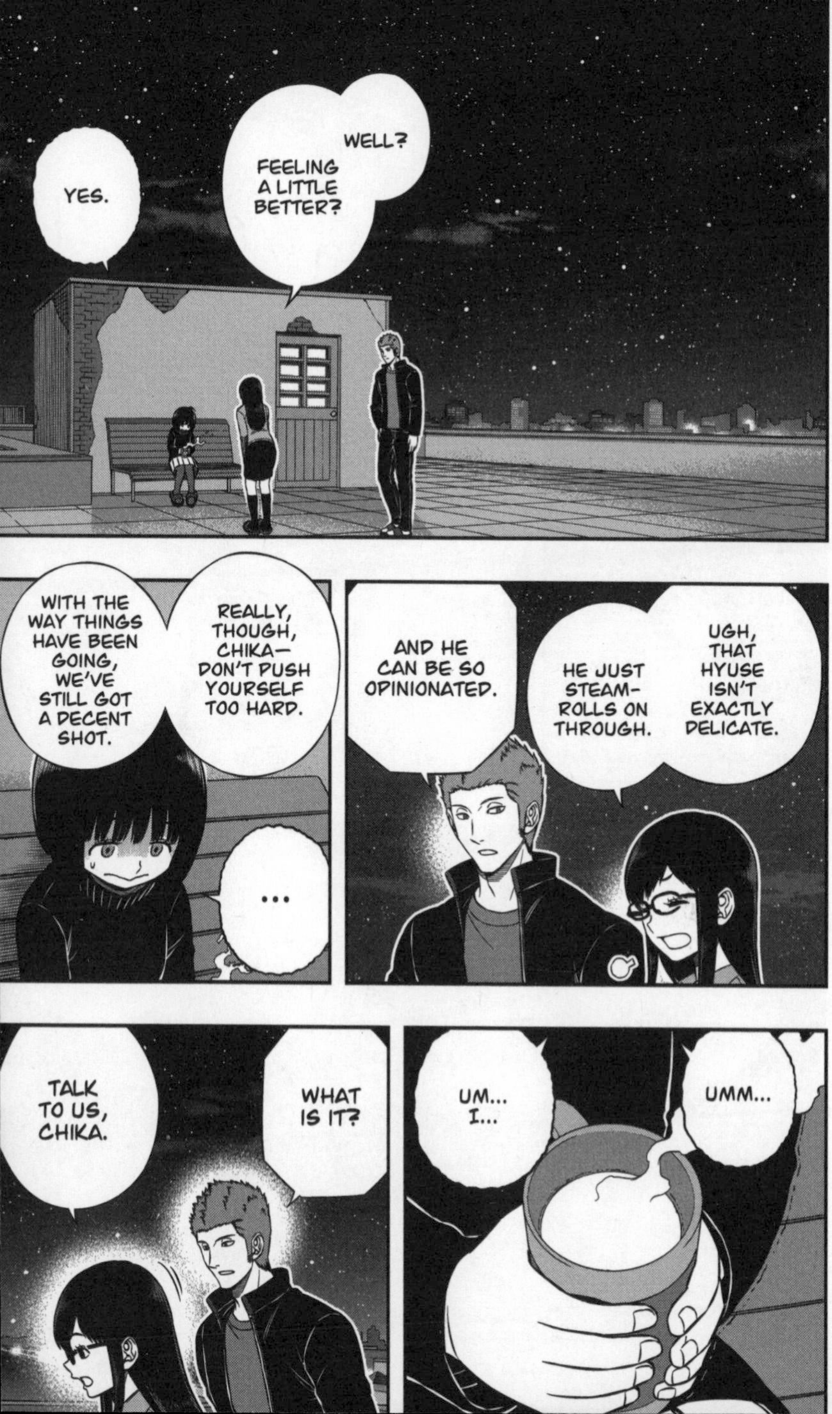
WELL?
FEELING A LITTLE BETTER?
YES.
UGH, THAT HYUSE ISN'T EXACTLY DELICATE.
HE JUST STEAM-ROLLS ON THROUGH.
AND HE CAN BE SO OPINIONATED.
REALLY, THOUGH, CHIKA— DON'T PUSH YOURSELF TOO HARD.
WITH THE WAY THINGS HAVE BEEN GOING, WE'VE STILL GOT A DECENT SHOT.
...
UMM...
UM... I...
WHAT IS IT?
TALK TO US, CHIKA.

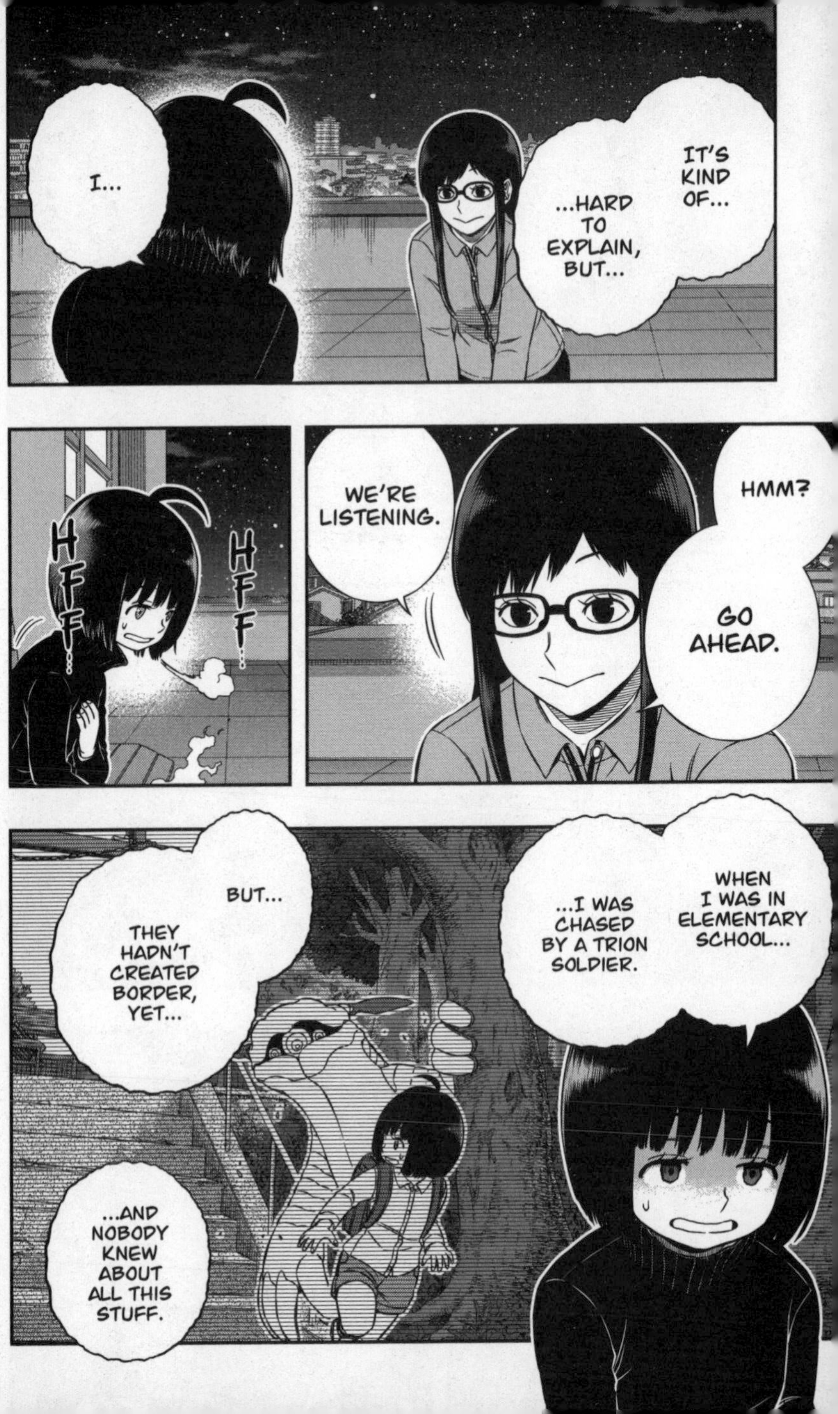
IT'S KIND OF...
...HARD TO EXPLAIN, BUT...
I...
HMM?
GO AHEAD.
WE'RE LISTENING.
HFF
HFF...
WHEN I WAS IN ELEMENTARY SCHOOL...
...I WAS CHASED BY A TRION SOLDIER.
BUT...
THEY HADN'T CREATED BORDER, YET...
...AND NOBODY KNEW ABOUT ALL THIS STUFF.

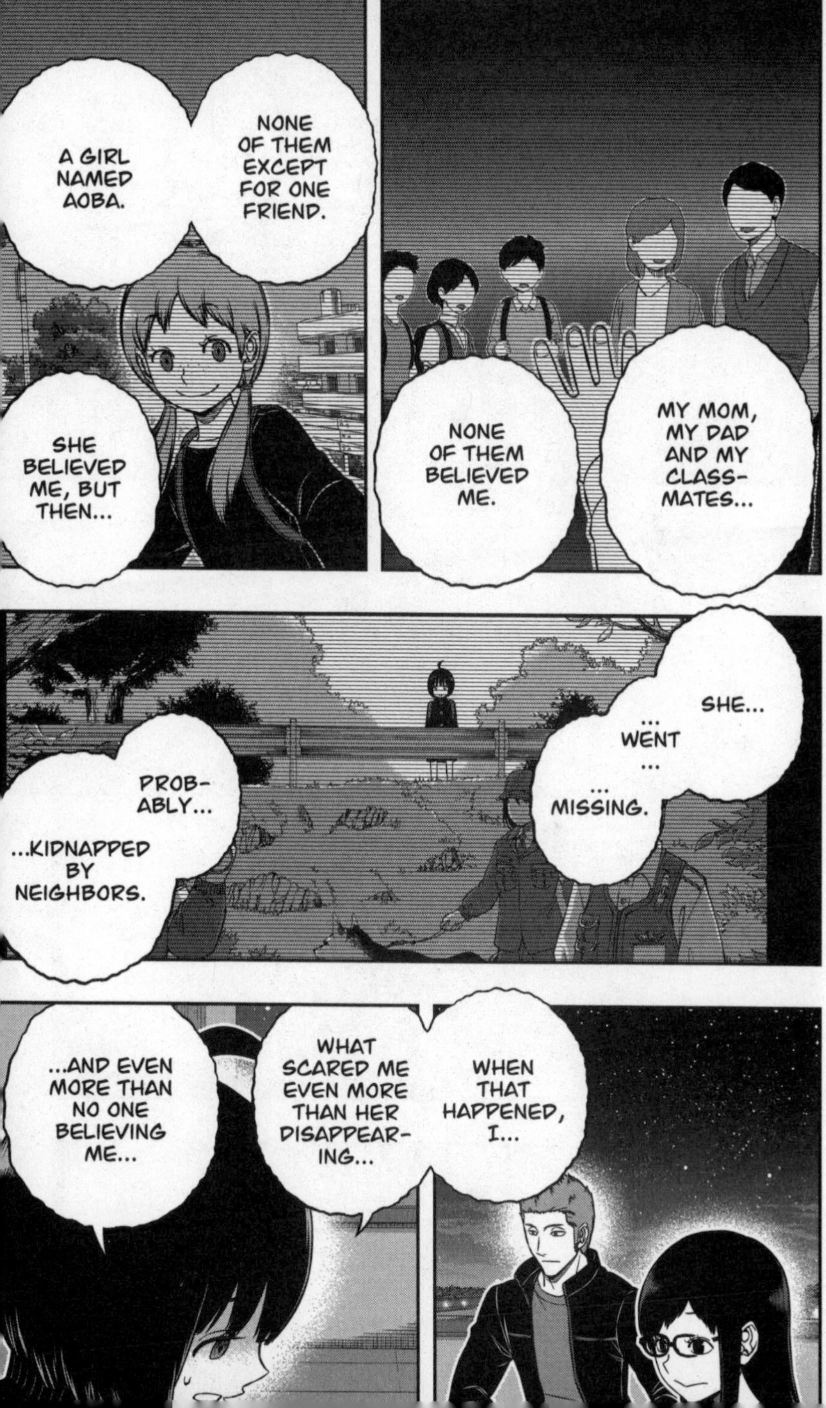
MY MOM, MY DAD AND MY CLASSMATES...
NONE OF THEM BELIEVED ME.
NONE OF THEM EXCEPT FOR ONE FRIEND.
A GIRL NAMED AOBA.
SHE BELIEVED ME, BUT THEN...
SHE... ...WENT... ...MISSING.
PROBABLY... ...KIDNAPPED BY NEIGHBORS.
WHEN THAT HAPPENED, I...
WHAT SCARED ME EVEN MORE THAN HER DISAPPEARING...
...AND EVEN MORE THAN NO ONE BELIEVING ME...

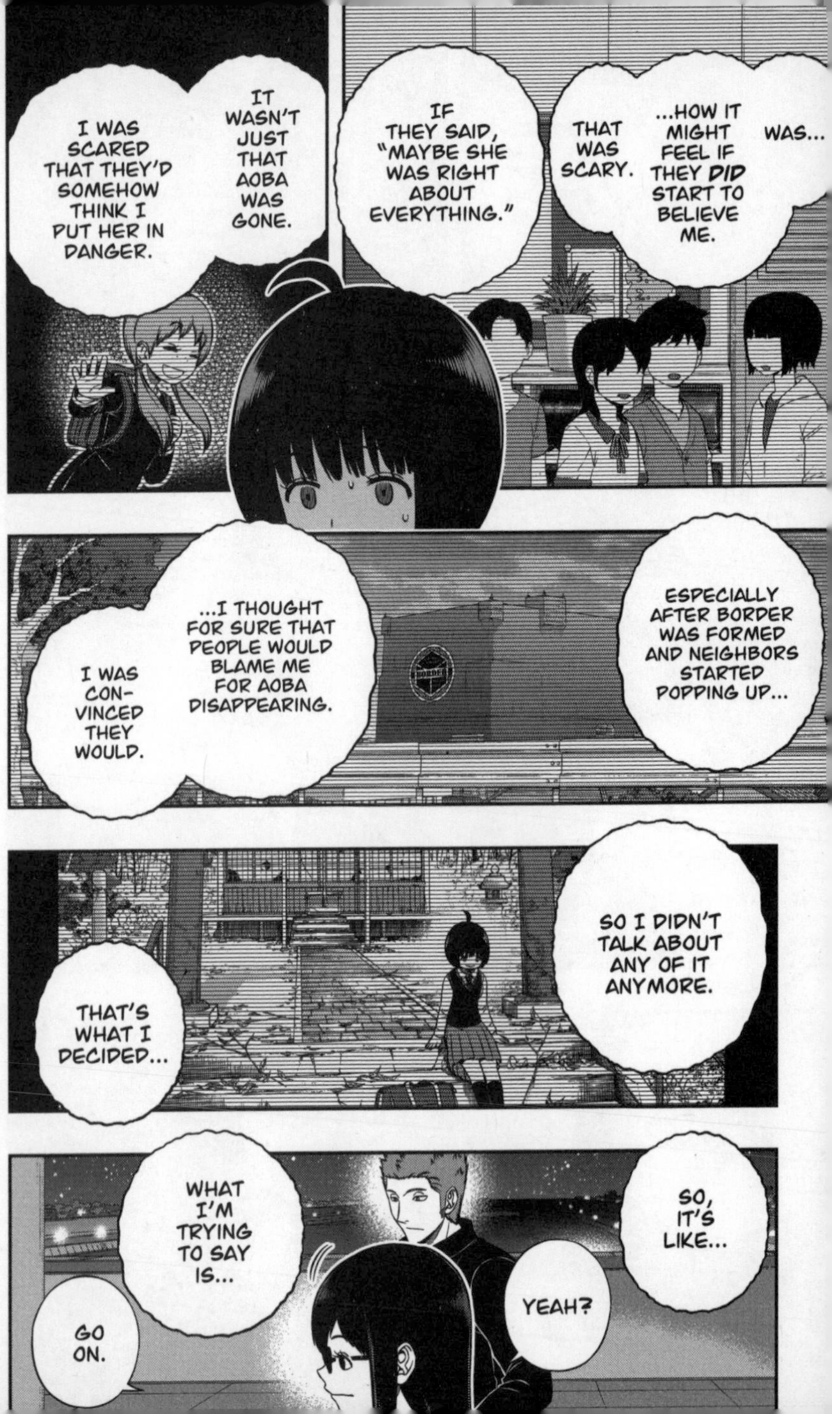
WAS...
...HOW IT MIGHT FEEL IF THEY *DID* START TO BELIEVE ME.
THAT WAS SCARY.
IF THEY SAID, "MAYBE SHE WAS RIGHT ABOUT EVERYTHING."
IT WASN'T JUST THAT AOBA WAS GONE.
I WAS SCARED THAT THEY'D SOMEHOW THINK I PUT HER IN DANGER.
ESPECIALLY AFTER BORDER WAS FORMED AND NEIGHBORS STARTED POPPING UP...
...I THOUGHT FOR SURE THAT PEOPLE WOULD BLAME ME FOR AOBA DISAPPEARING.
I WAS CON-VINCED THEY WOULD.
SO I DIDN'T TALK ABOUT ANY OF IT ANYMORE.
THAT'S WHAT I DECIDED...
SO, IT'S LIKE...
WHAT I'M TRYING TO SAY IS...
YEAH?
GO ON.

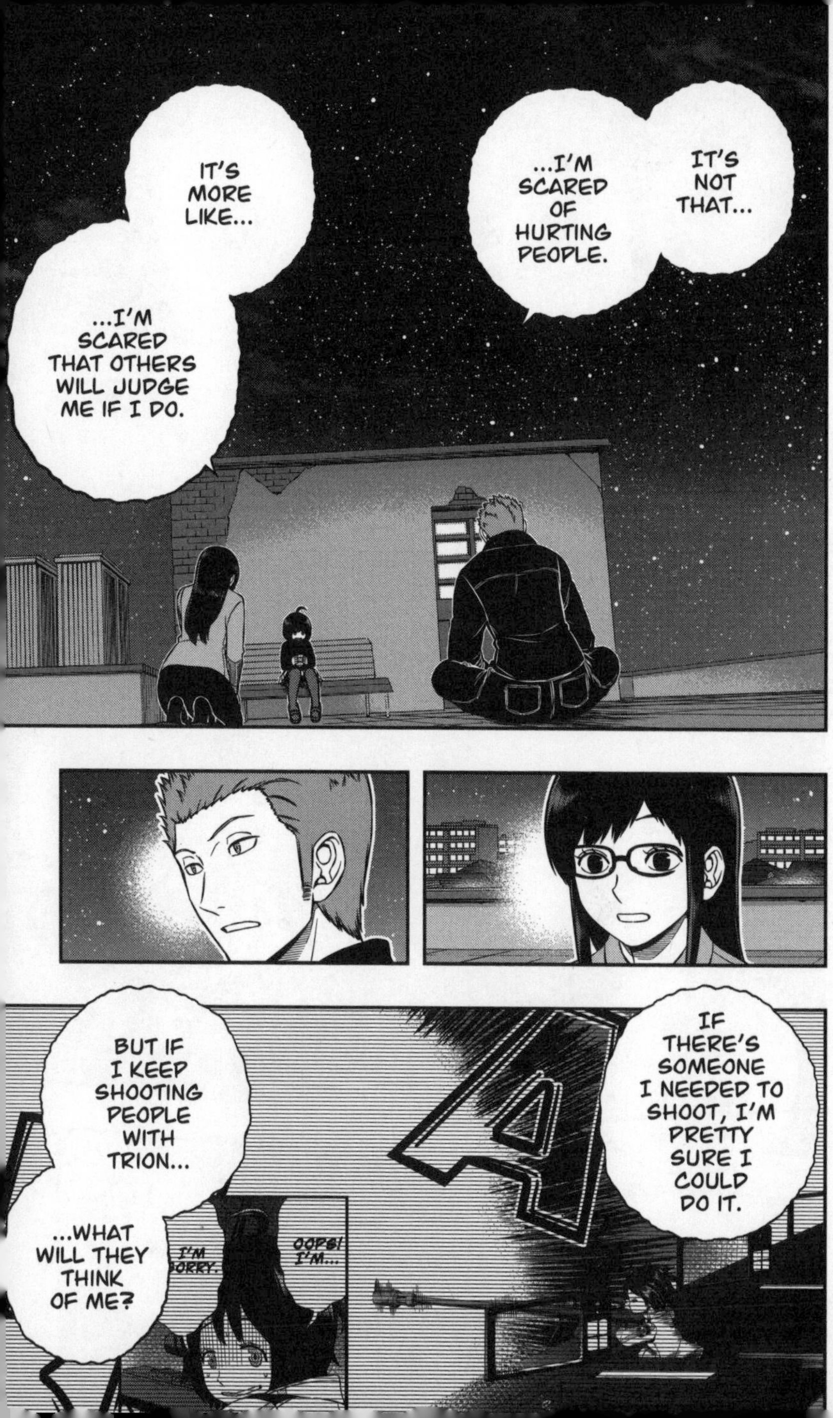
IT'S NOT THAT...
...I'M SCARED OF HURTING PEOPLE.
IT'S MORE LIKE...
...I'M SCARED THAT OTHERS WILL JUDGE ME IF I DO.
IF THERE'S SOMEONE I NEEDED TO SHOOT, I'M PRETTY SURE I COULD DO IT.
BUT IF I KEEP SHOOTING PEOPLE WITH TRION...
OOPS! I'M...
I'M ORRY.
...WHAT WILL THEY THINK OF ME?

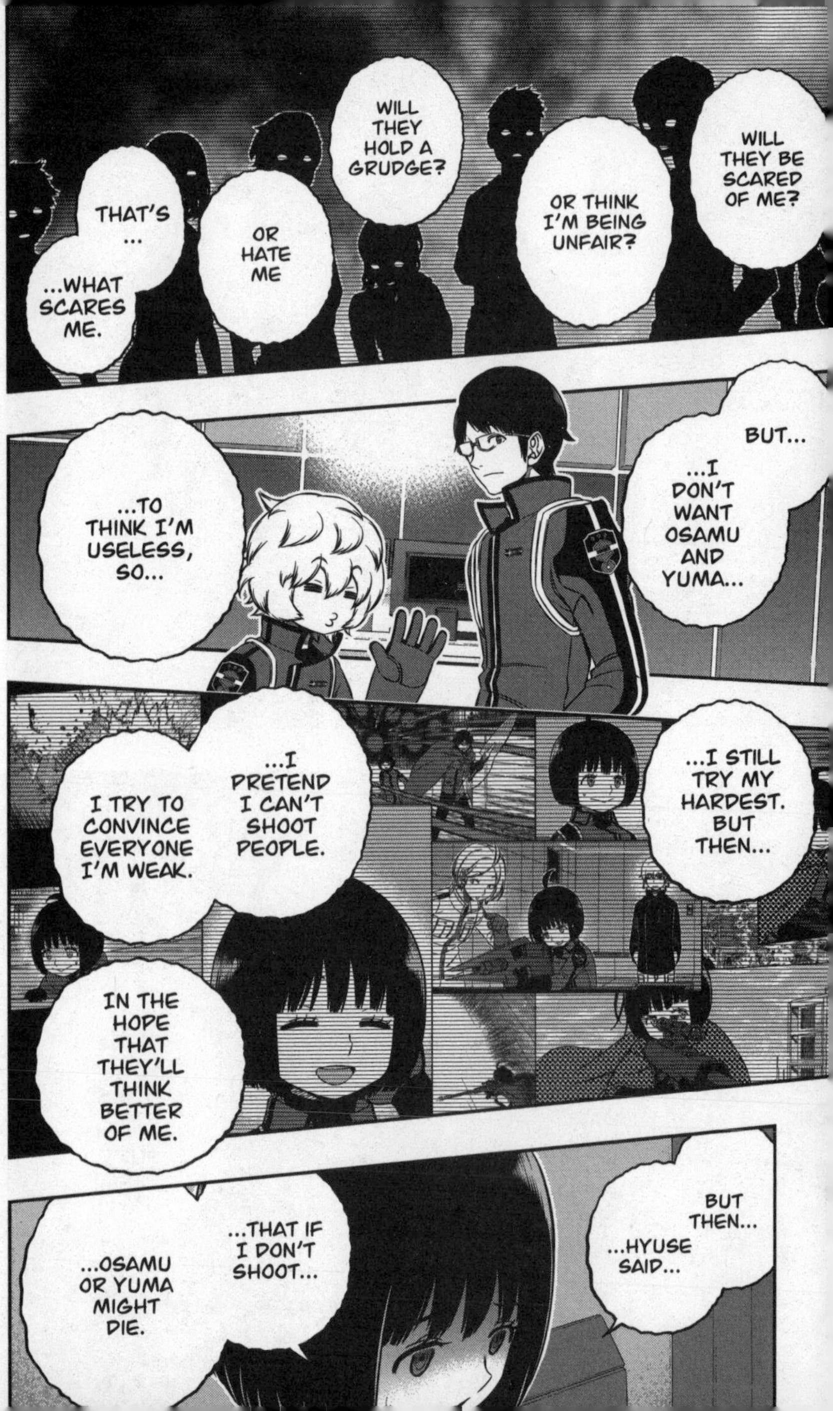
WILL THEY BE SCARED OF ME?
OR THINK I'M BEING UNFAIR?
WILL THEY HOLD A GRUDGE?
OR HATE ME
THAT'S ...
...WHAT SCARES ME.
BUT...
...I DON'T WANT OSAMU AND YUMA...
...TO THINK I'M USELESS, SO...
...I STILL TRY MY HARDEST. BUT THEN...
...I PRETEND I CAN'T SHOOT PEOPLE.
I TRY TO CONVINCE EVERYONE I'M WEAK.
IN THE HOPE THAT THEY'LL THINK BETTER OF ME.
BUT THEN...
...HYUSE SAID...
...THAT IF I DON'T SHOOT...
...OSAMU OR YUMA MIGHT DIE.

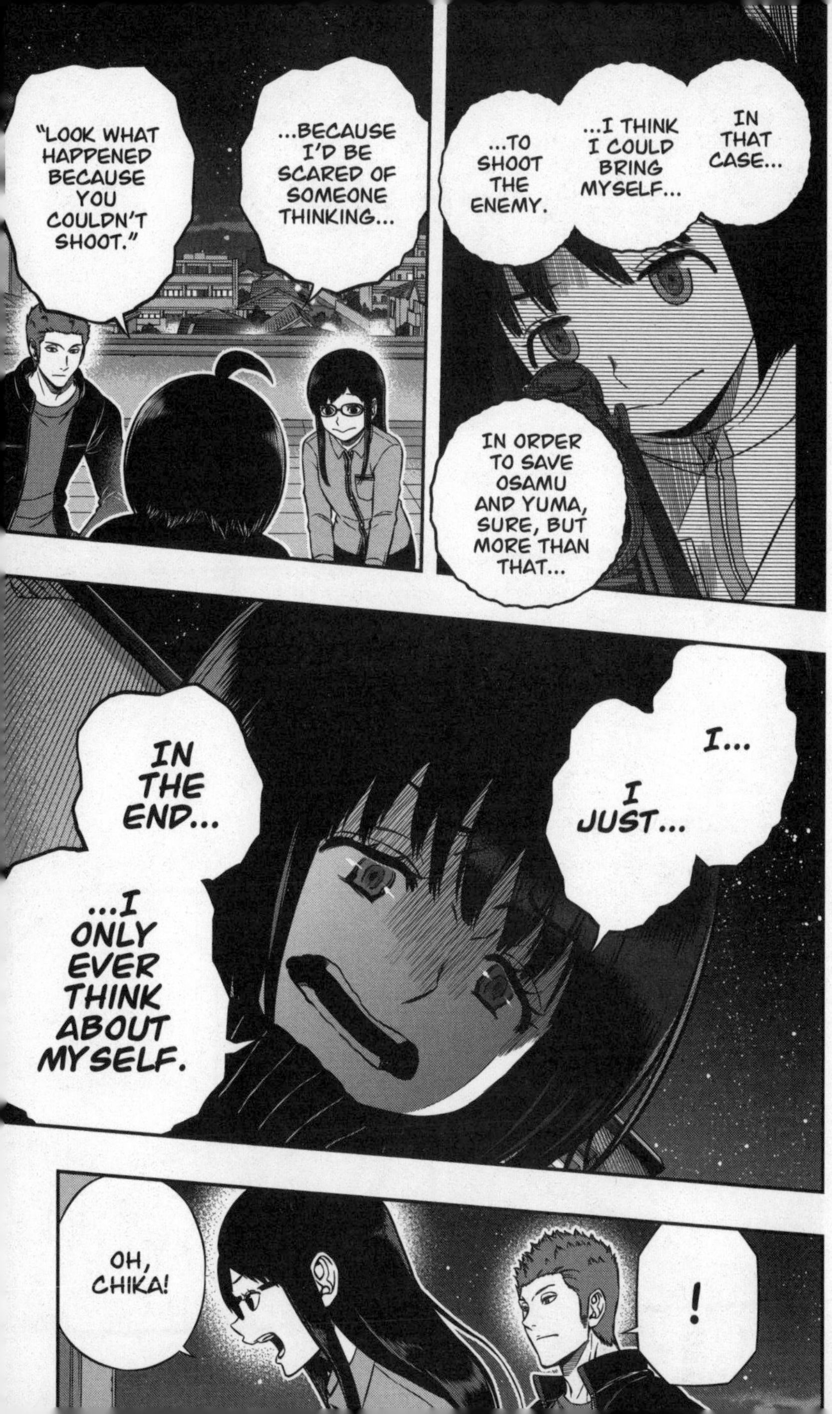
IN THAT CASE...
...I THINK I COULD BRING MYSELF...
...TO SHOOT THE ENEMY.
IN ORDER TO SAVE OSAMU AND YUMA, SURE, BUT MORE THAN THAT...
...BECAUSE I'D BE SCARED OF SOMEONE THINKING...
"LOOK WHAT HAPPENED BECAUSE YOU COULDN'T SHOOT."
I...
I JUST...
IN THE END...
...I ONLY EVER THINK ABOUT MYSELF.
!
OH, CHIKA!

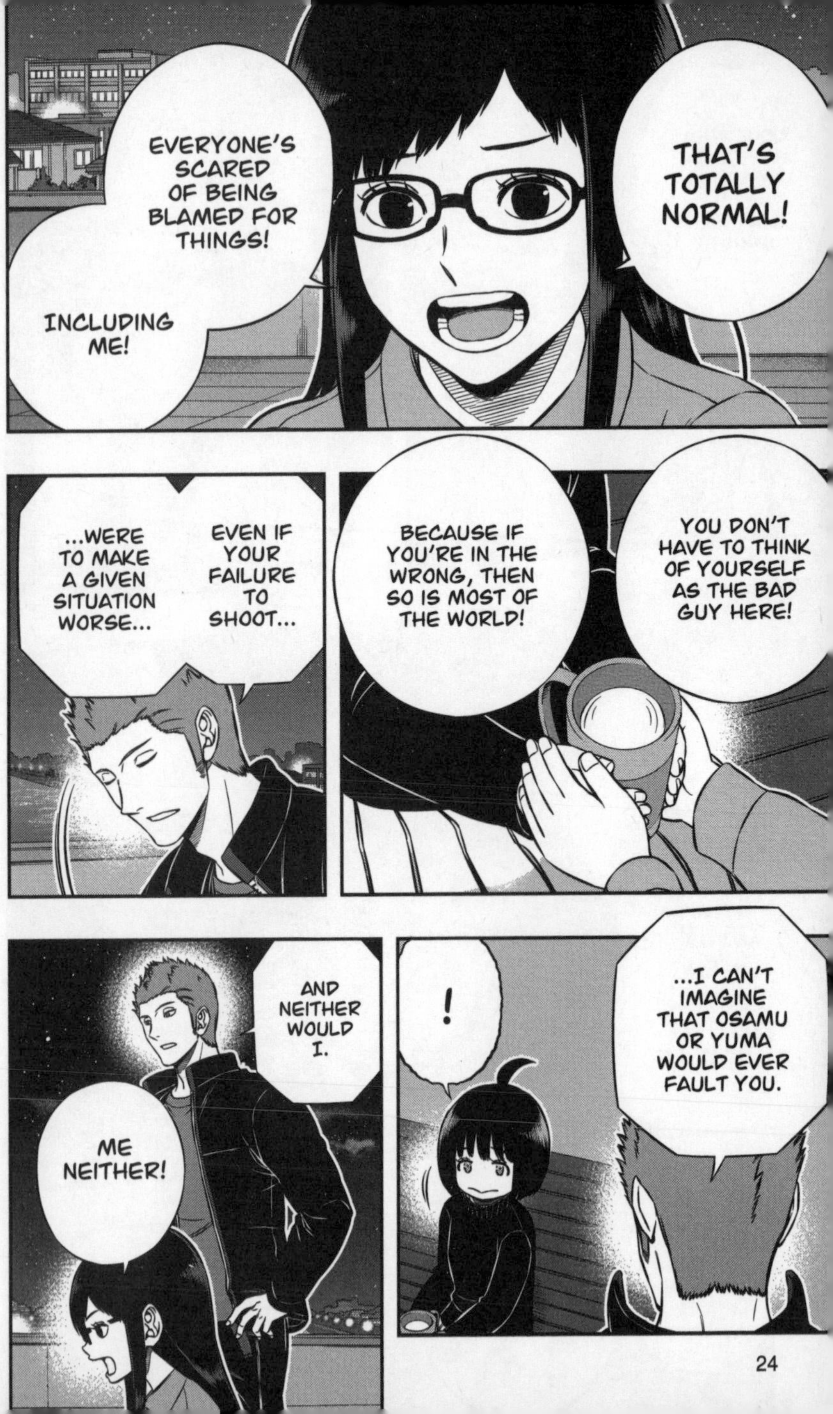
THAT'S TOTALLY NORMAL!
EVERYONE'S SCARED OF BEING BLAMED FOR THINGS!
INCLUDING ME!
YOU DON'T HAVE TO THINK OF YOURSELF AS THE BAD GUY HERE!
BECAUSE IF YOU'RE IN THE WRONG, THEN SO IS MOST OF THE WORLD!
EVEN IF YOUR FAILURE TO SHOOT...
...WERE TO MAKE A GIVEN SITUATION WORSE...
...I CAN'T IMAGINE THAT OSAMU OR YUMA WOULD EVER FAULT YOU.
!
AND NEITHER WOULD I.
ME NEITHER!

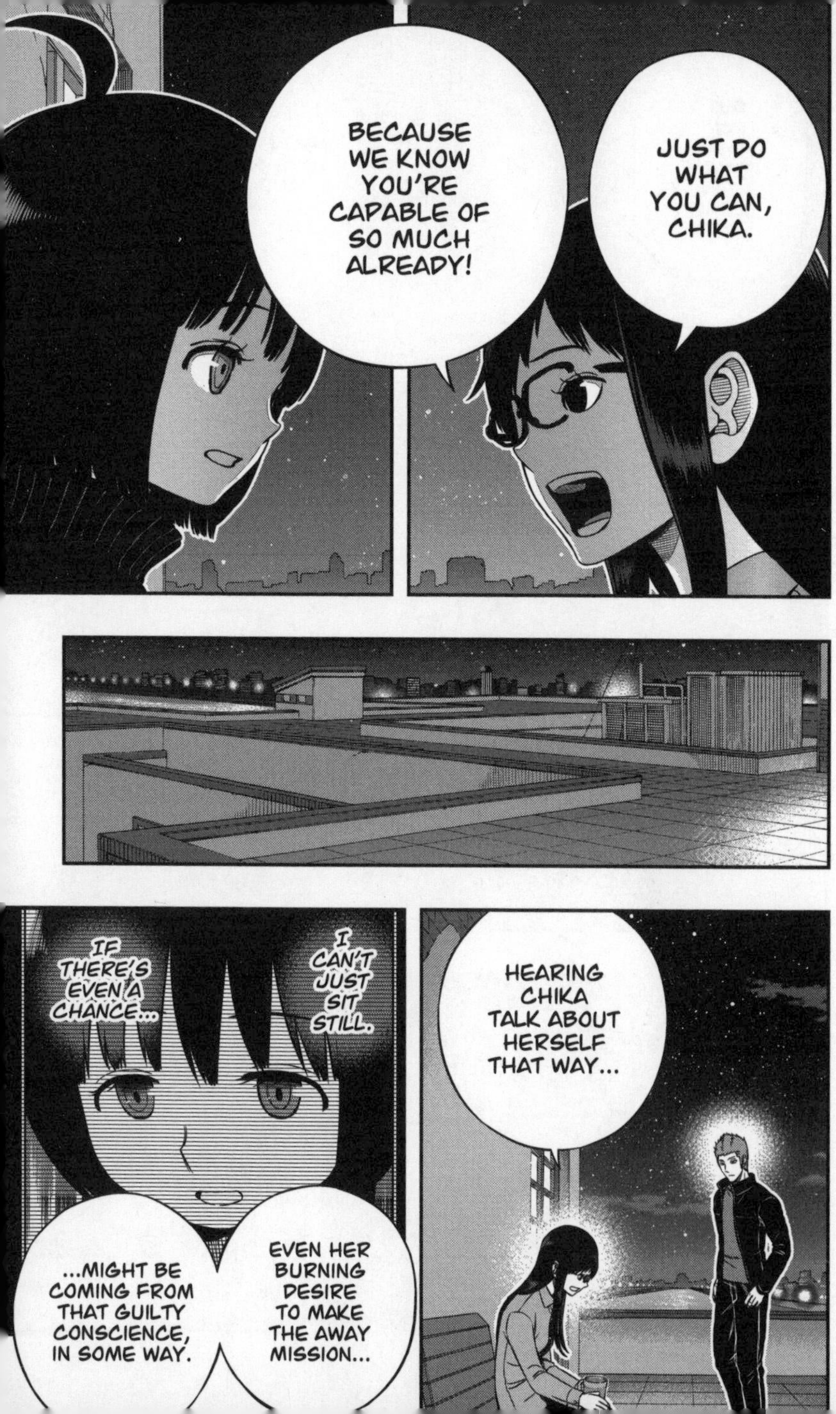
JUST DO WHAT YOU CAN, CHIKA.
BECAUSE WE KNOW YOU'RE CAPABLE OF SO MUCH ALREADY!
HEARING CHIKA TALK ABOUT HERSELF THAT WAY...
I CAN'T JUST SIT STILL.
IF THERE'S EVEN A CHANCE...
EVEN HER BURNING DESIRE TO MAKE THE AWAY MISSION...
...MIGHT BE COMING FROM THAT GUILTY CONSCIENCE, IN SOME WAY.

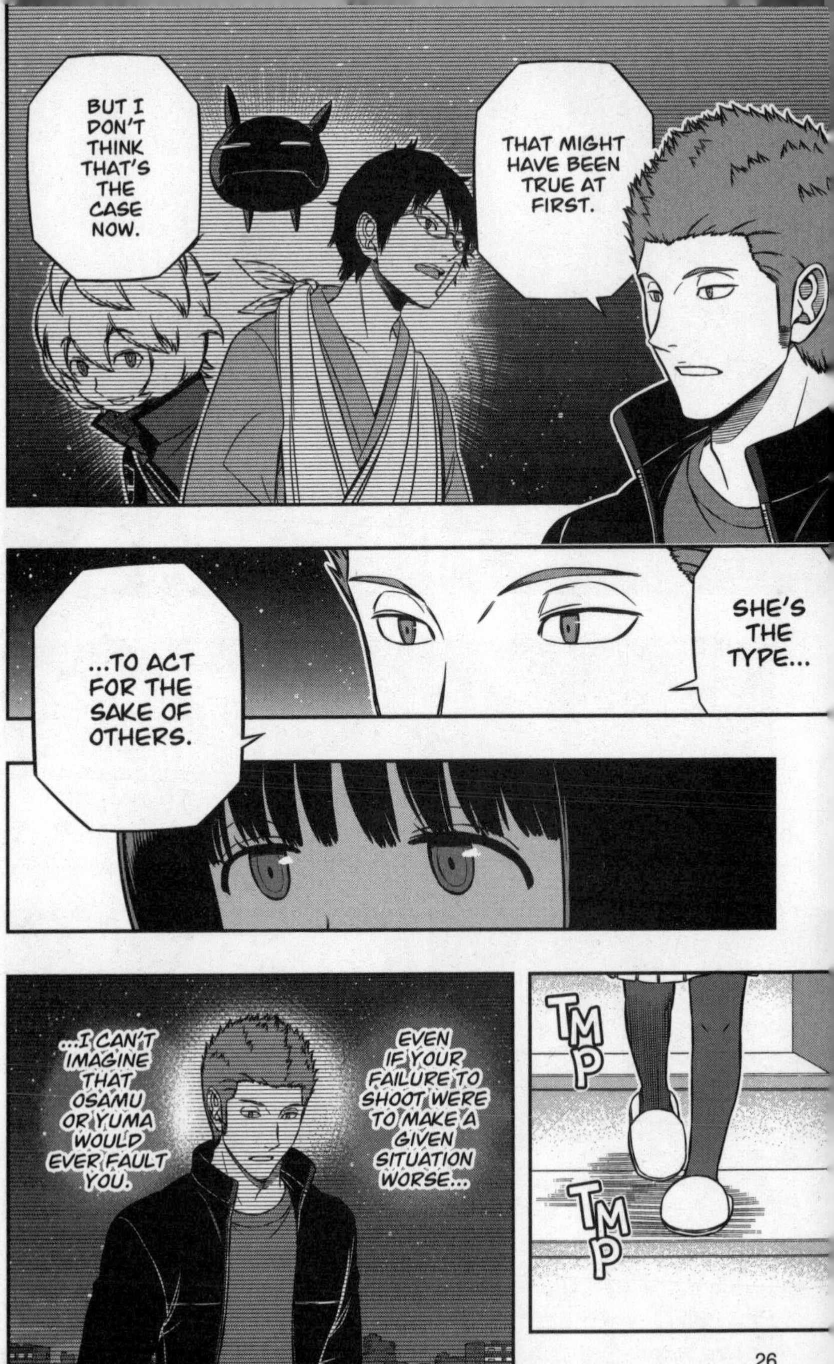
THAT MIGHT HAVE BEEN TRUE AT FIRST.
BUT I DON'T THINK THAT'S THE CASE NOW.
SHE'S THE TYPE...
...TO ACT FOR THE SAKE OF OTHERS.
TMP
TMP
EVEN IF YOUR FAILURE TO SHOOT WERE TO MAKE A GIVEN SITUATION WORSE...
...I CAN'T IMAGINE THAT OSAMU OR YUMA WOULD EVER FAULT YOU.

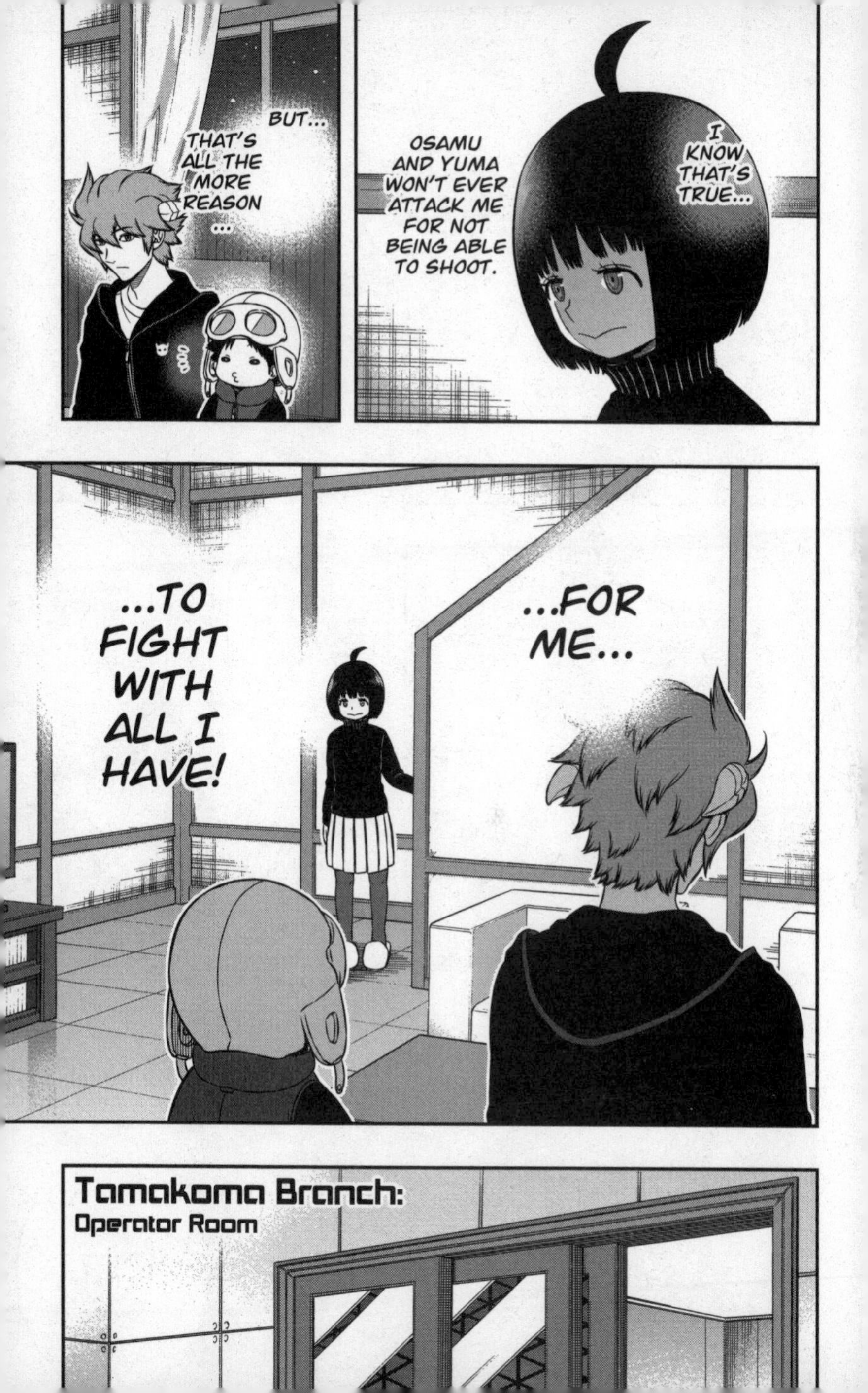
I KNOW THAT'S TRUE...
OSAMU AND YUMA WON'T EVER ATTACK ME FOR NOT BEING ABLE TO SHOOT.
BUT...
THAT'S ALL THE MORE REASON ...
...FOR ME...
...TO FIGHT WITH ALL I HAVE!
Tamakoma Branch:
Operator Room

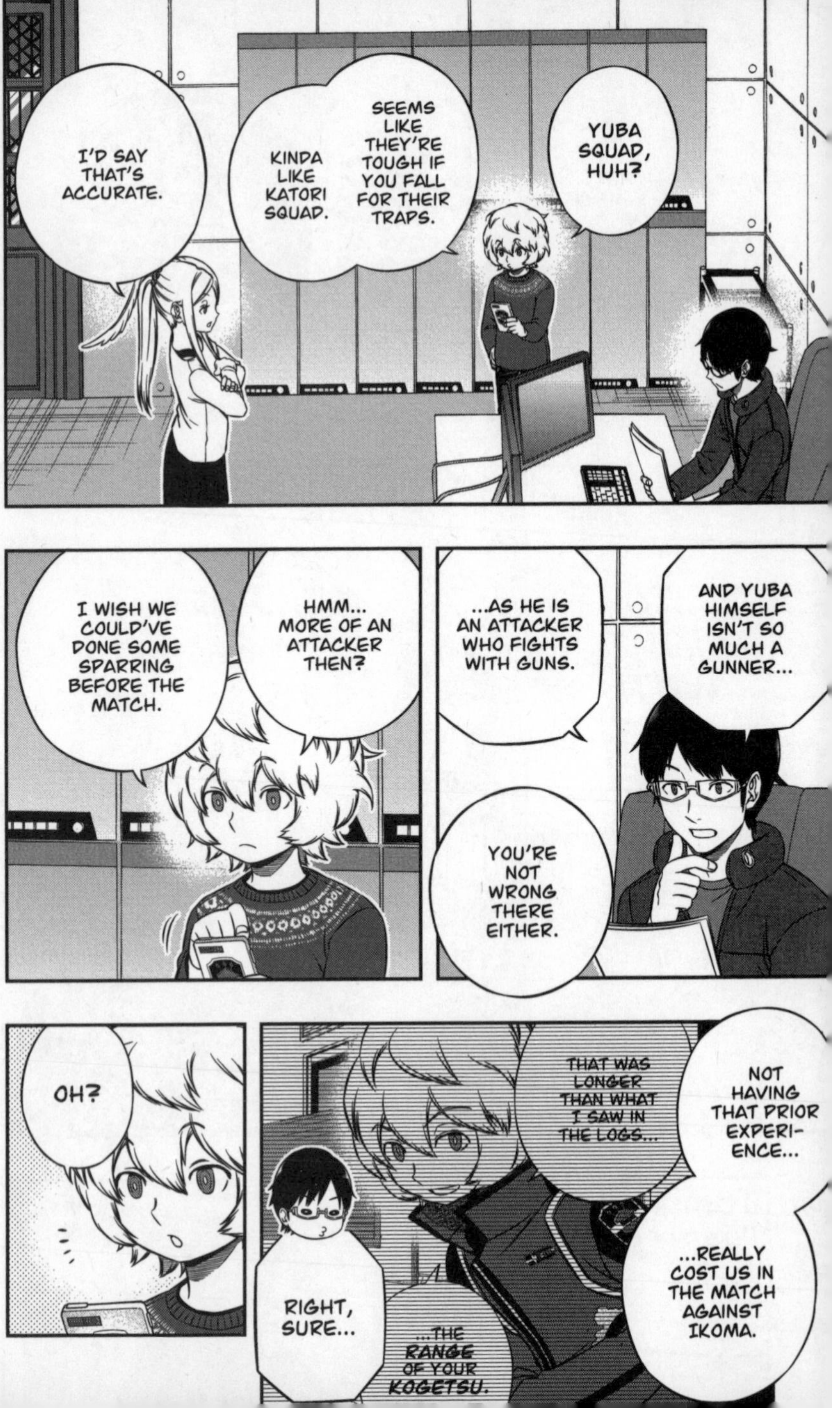
YUBA SQUAD, HUH?
SEEMS LIKE THEY'RE TOUGH IF YOU FALL FOR THEIR TRAPS.
KINDA LIKE KATORI SQUAD.
I'D SAY THAT'S ACCURATE.
AND YUBA HIMSELF ISN'T SO MUCH A GUNNER...
...AS HE IS AN ATTACKER WHO FIGHTS WITH GUNS.
YOU'RE NOT WRONG THERE EITHER.
HMM... MORE OF AN ATTACKER THEN?
I WISH WE COULD'VE DONE SOME SPARRING BEFORE THE MATCH.
NOT HAVING THAT PRIOR EXPERI-ENCE...
...REALLY COST US IN THE MATCH AGAINST IKOMA.
THAT WAS LONGER THAN WHAT I SAW IN THE LOGS...
...THE RANGE OF YOUR KOGETSU.
RIGHT, SURE...
OH?

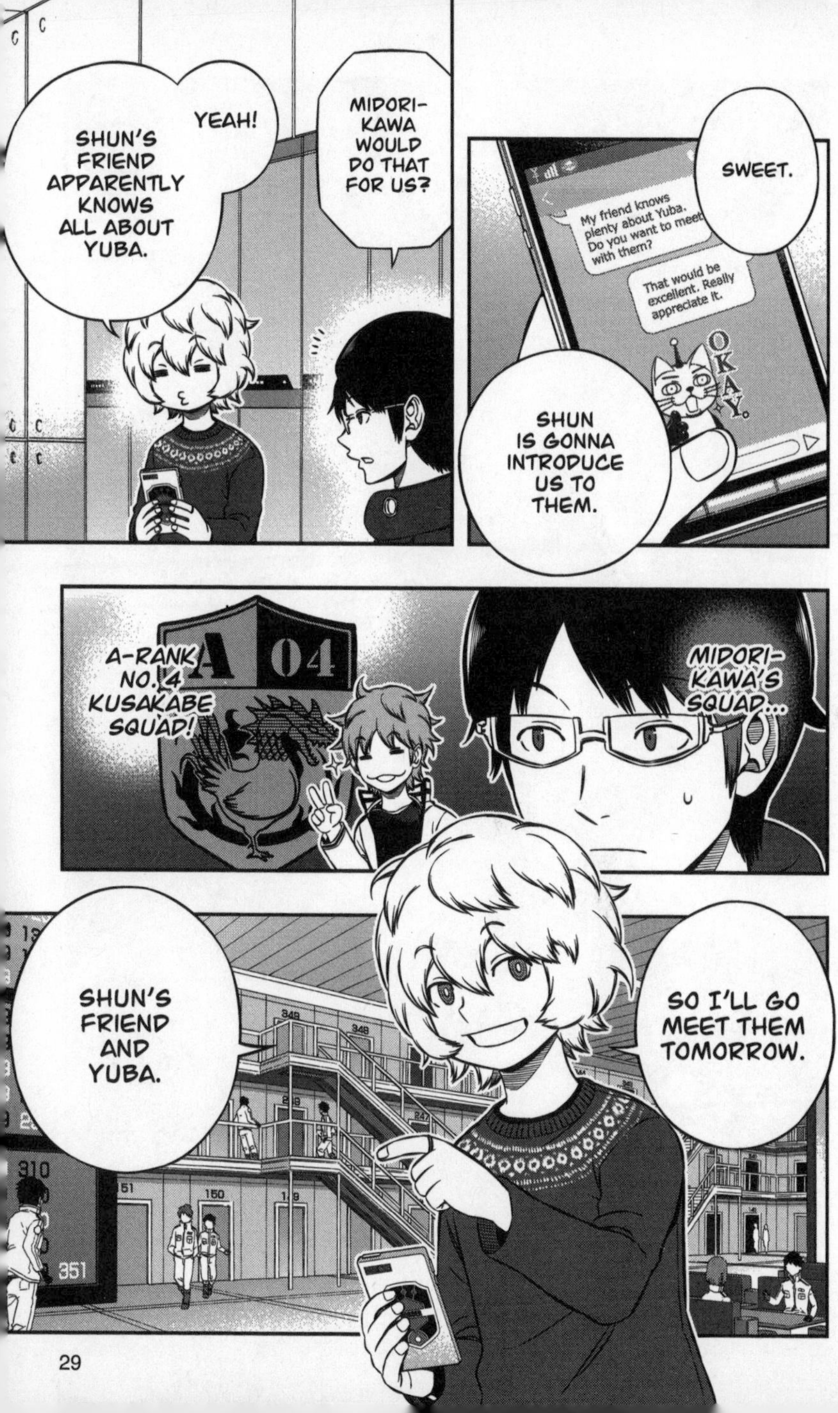
SWEET.
My friend knows plenty about Yuba. Do you want to meet with them?
That would be excellent. Really appreciate it.
OKAY.
SHUN IS GONNA INTRODUCE US TO THEM.
MIDORI-KAWA WOULD DO THAT FOR US?
YEAH!
SHUN'S FRIEND APPARENTLY KNOWS ALL ABOUT YUBA.
MIDORI-KAWA'S SQUAD...
A04
A-RANK NO. 4 KUSAKABE SQUAD!
SO I'LL GO MEET THEM TOMORROW.
SHUN'S FRIEND AND YUBA.

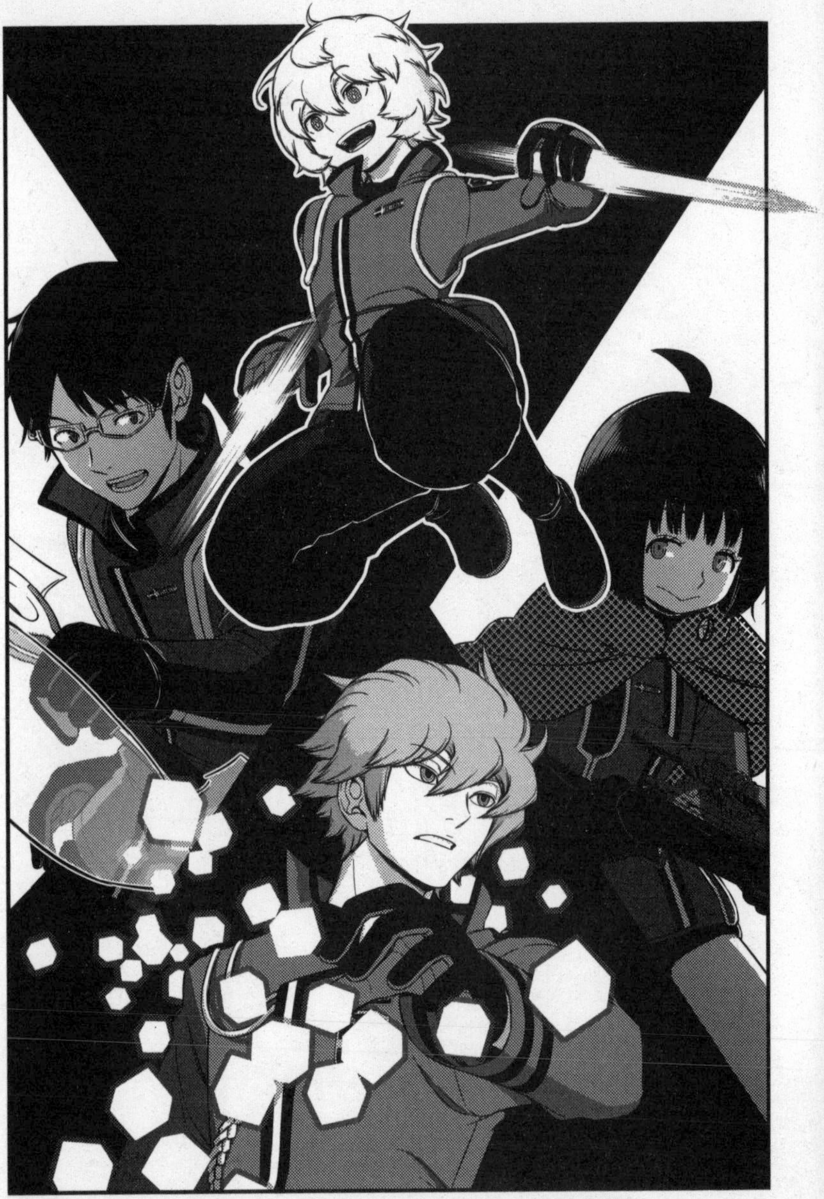

■ **Bonus Desk Mat included in *Jump SQ*, September 2019**

I had planned to use this color page in the July 2019 issue, but then I got sick out of nowhere and had to take the month off, so the magazine shifted this piece of art to September and made it a desk mat instead. I appreciated that.

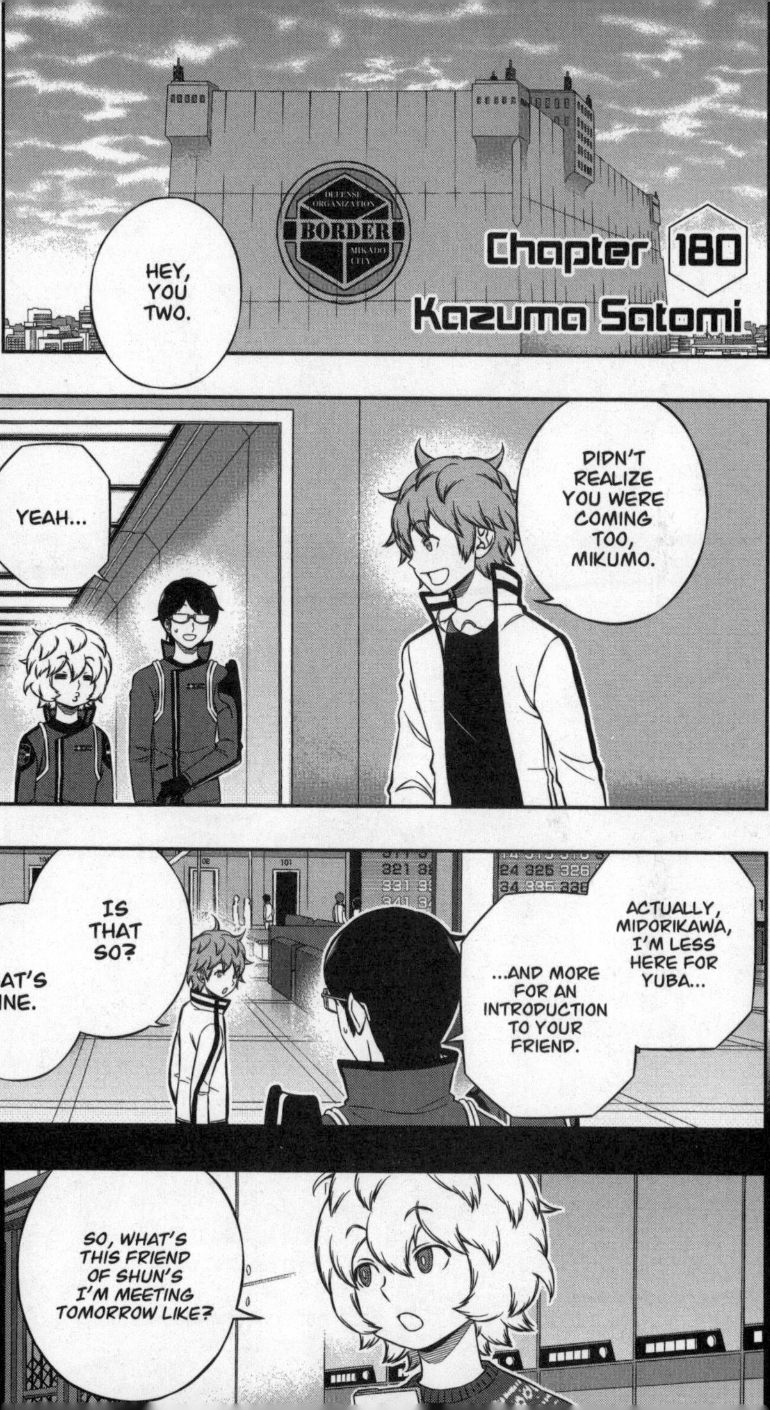
Chapter 180
Kazuma Satomi
DEFENSE ORGANIZATION BORDER MIKADO CITY
HEY, YOU TWO.
DIDN'T REALIZE YOU WERE COMING TOO, MIKUMO.
YEAH...
ACTUALLY, MIDORIKAWA, I'M LESS HERE FOR YUBA...
...AND MORE FOR AN INTRODUCTION TO YOUR FRIEND.
IS THAT SO?
THAT'S FINE.
SO, WHAT'S THIS FRIEND OF SHUN'S I'M MEETING TOMORROW LIKE?

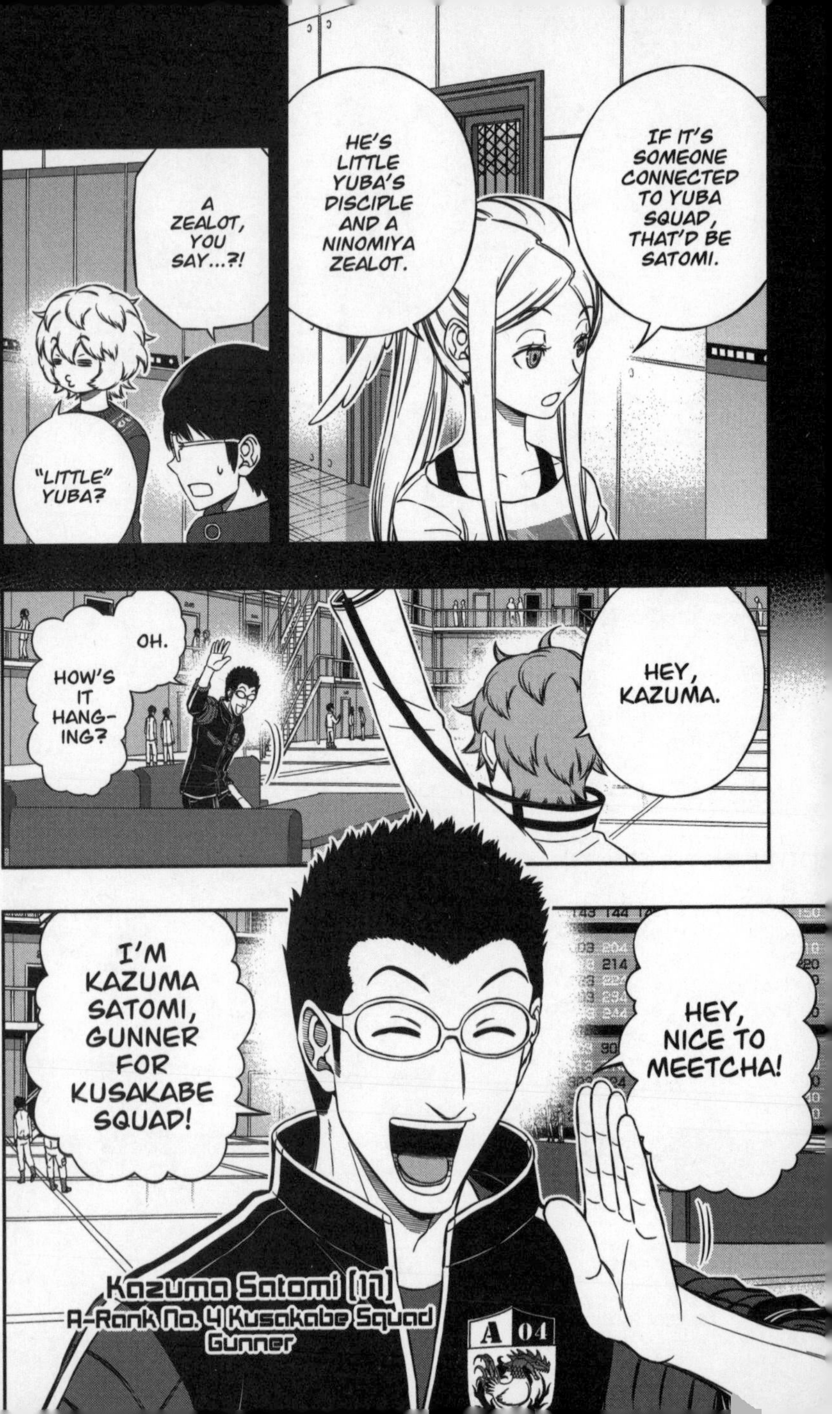
IF IT'S SOMEONE CONNECTED TO YUBA SQUAD, THAT'D BE SATOMI.
HE'S LITTLE YUBA'S DISCIPLE AND A NINOMIYA ZEALOT.
A ZEALOT, YOU SAY...?!
"LITTLE" YUBA?
HEY, KAZUMA.
OH.
HOW'S IT HANGING?
HEY, NICE TO MEETCHA!
I'M KAZUMA SATOMI, GUNNER FOR KUSAKABE SQUAD!
Kazuma Satomi (17)
A-Rank No. 4 Kusakabe Squad
Gunner
A 04

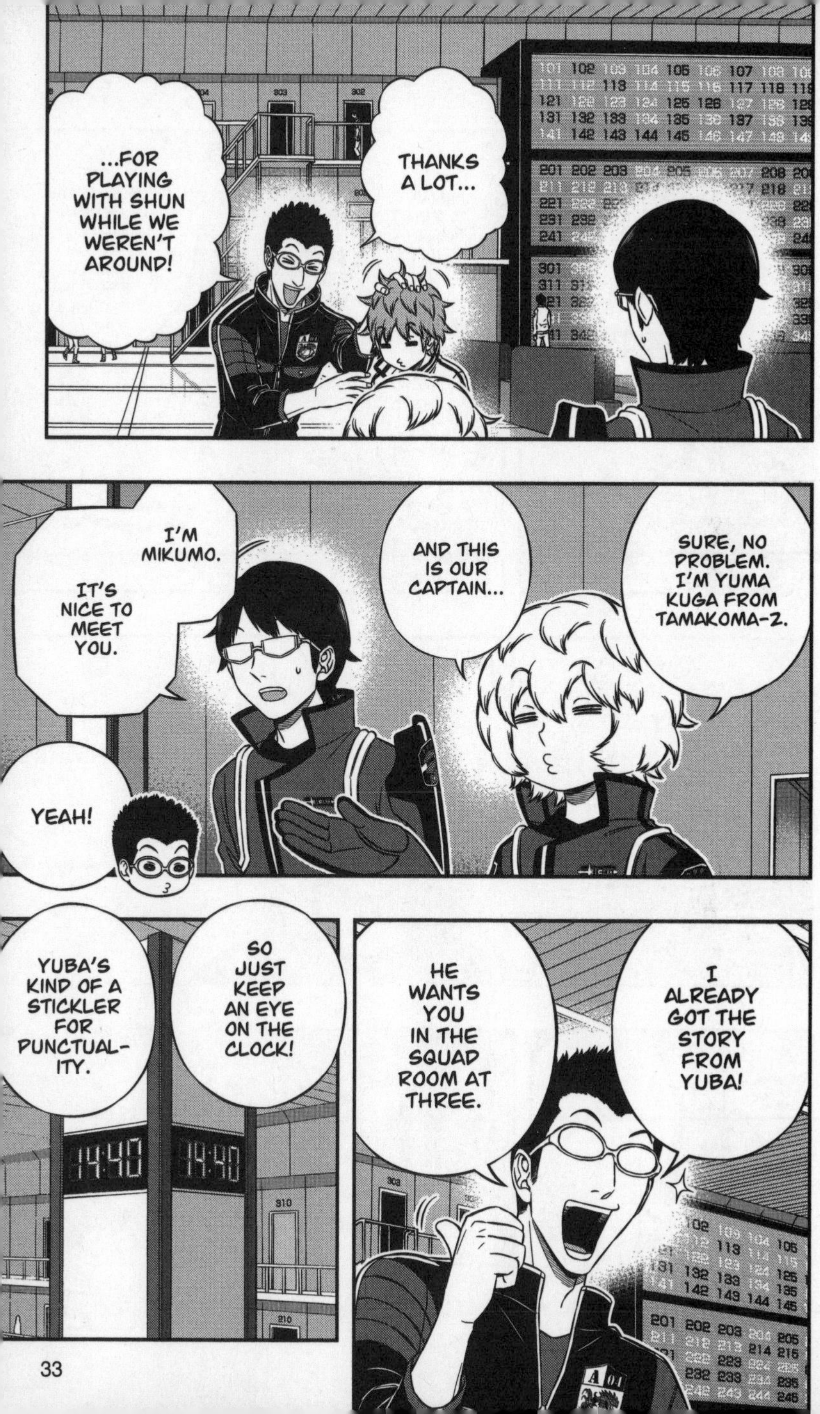
THANKS A LOT...
...FOR PLAYING WITH SHUN WHILE WE WEREN'T AROUND!
SURE, NO PROBLEM. I'M YUMA KUGA FROM TAMAKOMA-2.
AND THIS IS OUR CAPTAIN...
I'M MIKUMO.
IT'S NICE TO MEET YOU.
YEAH!
I ALREADY GOT THE STORY FROM YUBA!
HE WANTS YOU IN THE SQUAD ROOM AT THREE.
SO JUST KEEP AN EYE ON THE CLOCK!
YUBA'S KIND OF A STICKLER FOR PUNCTUAL-ITY.
14:40
14:40

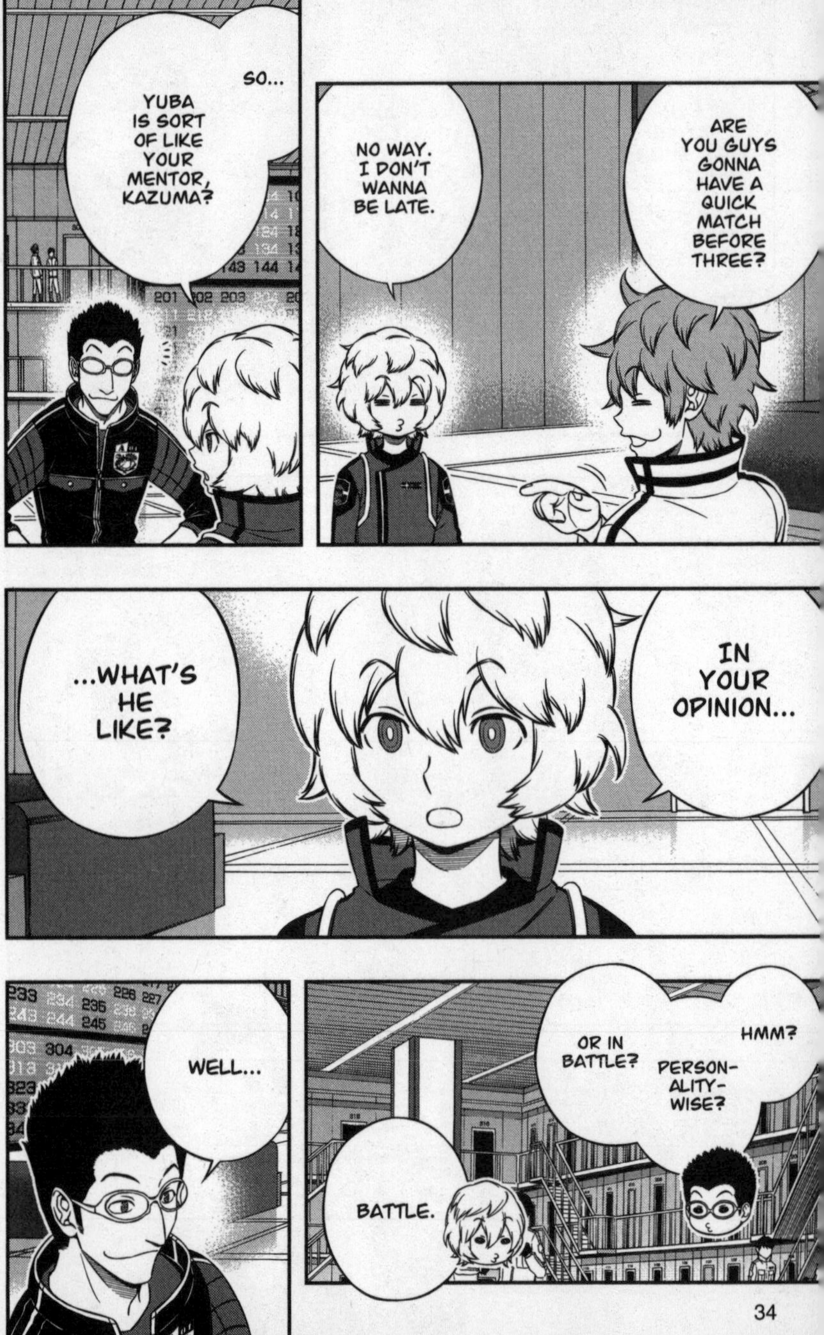
ARE YOU GUYS GONNA HAVE A QUICK MATCH BEFORE THREE?
NO WAY. I DON'T WANNA BE LATE.
SO...
YUBA IS SORT OF LIKE YOUR MENTOR, KAZUMA?
IN YOUR OPINION...
...WHAT'S HE LIKE?
HMM?
PERSON-ALITY-WISE?
OR IN BATTLE?
BATTLE.
WELL...

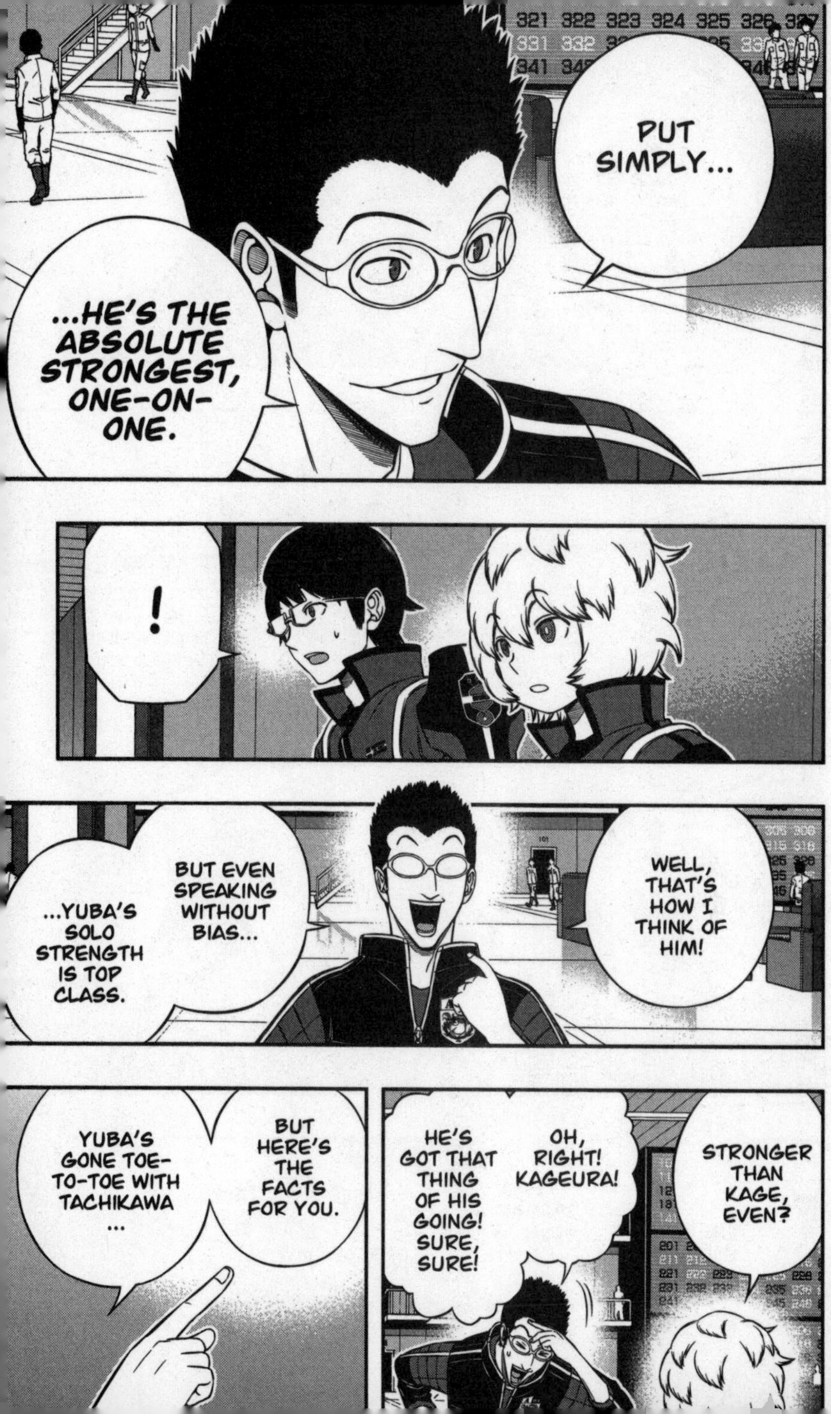
PUT SIMPLY...
...HE'S THE ABSOLUTE STRONGEST, ONE-ON-ONE.
!
WELL, THAT'S HOW I THINK OF HIM!
BUT EVEN SPEAKING WITHOUT BIAS...
...YUBA'S SOLO STRENGTH IS TOP CLASS.
STRONGER THAN KAGE, EVEN?
OH, RIGHT! KAGEURA!
HE'S GOT THAT THING OF HIS GOING! SURE, SURE!
BUT HERE'S THE FACTS FOR YOU.
YUBA'S GONE TOE-TO-TOE WITH TACHIKAWA...

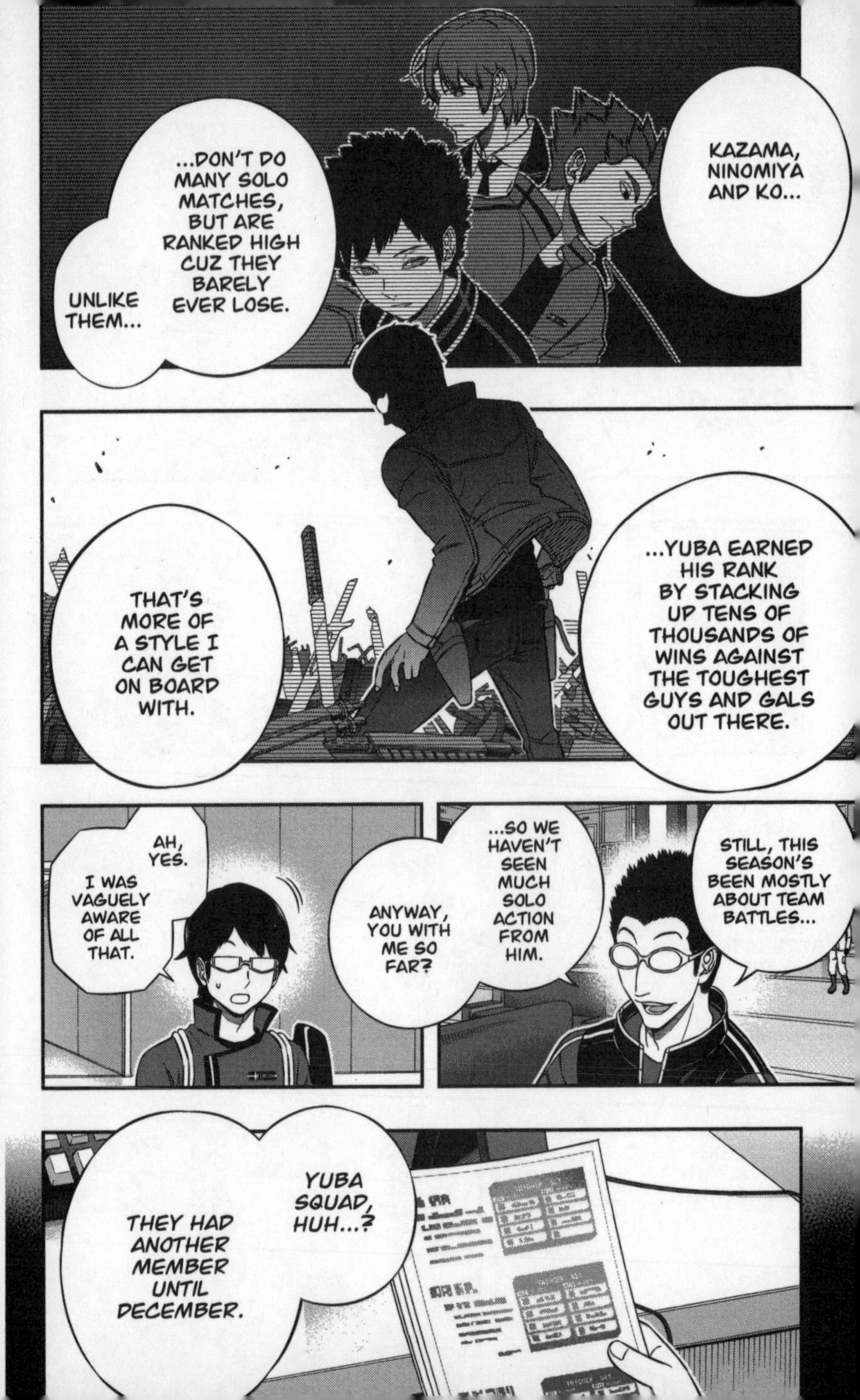
KAZAMA, NINOMIYA AND KO...
...DON'T DO MANY SOLO MATCHES, BUT ARE RANKED HIGH CUZ THEY BARELY EVER LOSE.
UNLIKE THEM...
...YUBA EARNED HIS RANK BY STACKING UP TENS OF THOUSANDS OF WINS AGAINST THE TOUGHEST GUYS AND GALS OUT THERE.
THAT'S MORE OF A STYLE I CAN GET ON BOARD WITH.
STILL, THIS SEASON'S BEEN MOSTLY ABOUT TEAM BATTLES...
...SO WE HAVEN'T SEEN MUCH SOLO ACTION FROM HIM.
ANYWAY, YOU WITH ME SO FAR?
AH, YES.
I WAS VAGUELY AWARE OF ALL THAT.
YUBA SQUAD, HUH...?
THEY HAD ANOTHER MEMBER UNTIL DECEMBER.

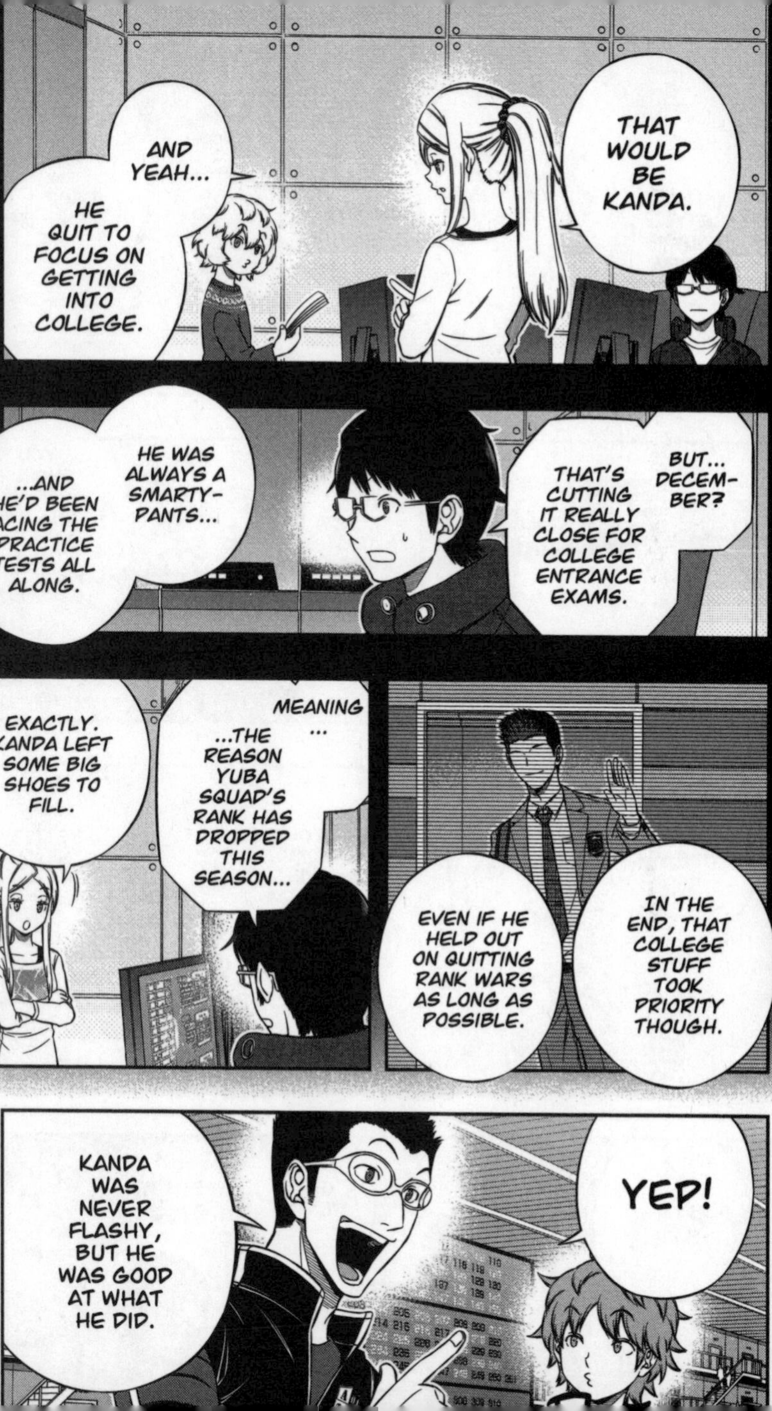
THAT WOULD BE KANDA.
AND YEAH...
HE QUIT TO FOCUS ON GETTING INTO COLLEGE.
BUT... DECEMBER?
THAT'S CUTTING IT REALLY CLOSE FOR COLLEGE ENTRANCE EXAMS.
HE WAS ALWAYS A SMARTY-PANTS...
...AND HE'D BEEN ACING THE PRACTICE TESTS ALL ALONG.
IN THE END, THAT COLLEGE STUFF TOOK PRIORITY THOUGH.
EVEN IF HE HELD OUT ON QUITTING RANK WARS AS LONG AS POSSIBLE.
MEANING...
...THE REASON YUBA SQUAD'S RANK HAS DROPPED THIS SEASON...
EXACTLY. KANDA LEFT SOME BIG SHOES TO FILL.
YEP!
KANDA WAS NEVER FLASHY, BUT HE WAS GOOD AT WHAT HE DID.

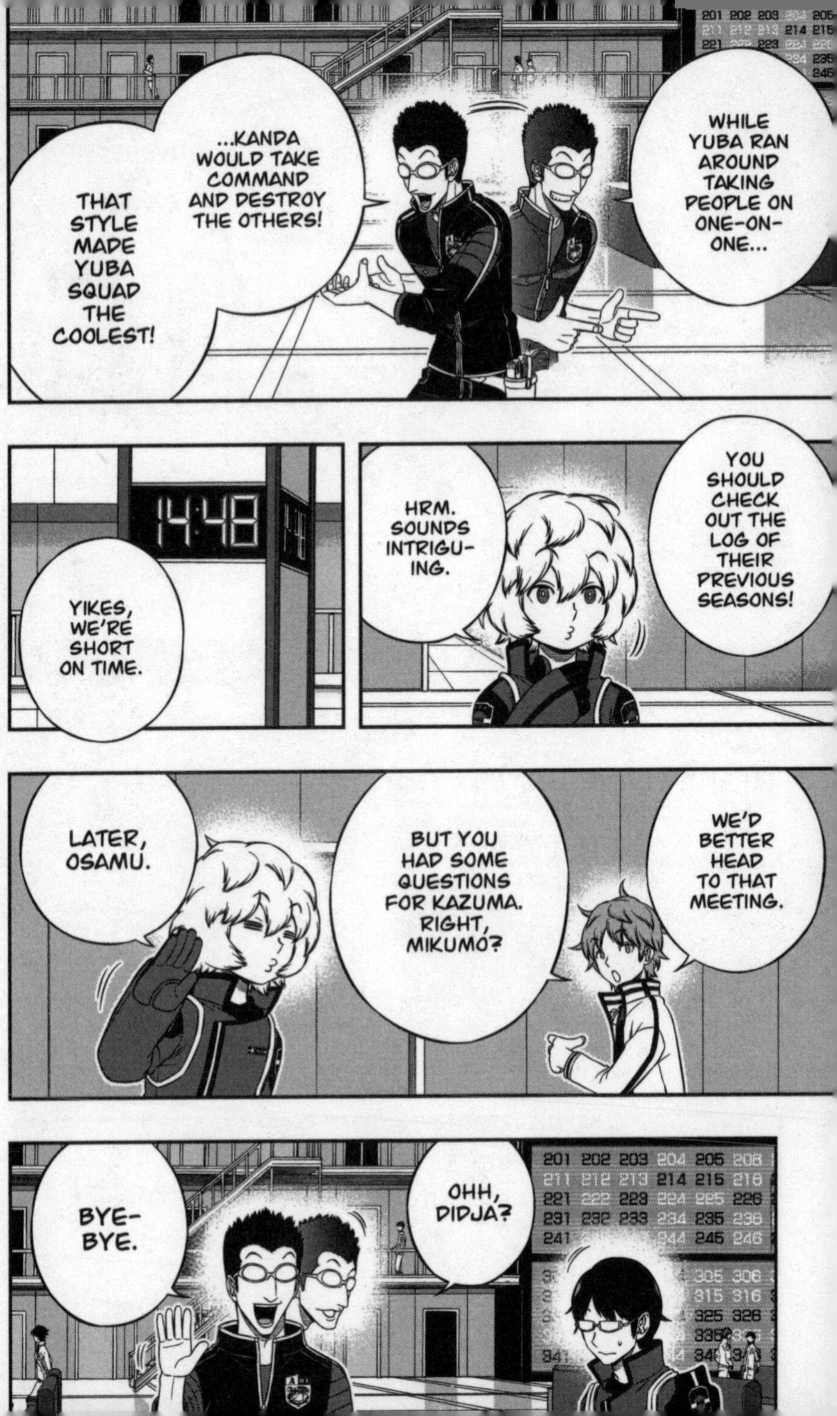
WHILE YUBA RAN AROUND TAKING PEOPLE ON ONE-ON-ONE...
...KANDA WOULD TAKE COMMAND AND DESTROY THE OTHERS!
THAT STYLE MADE YUBA SQUAD THE COOLEST!
YOU SHOULD CHECK OUT THE LOG OF THEIR PREVIOUS SEASONS!
HRM. SOUNDS INTRIGU-ING.
YIKES, WE'RE SHORT ON TIME.
WE'D BETTER HEAD TO THAT MEETING.
BUT YOU HAD SOME QUESTIONS FOR KAZUMA. RIGHT, MIKUMO?
LATER, OSAMU.
OHH, DIDJA?
BYE-BYE.

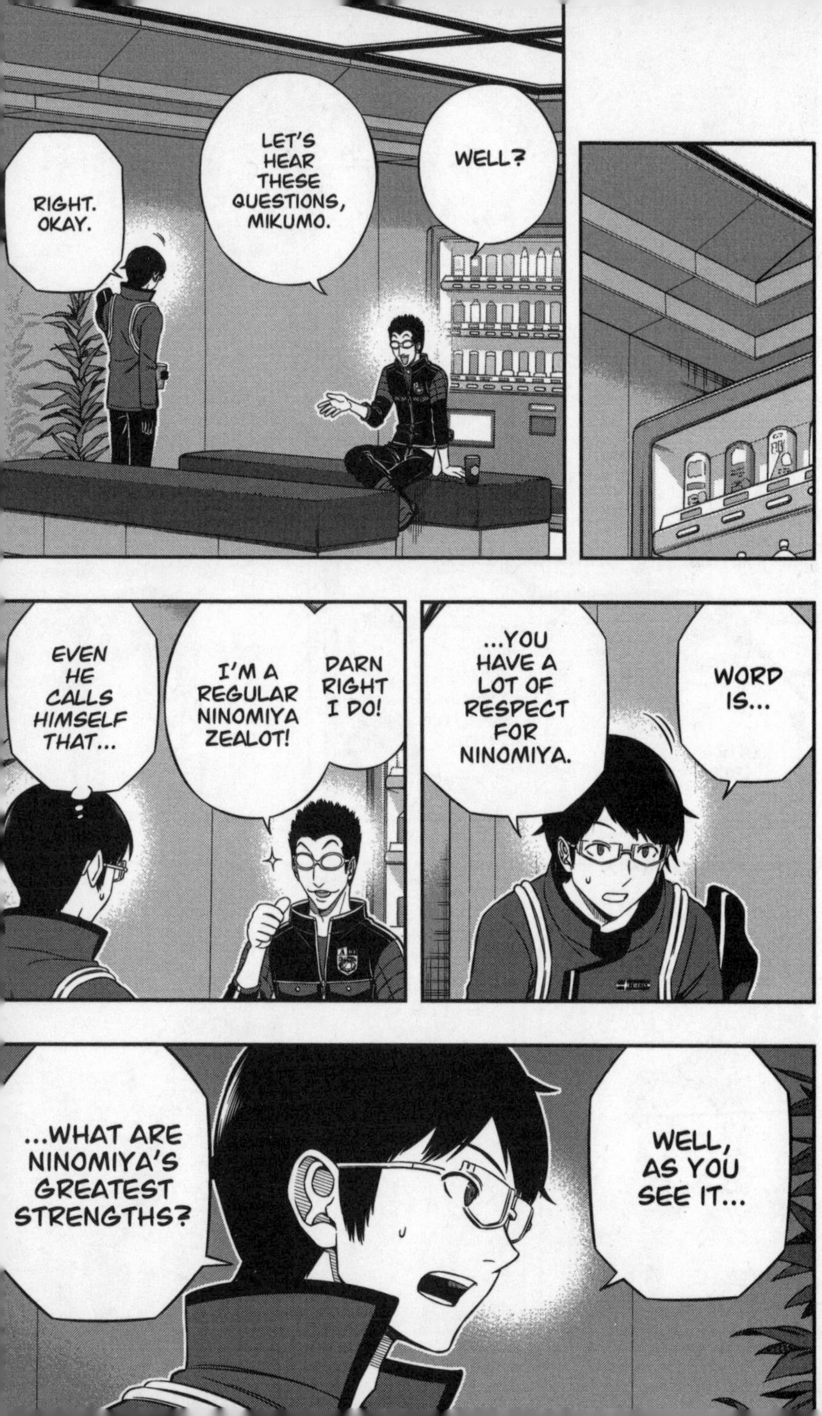
WELL?
LET'S HEAR THESE QUESTIONS, MIKUMO.
RIGHT. OKAY.
WORD IS...
...YOU HAVE A LOT OF RESPECT FOR NINOMIYA.
DARN RIGHT I DO!
I'M A REGULAR NINOMIYA ZEALOT!
EVEN HE CALLS HIMSELF THAT...
WELL, AS YOU SEE IT...
...WHAT ARE NINOMIYA'S GREATEST STRENGTHS?

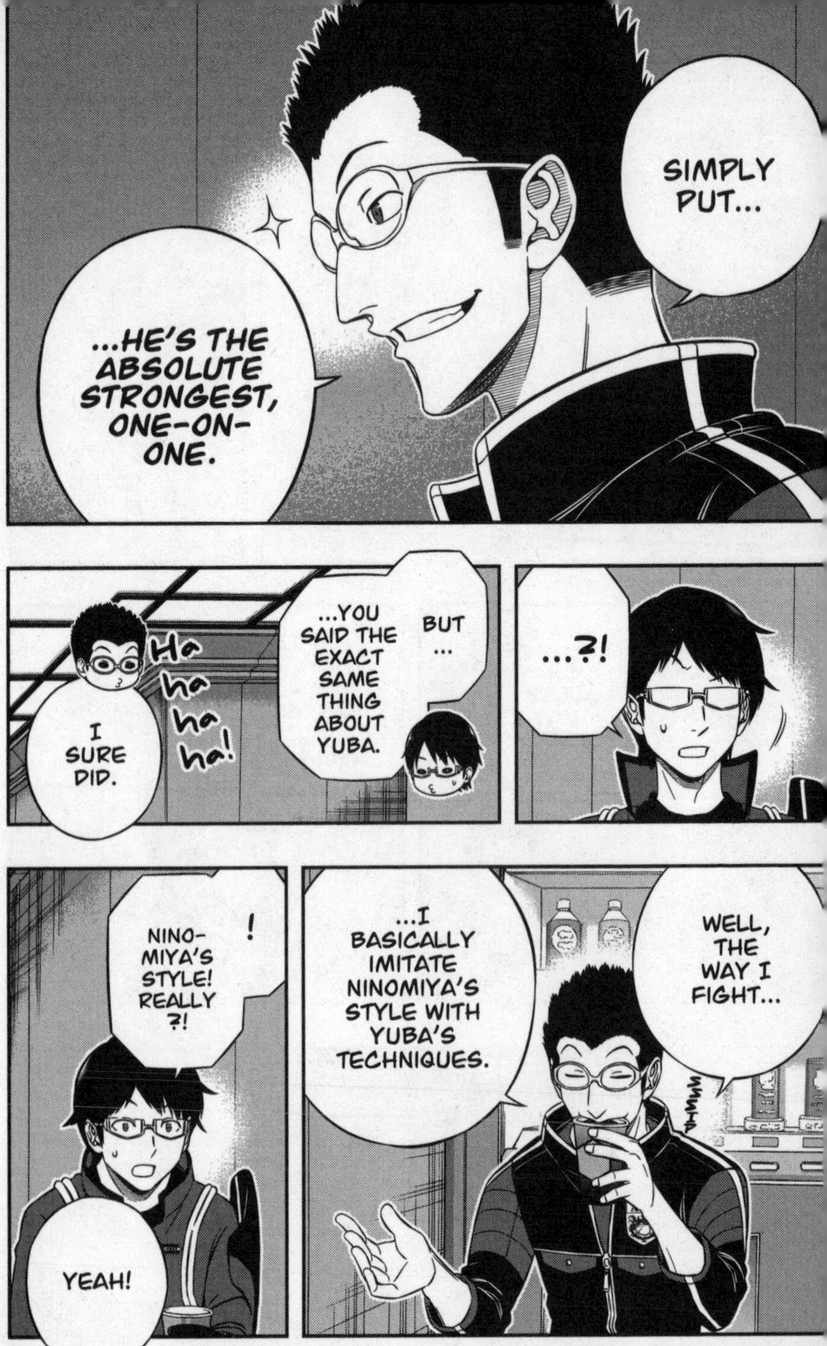
SIMPLY PUT...
...HE'S THE ABSOLUTE STRONGEST, ONE-ON-ONE.
...?!
BUT ...
...YOU SAID THE EXACT SAME THING ABOUT YUBA.
Ha ha ha ha!
I SURE DID.
WELL, THE WAY I FIGHT...
...I BASICALLY IMITATE NINOMIYA'S STYLE WITH YUBA'S TECHNIQUES.
!
NINO-MIYA'S STYLE! REALLY ?!
YEAH!

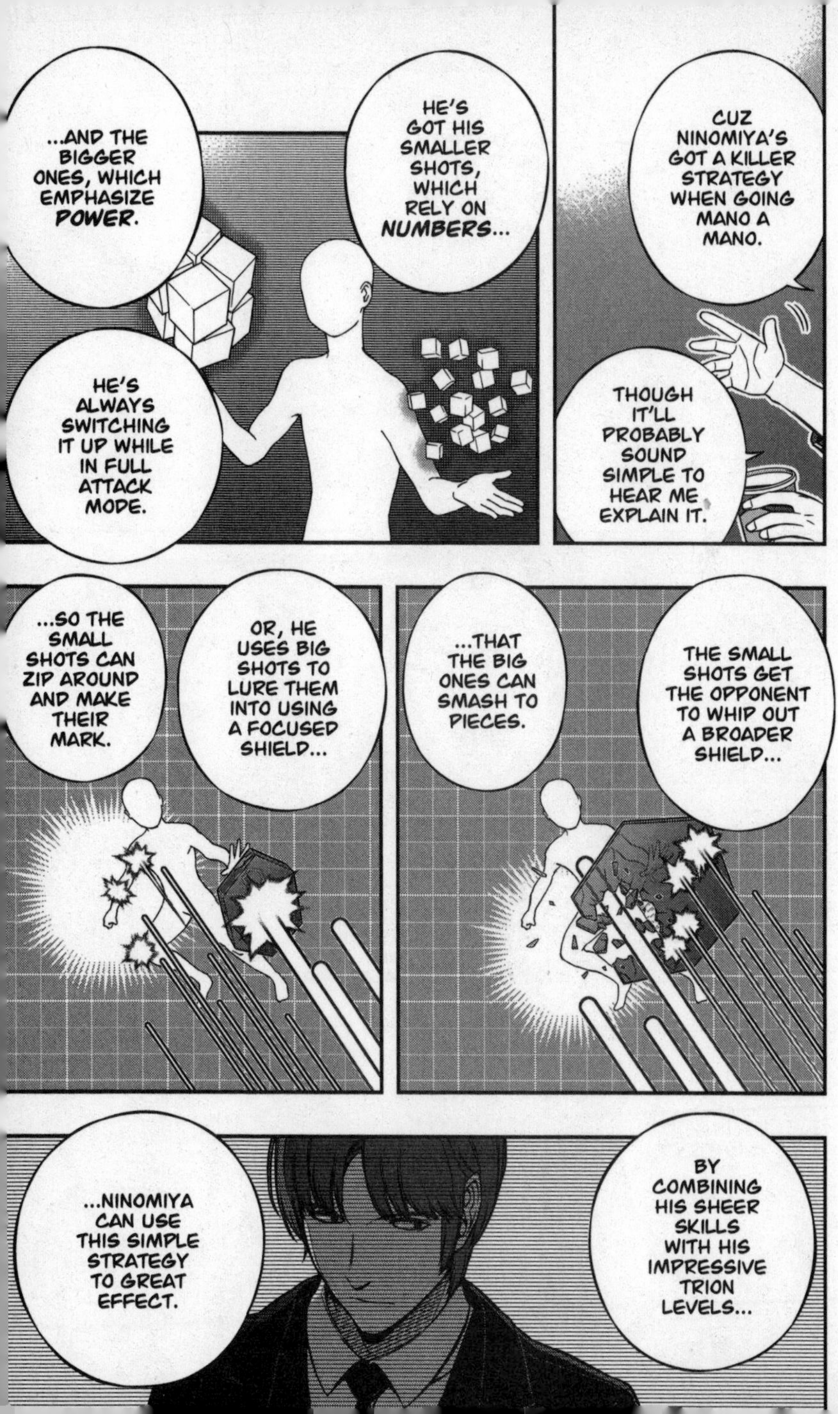
CUZ NINOMIYA'S GOT A KILLER STRATEGY WHEN GOING MANO A MANO.
THOUGH IT'LL PROBABLY SOUND SIMPLE TO HEAR ME EXPLAIN IT.
HE'S GOT HIS SMALLER SHOTS, WHICH RELY ON NUMBERS...
...AND THE BIGGER ONES, WHICH EMPHASIZE POWER.
HE'S ALWAYS SWITCHING IT UP WHILE IN FULL ATTACK MODE.
THE SMALL SHOTS GET THE OPPONENT TO WHIP OUT A BROADER SHIELD...
...THAT THE BIG ONES CAN SMASH TO PIECES.
OR, HE USES BIG SHOTS TO LURE THEM INTO USING A FOCUSED SHIELD...
...SO THE SMALL SHOTS CAN ZIP AROUND AND MAKE THEIR MARK.
BY COMBINING HIS SHEER SKILLS WITH HIS IMPRESSIVE TRION LEVELS...
...NINOMIYA CAN USE THIS SIMPLE STRATEGY TO GREAT EFFECT.

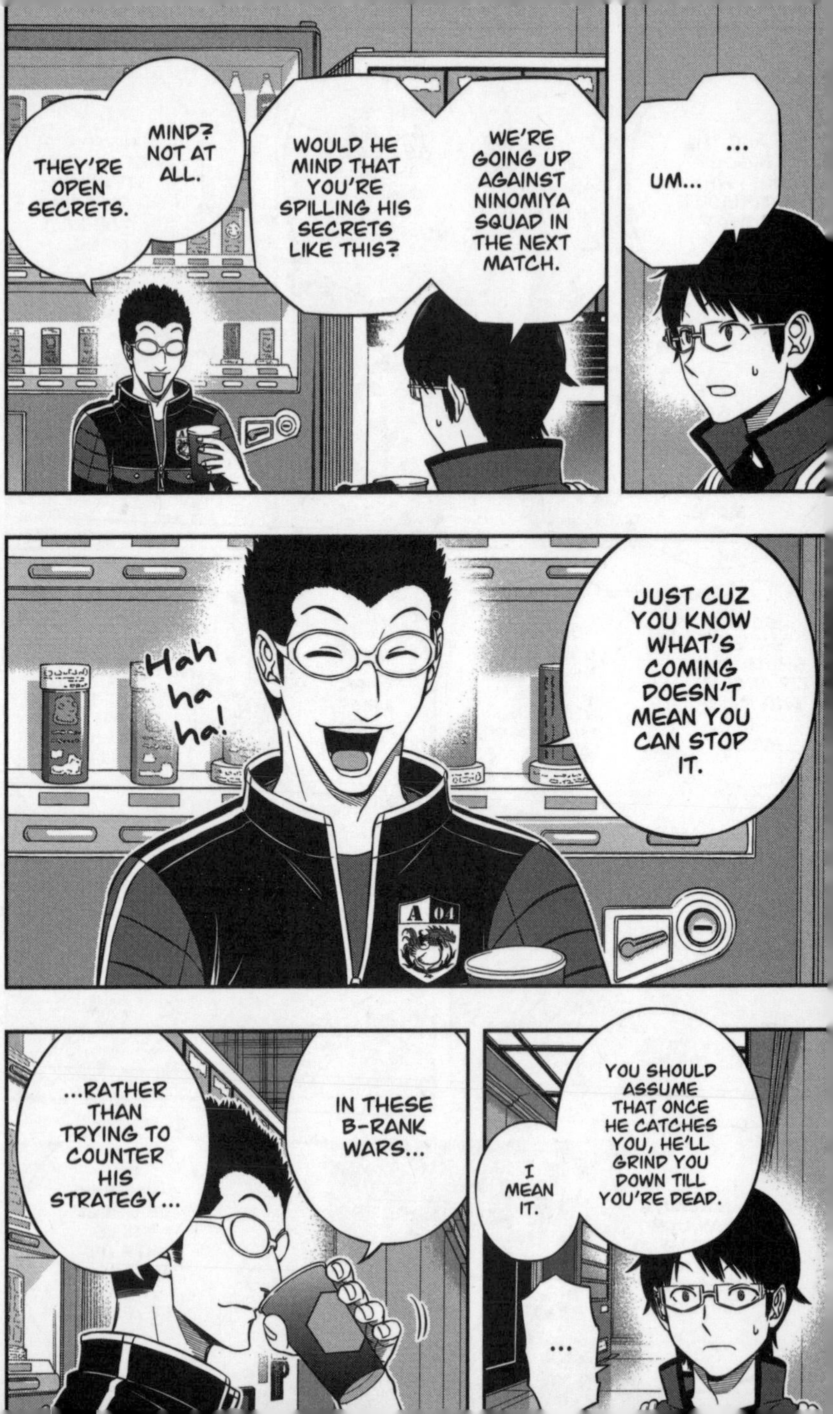
...
UM...
WE'RE GOING UP AGAINST NINOMIYA SQUAD IN THE NEXT MATCH.
WOULD HE MIND THAT YOU'RE SPILLING HIS SECRETS LIKE THIS?
MIND? NOT AT ALL.
THEY'RE OPEN SECRETS.
JUST CUZ YOU KNOW WHAT'S COMING DOESN'T MEAN YOU CAN STOP IT.
Hah ha ha!
YOU SHOULD ASSUME THAT ONCE HE CATCHES YOU, HE'LL GRIND YOU DOWN TILL YOU'RE DEAD.
I MEAN IT.
...
IN THESE B-RANK WARS...
...RATHER THAN TRYING TO COUNTER HIS STRATEGY...

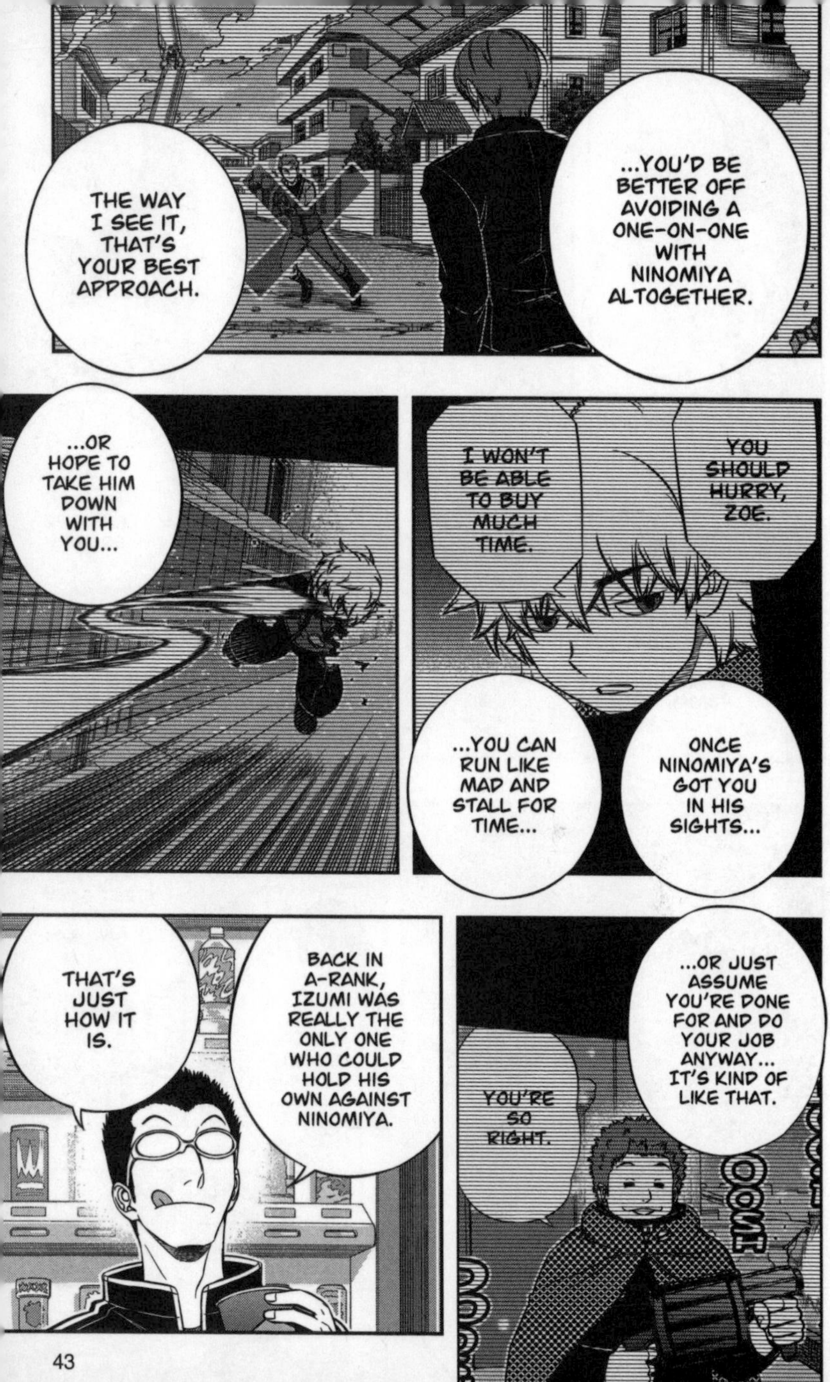
...YOU'D BE BETTER OFF AVOIDING A ONE-ON-ONE WITH NINOMIYA ALTOGETHER.
THE WAY I SEE IT, THAT'S YOUR BEST APPROACH.
YOU SHOULD HURRY, ZOE.
I WON'T BE ABLE TO BUY MUCH TIME.
ONCE NINOMIYA'S GOT YOU IN HIS SIGHTS...
...YOU CAN RUN LIKE MAD AND STALL FOR TIME...
...OR HOPE TO TAKE HIM DOWN WITH YOU...
...OR JUST ASSUME YOU'RE DONE FOR AND DO YOUR JOB ANYWAY... IT'S KIND OF LIKE THAT.
YOU'RE SO RIGHT.
BACK IN A-RANK, IZUMI WAS REALLY THE ONLY ONE WHO COULD HOLD HIS OWN AGAINST NINOMIYA.
THAT'S JUST HOW IT IS.

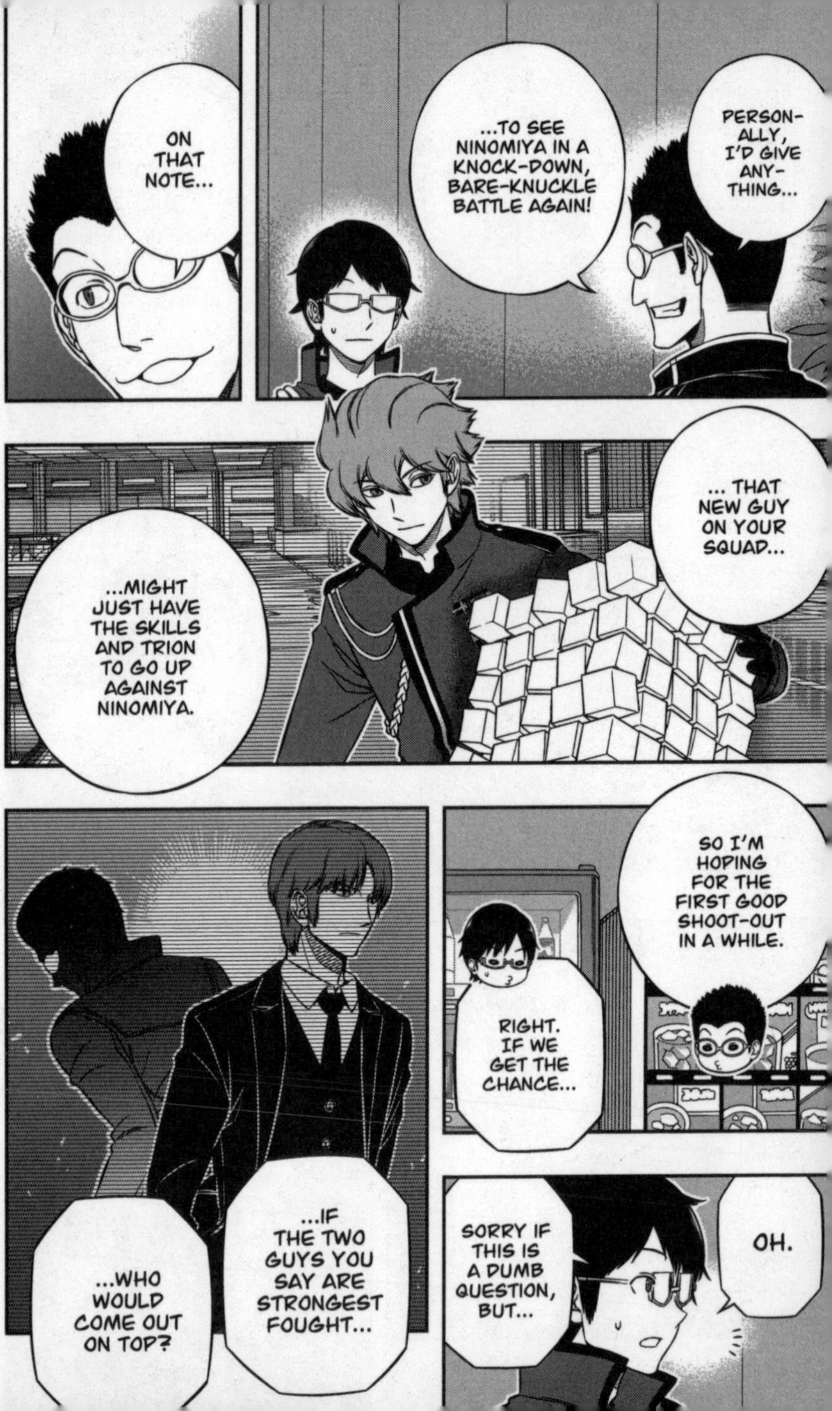
PERSON-ALLY, I'D GIVE ANY-THING...
...TO SEE NINOMIYA IN A KNOCK-DOWN, BARE-KNUCKLE BATTLE AGAIN!
ON THAT NOTE...
... THAT NEW GUY ON YOUR SQUAD...
...MIGHT JUST HAVE THE SKILLS AND TRION TO GO UP AGAINST NINOMIYA.
SO I'M HOPING FOR THE FIRST GOOD SHOOT-OUT IN A WHILE.
RIGHT. IF WE GET THE CHANCE...
OH.
SORRY IF THIS IS A DUMB QUESTION, BUT...
...IF THE TWO GUYS YOU SAY ARE STRONGEST FOUGHT...
...WHO WOULD COME OUT ON TOP?

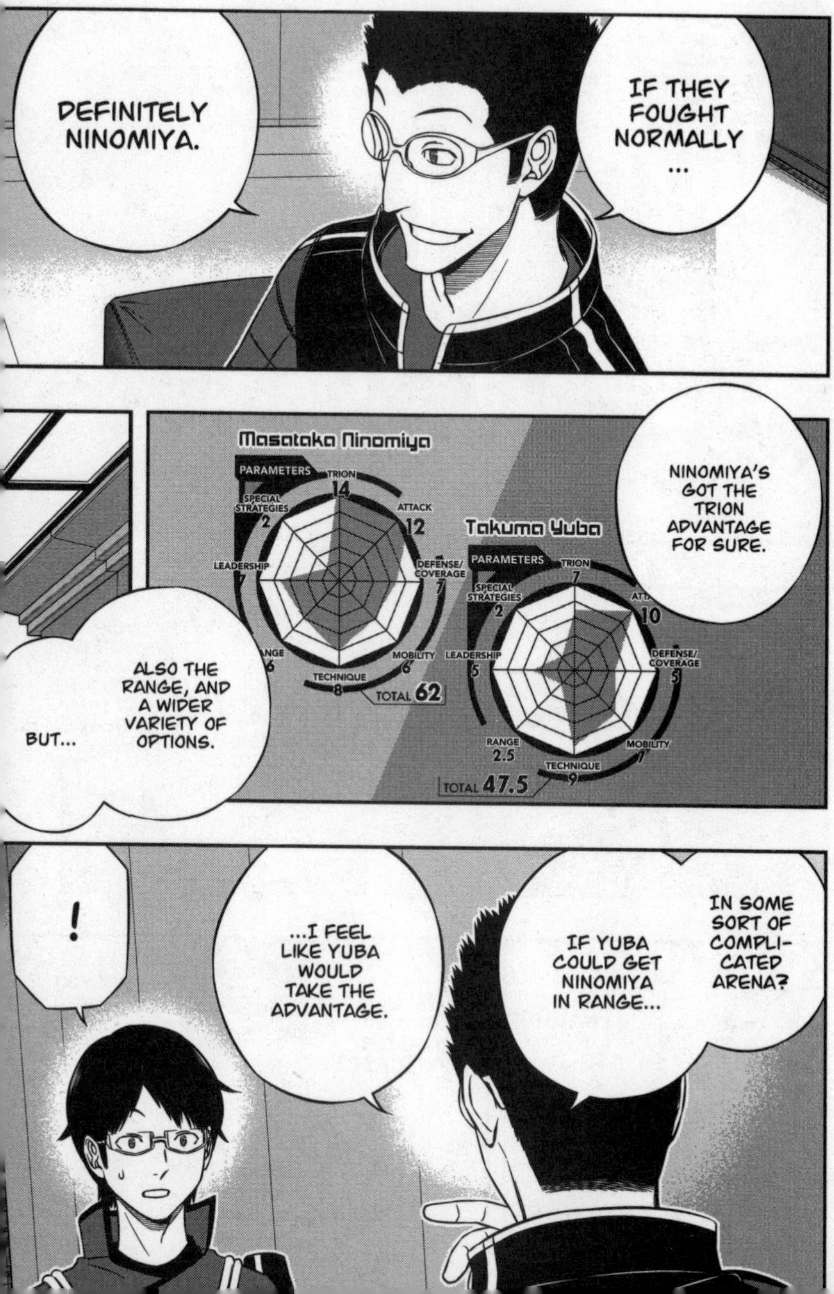
IF THEY FOUGHT NORMALLY ...
DEFINITELY NINOMIYA.
NINOMIYA'S GOT THE TRION ADVANTAGE FOR SURE.
Masataka Ninomiya
PARAMETERS
TRION 14
ATTACK 12
DEFENSE/COVERAGE 7
MOBILITY 6
TECHNIQUE 8
6
LEADERSHIP 7
SPECIAL STRATEGIES 2
TOTAL 62
Takuma Yuba
PARAMETERS
TRION 7
10
DEFENSE/COVERAGE 5
MOBILITY 7
TECHNIQUE 9
RANGE 2.5
LEADERSHIP 5
SPECIAL STRATEGIES 2
TOTAL 47.5
ALSO THE RANGE, AND A WIDER VARIETY OF OPTIONS.
BUT...
IN SOME SORT OF COMPLICATED ARENA?
IF YUBA COULD GET NINOMIYA IN RANGE...
...I FEEL LIKE YUBA WOULD TAKE THE ADVANTAGE.
!

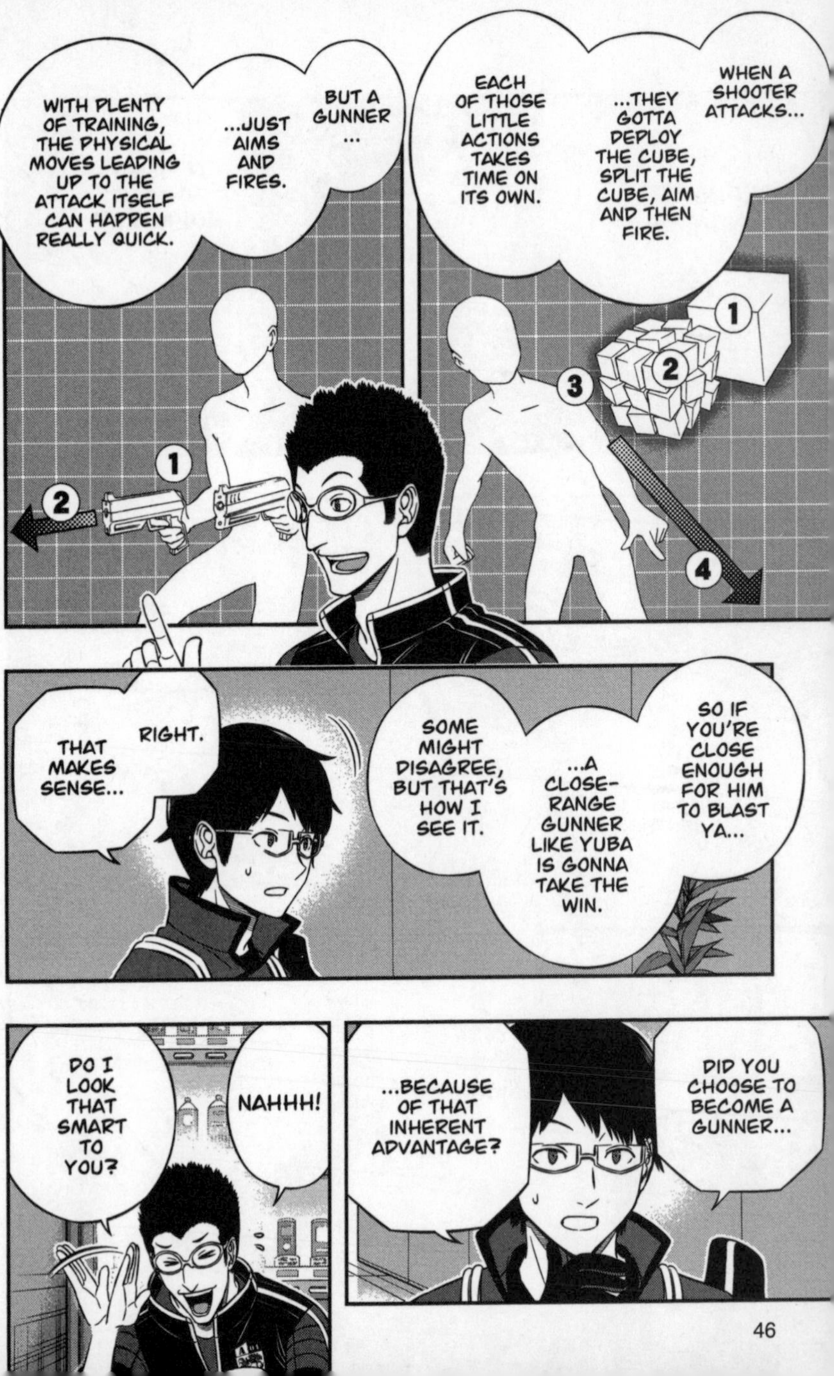
WHEN A SHOOTER ATTACKS...
...THEY GOTTA DEPLOY THE CUBE, SPLIT THE CUBE, AIM AND THEN FIRE.
EACH OF THOSE LITTLE ACTIONS TAKES TIME ON ITS OWN.
BUT A GUNNER...
...JUST AIMS AND FIRES.
WITH PLENTY OF TRAINING, THE PHYSICAL MOVES LEADING UP TO THE ATTACK ITSELF CAN HAPPEN REALLY QUICK.
SO IF YOU'RE CLOSE ENOUGH FOR HIM TO BLAST YA...
...A CLOSE-RANGE GUNNER LIKE YUBA IS GONNA TAKE THE WIN.
SOME MIGHT DISAGREE, BUT THAT'S HOW I SEE IT.
RIGHT.
THAT MAKES SENSE...
DID YOU CHOOSE TO BECOME A GUNNER...
...BECAUSE OF THAT INHERENT ADVANTAGE?
NAHHH!
DO I LOOK THAT SMART TO YOU?

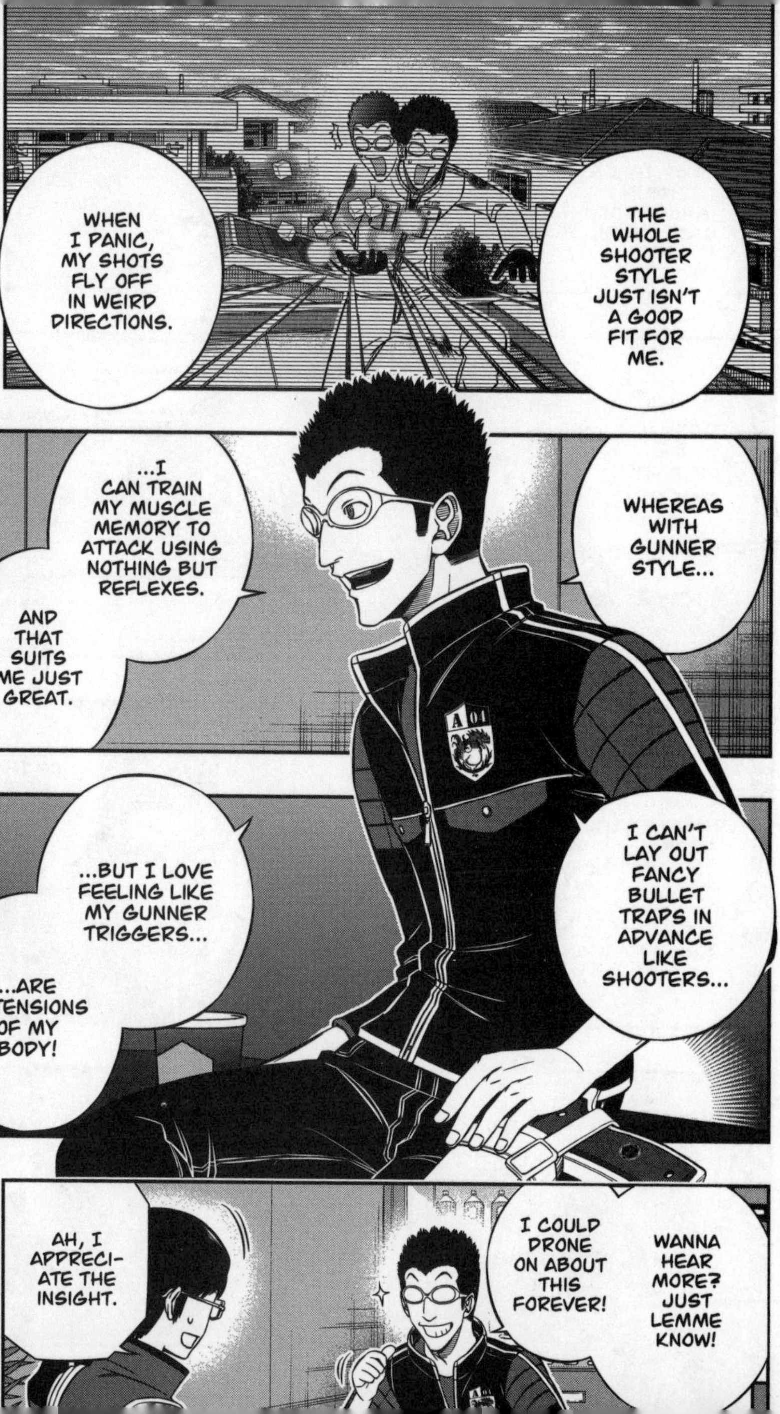
THE WHOLE SHOOTER STYLE JUST ISN'T A GOOD FIT FOR ME.
WHEN I PANIC, MY SHOTS FLY OFF IN WEIRD DIRECTIONS.
WHEREAS WITH GUNNER STYLE...
...I CAN TRAIN MY MUSCLE MEMORY TO ATTACK USING NOTHING BUT REFLEXES.
AND THAT SUITS ME JUST GREAT.
I CAN'T LAY OUT FANCY BULLET TRAPS IN ADVANCE LIKE SHOOTERS...
...BUT I LOVE FEELING LIKE MY GUNNER TRIGGERS...
...ARE EXTENSIONS OF MY BODY!
WANNA HEAR MORE? JUST LEMME KNOW!
I COULD DRONE ON ABOUT THIS FOREVER!
AH, I APPRECIATE THE INSIGHT.

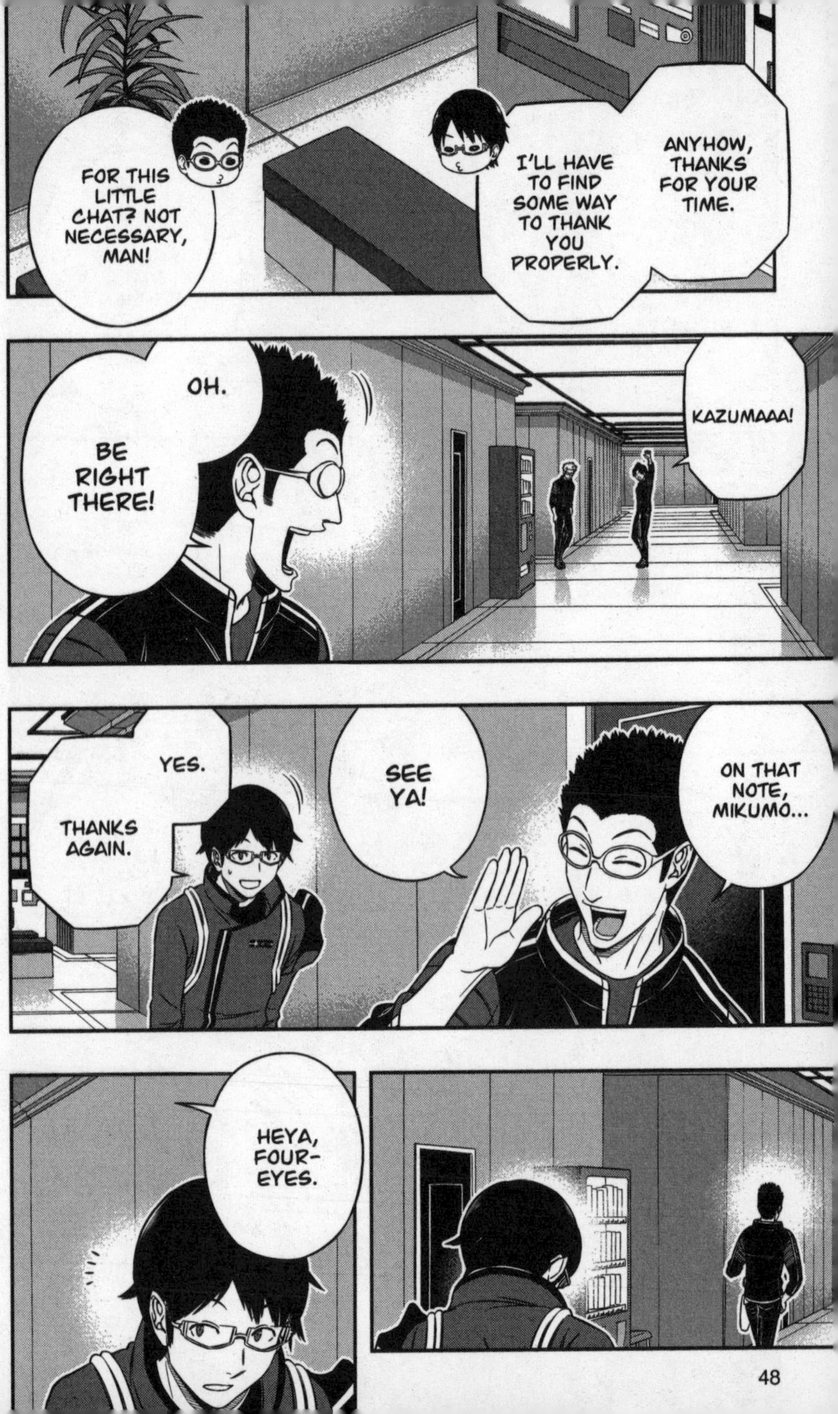
ANYHOW, THANKS FOR YOUR TIME.
I'LL HAVE TO FIND SOME WAY TO THANK YOU PROPERLY.
FOR THIS LITTLE CHAT? NOT NECESSARY, MAN!
KAZUMAAA!
OH.
BE RIGHT THERE!
ON THAT NOTE, MIKUMO...
SEE YA!
YES.
THANKS AGAIN.
HEYA, FOUR-EYES.

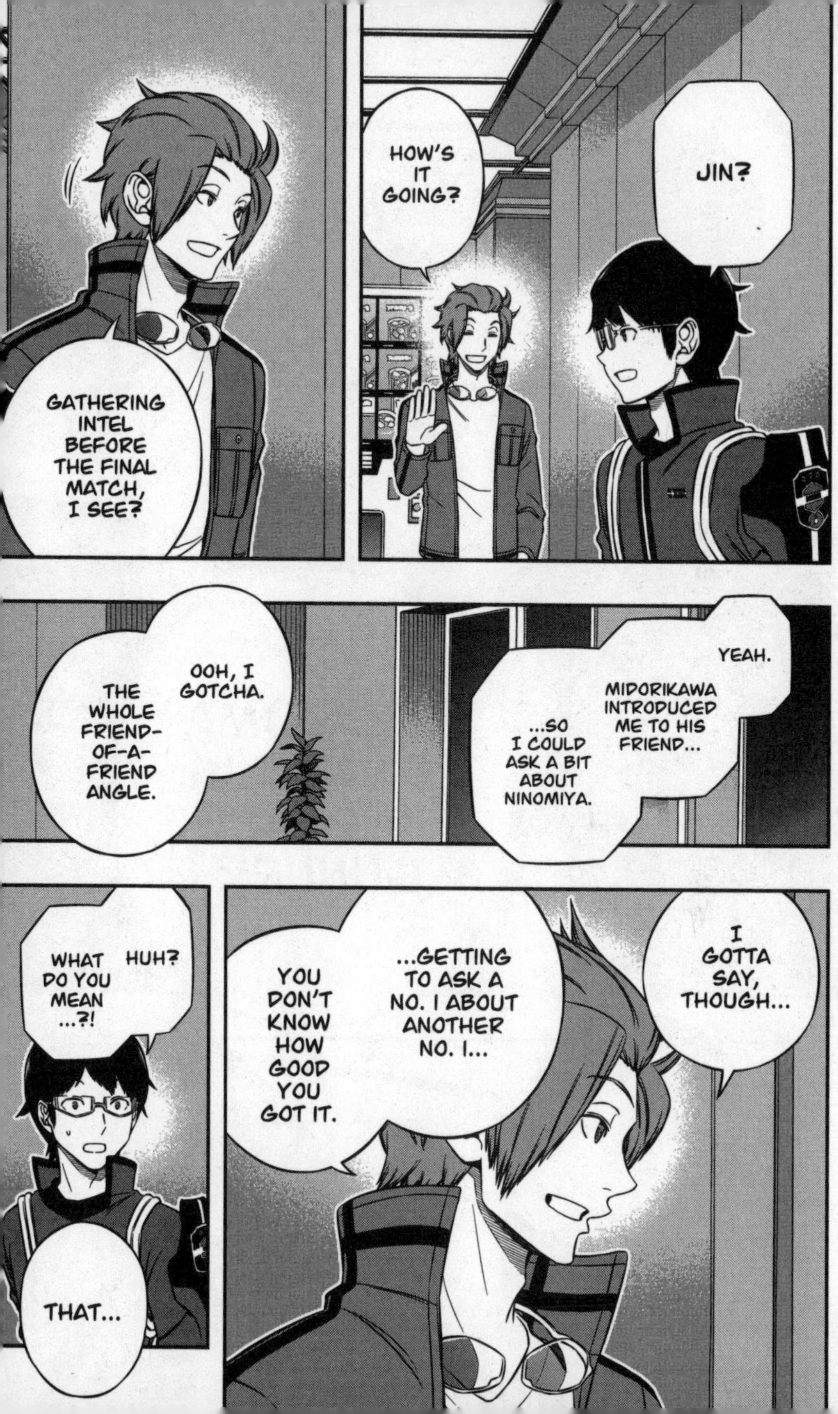
JIN?
HOW'S IT GOING?
GATHERING INTEL BEFORE THE FINAL MATCH, I SEE?
YEAH.
MIDORIKAWA INTRODUCED ME TO HIS FRIEND...
...SO I COULD ASK A BIT ABOUT NINOMIYA.
OOH, I GOTCHA.
THE WHOLE FRIEND-OF-A-FRIEND ANGLE.
I GOTTA SAY, THOUGH...
...GETTING TO ASK A NO. 1 ABOUT ANOTHER NO. 1...
YOU DON'T KNOW HOW GOOD YOU GOT IT.
HUH?
WHAT DO YOU MEAN ...?!
THAT...

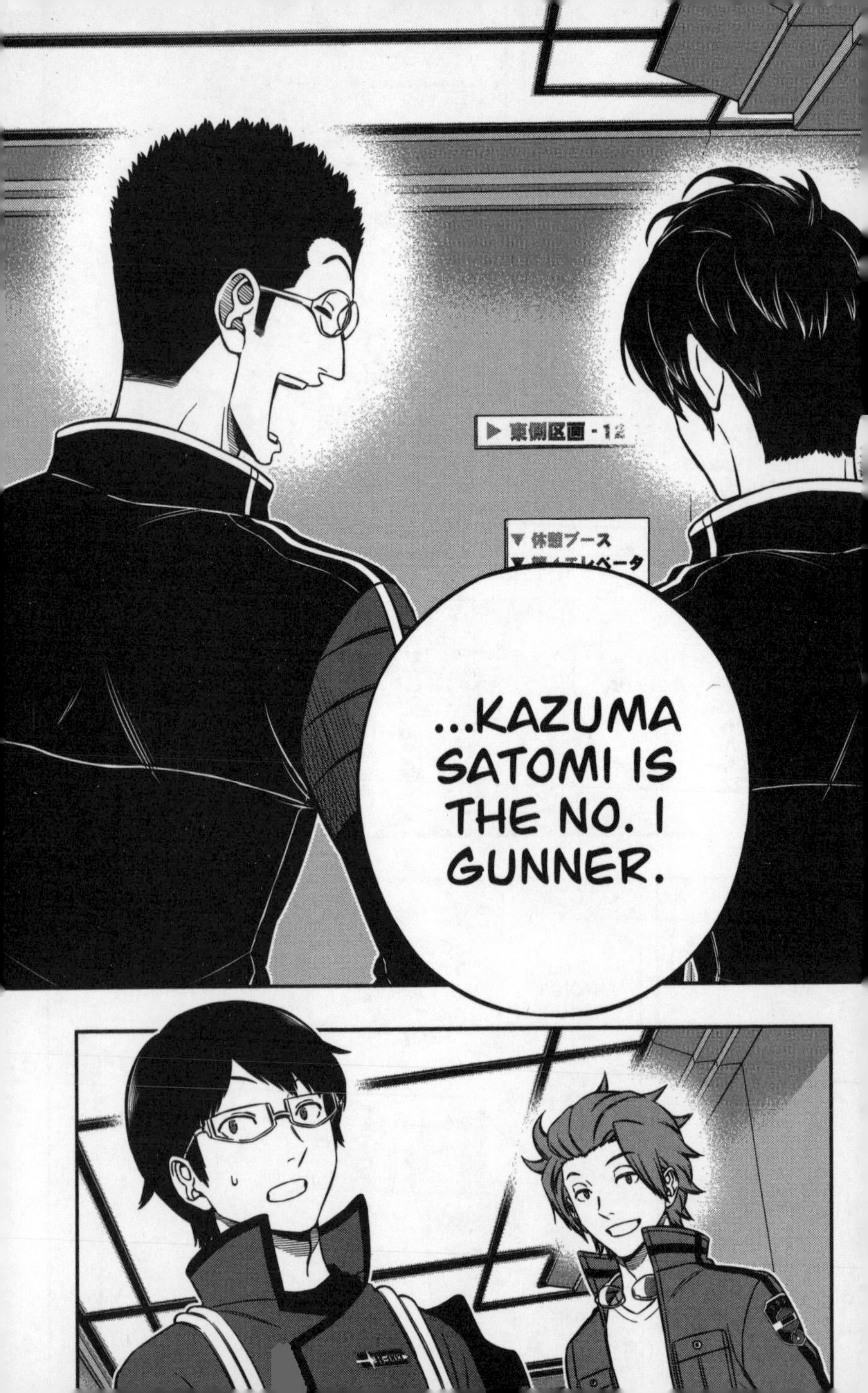
▶ 東側区画 - 12
▼ 休憩ブース
...KAZUMA SATOMI IS THE NO. 1 GUNNER.

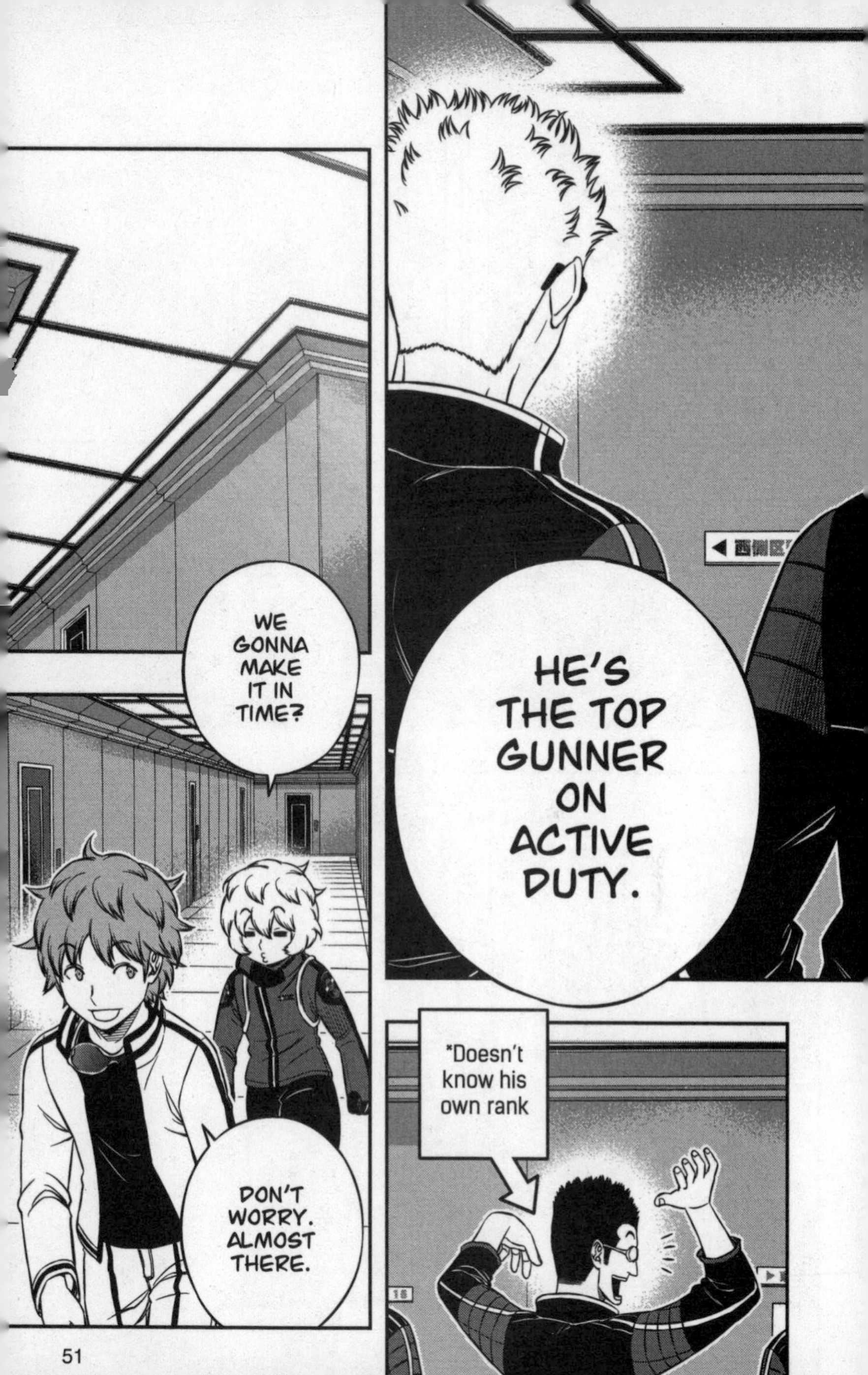
HE'S THE TOP GUNNER ON ACTIVE DUTY.
*Doesn't know his own rank
WE GONNA MAKE IT IN TIME?
DON'T WORRY. ALMOST THERE.

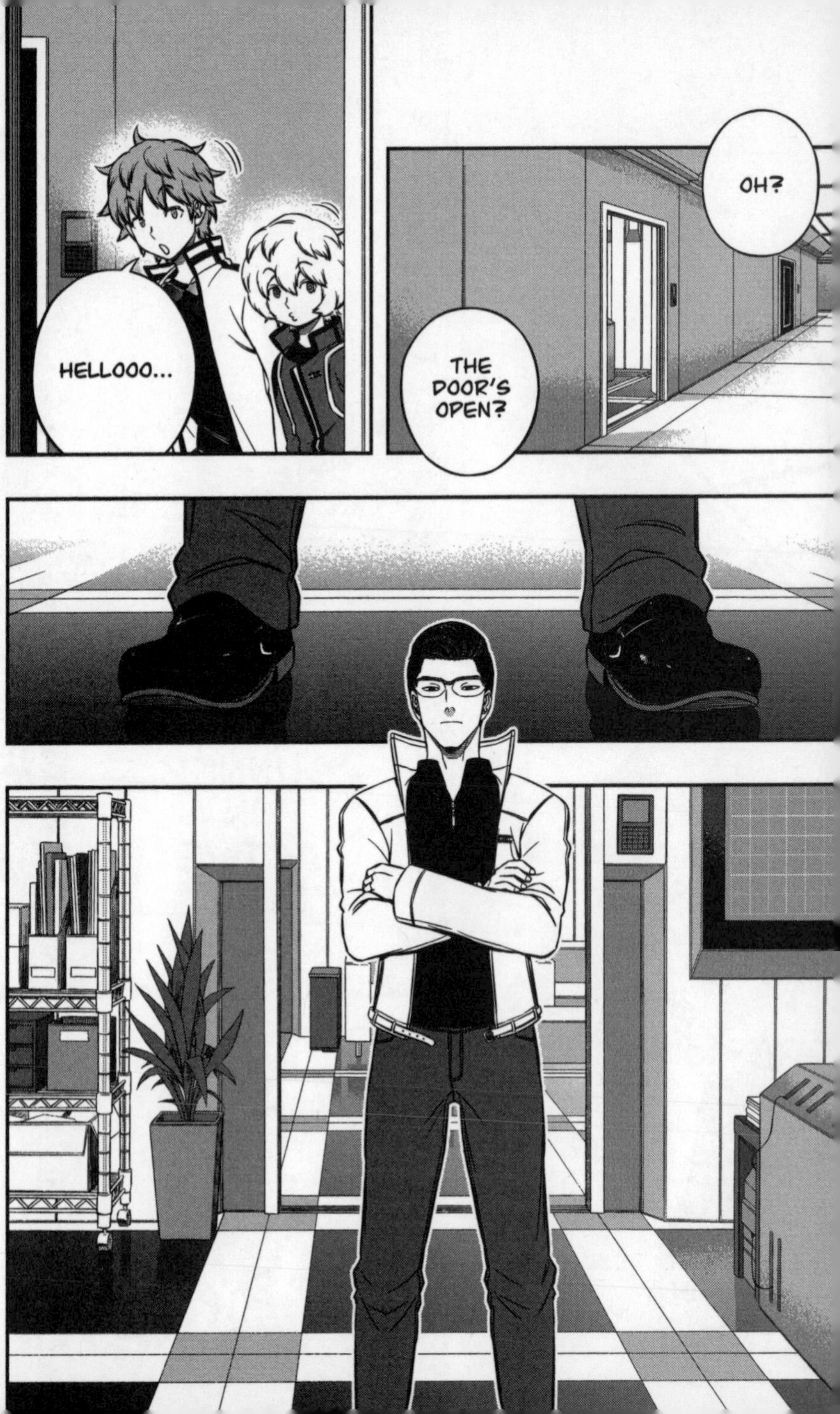
OH?
THE DOOR'S OPEN?
HELLOOO...

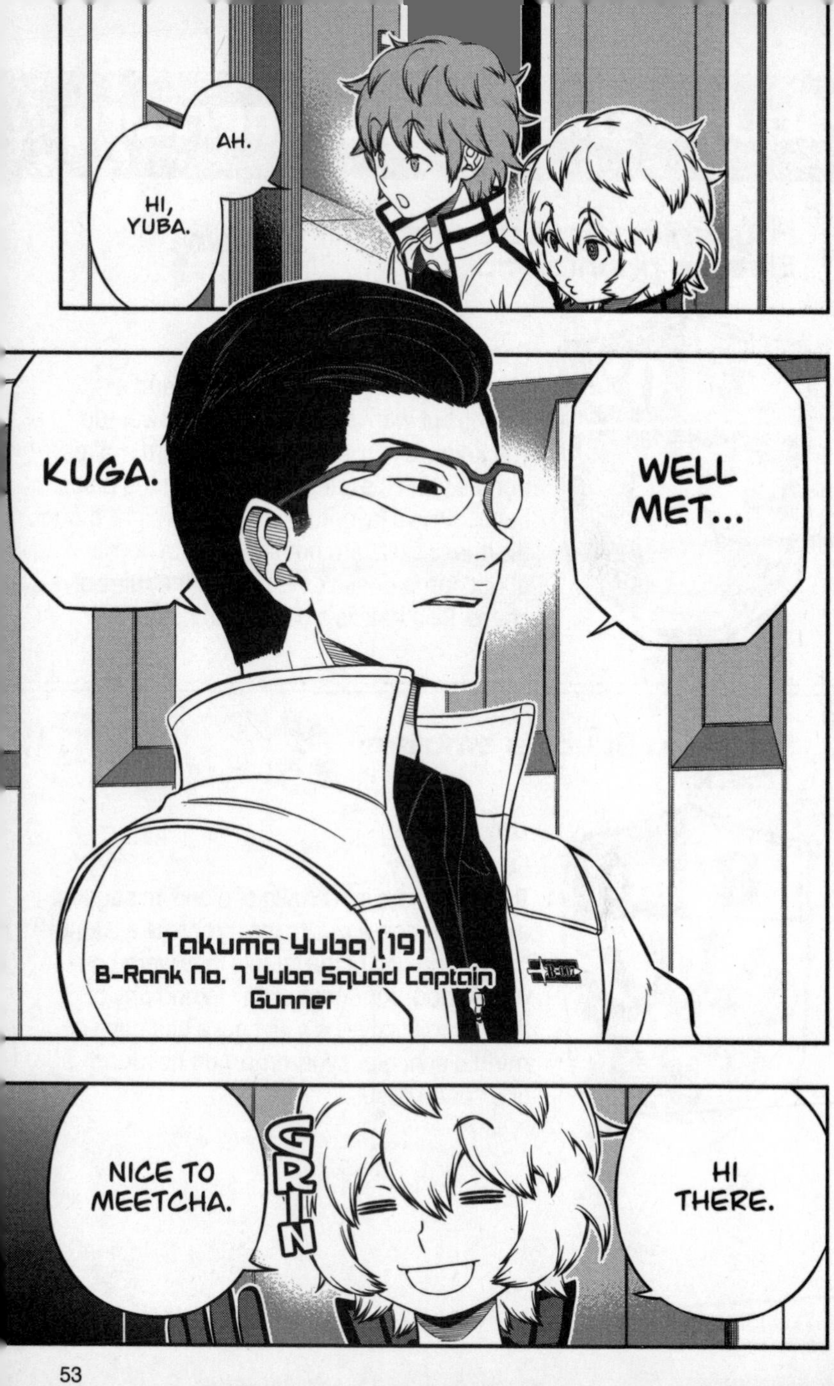
AH.
HI, YUBA.
WELL MET...
KUGA.
Takuma Yuba (19)
B-Rank No. 7 Yuba Squad Captain
Gunner
HI THERE.
GRIN
NICE TO MEETCHA.

Squad Emblem Commentary

Fuyushima Squad's emblem: Elusive, phantasmal

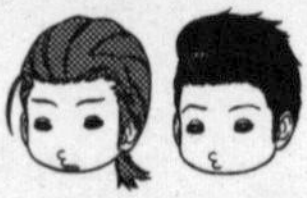

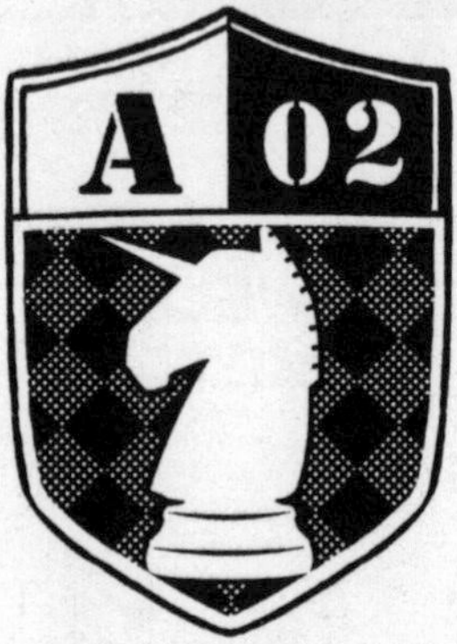
A
02

Commentary:
As you can see, it's a chessboard and a knight, but with a little horn, as a power-up. The knight's movement on the board makes people think it's teleporting all over the place. Fuyushima's favorite piece is the knight, though his chess skills are nothing to write home about. Toma doesn't even know the rules of chess. Risa Maki is a beast at chess.

Ninomiya Squad's emblem: Talent

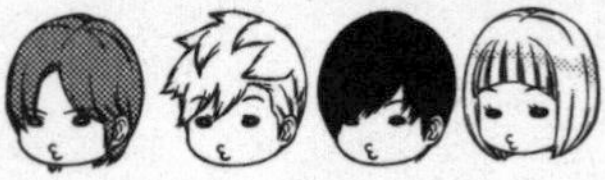

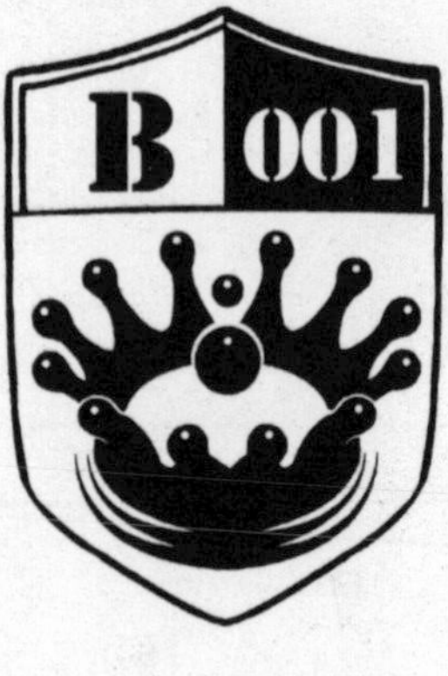
B
001

Commentary:
The motif here is a crown of blood, to suggest a squad that will rise to the throne (like a king) by making use of the talents they were born with (blood). Ninomiya didn't intend any of that, specifically—he's just got a bad case of middle schooler syndrome. And he's kind of a space case.

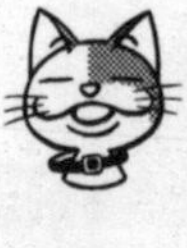

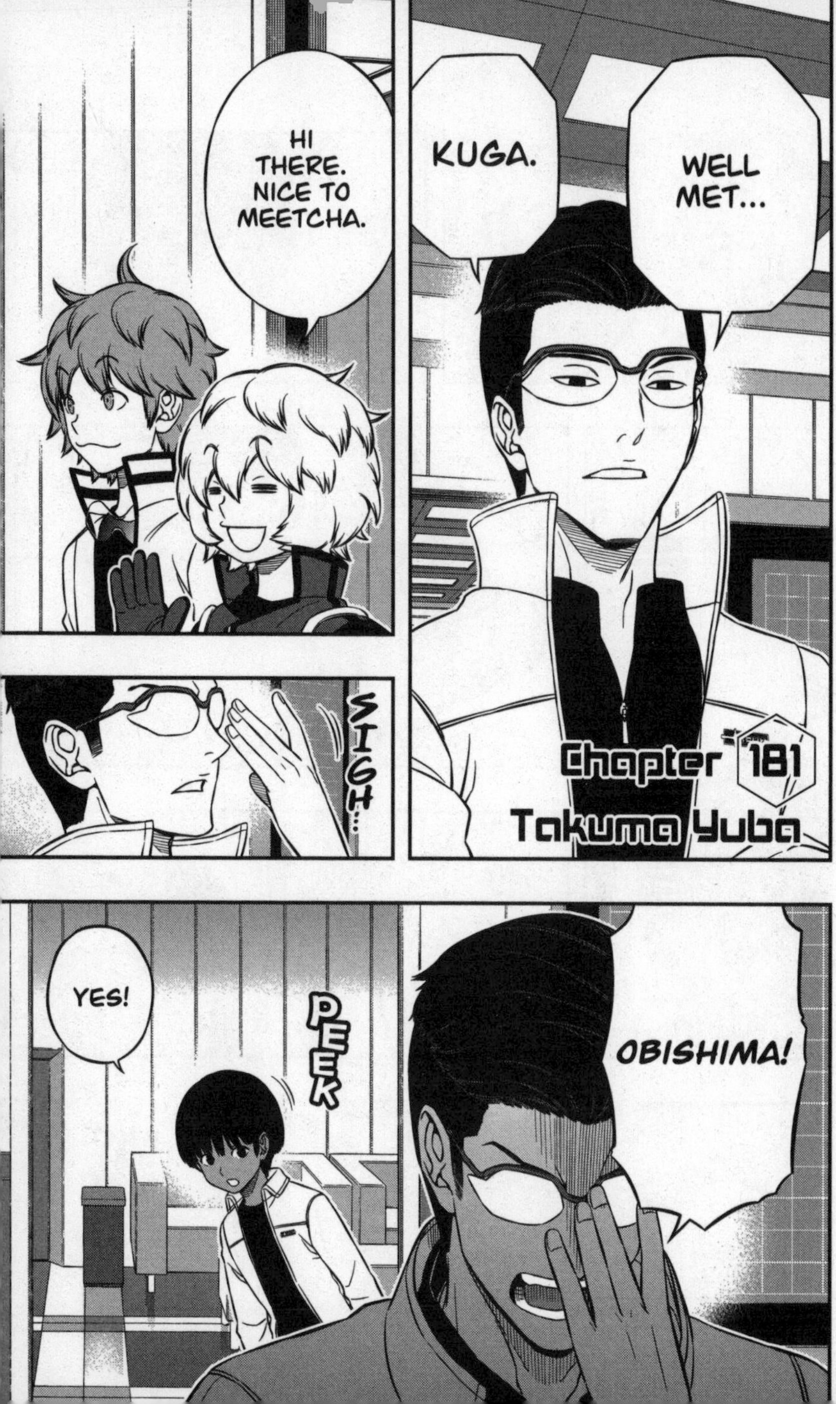
WELL MET...
KUGA.
Chapter 181
Takuma Yuba
HI THERE. NICE TO MEETCHA.
SIGH...
OBISHIMA!
PEEK
YES!

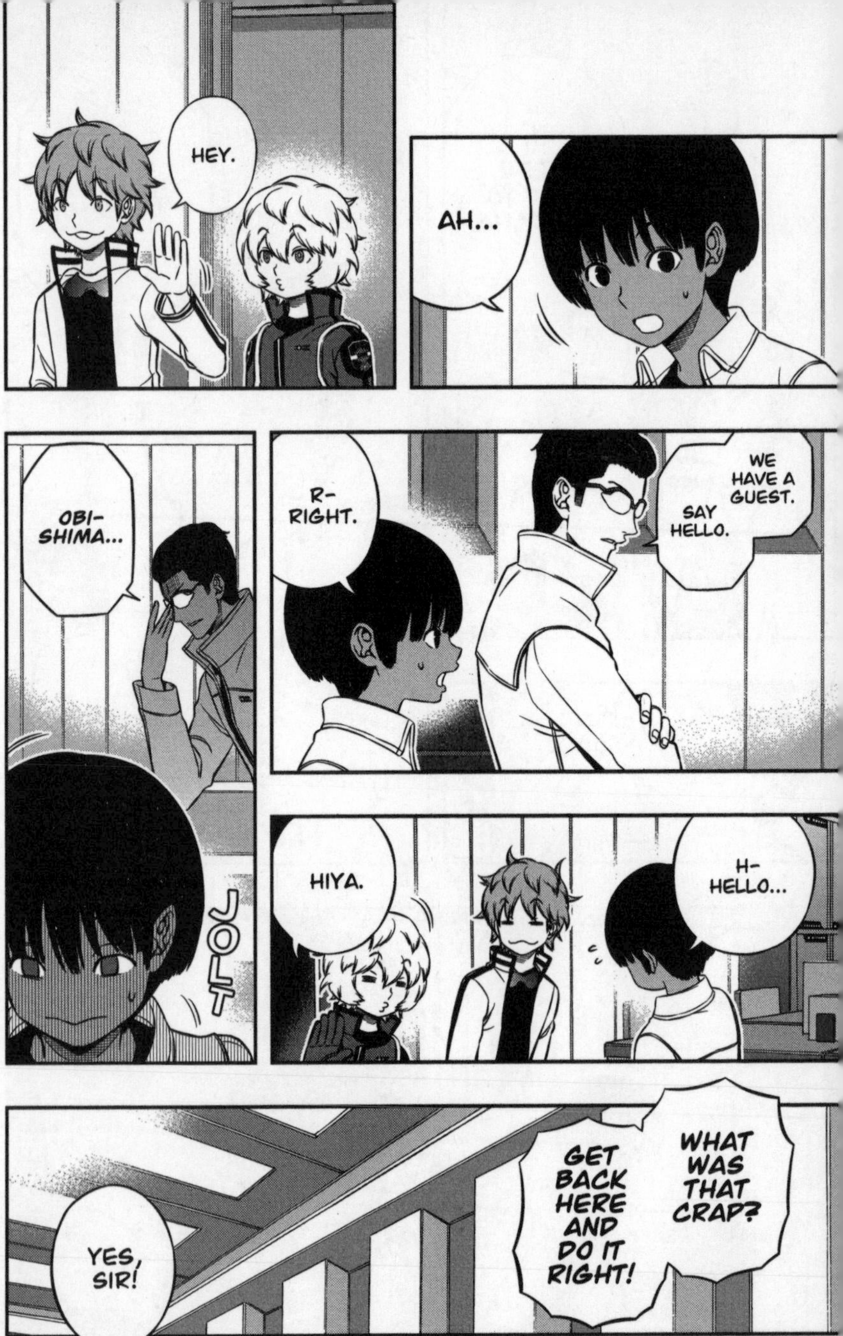

AH...
HEY.
WE HAVE A GUEST.
SAY HELLO.
R-RIGHT.
H-HELLO...
HIYA.
OBI-SHIMA...
JOLT
WHAT WAS THAT CRAP?
GET BACK HERE AND DO IT RIGHT!
YES, SIR!

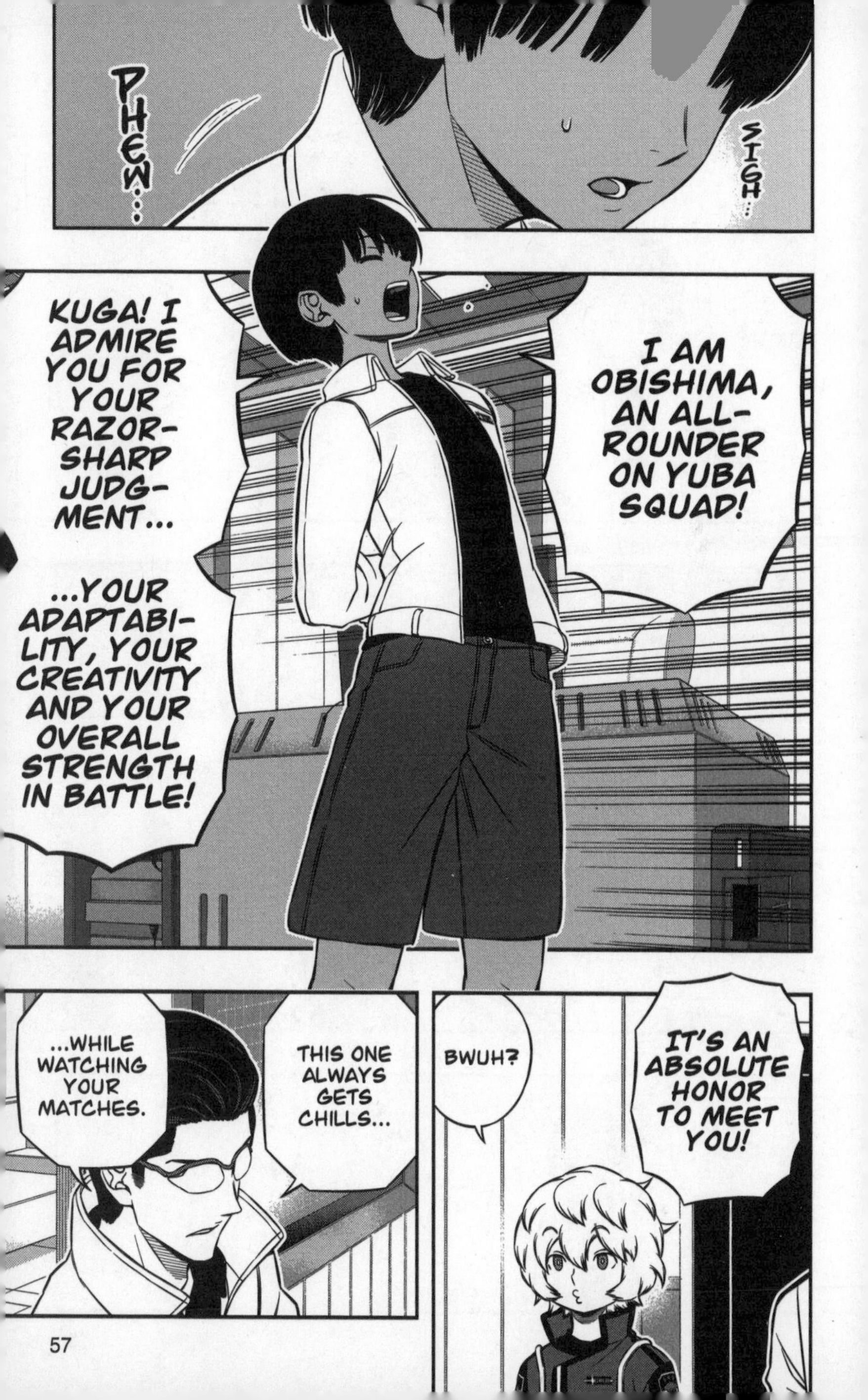
SIGH...
PHEW...
I AM OBISHIMA, AN ALL-ROUNDER ON YUBA SQUAD!
KUGA! I ADMIRE YOU FOR YOUR RAZOR-SHARP JUDGMENT...
...YOUR ADAPTABILITY, YOUR CREATIVITY AND YOUR OVERALL STRENGTH IN BATTLE!
IT'S AN ABSOLUTE HONOR TO MEET YOU!
BWUH?
THIS ONE ALWAYS GETS CHILLS...
...WHILE WATCHING YOUR MATCHES.

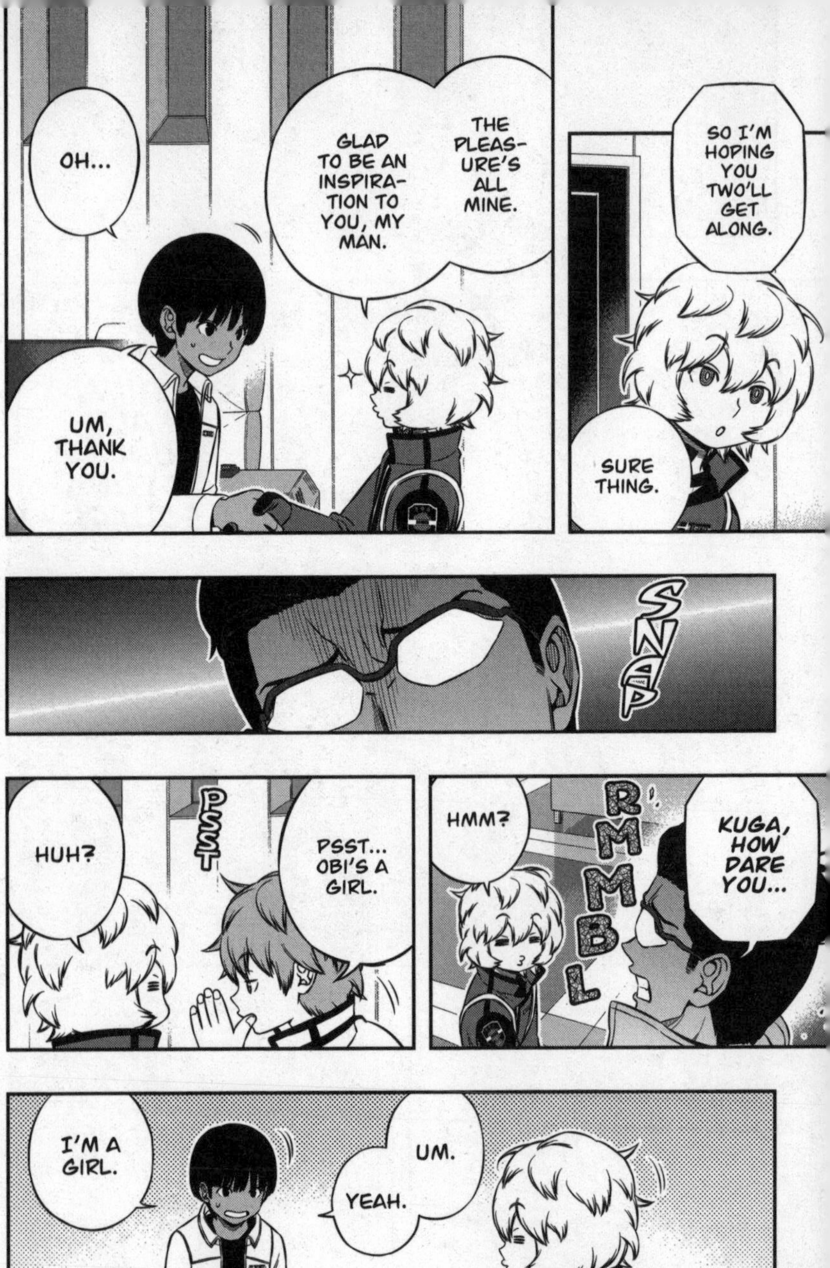
SO I'M HOPING YOU TWO'LL GET ALONG.
SURE THING.
THE PLEASURE'S ALL MINE.
GLAD TO BE AN INSPIRATION TO YOU, MY MAN.
OH...
UM, THANK YOU.
SNAP
KUGA, HOW DARE YOU...
RMMBL
HMM?
PSST... OBI'S A GIRL.
PSST
HUH?
UM. YEAH.
I'M A GIRL.

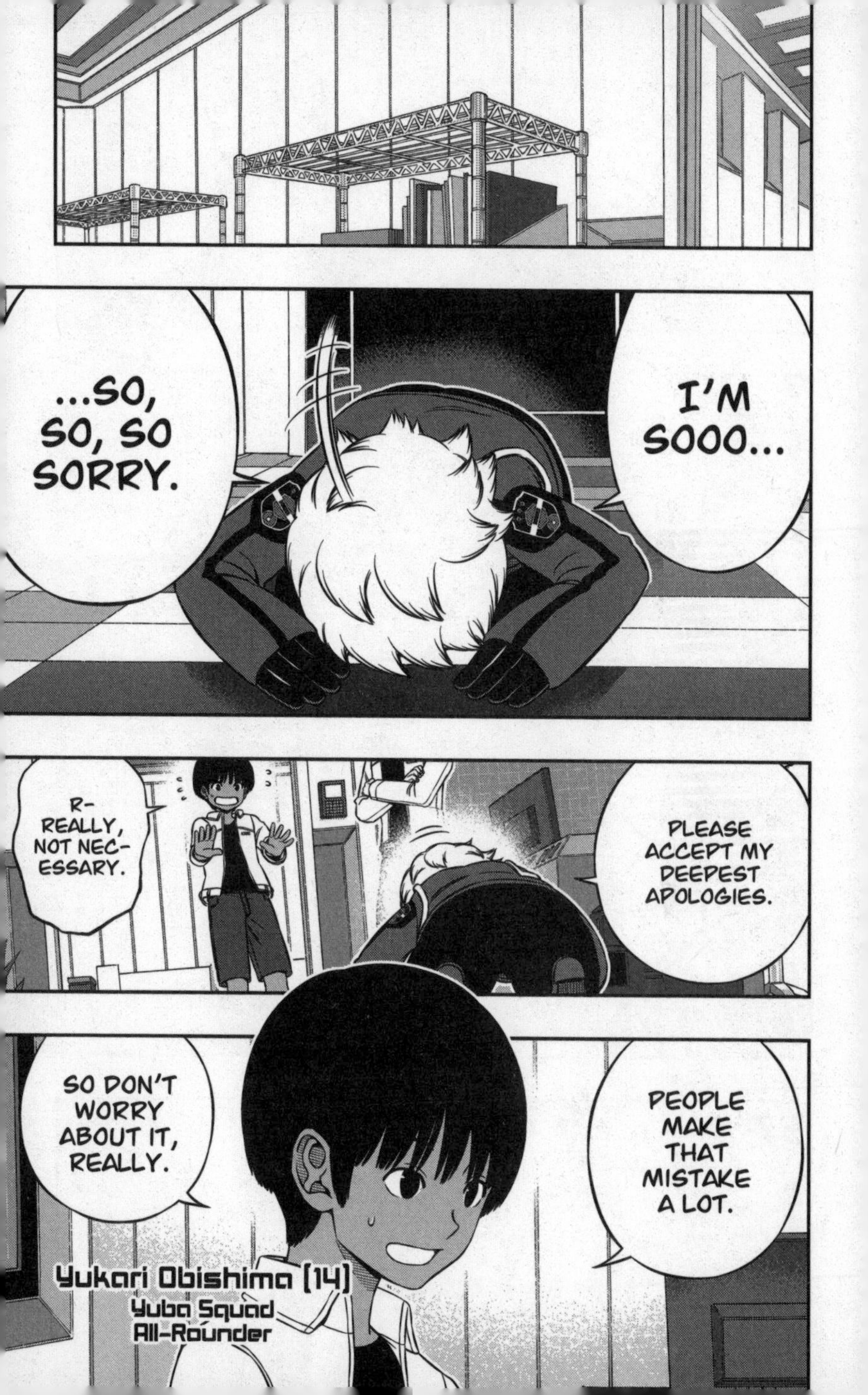
I'M SOOO...
...SO, SO, SO SORRY.
PLEASE ACCEPT MY DEEPEST APOLOGIES.
R-REALLY, NOT NEC-ESSARY.
PEOPLE MAKE THAT MISTAKE A LOT.
SO DON'T WORRY ABOUT IT, REALLY.
Yukari Obishima (14)
Yuba Squad All-Rounder

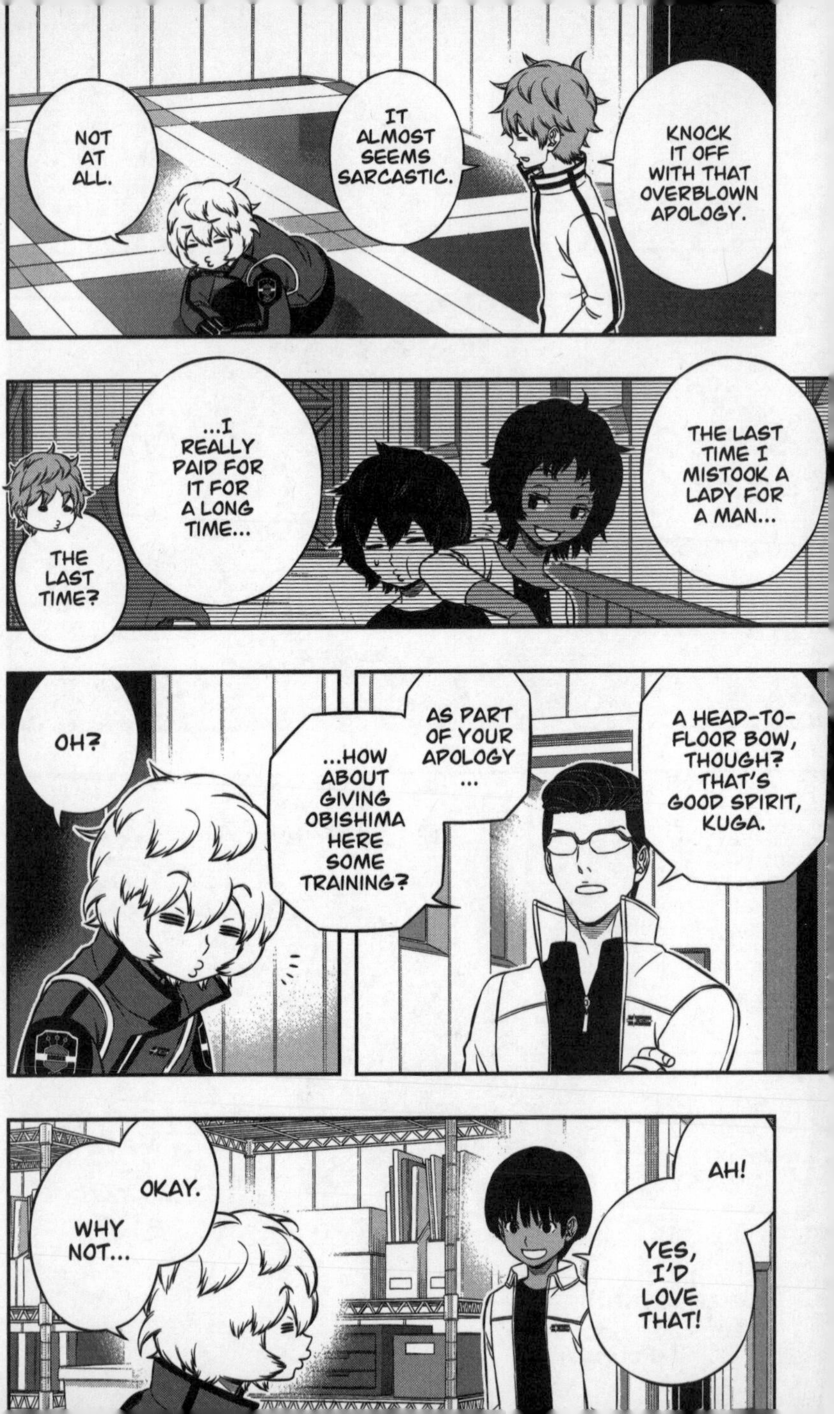
KNOCK IT OFF WITH THAT OVERBLOWN APOLOGY.
IT ALMOST SEEMS SARCASTIC.
NOT AT ALL.
THE LAST TIME I MISTOOK A LADY FOR A MAN...
...I REALLY PAID FOR IT FOR A LONG TIME...
THE LAST TIME?
A HEAD-TO-FLOOR BOW, THOUGH? THAT'S GOOD SPIRIT, KUGA.
AS PART OF YOUR APOLOGY...
...HOW ABOUT GIVING OBISHIMA HERE SOME TRAINING?
OH?
AH!
YES, I'D LOVE THAT!
OKAY.
WHY NOT...

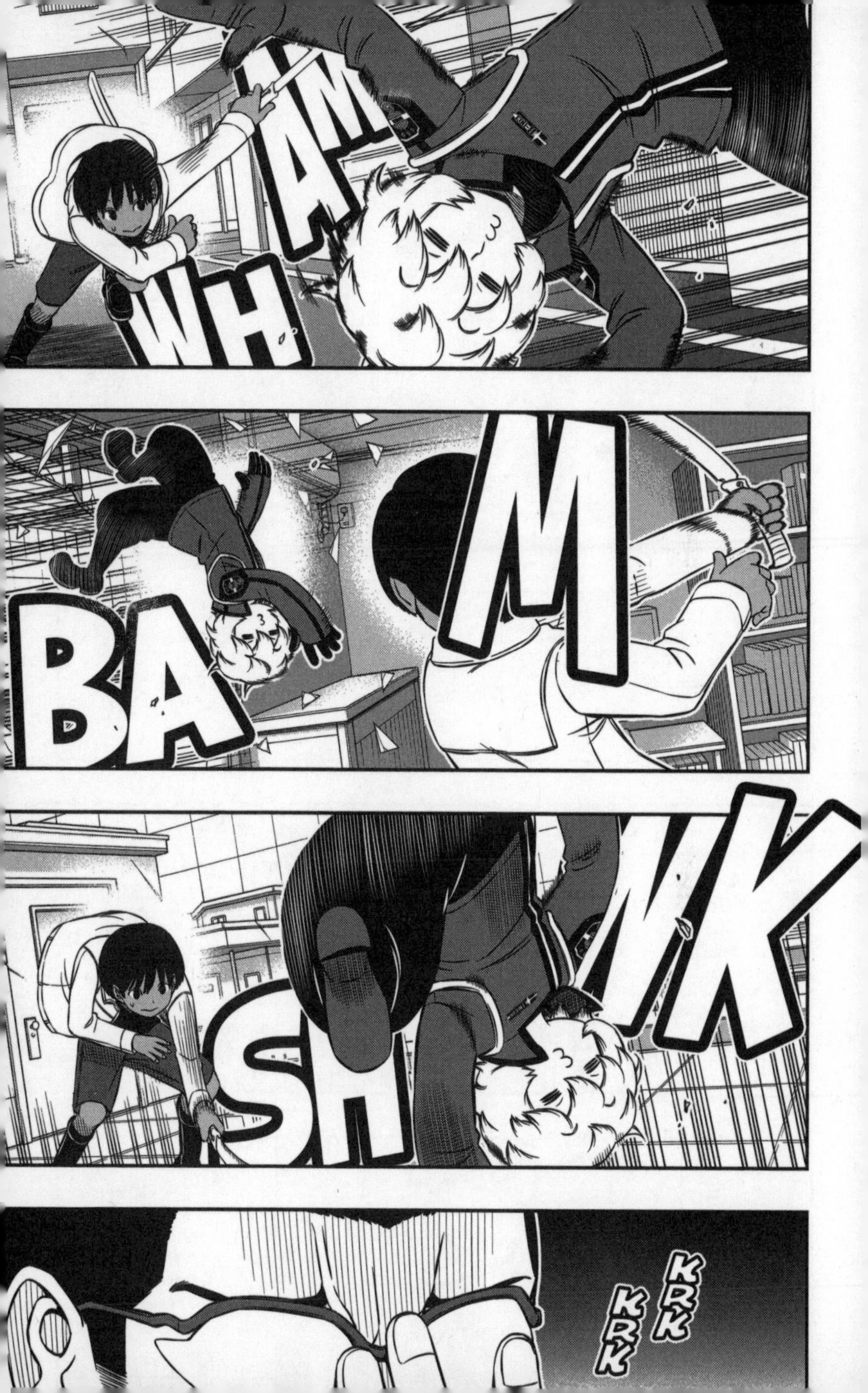
WHAM
BAM
SH
WK
KRK
KRK

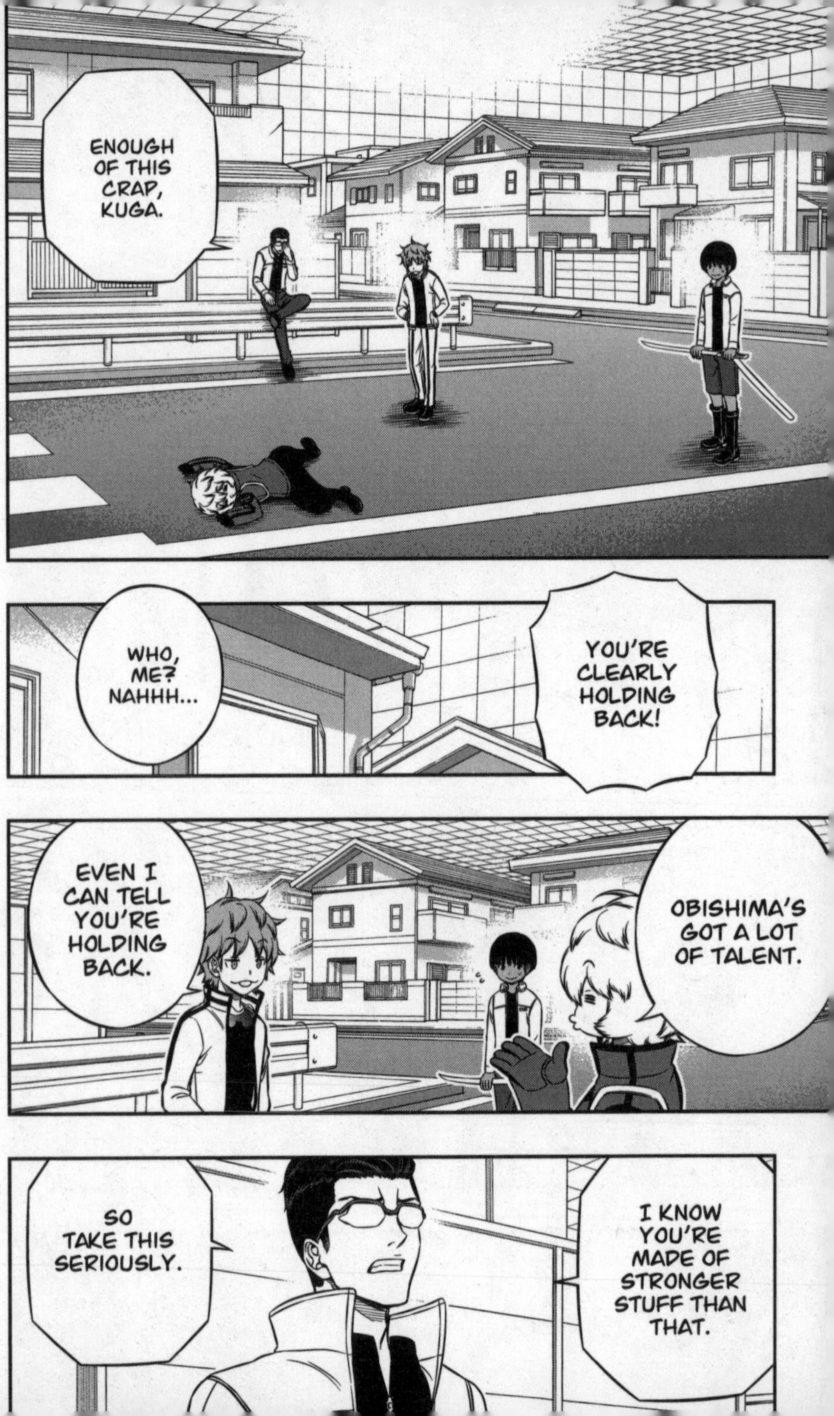
ENOUGH OF THIS CRAP, KUGA.
YOU'RE CLEARLY HOLDING BACK!
WHO, ME? NAHHH...
OBISHIMA'S GOT A LOT OF TALENT.
EVEN I CAN TELL YOU'RE HOLDING BACK.
I KNOW YOU'RE MADE OF STRONGER STUFF THAN THAT.
SO TAKE THIS SERIOUSLY.

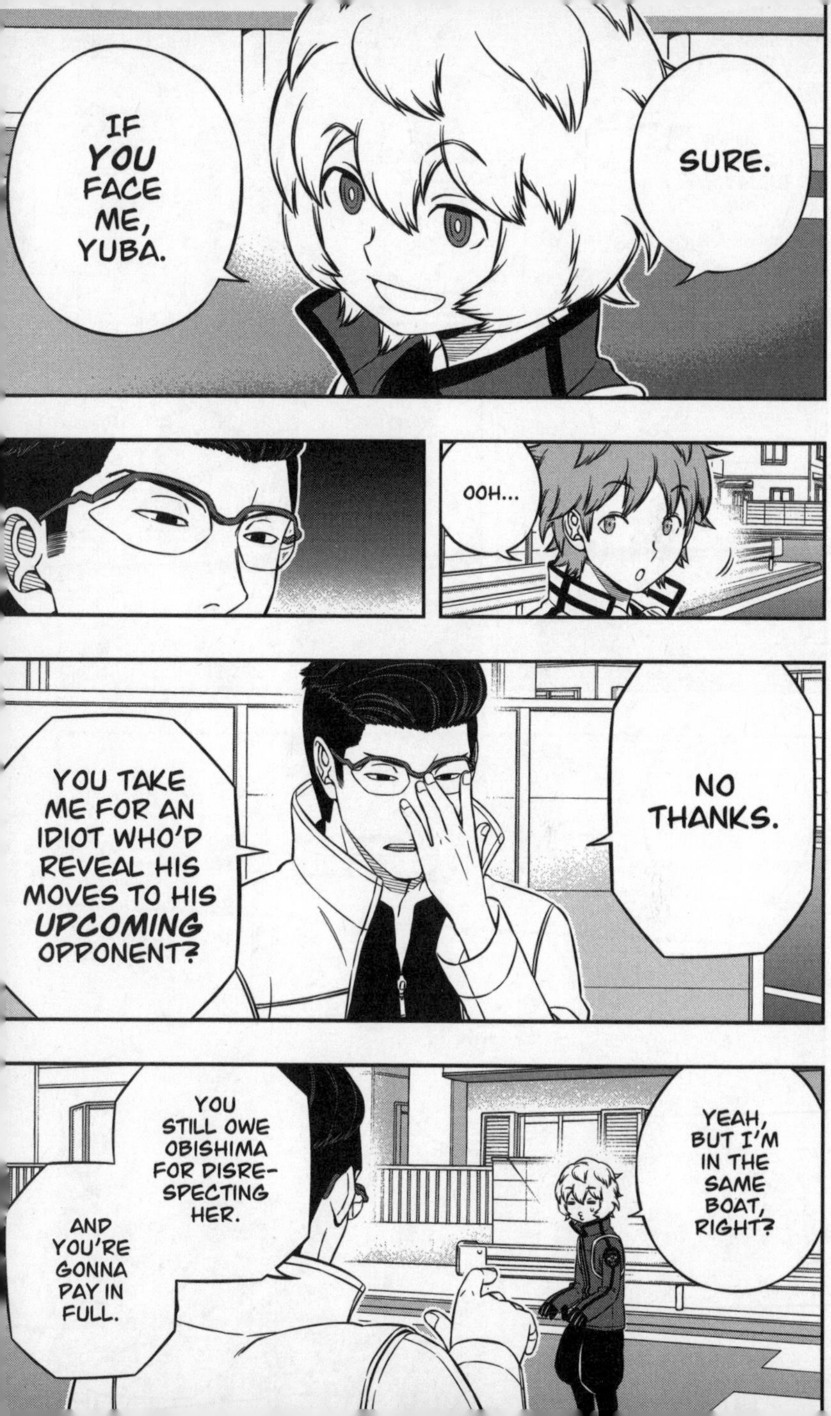
SURE.
IF *YOU* FACE ME, YUBA.
OOH...
NO THANKS.
YOU TAKE ME FOR AN IDIOT WHO'D REVEAL HIS MOVES TO HIS **UPCOMING** OPPONENT?
YEAH, BUT I'M IN THE SAME BOAT, RIGHT?
YOU STILL OWE OBISHIMA FOR DISRESPECTING HER.
AND YOU'RE GONNA PAY IN FULL.

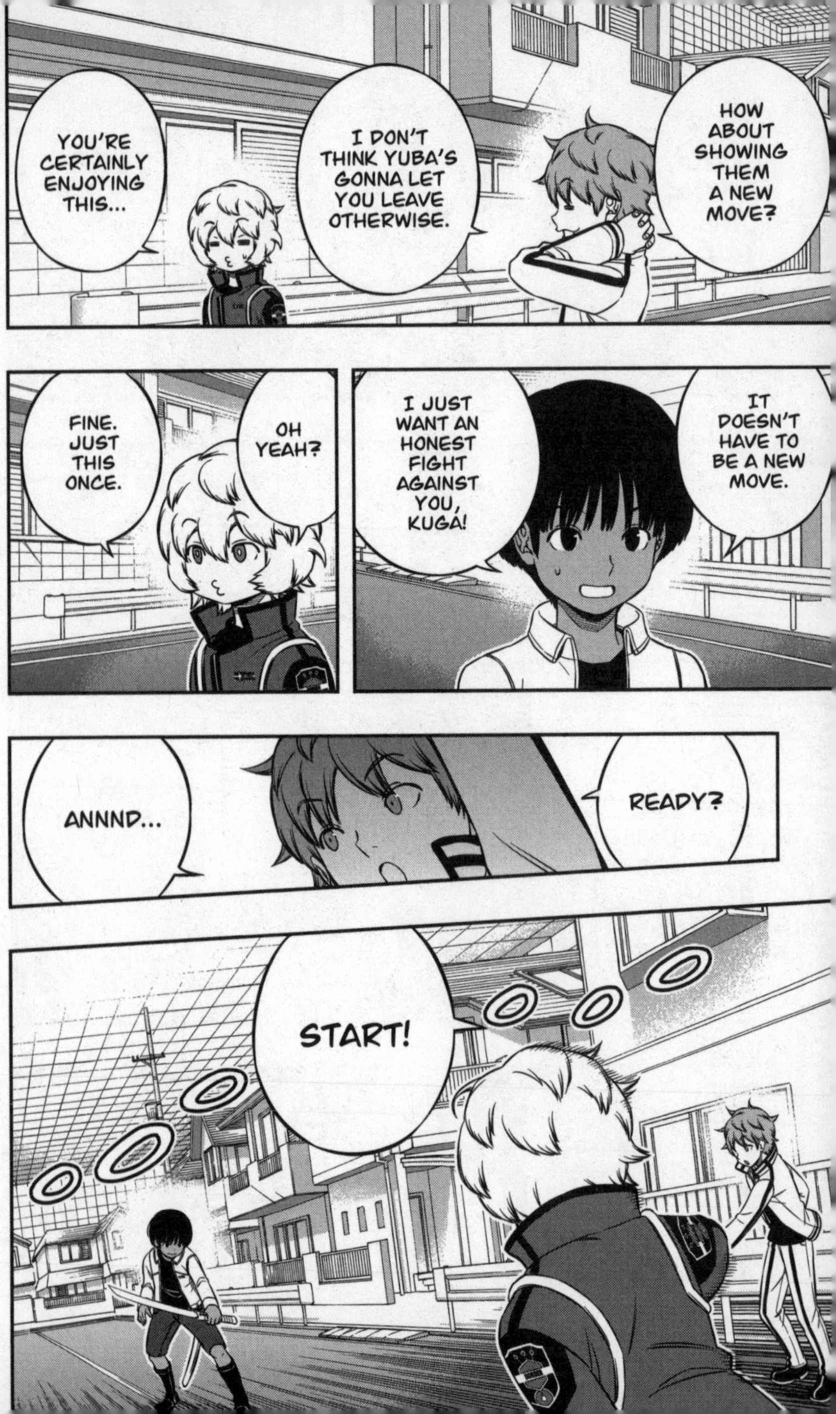
HOW ABOUT SHOWING THEM A NEW MOVE?
I DON'T THINK YUBA'S GONNA LET YOU LEAVE OTHERWISE.
YOU'RE CERTAINLY ENJOYING THIS...
IT DOESN'T HAVE TO BE A NEW MOVE.
I JUST WANT AN HONEST FIGHT AGAINST YOU, KUGA!
OH YEAH?
FINE. JUST THIS ONCE.
READY?
ANNND...
START!

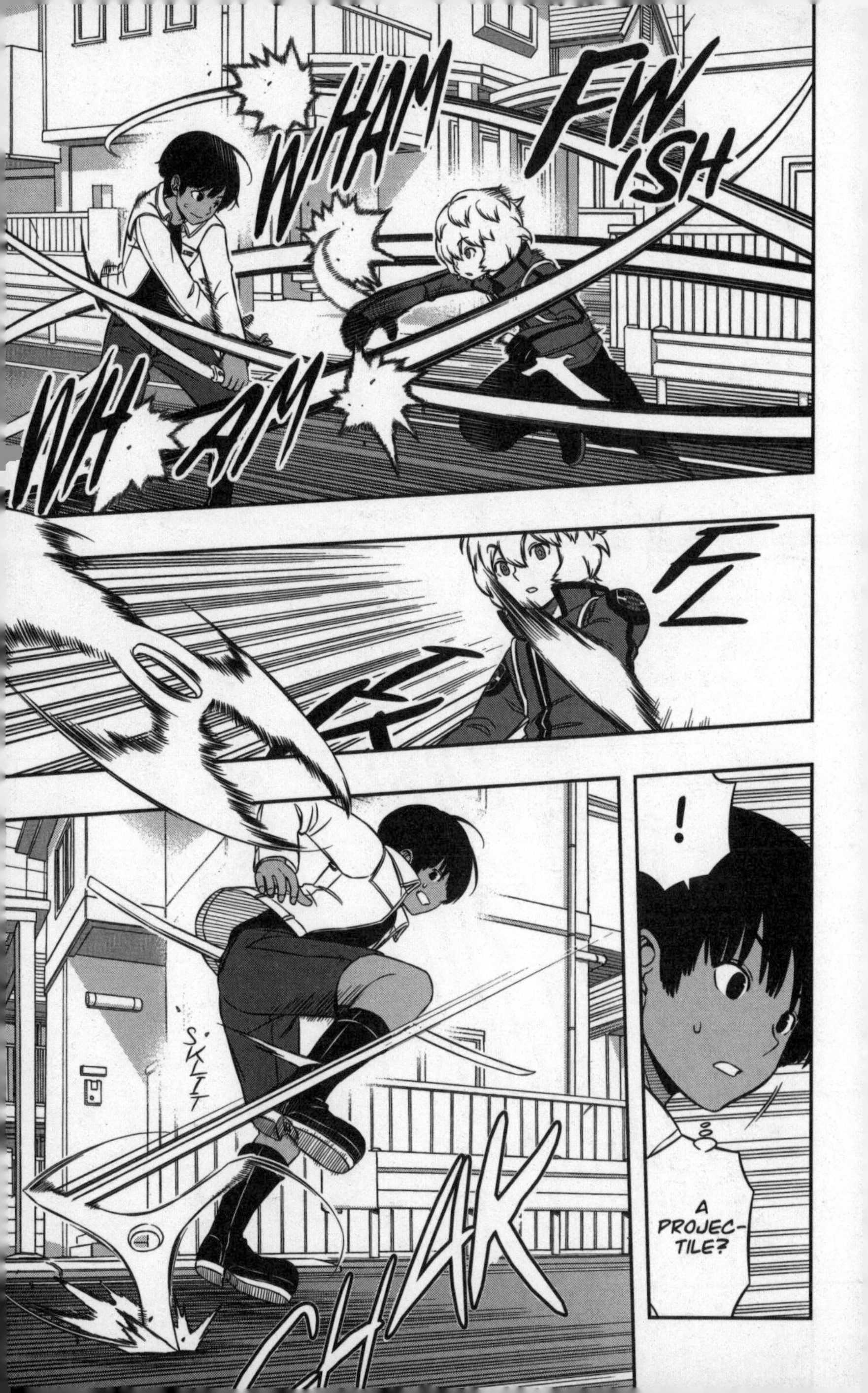

FWISH
WHAM
WHAM
!
A PROJEC-TILE?
SKLIT
CHAK

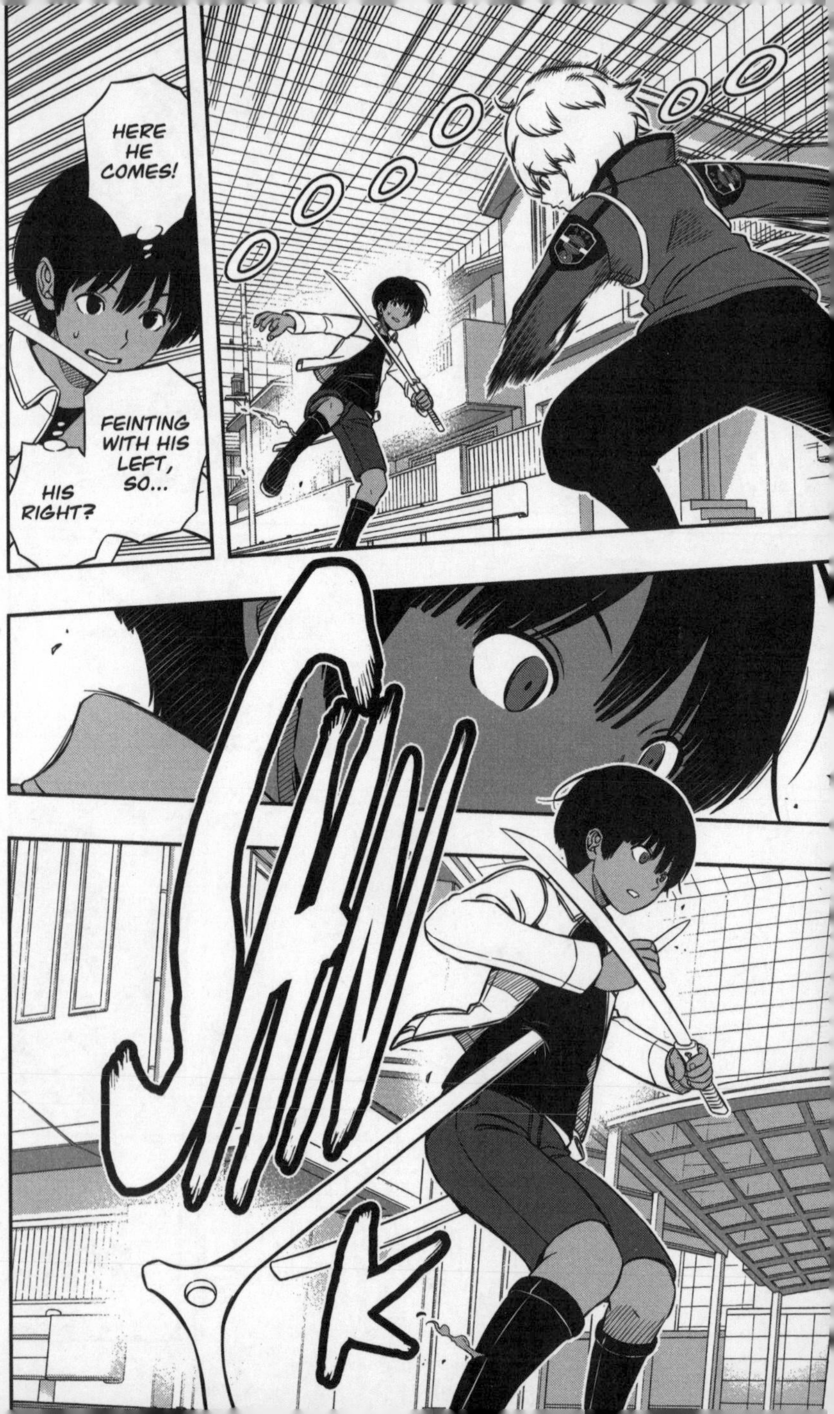
HERE HE COMES!
FEINTING WITH HIS LEFT, SO...
HIS RIGHT?

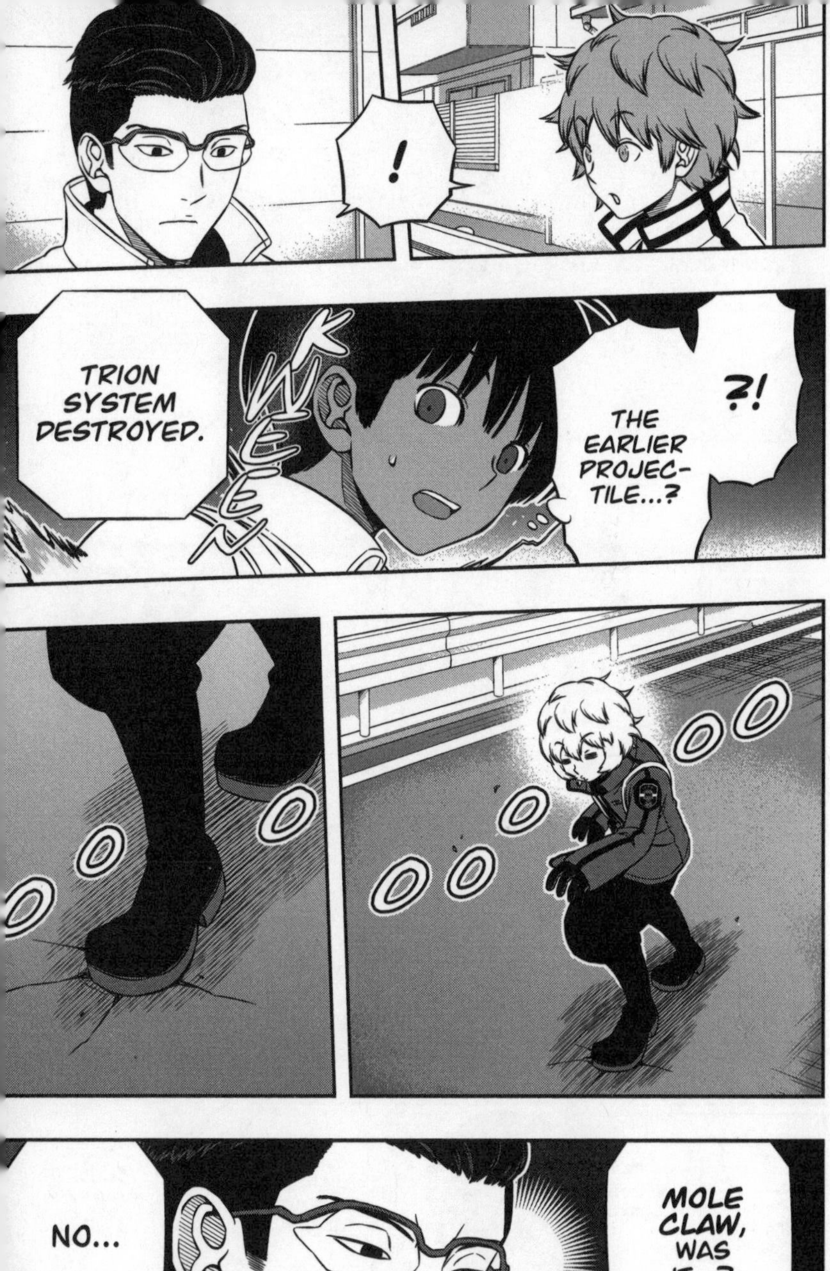
!
?!
THE EARLIER PROJEC-TILE...?
TRION SYSTEM DESTROYED.
MOLE CLAW, WAS IT...?
NO...

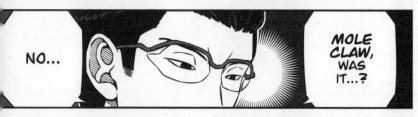

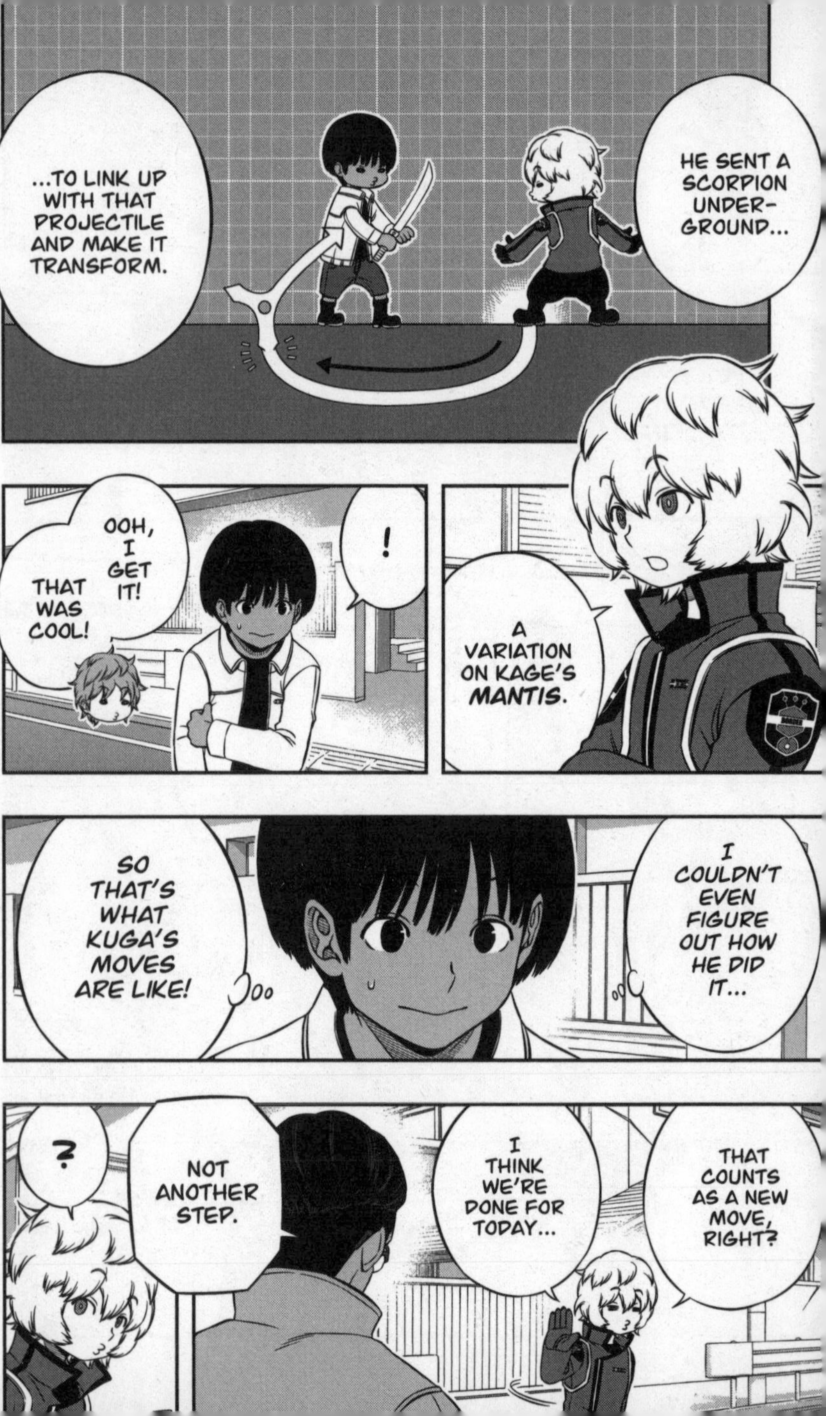
HE SENT A SCORPION UNDER-GROUND...
...TO LINK UP WITH THAT PROJECTILE AND MAKE IT TRANSFORM.
A VARIATION ON KAGE'S MANTIS.
!
OOH, I GET IT!
THAT WAS COOL!
I COULDN'T EVEN FIGURE OUT HOW HE DID IT...
SO THAT'S WHAT KUGA'S MOVES ARE LIKE!
THAT COUNTS AS A NEW MOVE, RIGHT?
I THINK WE'RE DONE FOR TODAY...
NOT ANOTHER STEP.
?

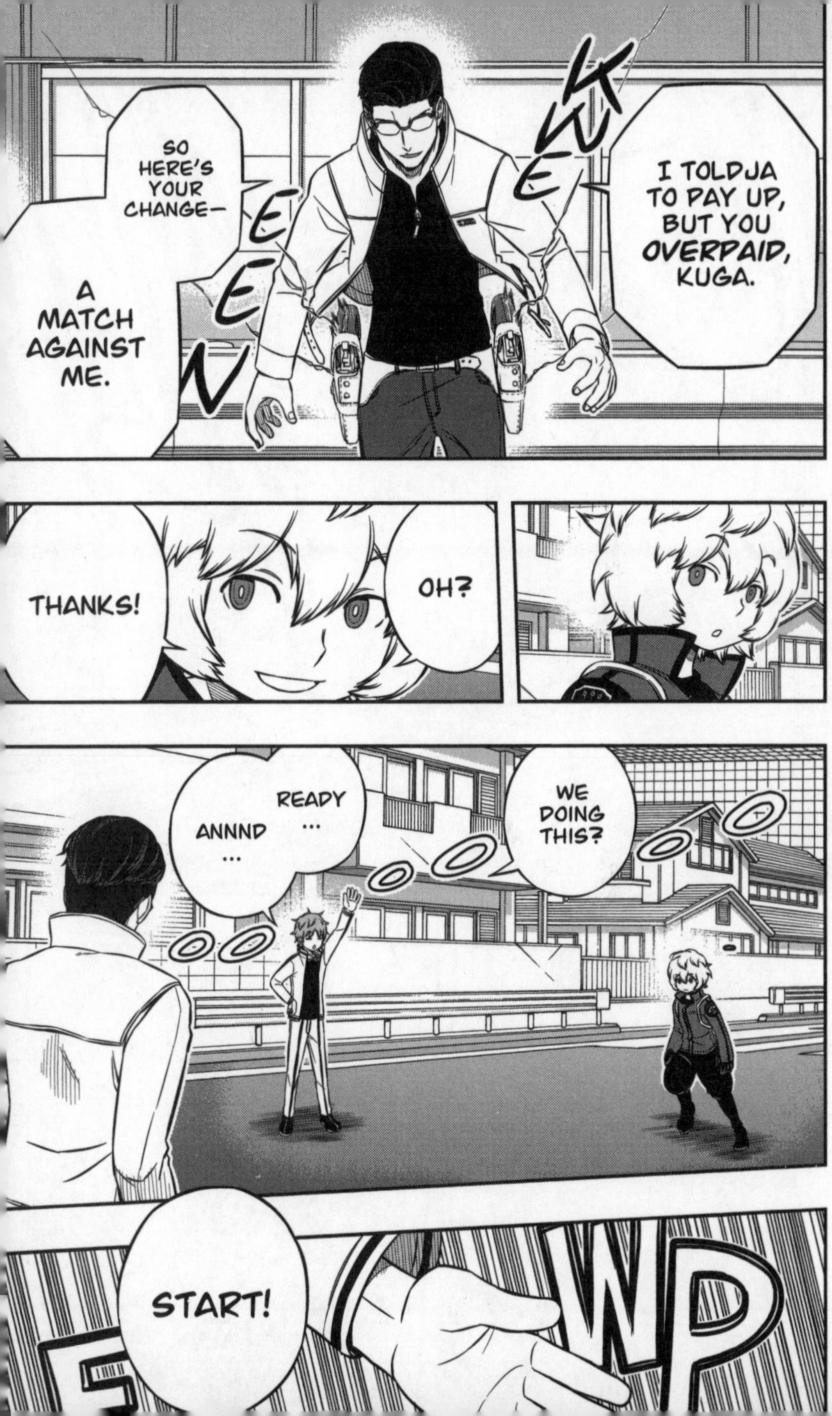
I TOLDJA TO PAY UP, BUT YOU OVERPAID, KUGA.
KWEEEN
SO HERE'S YOUR CHANGE—
A MATCH AGAINST ME.
OH?
THANKS!
WE DOING THIS?
READY ...
ANNND ...
WP
START!

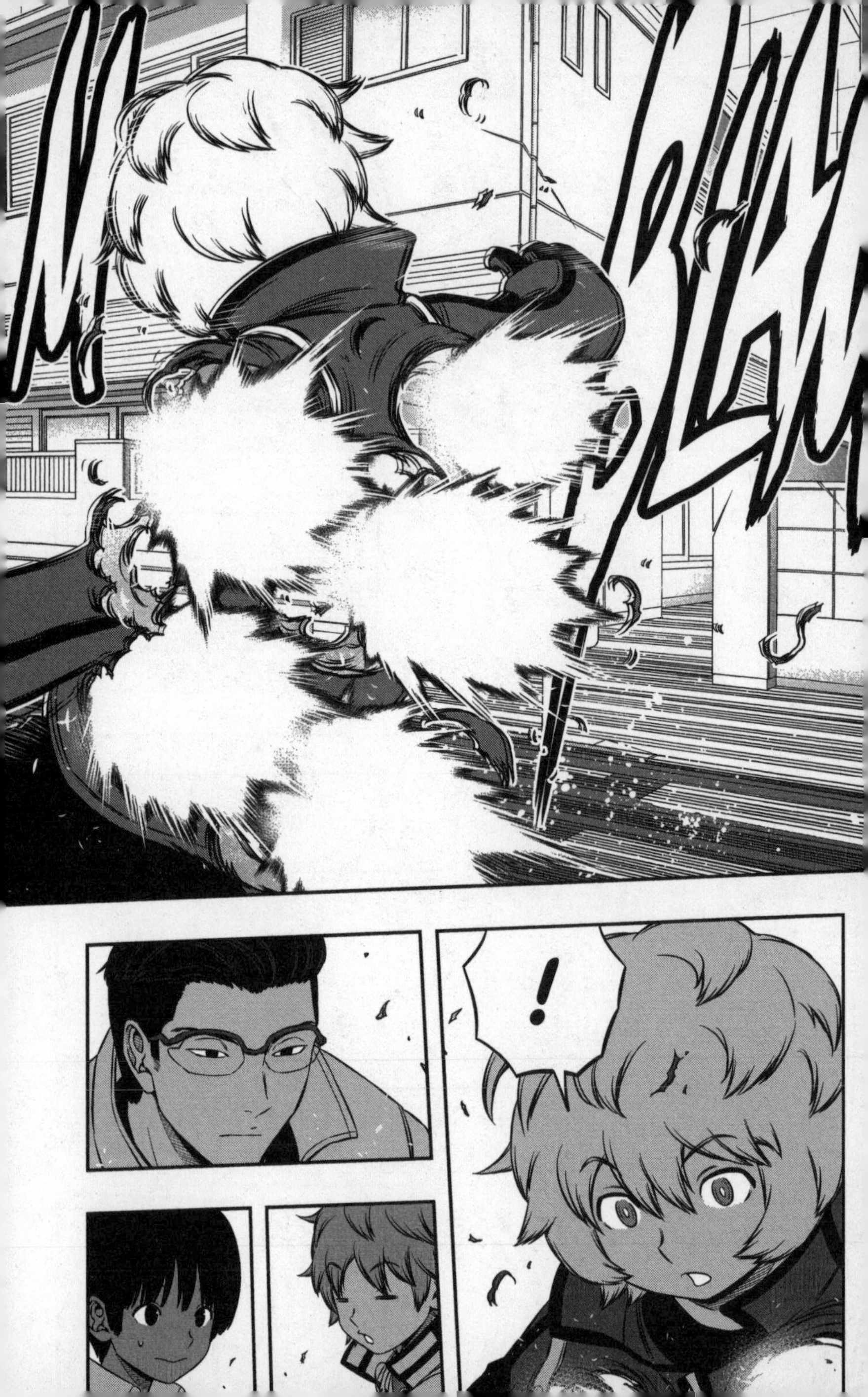
!

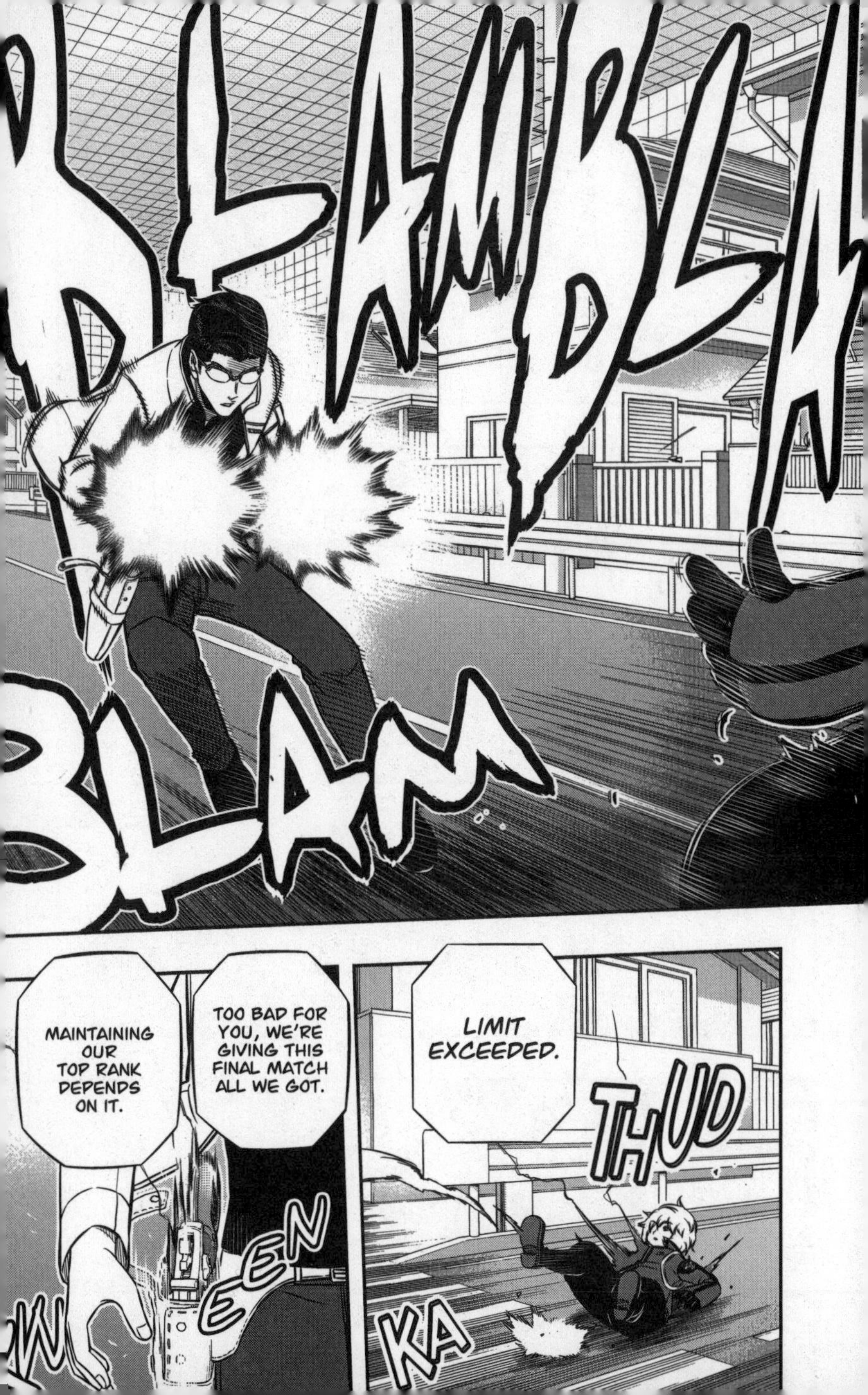
BLAM BLAM
BLAM
LIMIT EXCEEDED.
THUD
KA
TOO BAD FOR YOU, WE'RE GIVING THIS FINAL MATCH ALL WE GOT.
MAINTAINING OUR TOP RANK DEPENDS ON IT.
EEN
WN

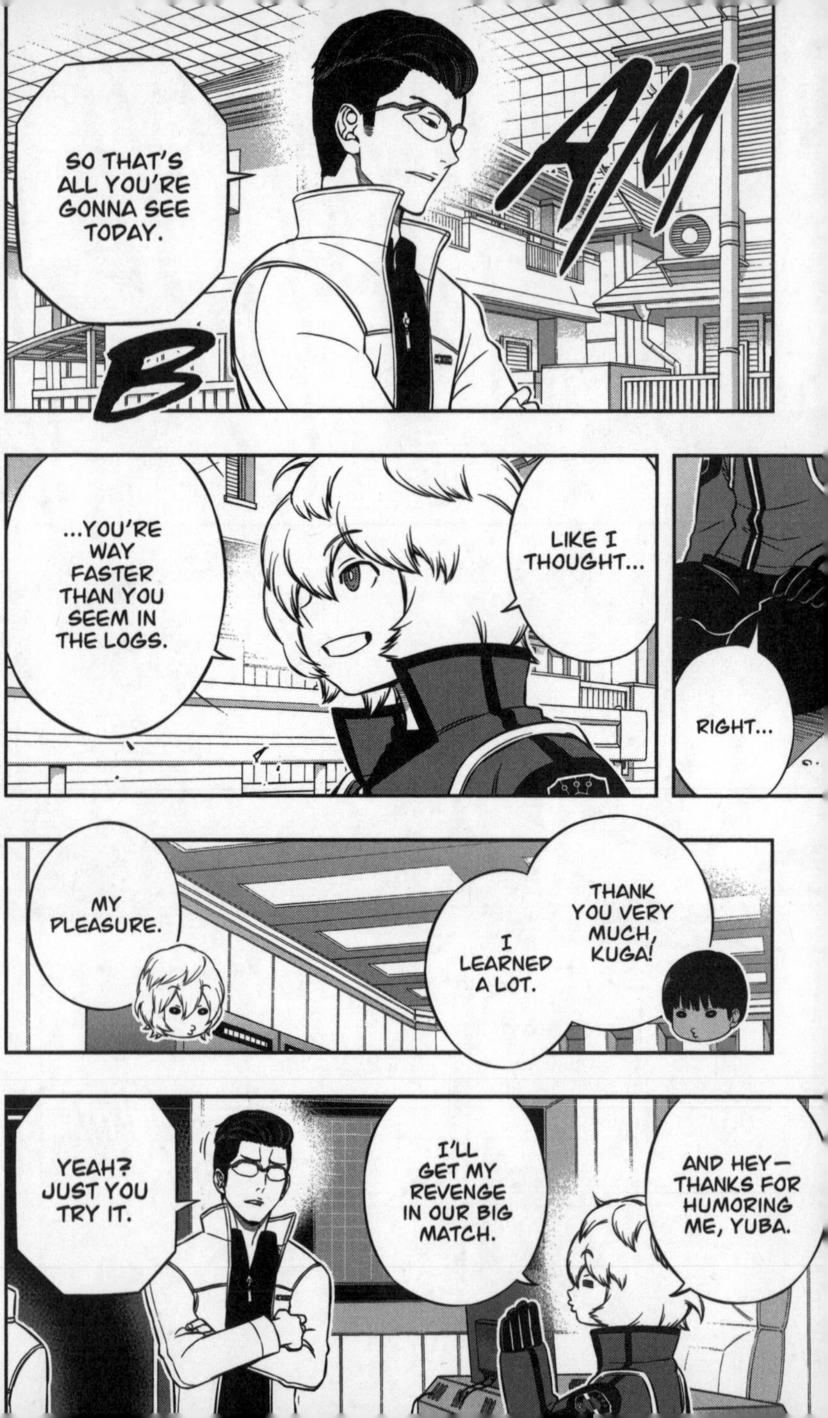

BAM
SO THAT'S ALL YOU'RE GONNA SEE TODAY.
RIGHT...
LIKE I THOUGHT...
...YOU'RE WAY FASTER THAN YOU SEEM IN THE LOGS.
THANK YOU VERY MUCH, KUGA!
I LEARNED A LOT.
MY PLEASURE.
AND HEY— THANKS FOR HUMORING ME, YUBA.
I'LL GET MY REVENGE IN OUR BIG MATCH.
YEAH? JUST YOU TRY IT.

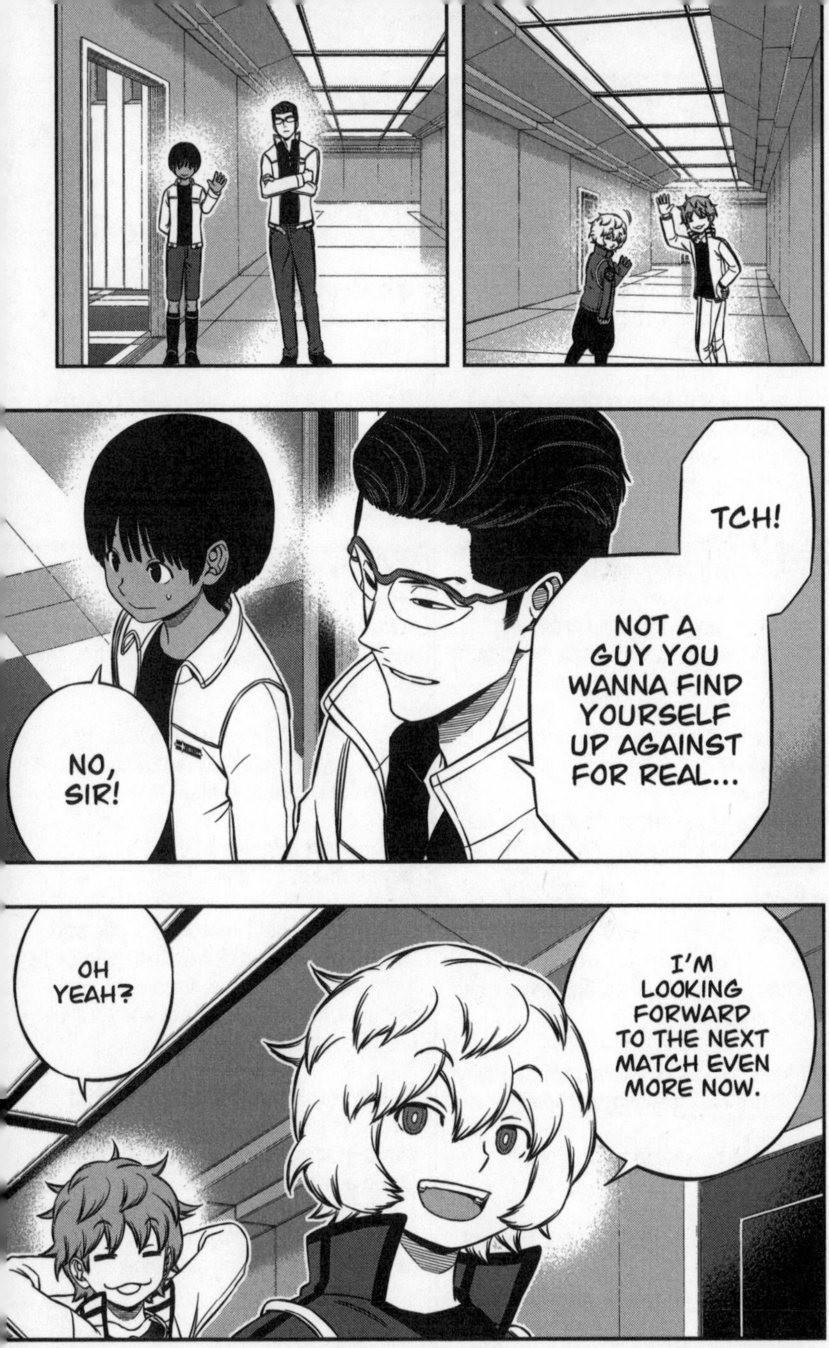
TCH!
NOT A GUY YOU WANNA FIND YOURSELF UP AGAINST FOR REAL...
NO, SIR!
I'M LOOKING FORWARD TO THE NEXT MATCH EVEN MORE NOW.
OH YEAH?

Q&A: Part 16

Selected from the questions answered during the hiatus.

■What would happen if Chika used Spider? Could she make a giant spider web all at once?

She could bust out one hundred times as many wires as Osamu in one go, but they'd be so dense they'd immobilize her, and they'd end up stabbing her and her allies.

■Does Kageura wear a mask in order to hide his sharp spiky teeth?

There's that, yes, but it's also to cover up more skin, which keeps his side effect from taking too much of a toll on him.

■Why would anyone ever recruit Taichi Betsuyaku?

For his youth, his decent Trion levels, his excitability and his dazzling eyes.

■Please tell me Tsuji's brothers' names.

His older brother is Ryotaro, and his younger brother is Sohei.

■If Tsuji is so awkward with women, why didn't he go to an all-boys school?

Because he needed to train his heart to cope.

■When will Suwa get a Black Trigger?

Who knows.? The future is vast and limitless.

■What do Trappers do, exactly? Do they forgo weapons altogether and just set traps?

Yes, they're dedicated to traps. The Switch Box trigger used by Trappers is not only tough to use, but it consumes a huge amount of Trion, so for the most part, Trappers don't equip ordinary attacking triggers.

■If someone tries removing the trion organ from a body, wouldn't they run into a wall of meat and bone? Is it possible to rip out the trion organ without killing the subject?

It's believed to be impossible with current technology. But surgically removing Black Triggers might be possible?

■Can other people not use Tamakoma-1's triggers?

Sure, they can, but Tamakoma's triggers are advanced enough to be hard to handle for the inexperienced. That said, Arashiyama could use Geist, Nasu could use Axe, and Iko could use Full-Arms.

■Half a year before the story started, Rinji was 20 years old, but was he in the same grade as Ninomiya? Or the same grade as Kazama?

Same grade as Ninomiya. Maybe they kept passing by and missing each other in high school and college?

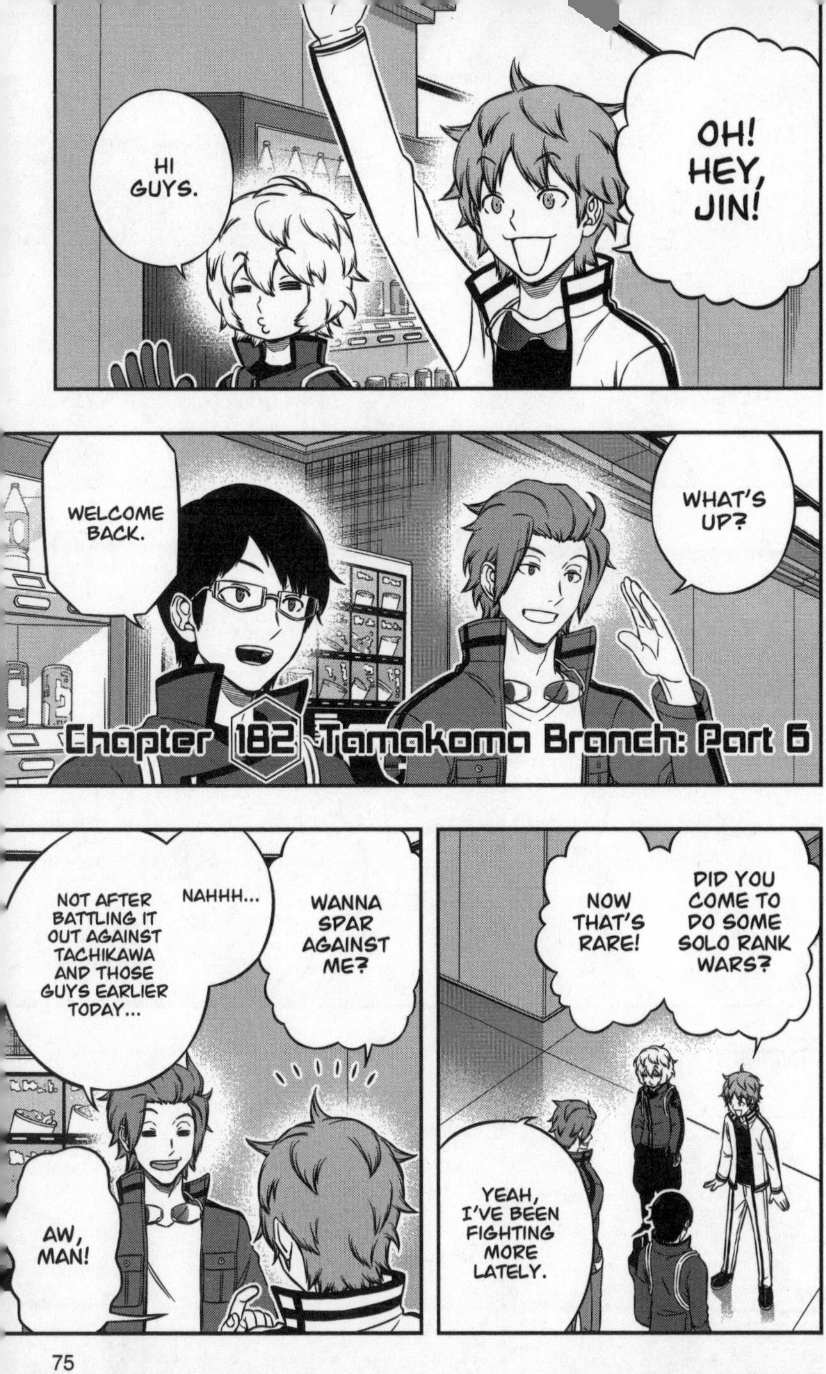
OH! HEY, JIN!
HI GUYS.
WHAT'S UP?
WELCOME BACK.
Chapter 182 Tamakoma Branch: Part 6
DID YOU COME TO DO SOME SOLO RANK WARS?
NOW THAT'S RARE!
YEAH, I'VE BEEN FIGHTING MORE LATELY.
WANNA SPAR AGAINST ME?
NAHHH...
NOT AFTER BATTLING IT OUT AGAINST TACHIKAWA AND THOSE GUYS EARLIER TODAY...
AW, MAN!

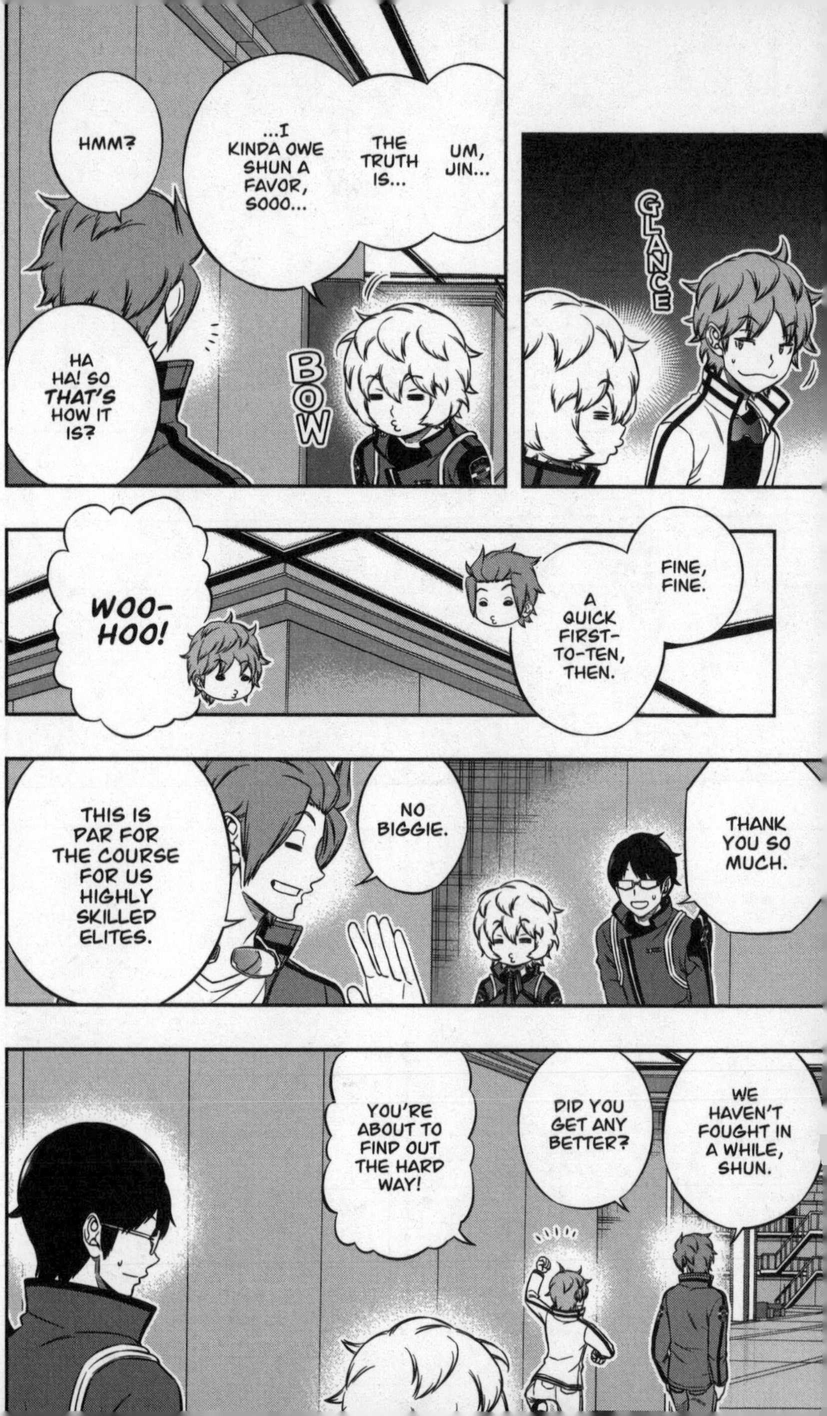
GLANCE
UM, JIN...
THE TRUTH IS...
...I KINDA OWE SHUN A FAVOR, SOOO...
HMM?
BOW
HA HA! SO *THAT'S* HOW IT IS?
FINE, FINE.
A QUICK FIRST-TO-TEN, THEN.
WOO-HOO!
THANK YOU SO MUCH.
NO BIGGIE.
THIS IS PAR FOR THE COURSE FOR US HIGHLY SKILLED ELITES.
WE HAVEN'T FOUGHT IN A WHILE, SHUN.
DID YOU GET ANY BETTER?
YOU'RE ABOUT TO FIND OUT THE HARD WAY!

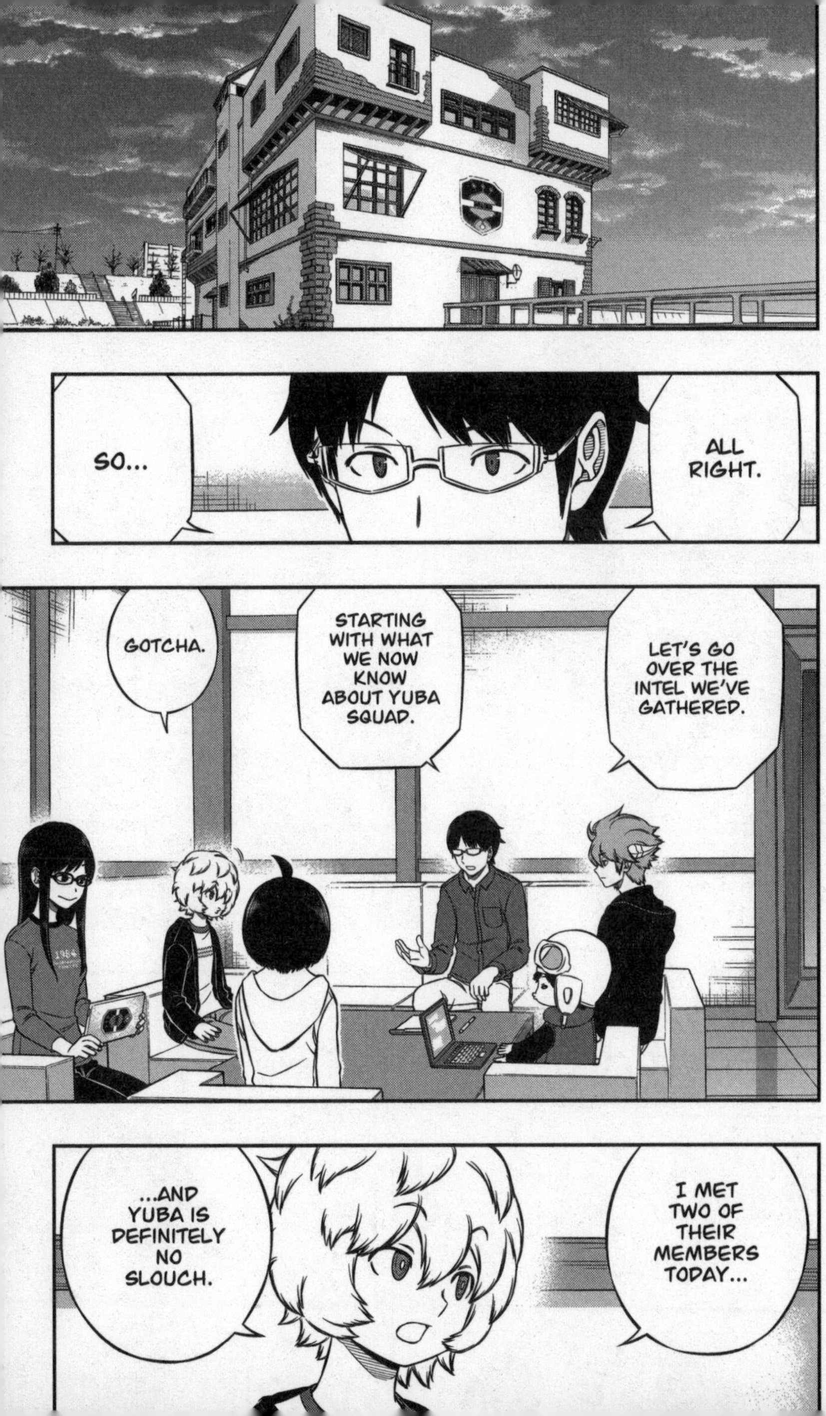
ALL RIGHT.
SO...
LET'S GO OVER THE INTEL WE'VE GATHERED.
STARTING WITH WHAT WE NOW KNOW ABOUT YUBA SQUAD.
GOTCHA.
I MET TWO OF THEIR MEMBERS TODAY...
...AND YUBA IS DEFINITELY NO SLOUCH.

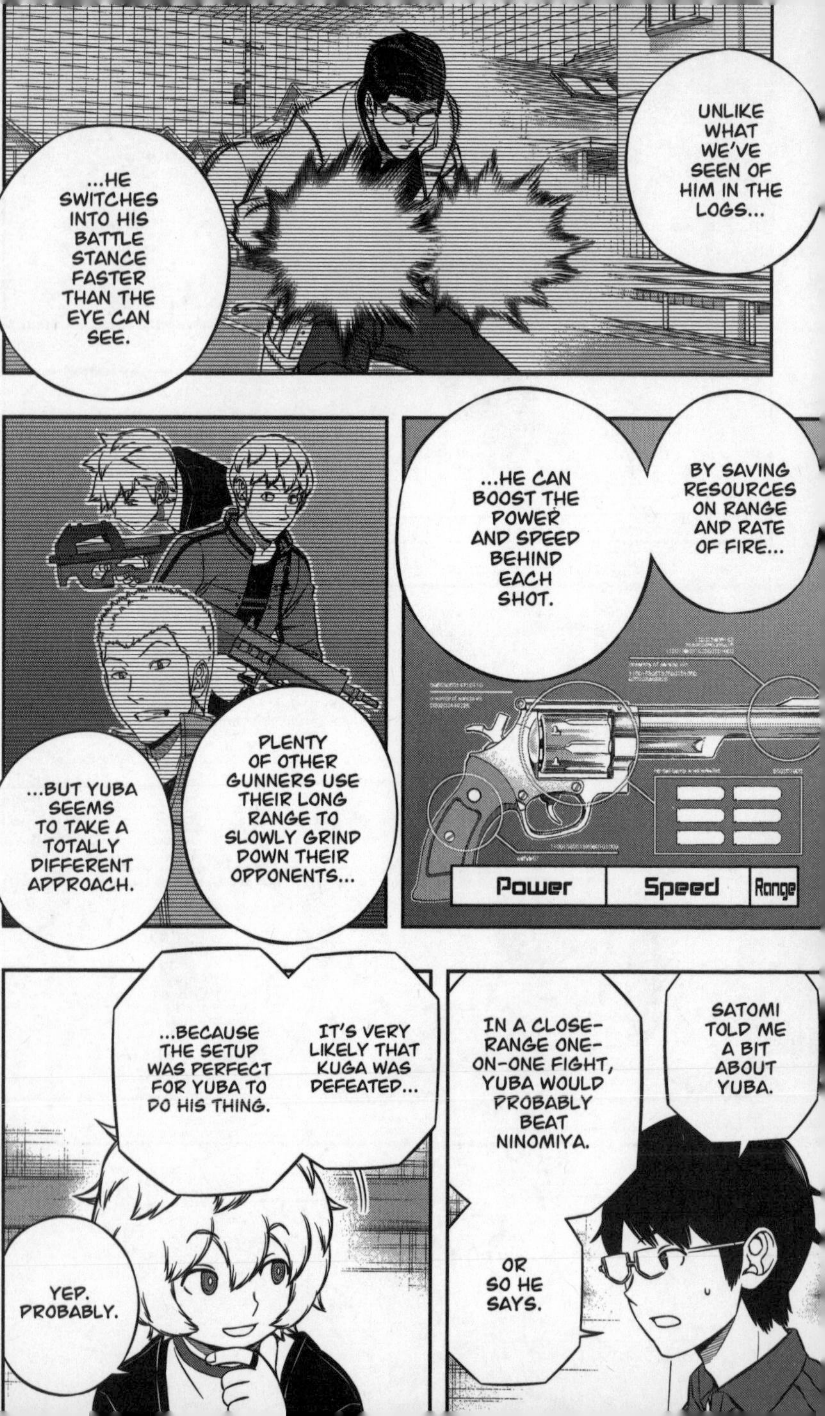
UNLIKE WHAT WE'VE SEEN OF HIM IN THE LOGS...
...HE SWITCHES INTO HIS BATTLE STANCE FASTER THAN THE EYE CAN SEE.
BY SAVING RESOURCES ON RANGE AND RATE OF FIRE...
...HE CAN BOOST THE POWER AND SPEED BEHIND EACH SHOT.
Power
Speed
Range
PLENTY OF OTHER GUNNERS USE THEIR LONG RANGE TO SLOWLY GRIND DOWN THEIR OPPONENTS...
...BUT YUBA SEEMS TO TAKE A TOTALLY DIFFERENT APPROACH.
SATOMI TOLD ME A BIT ABOUT YUBA.
IN A CLOSE-RANGE ONE-ON-ONE FIGHT, YUBA WOULD PROBABLY BEAT NINOMIYA.
OR SO HE SAYS.
IT'S VERY LIKELY THAT KUGA WAS DEFEATED...
...BECAUSE THE SETUP WAS PERFECT FOR YUBA TO DO HIS THING.
YEP. PROBABLY.

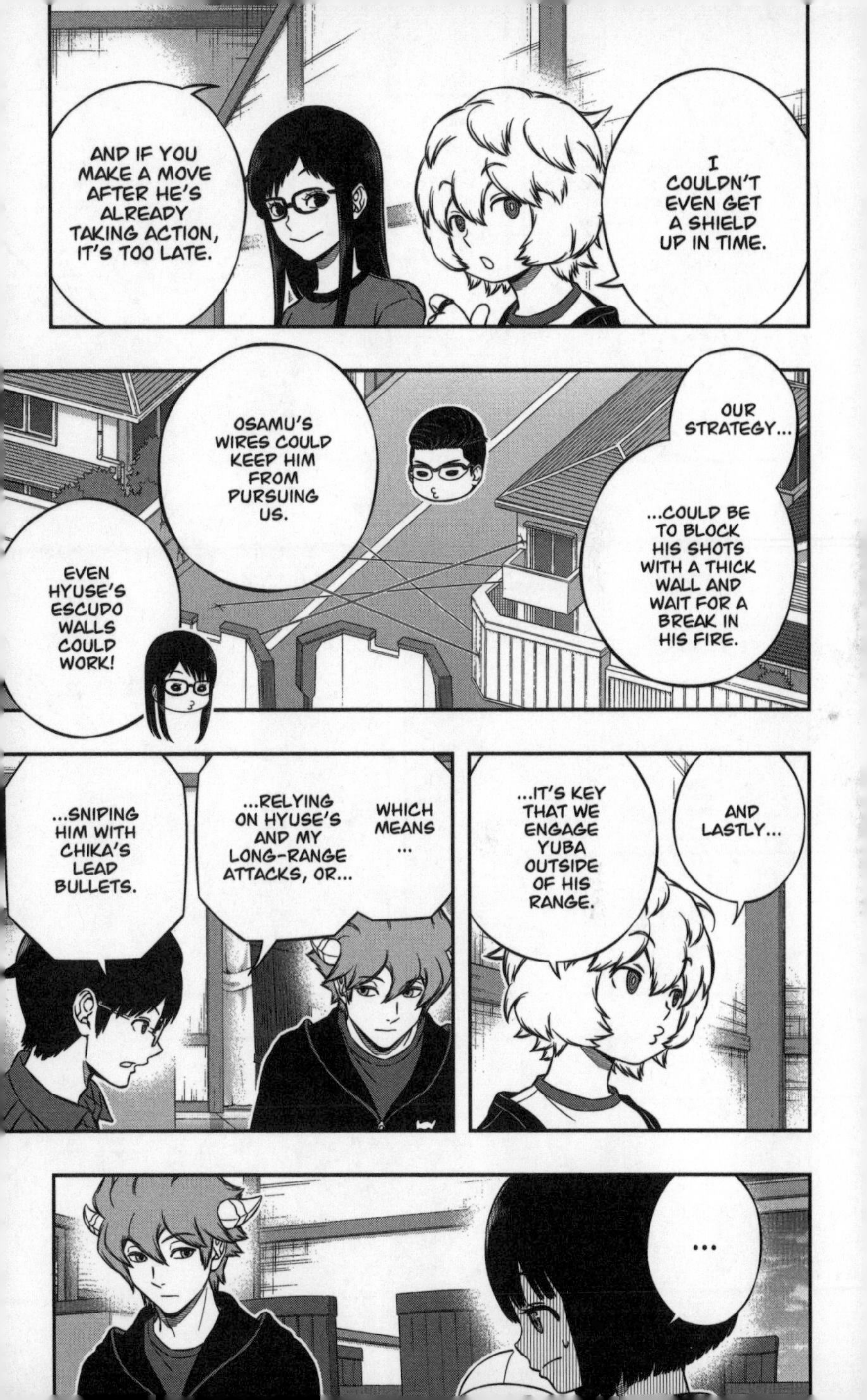
I COULDN'T EVEN GET A SHIELD UP IN TIME.
AND IF YOU MAKE A MOVE AFTER HE'S ALREADY TAKING ACTION, IT'S TOO LATE.
OUR STRATEGY...
...COULD BE TO BLOCK HIS SHOTS WITH A THICK WALL AND WAIT FOR A BREAK IN HIS FIRE.
OSAMU'S WIRES COULD KEEP HIM FROM PURSUING US.
EVEN HYUSE'S ESCUDO WALLS COULD WORK!
AND LASTLY...
...IT'S KEY THAT WE ENGAGE YUBA OUTSIDE OF HIS RANGE.
WHICH MEANS...
...RELYING ON HYUSE'S AND MY LONG-RANGE ATTACKS, OR...
...SNIPING HIM WITH CHIKA'S LEAD BULLETS.
...

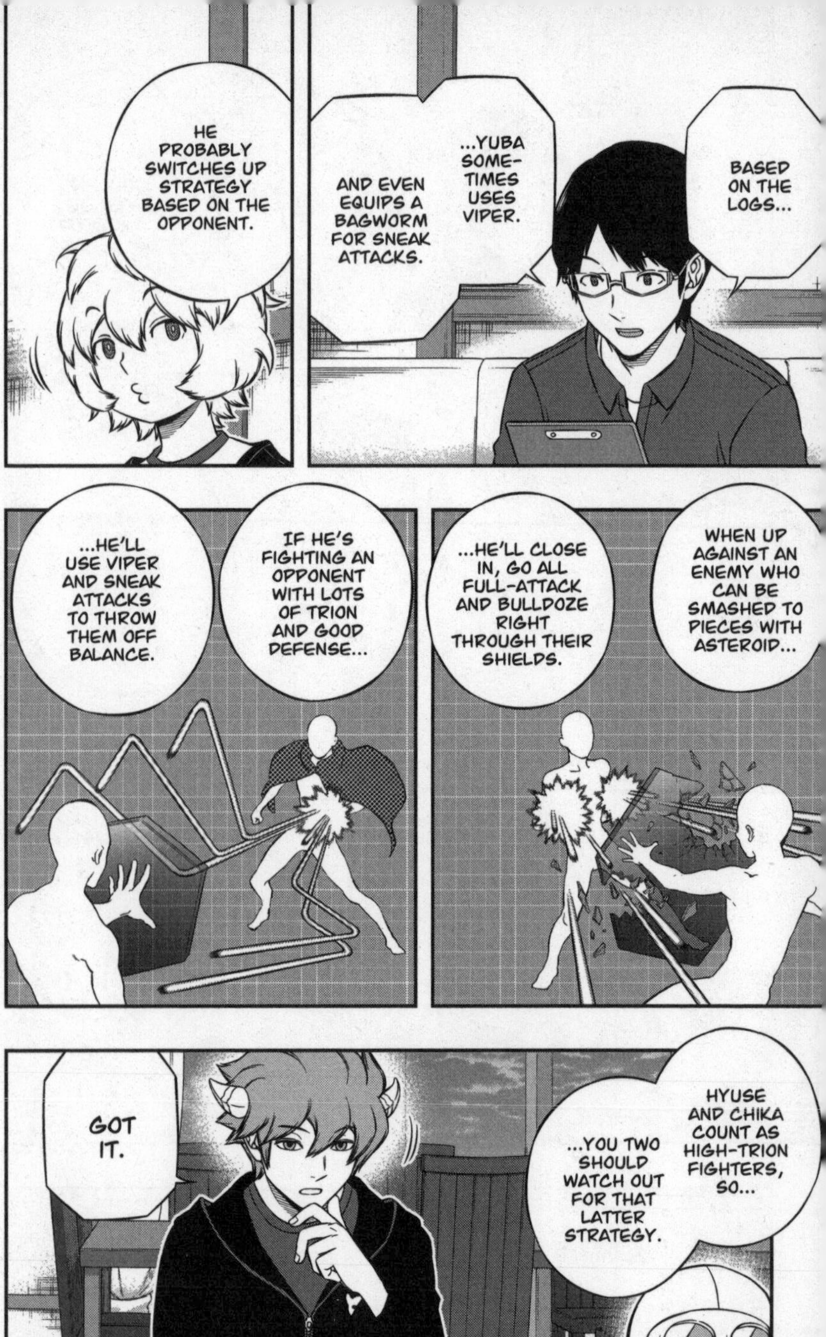
BASED ON THE LOGS...
...YUBA SOMETIMES USES VIPER.
AND EVEN EQUIPS A BAGWORM FOR SNEAK ATTACKS.
HE PROBABLY SWITCHES UP STRATEGY BASED ON THE OPPONENT.
WHEN UP AGAINST AN ENEMY WHO CAN BE SMASHED TO PIECES WITH ASTEROID...
...HE'LL CLOSE IN, GO ALL FULL-ATTACK AND BULLDOZE RIGHT THROUGH THEIR SHIELDS.
IF HE'S FIGHTING AN OPPONENT WITH LOTS OF TRION AND GOOD DEFENSE...
...HE'LL USE VIPER AND SNEAK ATTACKS TO THROW THEM OFF BALANCE.
HYUSE AND CHIKA COUNT AS HIGH-TRION FIGHTERS, SO...
...YOU TWO SHOULD WATCH OUT FOR THAT LATTER STRATEGY.
GOT IT.

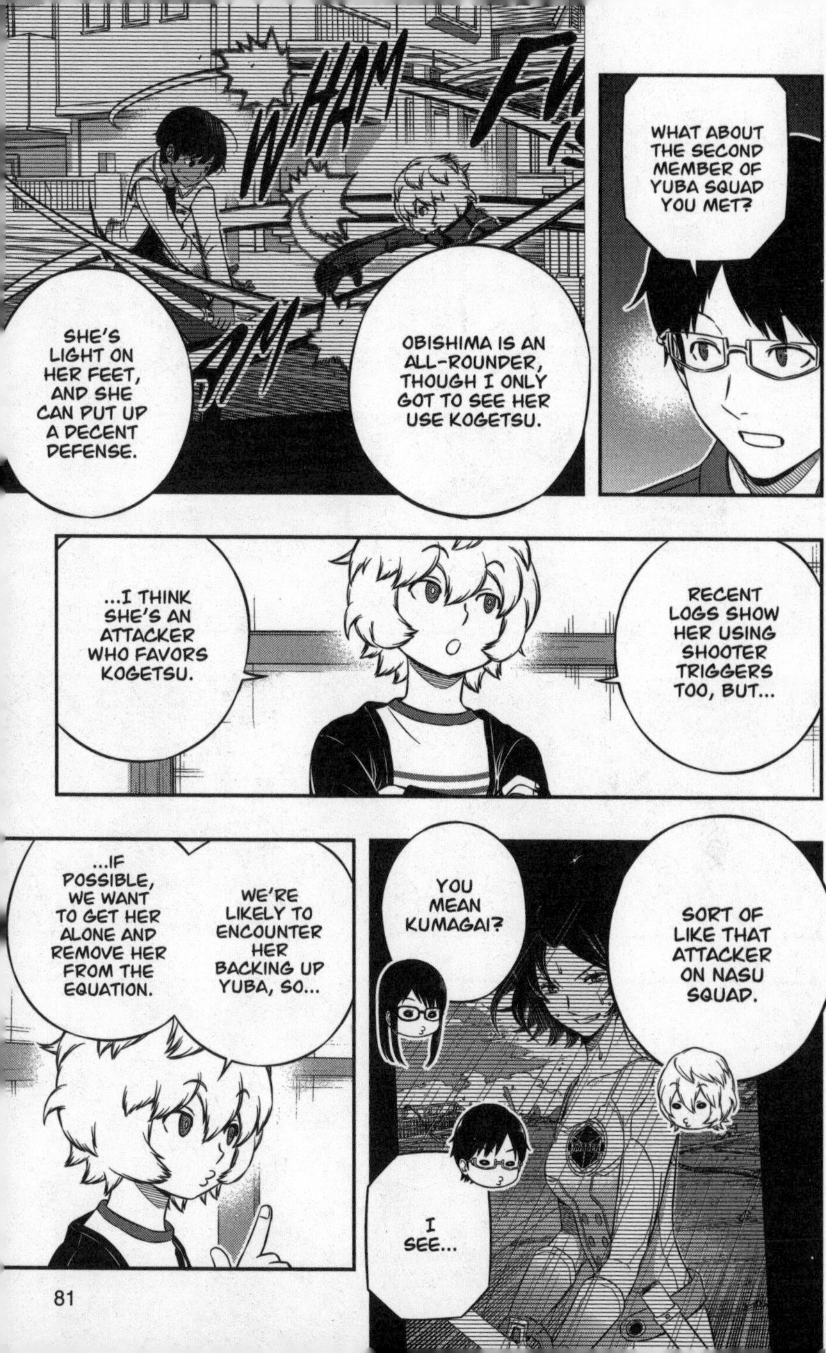
WHAT ABOUT THE SECOND MEMBER OF YUBA SQUAD YOU MET?
WHAM
OBISHIMA IS AN ALL-ROUNDER, THOUGH I ONLY GOT TO SEE HER USE KOGETSU.
SHE'S LIGHT ON HER FEET, AND SHE CAN PUT UP A DECENT DEFENSE.
RECENT LOGS SHOW HER USING SHOOTER TRIGGERS TOO, BUT...
...I THINK SHE'S AN ATTACKER WHO FAVORS KOGETSU.
SORT OF LIKE THAT ATTACKER ON NASU SQUAD.
YOU MEAN KUMAGAI?
I SEE...
WE'RE LIKELY TO ENCOUNTER HER BACKING UP YUBA, SO...
...IF POSSIBLE, WE WANT TO GET HER ALONE AND REMOVE HER FROM THE EQUATION.

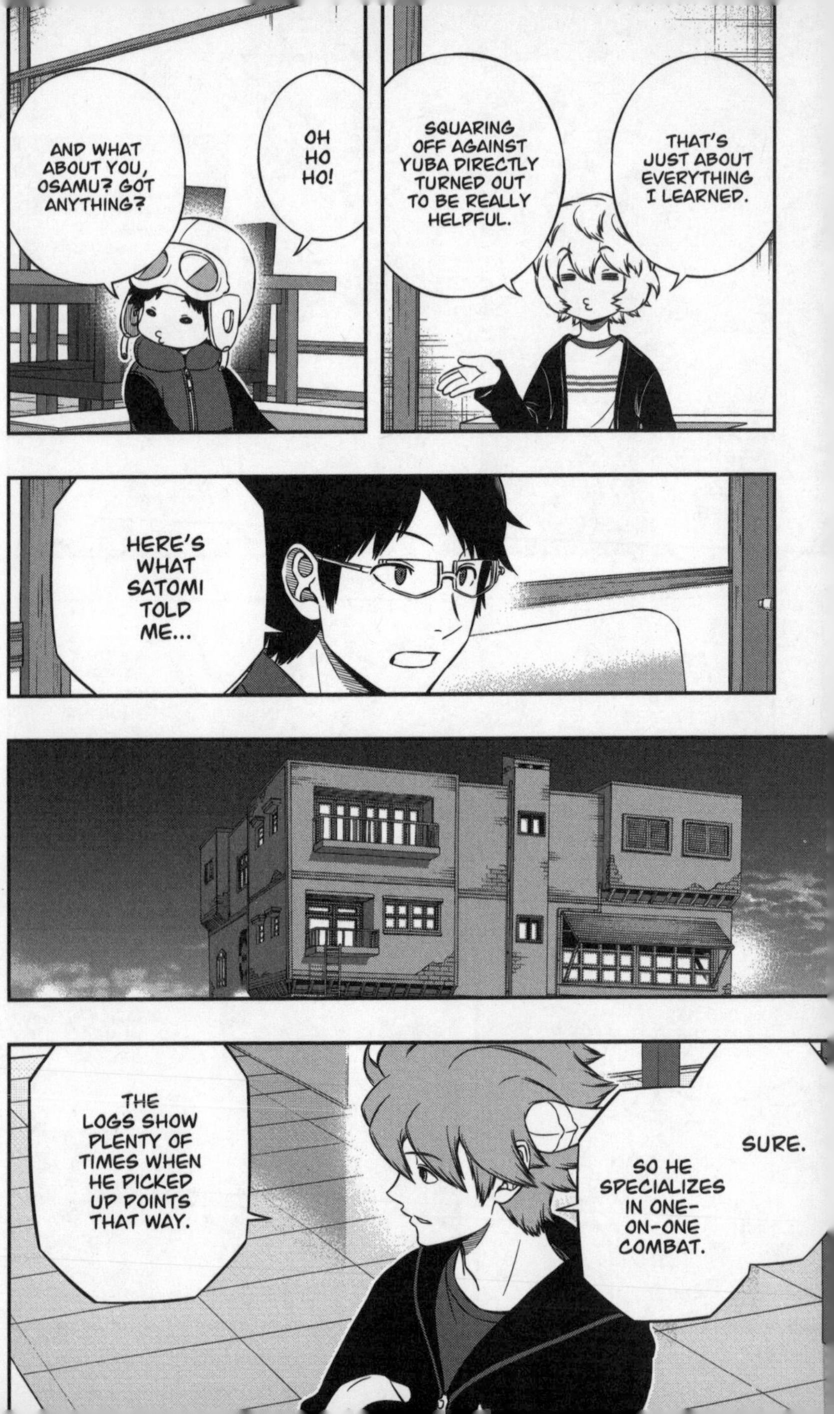
THAT'S JUST ABOUT EVERYTHING I LEARNED.
SQUARING OFF AGAINST YUBA DIRECTLY TURNED OUT TO BE REALLY HELPFUL.
OH HO HO!
AND WHAT ABOUT YOU, OSAMU? GOT ANYTHING?
HERE'S WHAT SATOMI TOLD ME...
SURE.
SO HE SPECIALIZES IN ONE-ON-ONE COMBAT.
THE LOGS SHOW PLENTY OF TIMES WHEN HE PICKED UP POINTS THAT WAY.

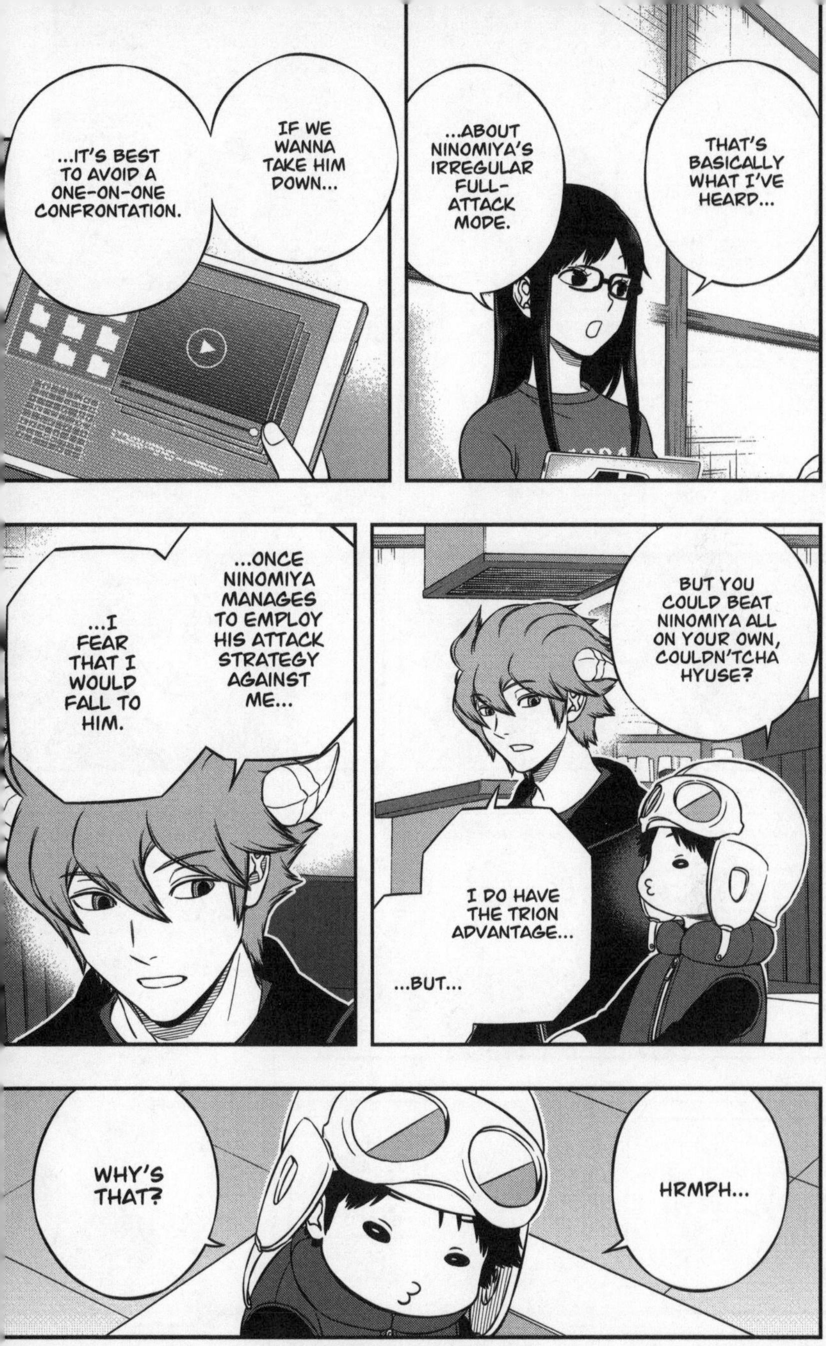
THAT'S BASICALLY WHAT I'VE HEARD...
...ABOUT NINOMIYA'S IRREGULAR FULL-ATTACK MODE.
IF WE WANNA TAKE HIM DOWN...
...IT'S BEST TO AVOID A ONE-ON-ONE CONFRONTATION.
BUT YOU COULD BEAT NINOMIYA ALL ON YOUR OWN, COULDN'TCHA HYUSE?
I DO HAVE THE TRION ADVANTAGE...
...BUT...
...ONCE NINOMIYA MANAGES TO EMPLOY HIS ATTACK STRATEGY AGAINST ME...
...I FEAR THAT I WOULD FALL TO HIM.
HRMPH...
WHY'S THAT?

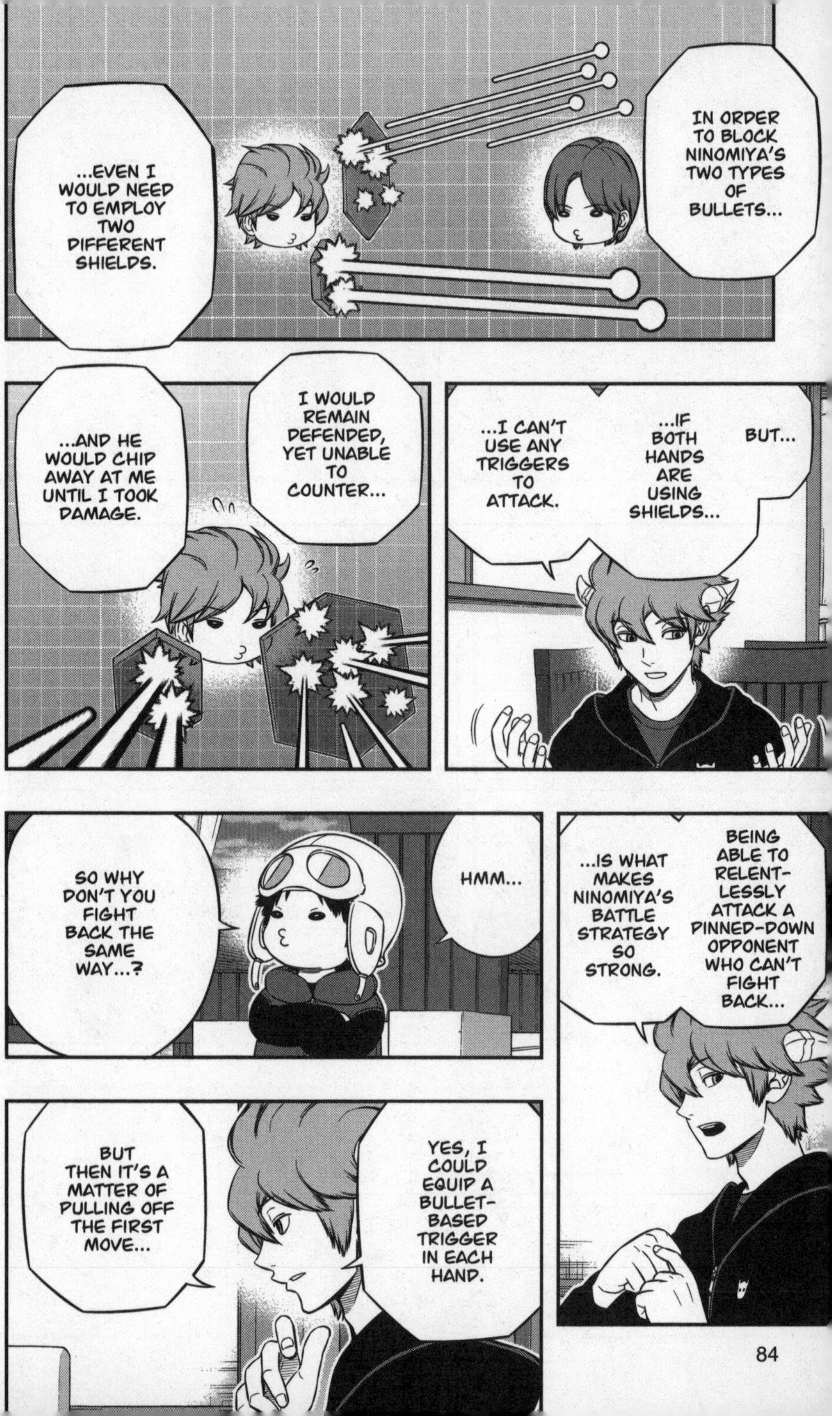
IN ORDER TO BLOCK NINOMIYA'S TWO TYPES OF BULLETS...
...EVEN I WOULD NEED TO EMPLOY TWO DIFFERENT SHIELDS.
BUT...
...IF BOTH HANDS ARE USING SHIELDS...
...I CAN'T USE ANY TRIGGERS TO ATTACK.
I WOULD REMAIN DEFENDED, YET UNABLE TO COUNTER...
...AND HE WOULD CHIP AWAY AT ME UNTIL I TOOK DAMAGE.
BEING ABLE TO RELENT-LESSLY ATTACK A PINNED-DOWN OPPONENT WHO CAN'T FIGHT BACK...
...IS WHAT MAKES NINOMIYA'S BATTLE STRATEGY SO STRONG.
HMM...
SO WHY DON'T YOU FIGHT BACK THE SAME WAY...?
YES, I COULD EQUIP A BULLET-BASED TRIGGER IN EACH HAND.
BUT THEN IT'S A MATTER OF PULLING OFF THE FIRST MOVE...

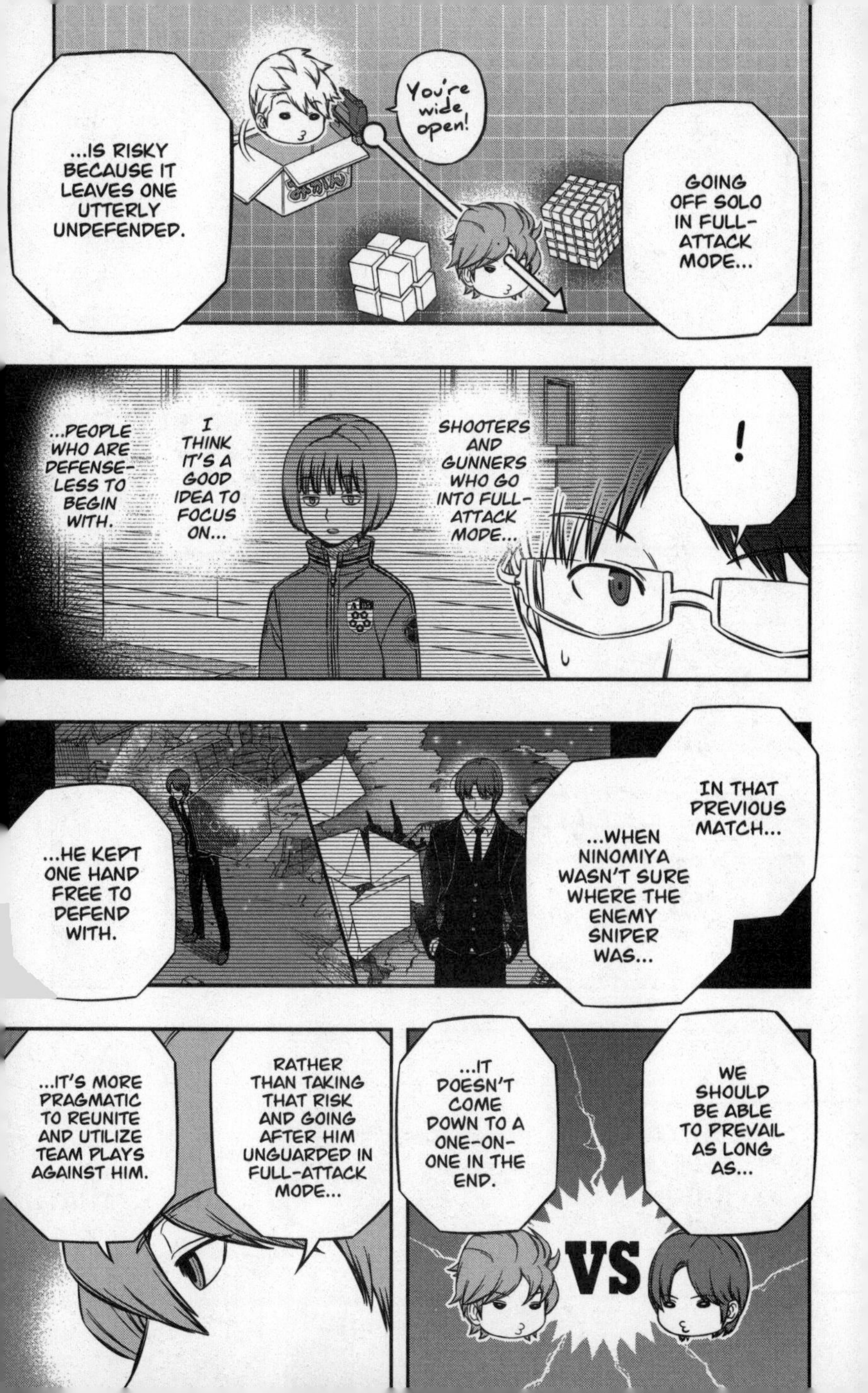
GOING OFF SOLO IN FULL-ATTACK MODE...
You're wide open!
...IS RISKY BECAUSE IT LEAVES ONE UTTERLY UNDEFENDED.
!
SHOOTERS AND GUNNERS WHO GO INTO FULL-ATTACK MODE...
I THINK IT'S A GOOD IDEA TO FOCUS ON...
...PEOPLE WHO ARE DEFENSE-LESS TO BEGIN WITH.
IN THAT PREVIOUS MATCH...
...WHEN NINOMIYA WASN'T SURE WHERE THE ENEMY SNIPER WAS...
...HE KEPT ONE HAND FREE TO DEFEND WITH.
WE SHOULD BE ABLE TO PREVAIL AS LONG AS...
...IT DOESN'T COME DOWN TO A ONE-ON-ONE IN THE END.
VS
RATHER THAN TAKING THAT RISK AND GOING AFTER HIM UNGUARDED IN FULL-ATTACK MODE...
...IT'S MORE PRAGMATIC TO REUNITE AND UTILIZE TEAM PLAYS AGAINST HIM.

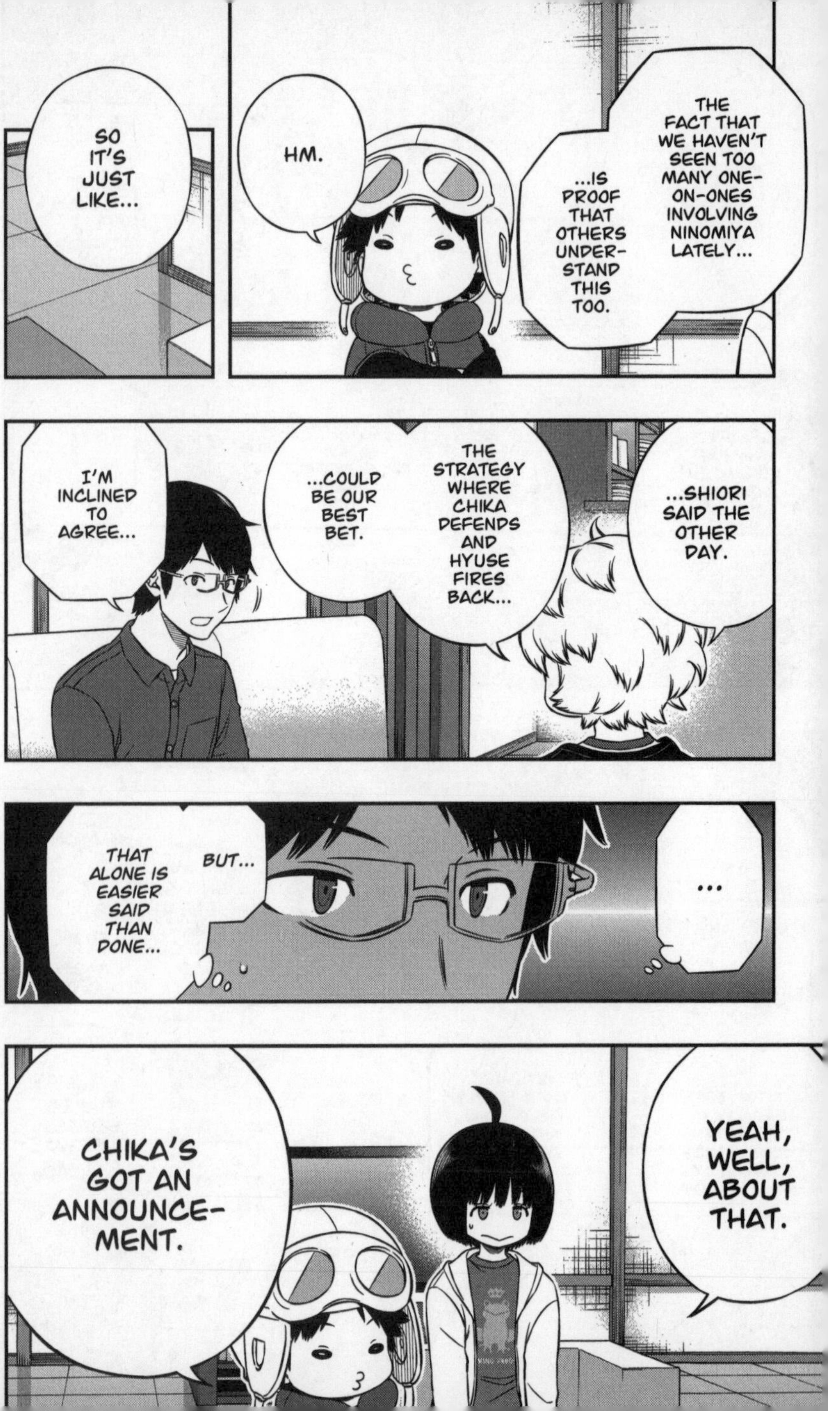
THE FACT THAT WE HAVEN'T SEEN TOO MANY ONE-ON-ONES INVOLVING NINOMIYA LATELY...
...IS PROOF THAT OTHERS UNDER-STAND THIS TOO.
HM.
SO IT'S JUST LIKE...
...SHIORI SAID THE OTHER DAY.
THE STRATEGY WHERE CHIKA DEFENDS AND HYUSE FIRES BACK...
...COULD BE OUR BEST BET.
I'M INCLINED TO AGREE...
...
BUT...
THAT ALONE IS EASIER SAID THAN DONE...
YEAH, WELL, ABOUT THAT.
CHIKA'S GOT AN ANNOUNCE-MENT.

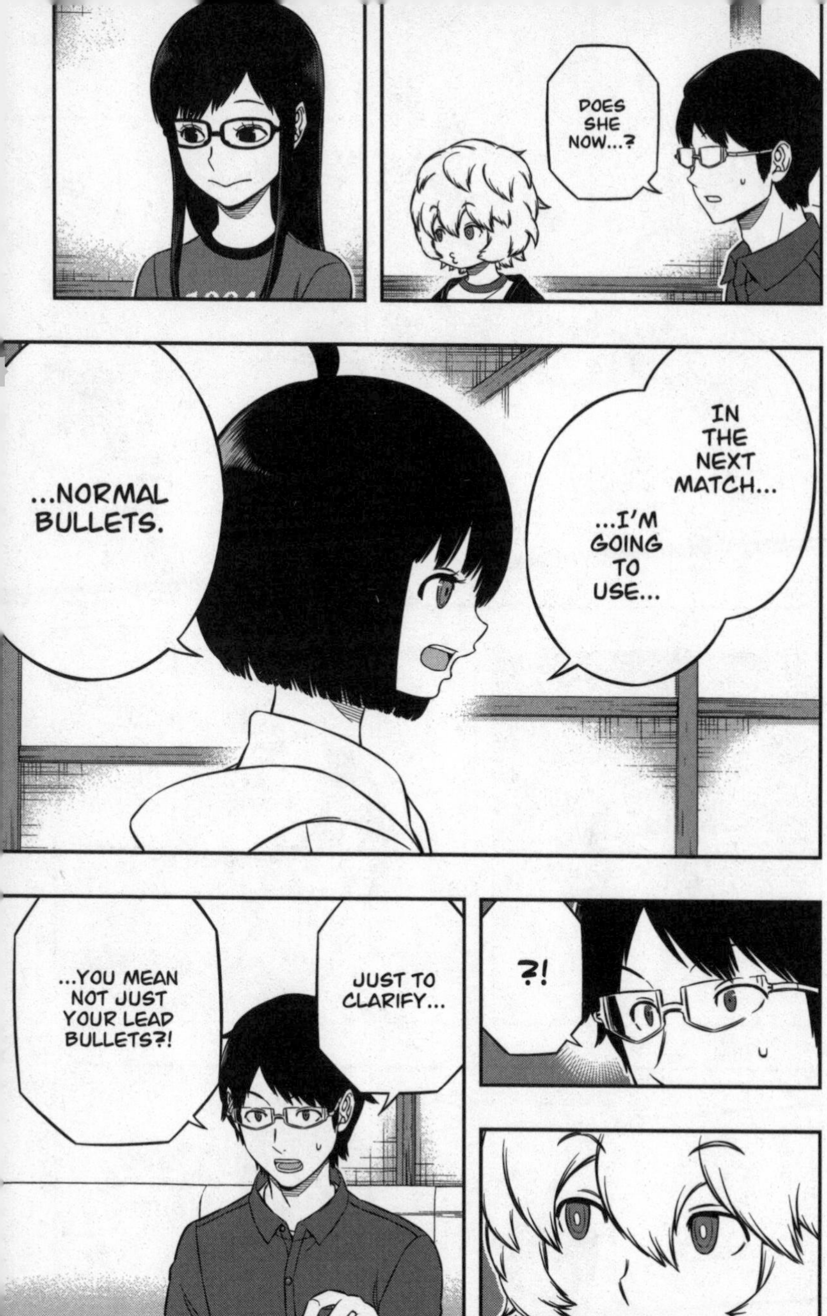
DOES SHE NOW...?
IN THE NEXT MATCH...
...I'M GOING TO USE...
...NORMAL BULLETS.
?!
JUST TO CLARIFY...
...YOU MEAN NOT JUST YOUR LEAD BULLETS?!

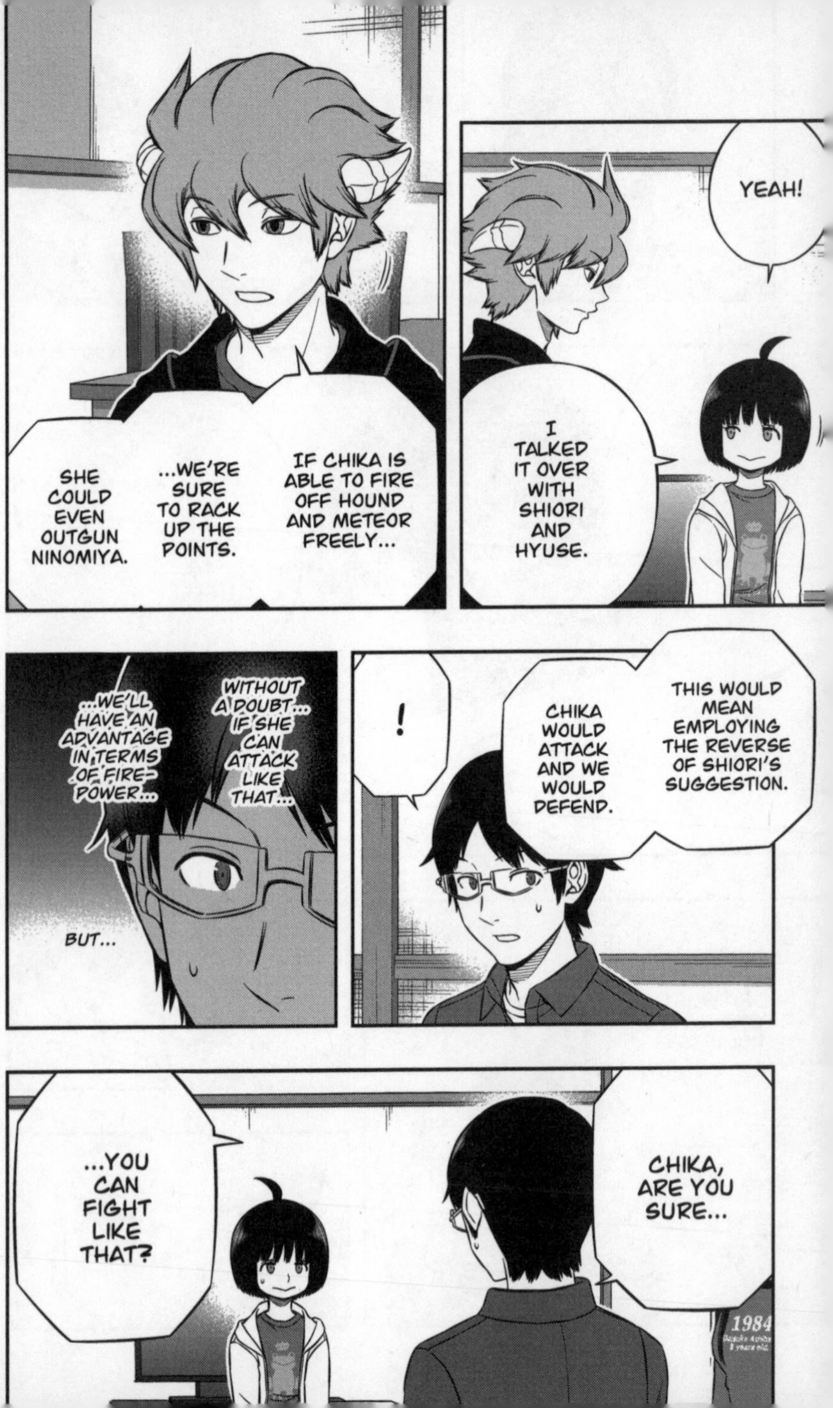
YEAH!
I TALKED IT OVER WITH SHIORI AND HYUSE.
IF CHIKA IS ABLE TO FIRE OFF HOUND AND METEOR FREELY...
...WE'RE SURE TO RACK UP THE POINTS.
SHE COULD EVEN OUTGUN NINOMIYA.
THIS WOULD MEAN EMPLOYING THE REVERSE OF SHIORI'S SUGGESTION.
CHIKA WOULD ATTACK AND WE WOULD DEFEND.
!
WITHOUT A DOUBT... IF SHE CAN ATTACK LIKE THAT...
...WE'LL HAVE AN ADVANTAGE IN TERMS OF FIRE-POWER...
BUT...
CHIKA, ARE YOU SURE...
...YOU CAN FIGHT LIKE THAT?
1984

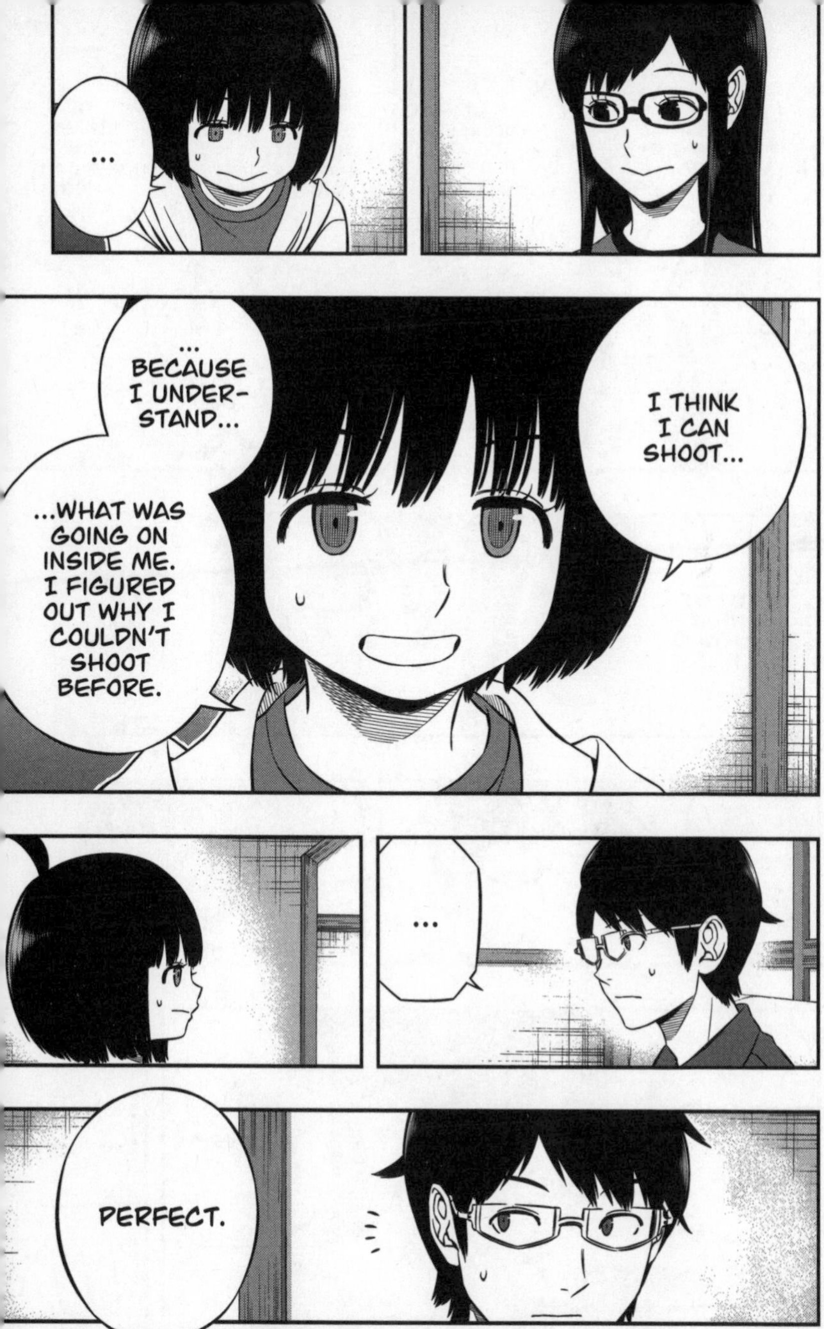
...
I THINK I CAN SHOOT...
... BECAUSE I UNDER-STAND...
...WHAT WAS GOING ON INSIDE ME. I FIGURED OUT WHY I COULDN'T SHOOT BEFORE.
...
PERFECT.

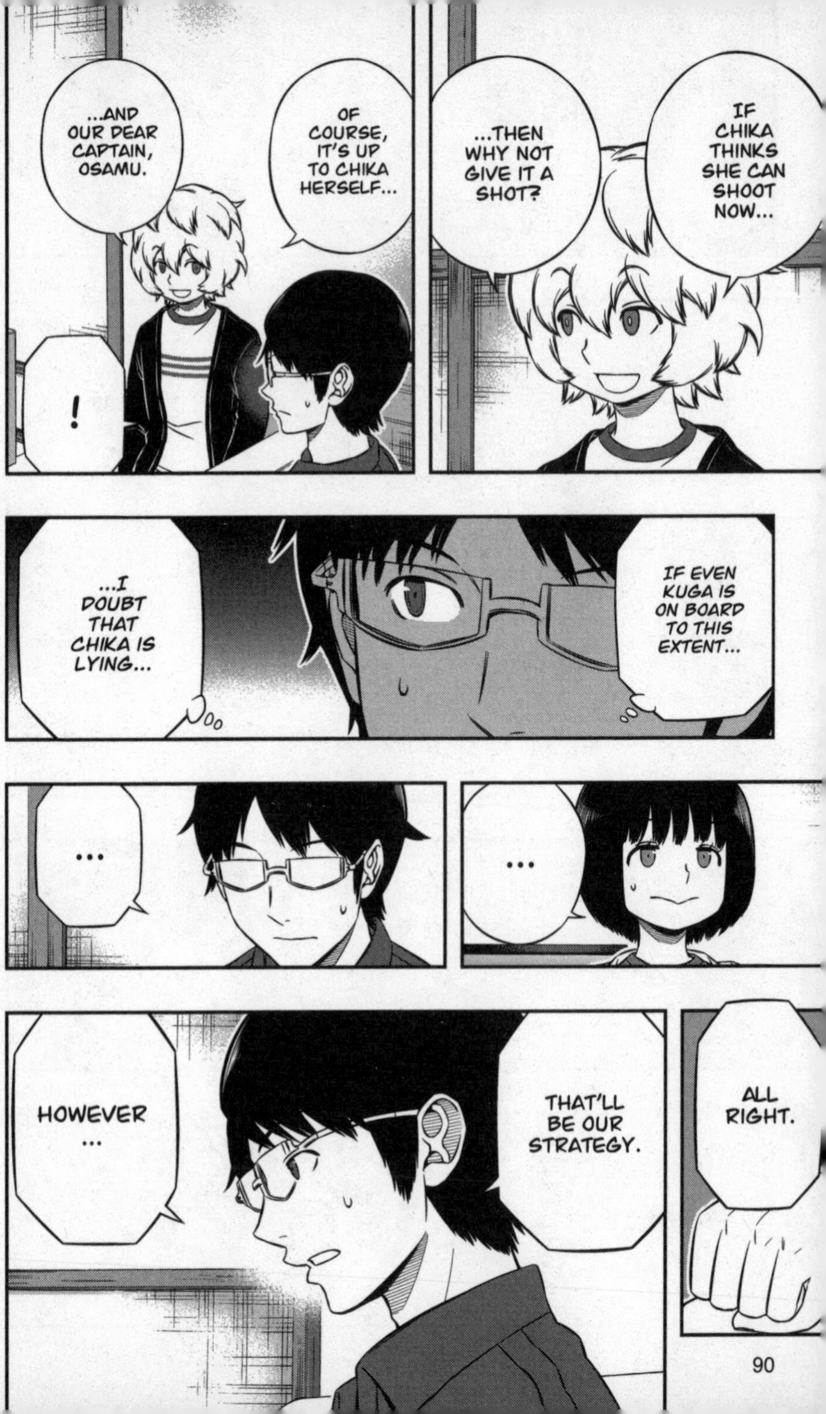
IF CHIKA THINKS SHE CAN SHOOT NOW...
...THEN WHY NOT GIVE IT A SHOT?
OF COURSE, IT'S UP TO CHIKA HERSELF...
...AND OUR DEAR CAPTAIN, OSAMU.
!
IF EVEN KUGA IS ON BOARD TO THIS EXTENT...
...I DOUBT THAT CHIKA IS LYING...
...
...
ALL RIGHT.
THAT'LL BE OUR STRATEGY.
HOWEVER...

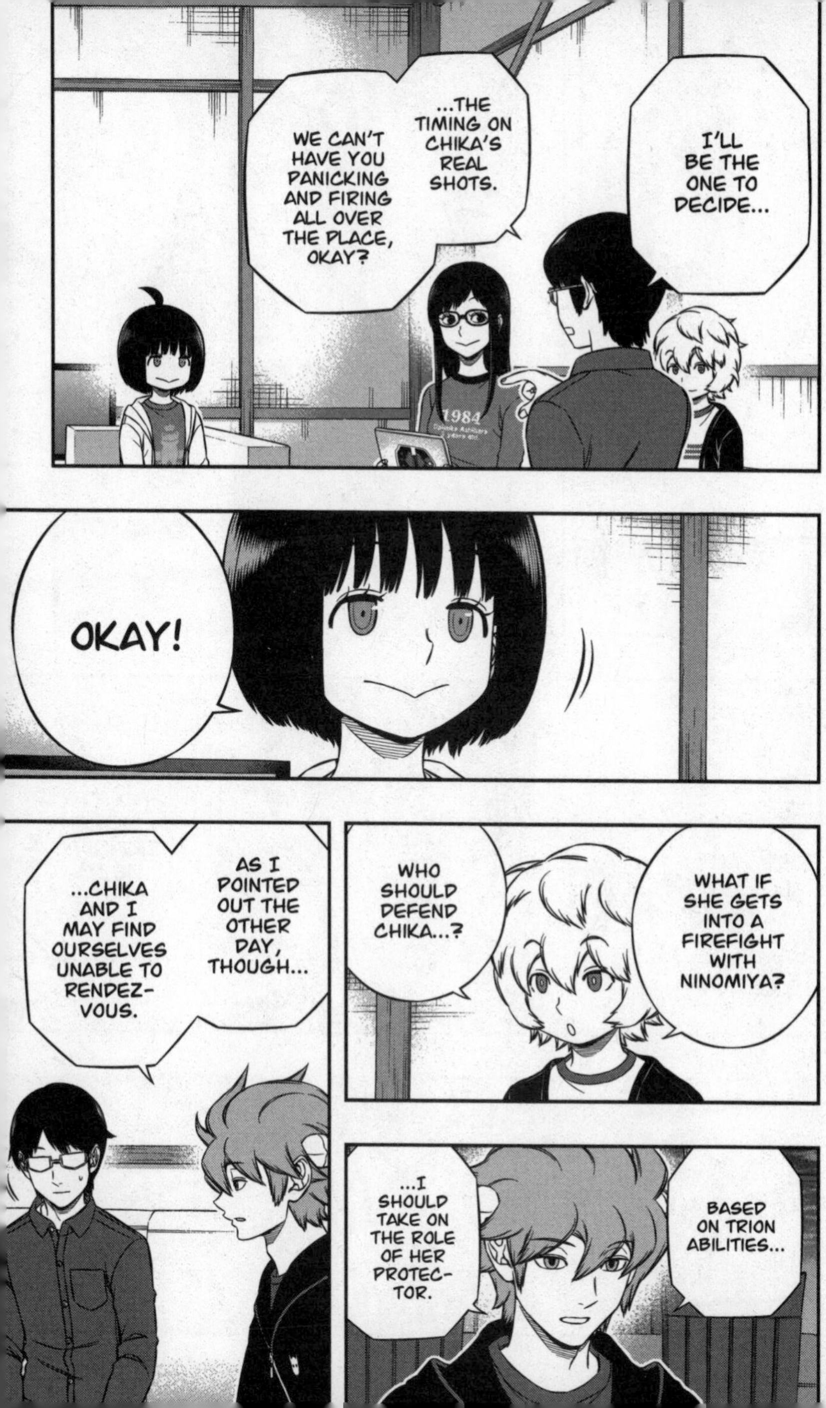
I'LL BE THE ONE TO DECIDE...
...THE TIMING ON CHIKA'S REAL SHOTS.
WE CAN'T HAVE YOU PANICKING AND FIRING ALL OVER THE PLACE, OKAY?
OKAY!
WHAT IF SHE GETS INTO A FIREFIGHT WITH NINOMIYA?
WHO SHOULD DEFEND CHIKA...?
BASED ON TRION ABILITIES...
...I SHOULD TAKE ON THE ROLE OF HER PROTECTOR.
AS I POINTED OUT THE OTHER DAY, THOUGH...
...CHIKA AND I MAY FIND OURSELVES UNABLE TO RENDEZVOUS.

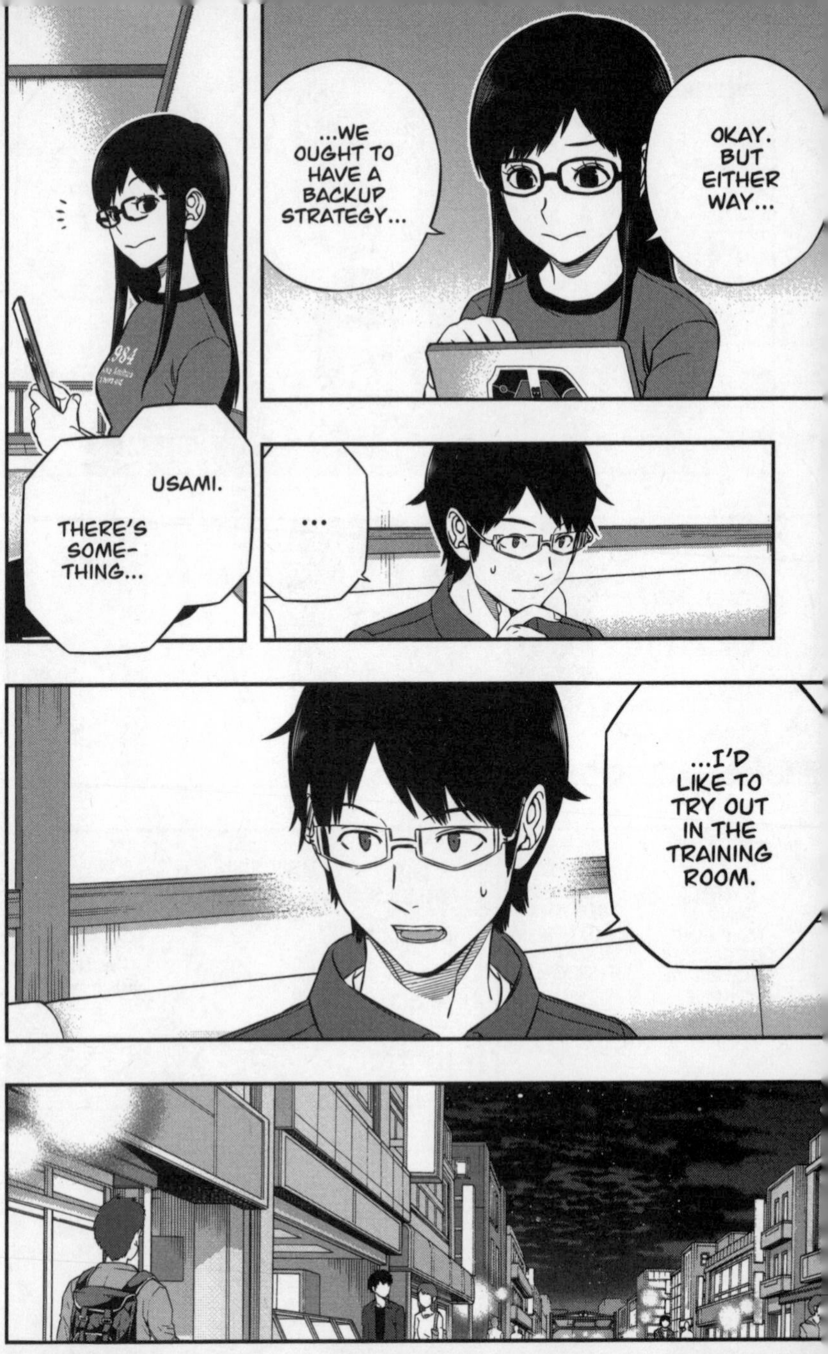
OKAY. BUT EITHER WAY...
...WE OUGHT TO HAVE A BACKUP STRATEGY...
...
USAMI.
THERE'S SOME- THING...
...I'D LIKE TO TRY OUT IN THE TRAINING ROOM.

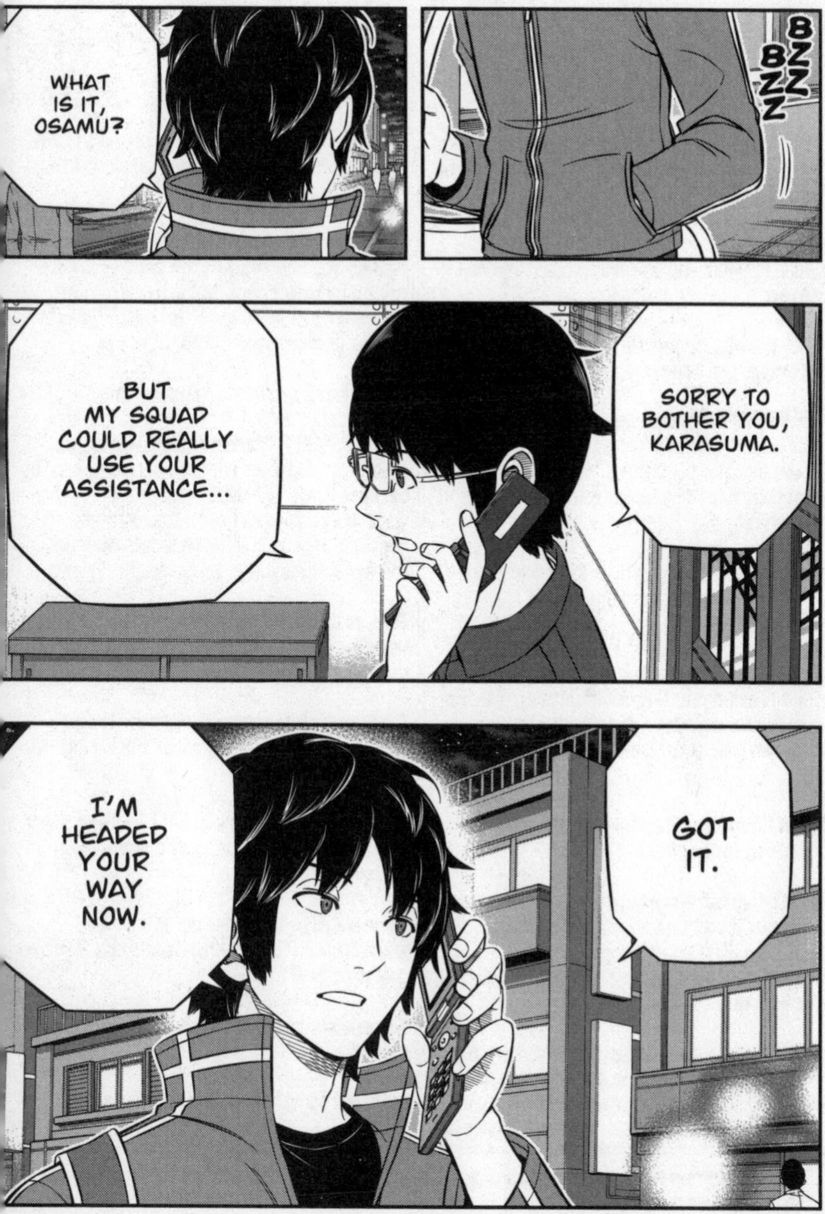
BZZ BZZ
WHAT IS IT, OSAMU?
SORRY TO BOTHER YOU, KARASUMA.
BUT MY SQUAD COULD REALLY USE YOUR ASSISTANCE...
GOT IT.
I'M HEADED YOUR WAY NOW.

Q&A: Part 17

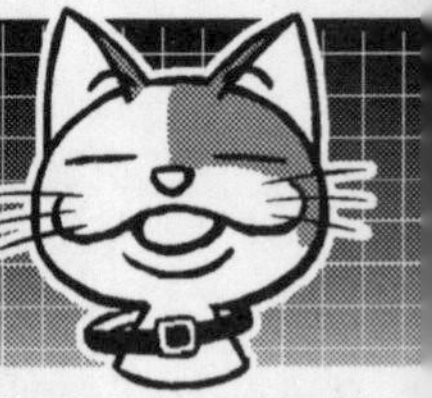

And a few first-time questions.

■What were Ikoma Squad and Oji Squad doing when Galopoula showed up? I guess they were off duty?

In chapter 124, when Shinoda said, "Leave one squad in the west and one in the south," that was those two.

■Of all the nicknames Oji has given people, what are his top three?

He doesn't think too hard about them. He just sort of comes up with them in a very Oji-esque way. Two that have become popular are "Mikamika" and "Pokari," and the one that's spread the least is "Jackson," for Wakamura.

■When someone is using a Trion body, can they take off their clothes and shoes?

There are settings that allow that and settings that don't. Not allowing it saves on Trion costs since constructing the body is simpler. For official Border purposes, the standard setting only allows one to remove outerwear but nothing else.

■What do the other agents think about Oji's nicknames for people?

"As long as we can figure out who he's talking about, it's whatever." Except in the case of Wakamura.

■What sort of gifts are you happy to receive? And which ones, not so much?

When I was hospitalized, I hated the flavorless okayu (rice gruel), so I got a lot of use out of the bottled kaisen-tsukudani (seafood preserves) sent to me by fans (with hospital permission, of course). There's no gift I wasn't happy to receive, though the editorial staff wouldn't let me eat homemade food from fans, as a rule.

■During the Galopoula attack, Kuruma mentioned how leaders are usually determined by rank or age, but are there more formalized military ranks for individuals in Border (like sergeant, colonel, etc.)?

Since the organization is still pretty small, different agents' duties don't differ that much. Besides Commander, HQ Director, Branch Director, and squad captains, there are no individual ranks. Also, because Border is a civilian organization, they're wary about pushback from the government and populace in general if they were to implement more of a military-style hierarchy.

■Does the internal communicator function transmit all of one's thoughts? Or just the thoughts that one wants to broadcast?

The latter. It won't transmit unless you have a recipient in mind and put those thoughts into clear words.

■Satori's ultimate move isn't "Double Snipe," but rather, "Twin Snipe." Any special reason for that name?

Satori once played a video game that had a weapon called "Twin Cannon," and that's where he got the name.

■Please tell me why Satori chose to be a sniper.

So that he could help people over the widest range possible.

■ Sometimes we answer questions asked in fan letters on Twitter. My editor promised to do a mysterious giveaway if we get a lot more followers.
World Trigger Official Twitter Account: @W_Trigger_off

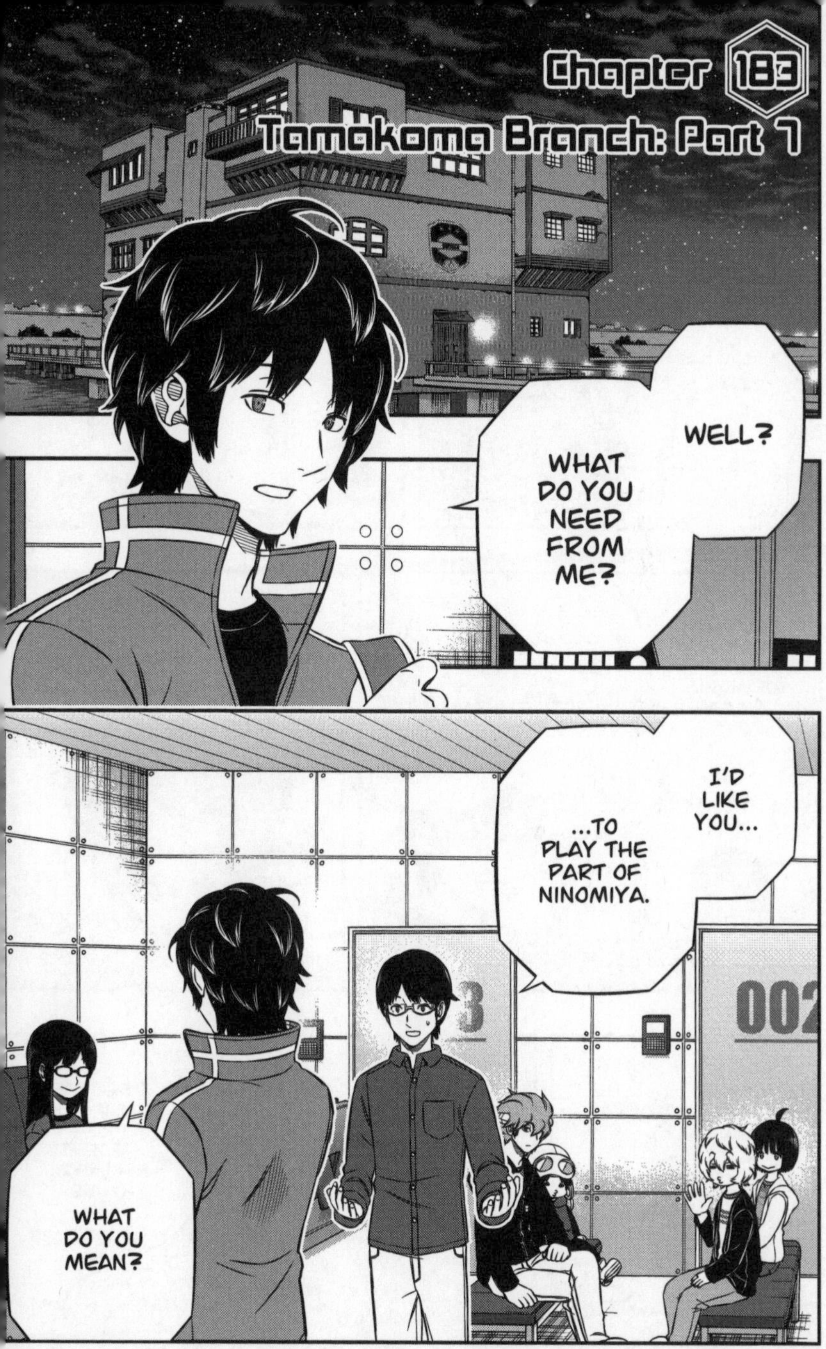

Chapter 183
Tamakoma Branch: Part 7
WELL?
WHAT DO YOU NEED FROM ME?
I'D LIKE YOU...
...TO PLAY THE PART OF NINOMIYA.
002
WHAT DO YOU MEAN?

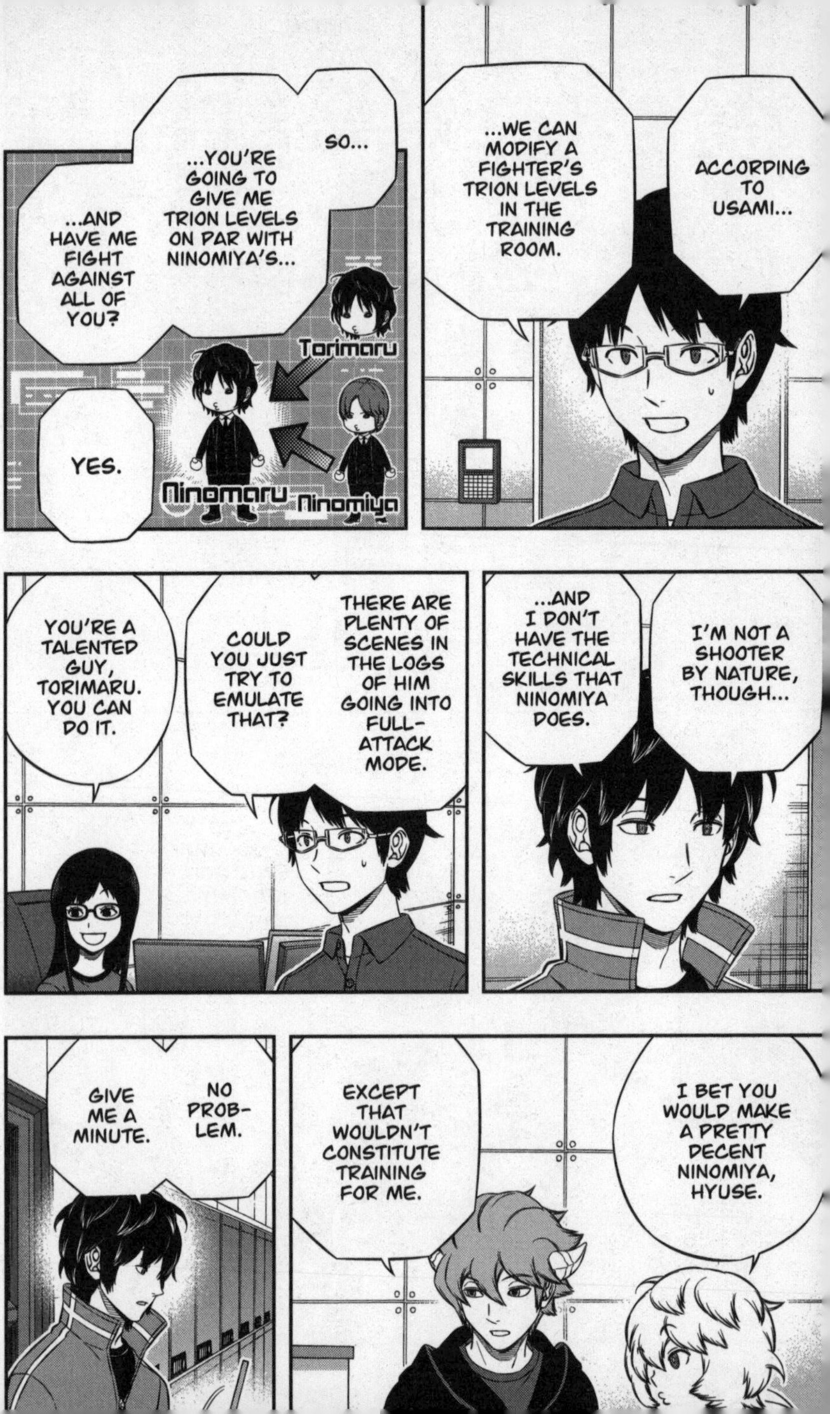
ACCORDING TO USAMI...
...WE CAN MODIFY A FIGHTER'S TRION LEVELS IN THE TRAINING ROOM.
SO...
...YOU'RE GOING TO GIVE ME TRION LEVELS ON PAR WITH NINOMIYA'S...
...AND HAVE ME FIGHT AGAINST ALL OF YOU?
Torimaru
Ninomaru
Ninomiya
YES.
I'M NOT A SHOOTER BY NATURE, THOUGH...
...AND I DON'T HAVE THE TECHNICAL SKILLS THAT NINOMIYA DOES.
THERE ARE PLENTY OF SCENES IN THE LOGS OF HIM GOING INTO FULL-ATTACK MODE.
COULD YOU JUST TRY TO EMULATE THAT?
YOU'RE A TALENTED GUY, TORIMARU. YOU CAN DO IT.
I BET YOU WOULD MAKE A PRETTY DECENT NINOMIYA, HYUSE.
EXCEPT THAT WOULDN'T CONSTITUTE TRAINING FOR ME.
NO PROB-LEM.
GIVE ME A MINUTE.

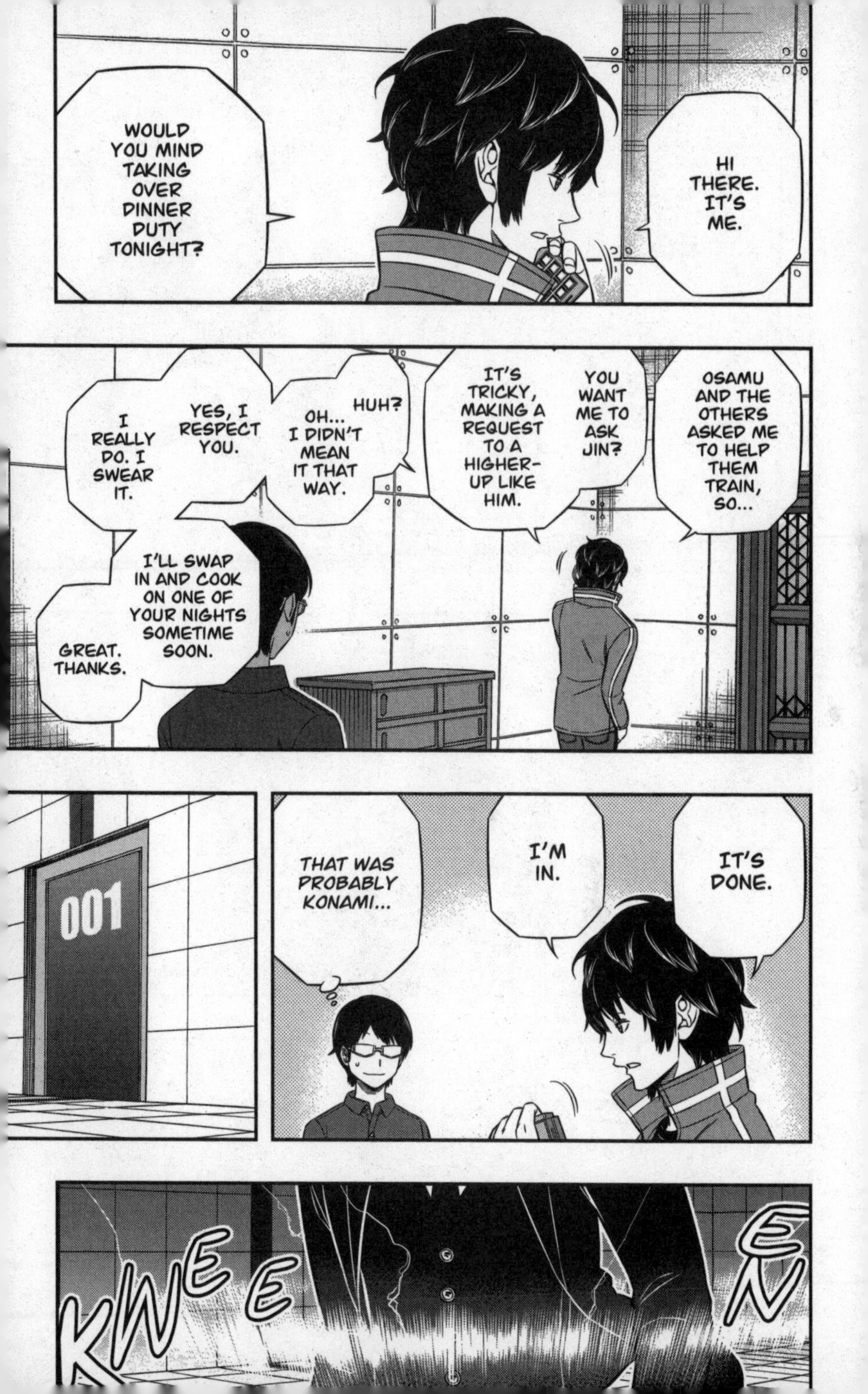
HI THERE. IT'S ME.
WOULD YOU MIND TAKING OVER DINNER DUTY TONIGHT?
OSAMU AND THE OTHERS ASKED ME TO HELP THEM TRAIN, SO...
YOU WANT ME TO ASK JIN?
IT'S TRICKY, MAKING A REQUEST TO A HIGHER-UP LIKE HIM.
HUH?
OH... I DIDN'T MEAN IT THAT WAY.
YES, I RESPECT YOU.
I REALLY DO. I SWEAR IT.
I'LL SWAP IN AND COOK ON ONE OF YOUR NIGHTS SOMETIME SOON.
GREAT. THANKS.
IT'S DONE.
I'M IN.
THAT WAS PROBABLY KONAMI...
001
KWEEEN

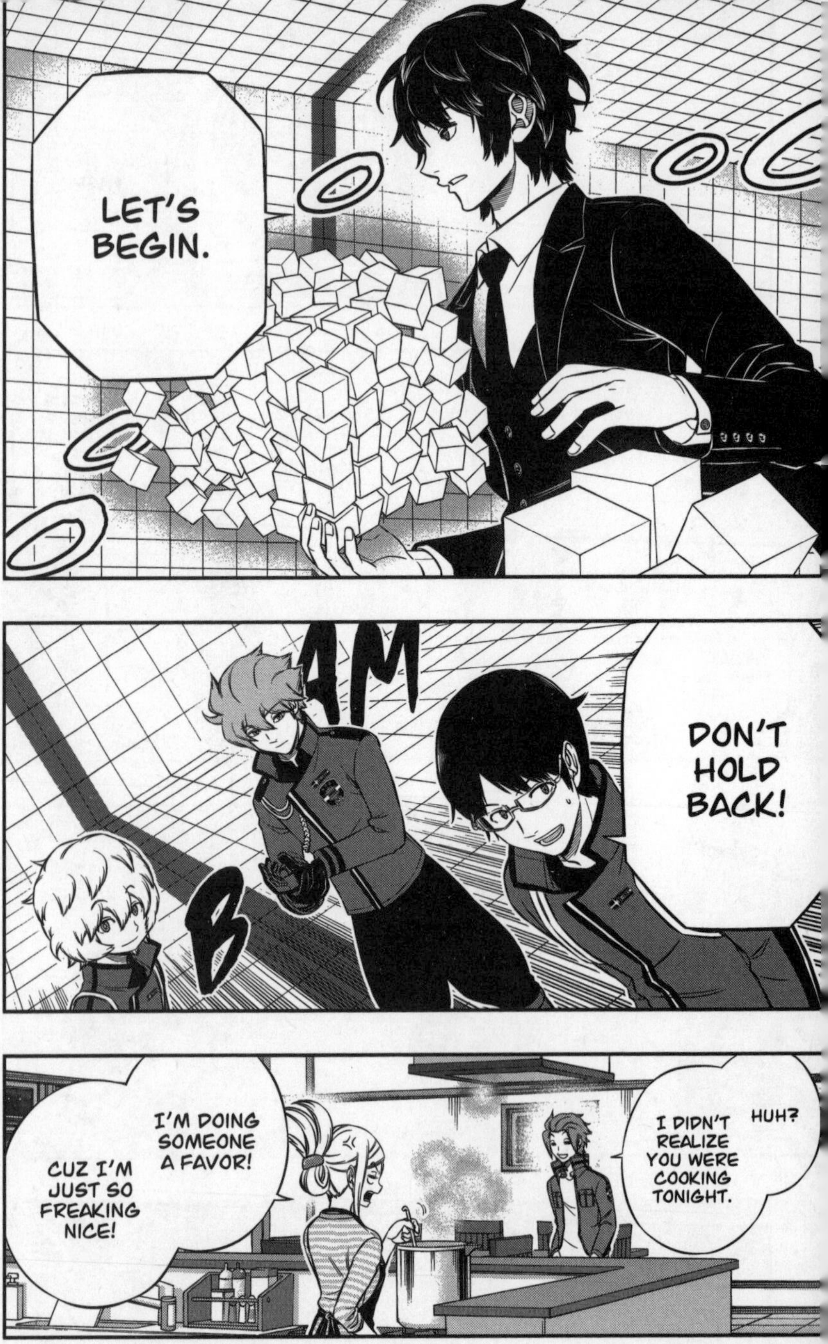
LET'S BEGIN.
DON'T HOLD BACK!
BAM
HUH?
I DIDN'T REALIZE YOU WERE COOKING TONIGHT.
I'M DOING SOMEONE A FAVOR!
CUZ I'M JUST SO FREAKING NICE!

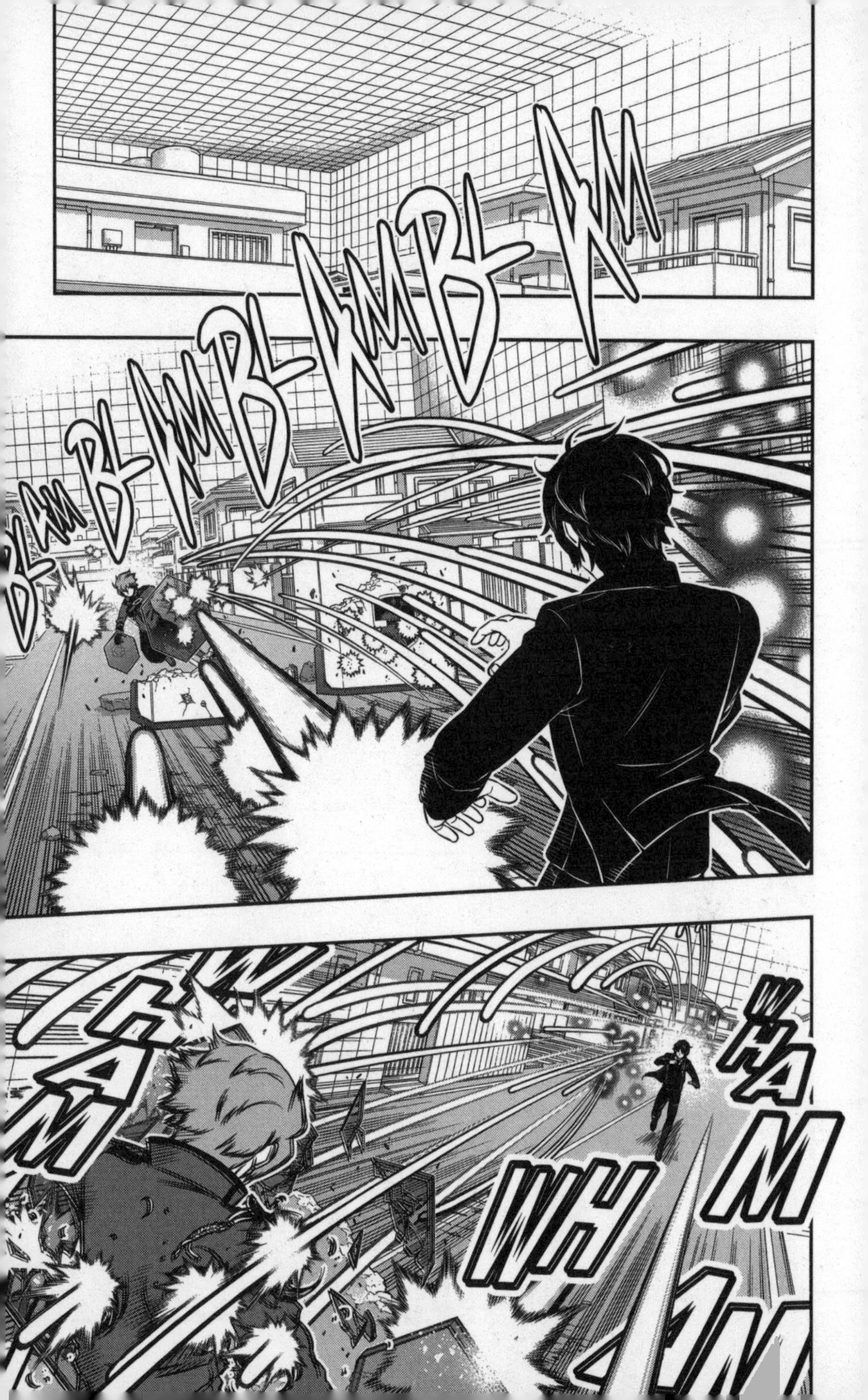
BLAMBLAMBLAMBLAM
WHAM

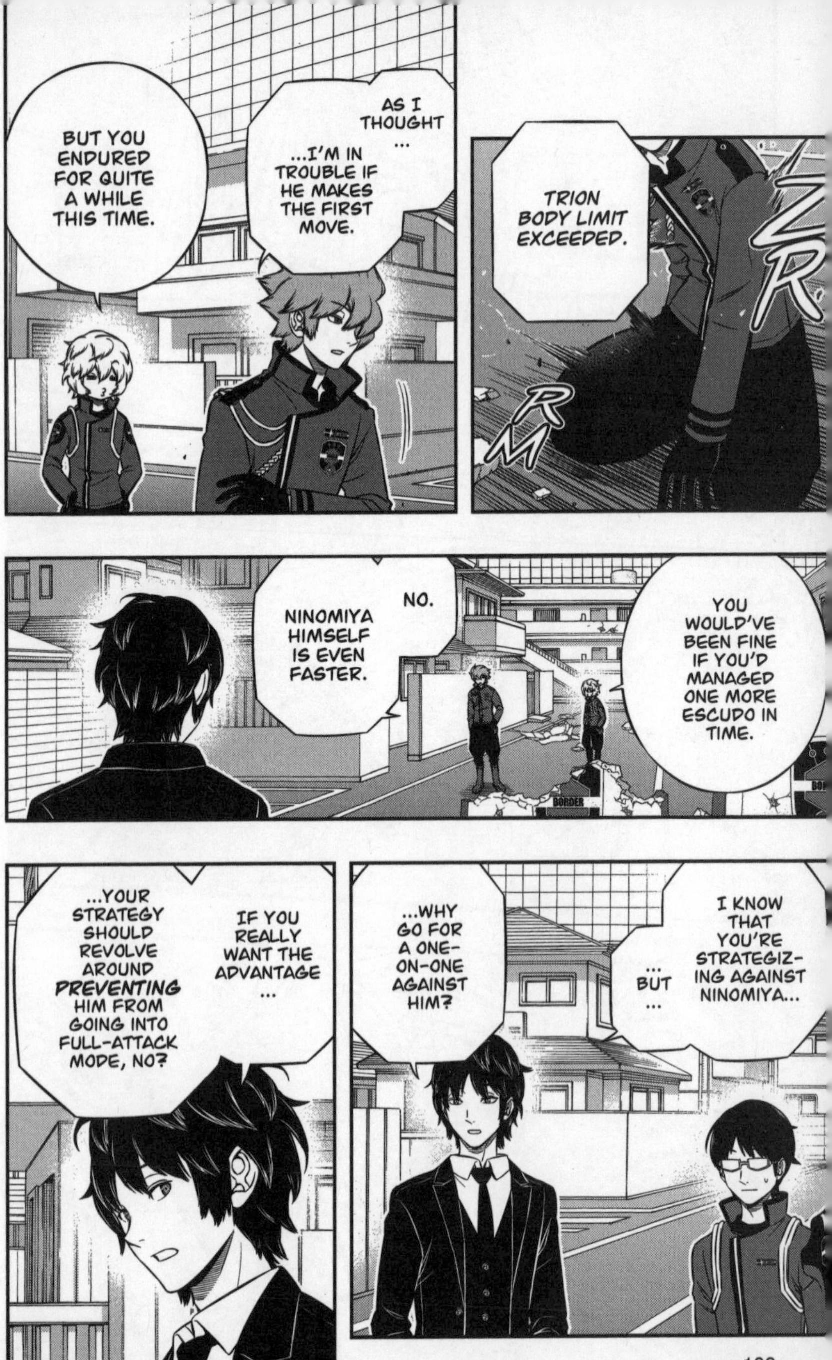
TRION BODY LIMIT EXCEEDED.
AS I THOUGHT ...
...I'M IN TROUBLE IF HE MAKES THE FIRST MOVE.
BUT YOU ENDURED FOR QUITE A WHILE THIS TIME.
YOU WOULD'VE BEEN FINE IF YOU'D MANAGED ONE MORE ESCUDO IN TIME.
NO.
NINOMIYA HIMSELF IS EVEN FASTER.
I KNOW THAT YOU'RE STRATEGIZING AGAINST NINOMIYA...
... BUT ...
...WHY GO FOR A ONE-ON-ONE AGAINST HIM?
IF YOU REALLY WANT THE ADVANTAGE ...
...YOUR STRATEGY SHOULD REVOLVE AROUND PREVENTING HIM FROM GOING INTO FULL-ATTACK MODE, NO?

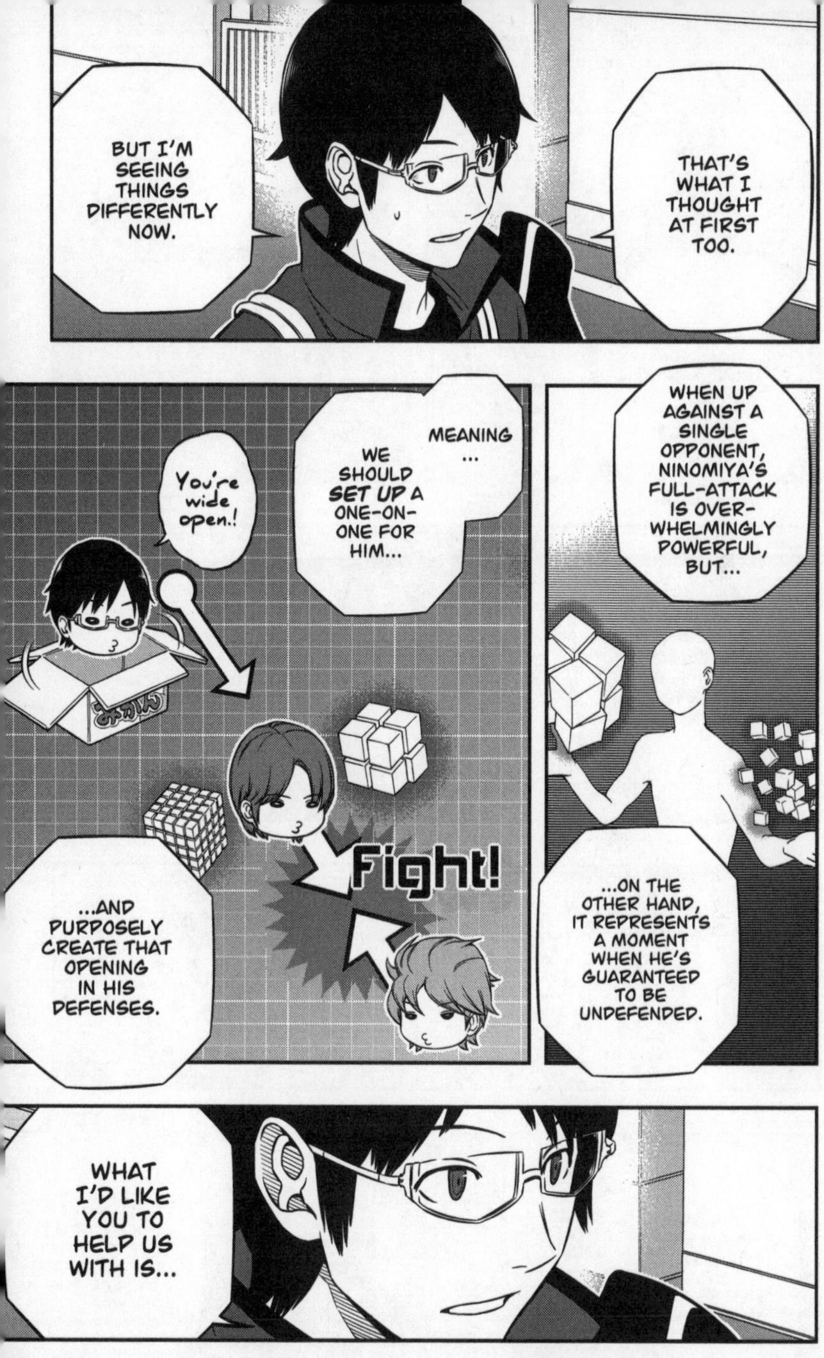

THAT'S WHAT I THOUGHT AT FIRST TOO.
BUT I'M SEEING THINGS DIFFERENTLY NOW.
WHEN UP AGAINST A SINGLE OPPONENT, NINOMIYA'S FULL-ATTACK IS OVER-WHELMINGLY POWERFUL, BUT...
...ON THE OTHER HAND, IT REPRESENTS A MOMENT WHEN HE'S GUARANTEED TO BE UNDEFENDED.
MEANING...
WE SHOULD SET UP A ONE-ON-ONE FOR HIM...
You're wide open.!
Fight!
...AND PURPOSELY CREATE THAT OPENING IN HIS DEFENSES.
WHAT I'D LIKE YOU TO HELP US WITH IS...

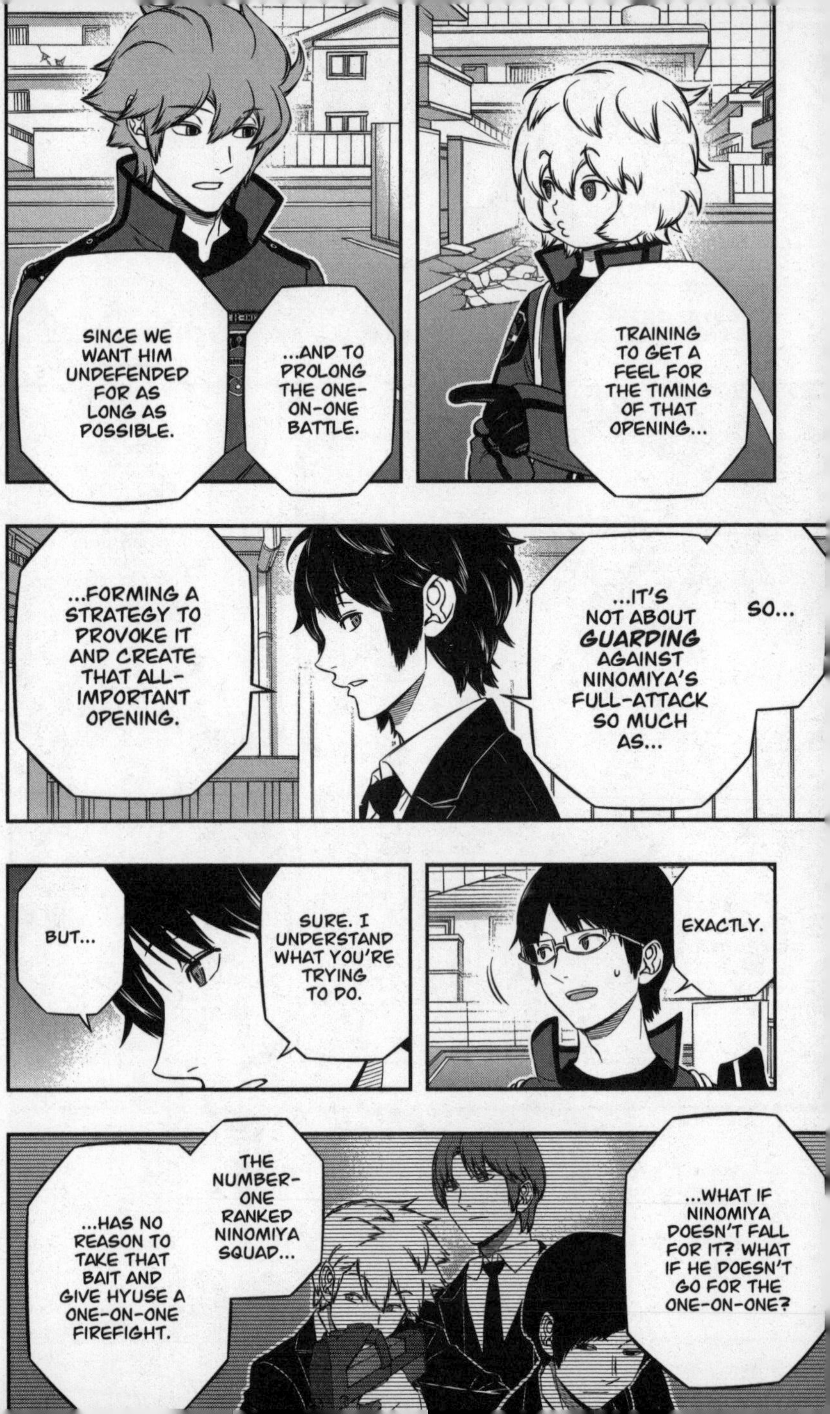
TRAINING TO GET A FEEL FOR THE TIMING OF THAT OPENING...
...AND TO PROLONG THE ONE-ON-ONE BATTLE.
SINCE WE WANT HIM UNDEFENDED FOR AS LONG AS POSSIBLE.
SO...
...IT'S NOT ABOUT **GUARDING** AGAINST NINOMIYA'S FULL-ATTACK SO MUCH AS...
...FORMING A STRATEGY TO PROVOKE IT AND CREATE THAT ALL-IMPORTANT OPENING.
EXACTLY.
SURE. I UNDERSTAND WHAT YOU'RE TRYING TO DO.
BUT...
...WHAT IF NINOMIYA DOESN'T FALL FOR IT? WHAT IF HE DOESN'T GO FOR THE ONE-ON-ONE?
THE NUMBER-ONE RANKED NINOMIYA SQUAD...
...HAS NO REASON TO TAKE THAT BAIT AND GIVE HYUSE A ONE-ON-ONE FIREFIGHT.

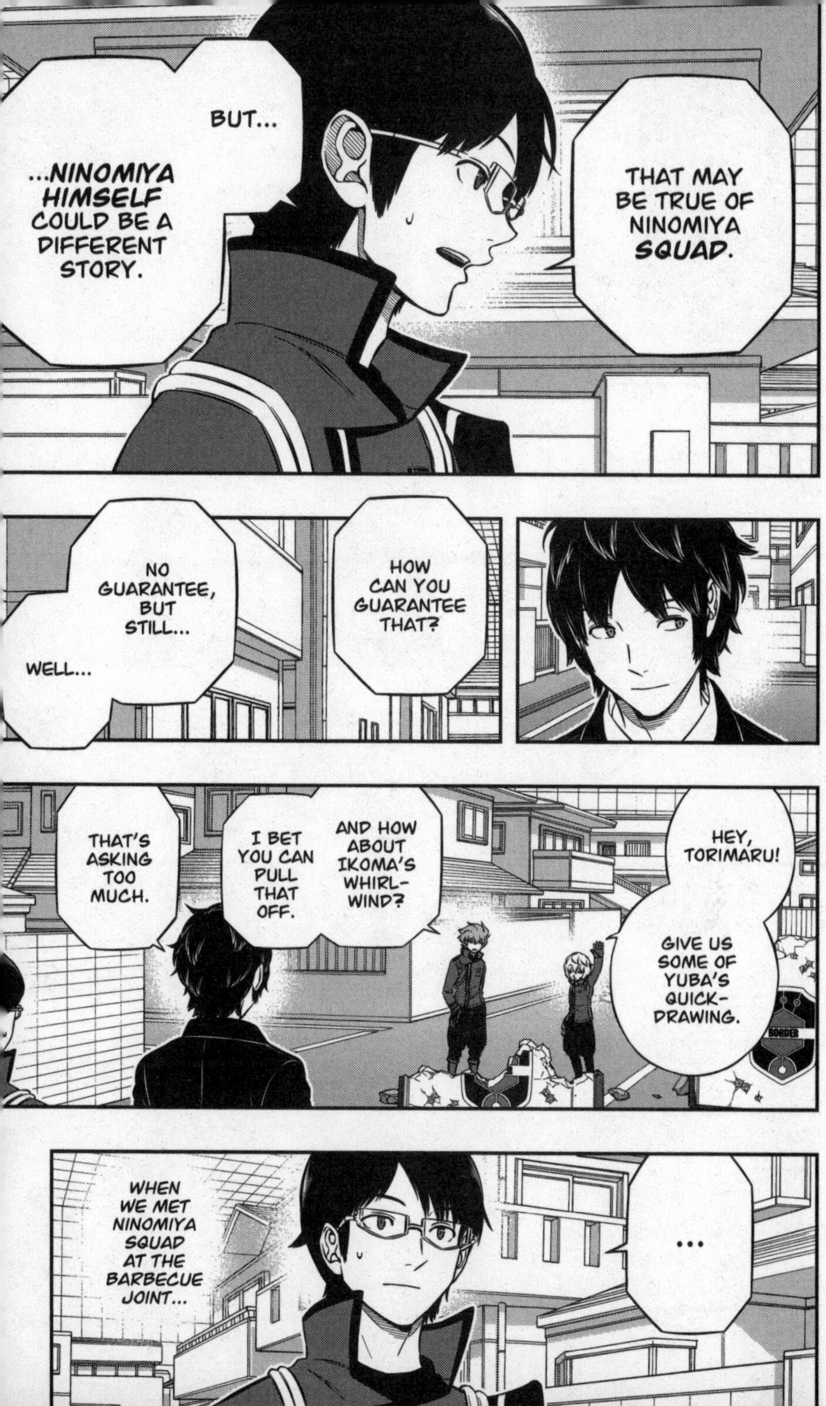
THAT MAY BE TRUE OF NINOMIYA SQUAD.
BUT...
...NINOMIYA HIMSELF COULD BE A DIFFERENT STORY.
HOW CAN YOU GUARANTEE THAT?
NO GUARANTEE, BUT STILL...
WELL...
HEY, TORIMARU!
GIVE US SOME OF YUBA'S QUICK-DRAWING.
AND HOW ABOUT IKOMA'S WHIRLWIND?
I BET YOU CAN PULL THAT OFF.
THAT'S ASKING TOO MUCH.
BORDER
...
WHEN WE MET NINOMIYA SQUAD AT THE BARBECUE JOINT...

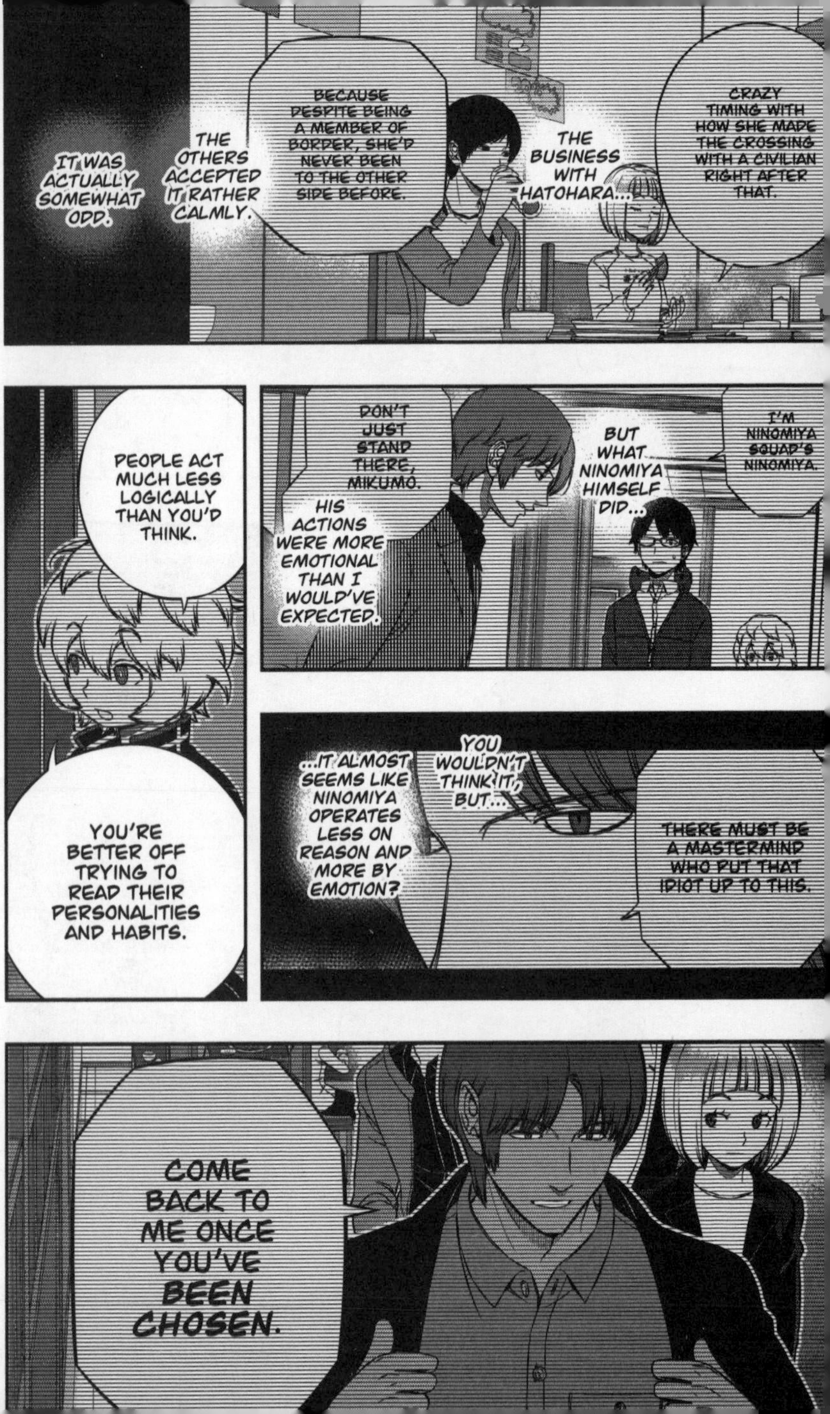
CRAZY TIMING WITH HOW SHE MADE THE CROSSING WITH A CIVILIAN RIGHT AFTER THAT.
THE BUSINESS WITH HATOHARA...
BECAUSE DESPITE BEING A MEMBER OF BORDER, SHE'D NEVER BEEN TO THE OTHER SIDE BEFORE.
THE OTHERS ACCEPTED IT RATHER CALMLY.
IT WAS ACTUALLY SOMEWHAT ODD.
I'M NINOMIYA SQUAD'S NINOMIYA.
BUT WHAT NINOMIYA HIMSELF DID...
DON'T JUST STAND THERE, MIKUMO.
HIS ACTIONS WERE MORE EMOTIONAL THAN I WOULD'VE EXPECTED.
THERE MUST BE A MASTERMIND WHO PUT THAT IDIOT UP TO THIS.
YOU WOULDN'T THINK IT, BUT...
...IT ALMOST SEEMS LIKE NINOMIYA OPERATES LESS ON REASON AND MORE BY EMOTION?
PEOPLE ACT MUCH LESS LOGICALLY THAN YOU'D THINK.
YOU'RE BETTER OFF TRYING TO READ THEIR PERSONALITIES AND HABITS.
COME BACK TO ME ONCE YOU'VE BEEN CHOSEN.

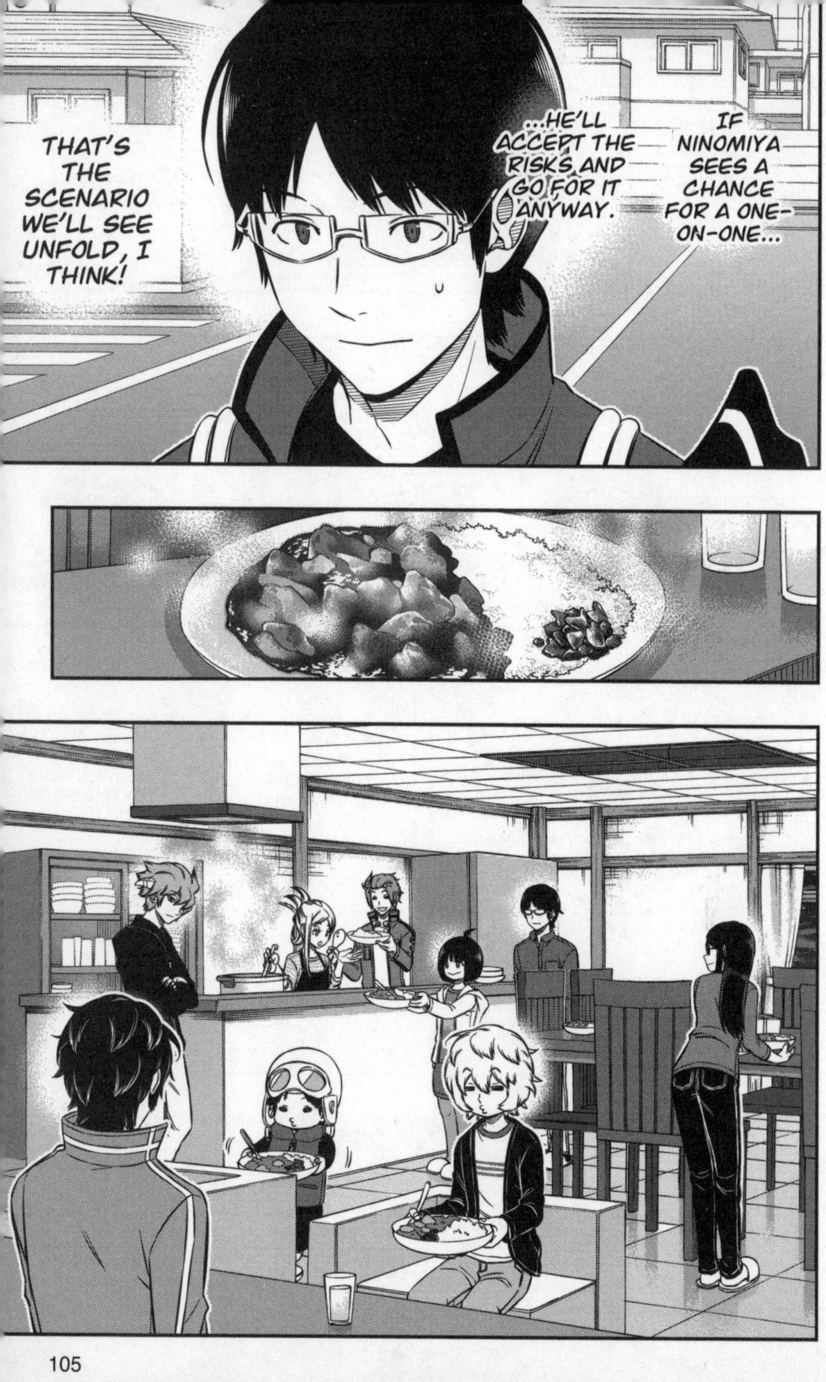
IF NINOMIYA SEES A CHANCE FOR A ONE-ON-ONE...
...HE'LL ACCEPT THE RISKS AND GO FOR IT ANYWAY.
THAT'S THE SCENARIO WE'LL SEE UNFOLD, I THINK!

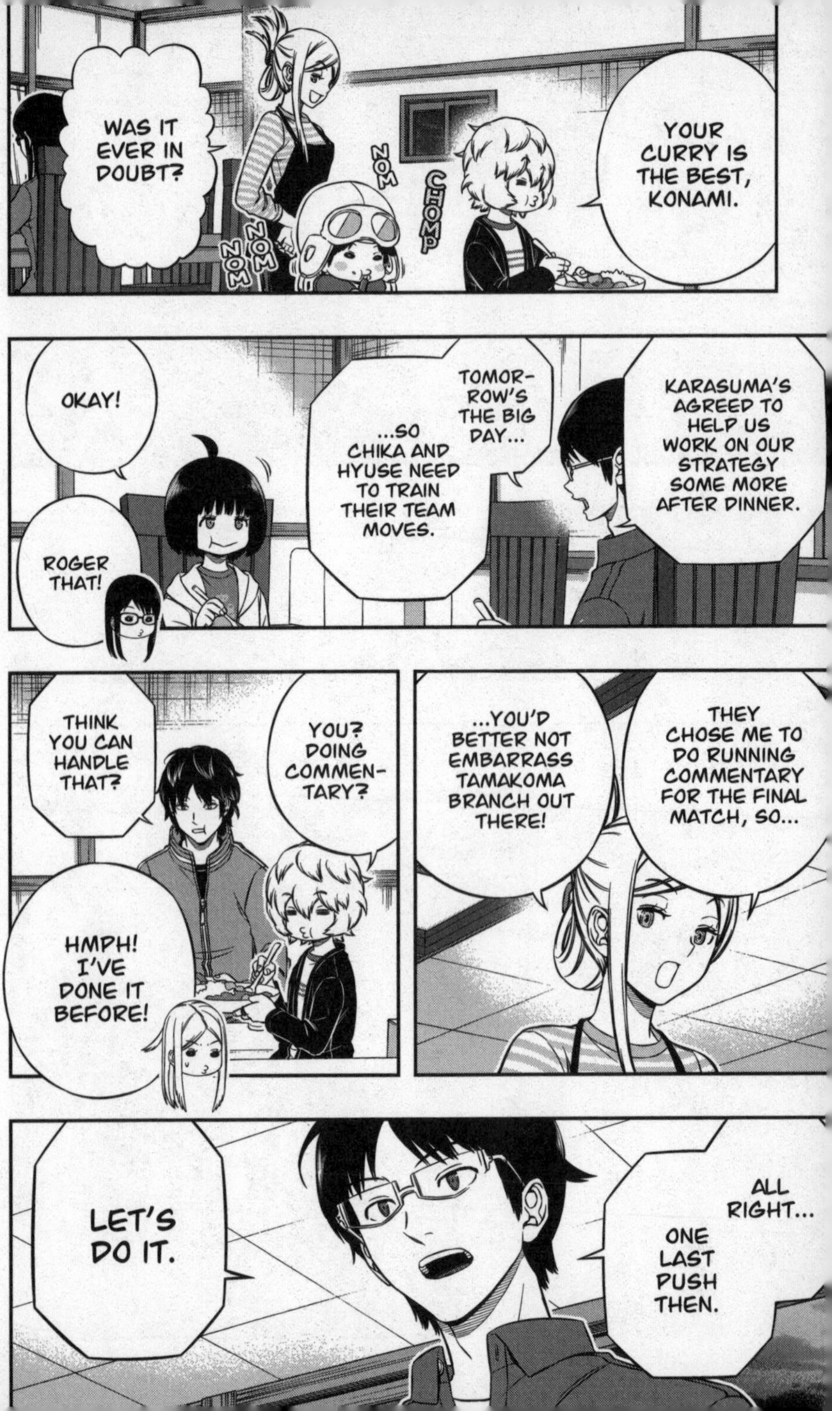
YOUR CURRY IS THE BEST, KONAMI.
CHOMP
NOM
NOM NOM
WAS IT EVER IN DOUBT?
KARASUMA'S AGREED TO HELP US WORK ON OUR STRATEGY SOME MORE AFTER DINNER.
TOMOR-ROW'S THE BIG DAY...
...SO CHIKA AND HYUSE NEED TO TRAIN THEIR TEAM MOVES.
OKAY!
ROGER THAT!
THEY CHOSE ME TO DO RUNNING COMMENTARY FOR THE FINAL MATCH, SO...
...YOU'D BETTER NOT EMBARRASS TAMAKOMA BRANCH OUT THERE!
YOU? DOING COMMEN-TARY?
THINK YOU CAN HANDLE THAT?
HMPH! I'VE DONE IT BEFORE!
ALL RIGHT...
ONE LAST PUSH THEN.
LET'S DO IT.

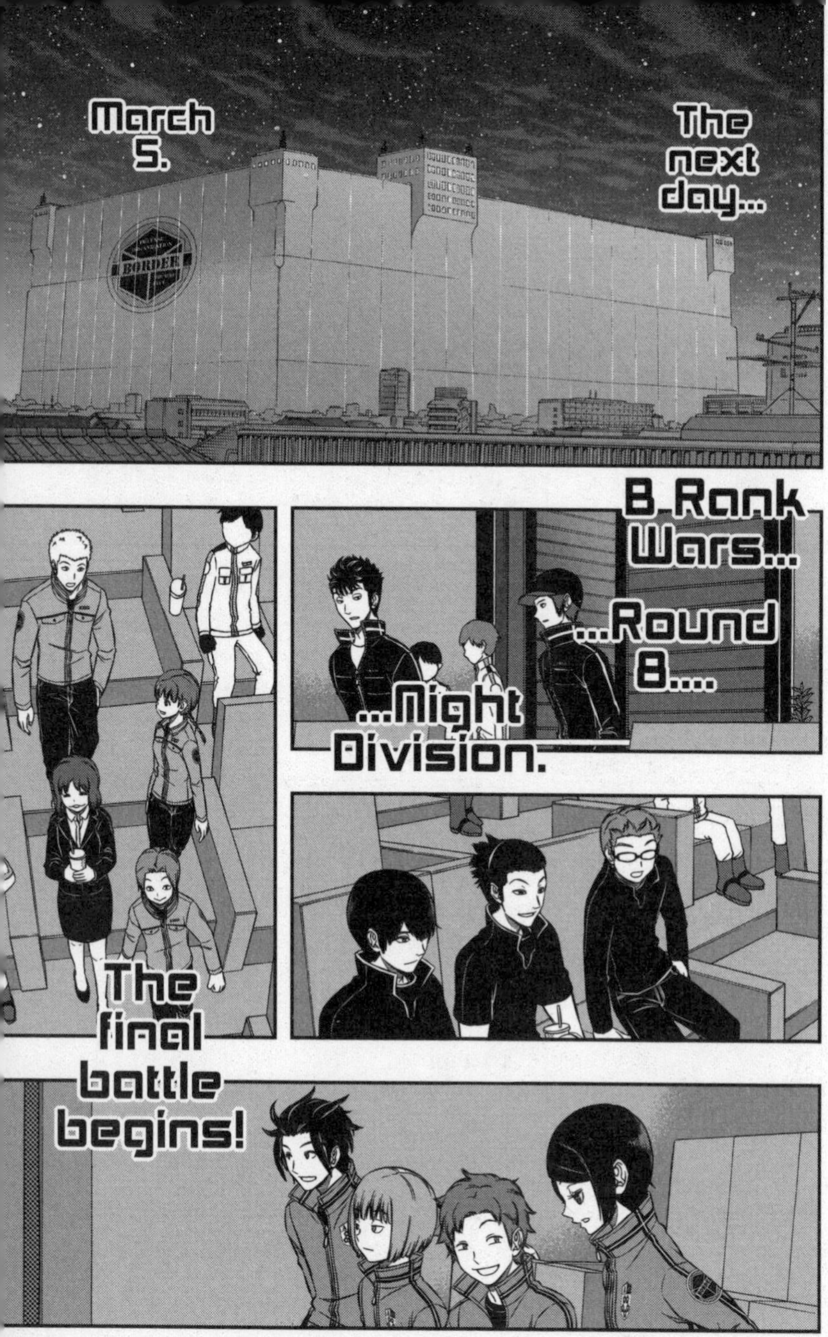
The next day...
March 5.
B Rank Wars...
...Round 8....
...Night Division.
The final battle begins!

Yuba Squad

Border HQ B-Rank #7

B-007

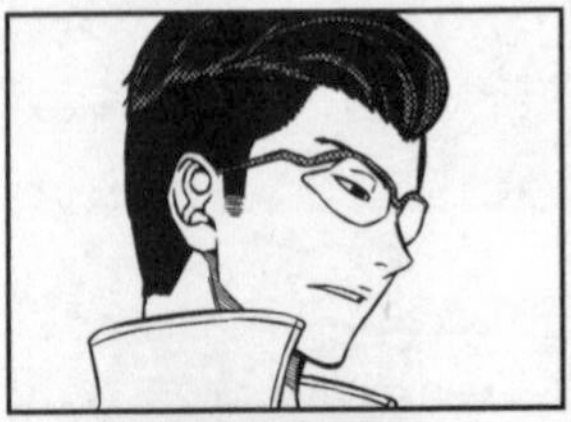

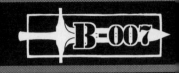

Takuma Yuba

Captain, Gunner

■19 years old (College student)

■Born April 30

■Felis Blood type AB

■Height: 5′1″

■Likes: One-on-one matches, family, friends, pound cake

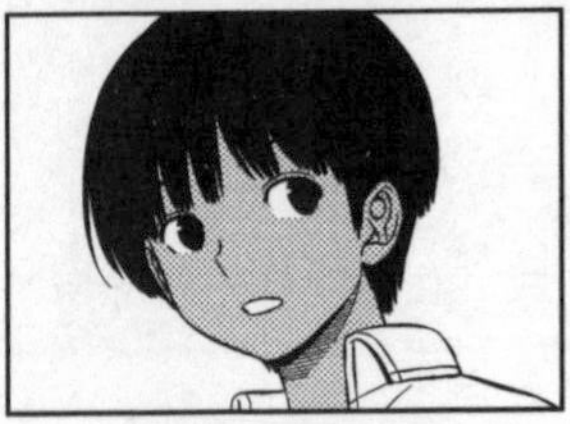

Yukari Obishima

All-Rounder

■14 years old (Middle school student)

■Born February 4

■Amphibious Blood type B

■Height: 5′0″

■Likes: Exercise, black sesame dango, mikan, dogs

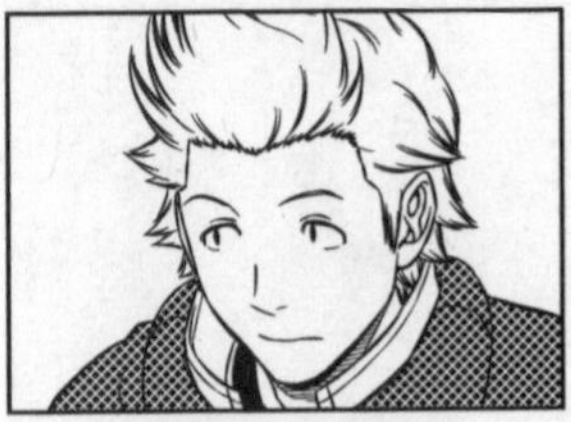

Kazuto Tonooka

Sniper

■16 years old (High school student)

■Born November 21

■Chronos Blood type B

■Height: 5′6″

■Likes: Kashiwa tempura, roasted green tea, alone time

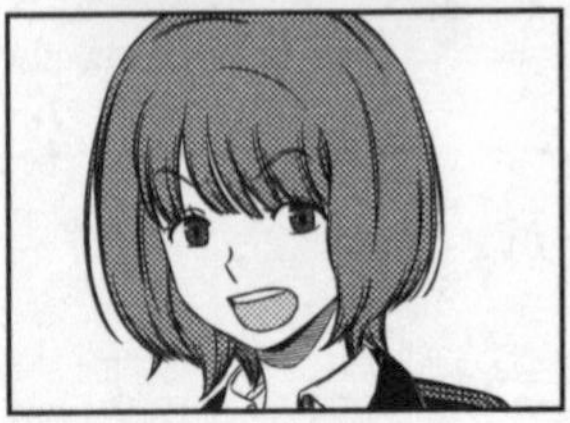

Nono Fujimaru

Operator

■19 years old (College student)

■Born October 24

■Chronos Blood type A

■Height: 5′4″

■Likes: Chocolate, carbonated beverages, comics

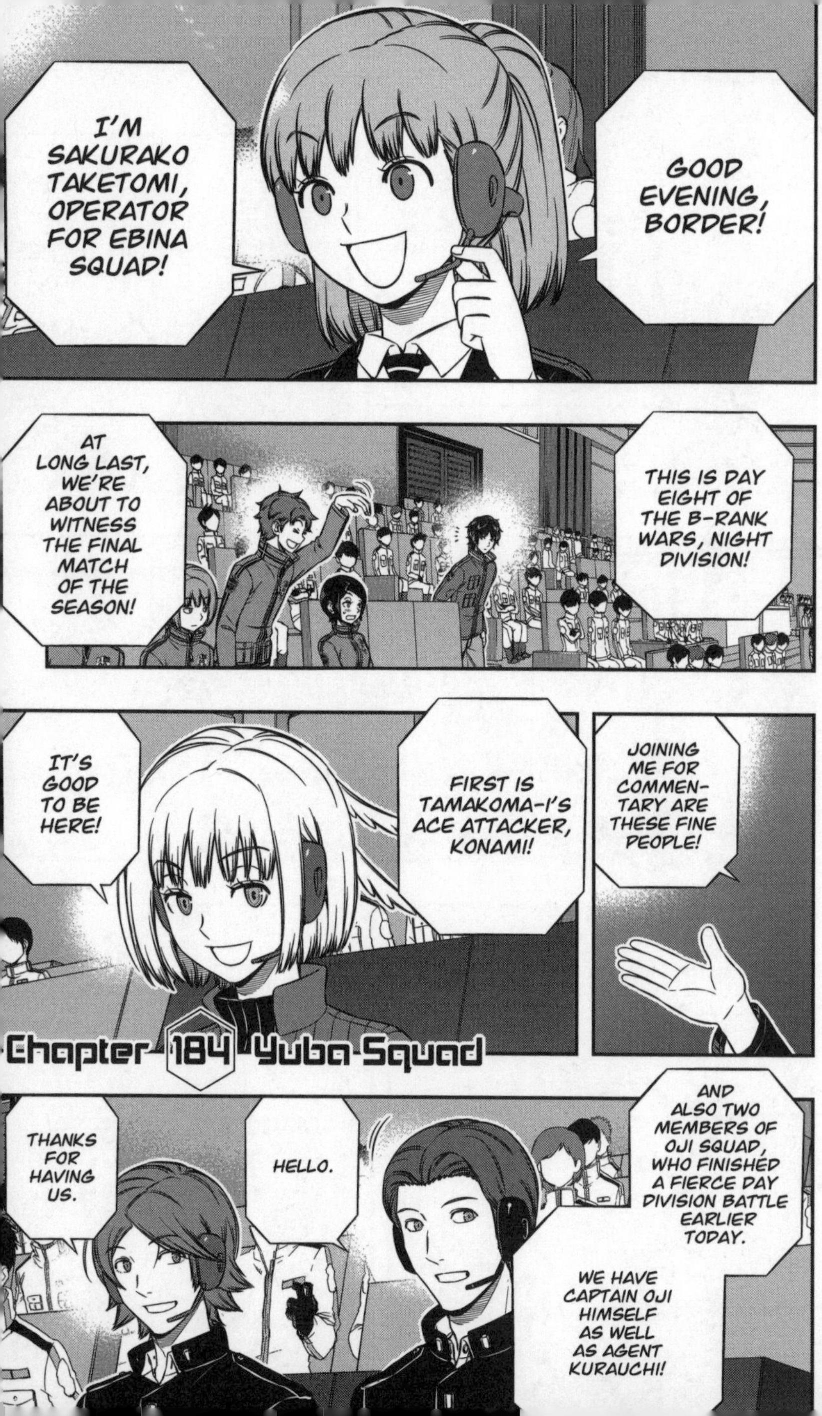
GOOD EVENING, BORDER!
I'M SAKURAKO TAKETOMI, OPERATOR FOR EBINA SQUAD!
THIS IS DAY EIGHT OF THE B-RANK WARS, NIGHT DIVISION!
AT LONG LAST, WE'RE ABOUT TO WITNESS THE FINAL MATCH OF THE SEASON!
JOINING ME FOR COMMENTARY ARE THESE FINE PEOPLE!
FIRST IS TAMAKOMA-1'S ACE ATTACKER, KONAMI!
IT'S GOOD TO BE HERE!
Chapter 184 Yuba Squad
AND ALSO TWO MEMBERS OF OJI SQUAD, WHO FINISHED A FIERCE DAY DIVISION BATTLE EARLIER TODAY.
WE HAVE CAPTAIN OJI HIMSELF AS WELL AS AGENT KURAUCHI!
HELLO.
THANKS FOR HAVING US.

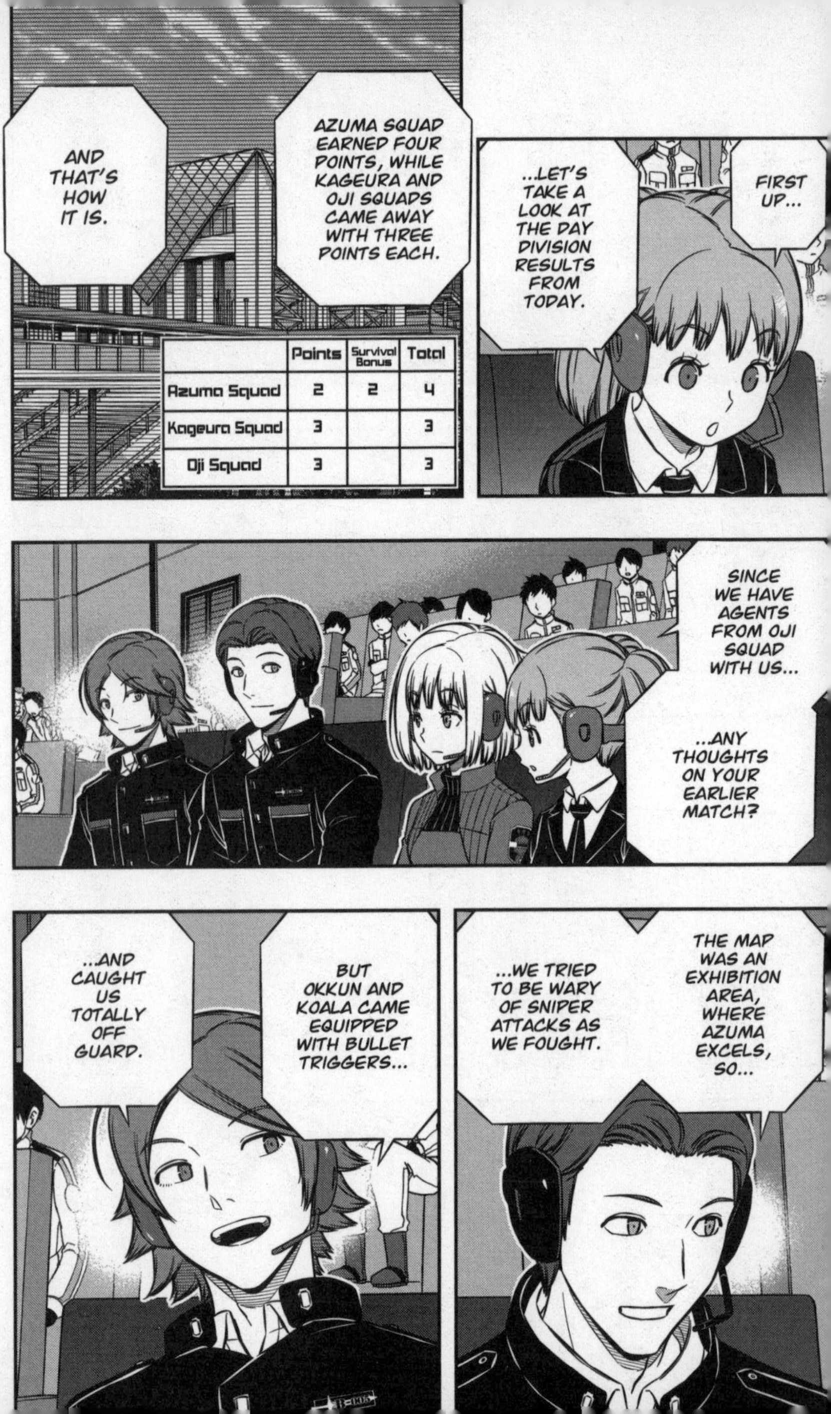
FIRST UP...
...LET'S TAKE A LOOK AT THE DAY DIVISION RESULTS FROM TODAY.
AZUMA SQUAD EARNED FOUR POINTS, WHILE KAGEURA AND OJI SQUADS CAME AWAY WITH THREE POINTS EACH.
AND THAT'S HOW IT IS.
Points / Survival Bonus / Total
Azuma Squad 2 2 4
Kageura Squad 3 3
Oji Squad 3 3
SINCE WE HAVE AGENTS FROM OJI SQUAD WITH US...
...ANY THOUGHTS ON YOUR EARLIER MATCH?
THE MAP WAS AN EXHIBITION AREA, WHERE AZUMA EXCELS, SO...
...WE TRIED TO BE WARY OF SNIPER ATTACKS AS WE FOUGHT.
BUT OKKUN AND KOALA CAME EQUIPPED WITH BULLET TRIGGERS...
...AND CAUGHT US TOTALLY OFF GUARD.

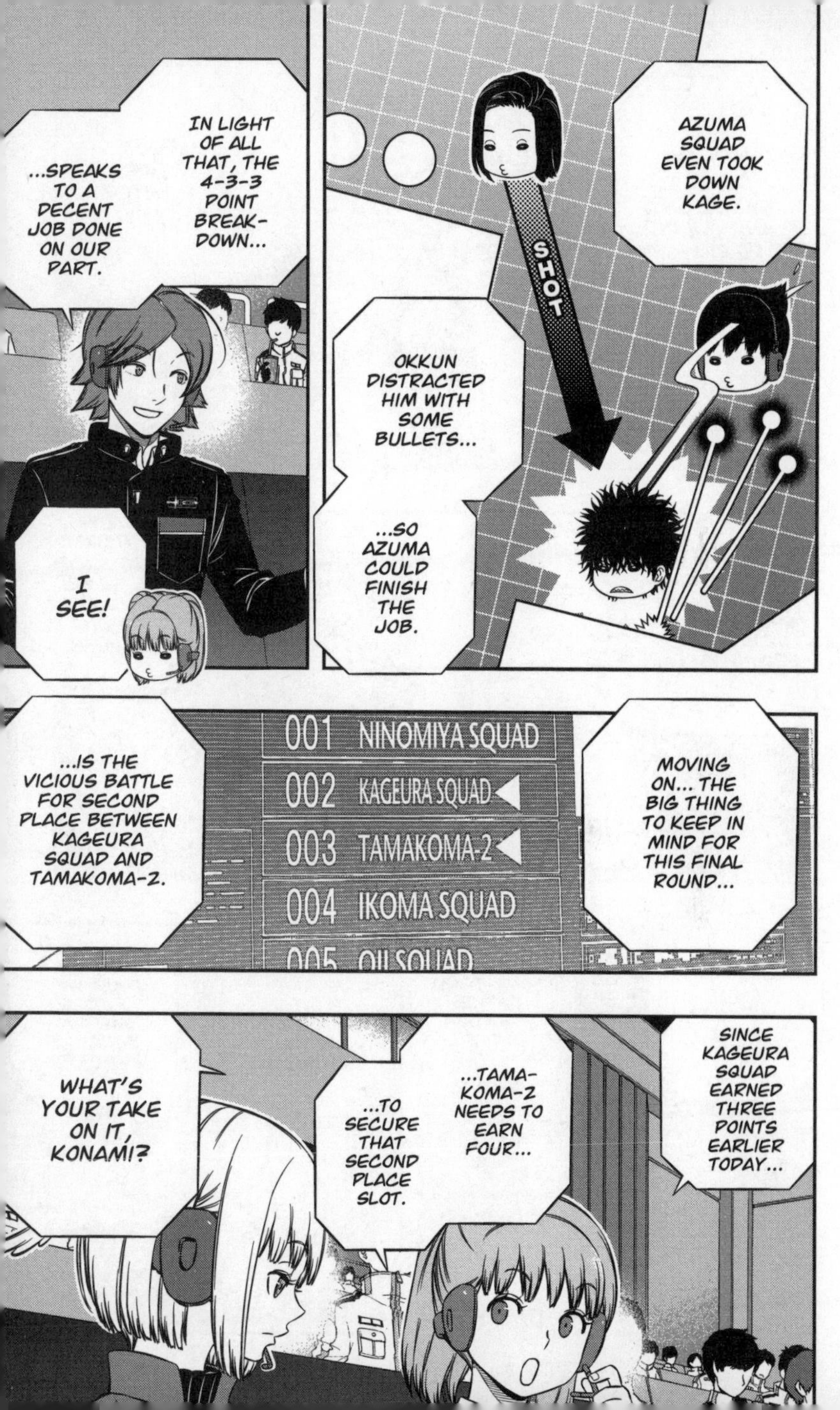
AZUMA SQUAD EVEN TOOK DOWN KAGE.
SHOT
OKKUN DISTRACTED HIM WITH SOME BULLETS...
...SO AZUMA COULD FINISH THE JOB.
IN LIGHT OF ALL THAT, THE 4-3-3 POINT BREAK-DOWN...
...SPEAKS TO A DECENT JOB DONE ON OUR PART.
I SEE!
MOVING ON... THE BIG THING TO KEEP IN MIND FOR THIS FINAL ROUND...
001 NINOMIYA SQUAD
002 KAGEURA SQUAD
003 TAMAKOMA-2
004 IKOMA SQUAD
...IS THE VICIOUS BATTLE FOR SECOND PLACE BETWEEN KAGEURA SQUAD AND TAMAKOMA-2.
SINCE KAGEURA SQUAD EARNED THREE POINTS EARLIER TODAY...
...TAMA-KOMA-2 NEEDS TO EARN FOUR...
...TO SECURE THAT SECOND PLACE SLOT.
WHAT'S YOUR TAKE ON IT, KONAMI?

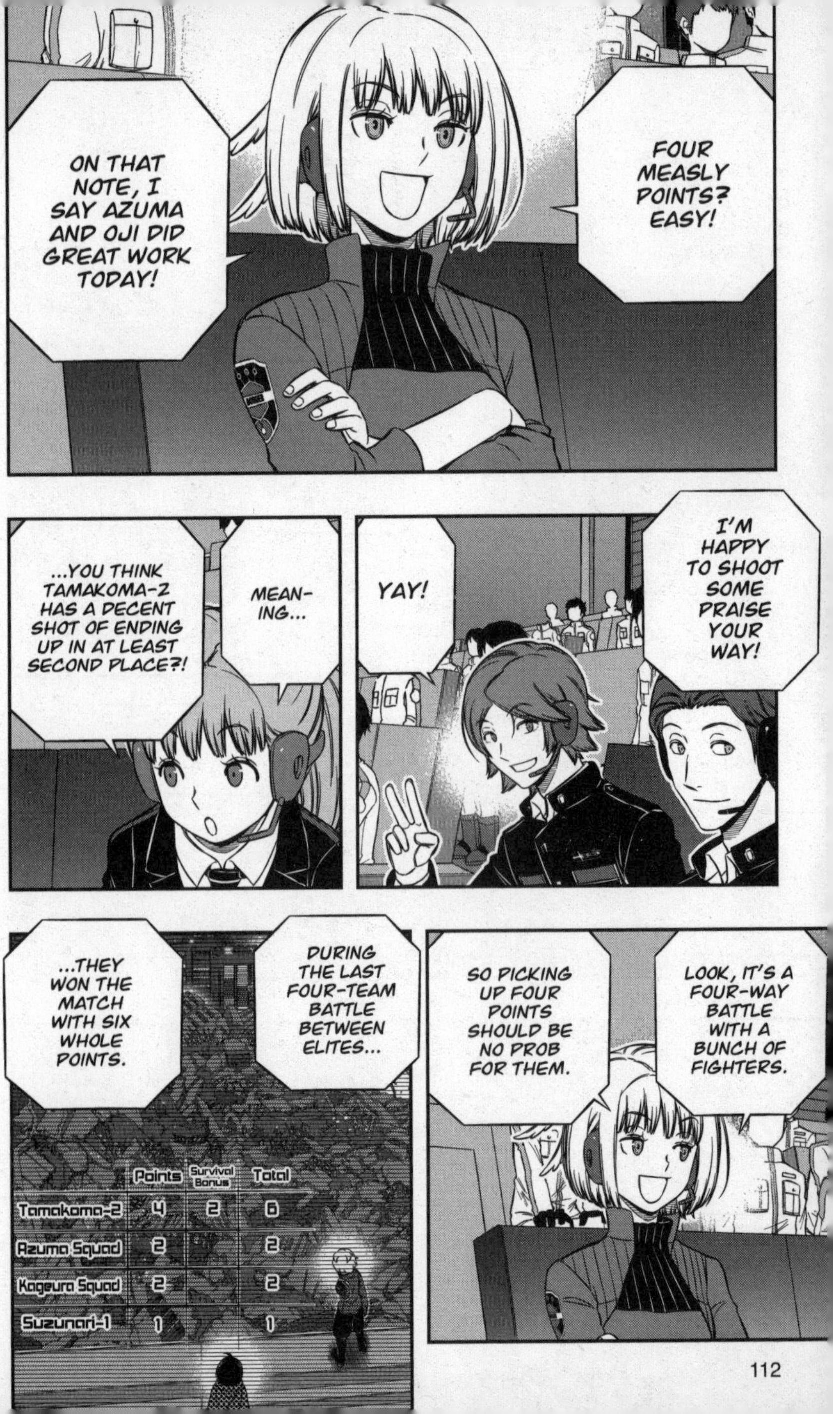
FOUR MEASLY POINTS? EASY!
ON THAT NOTE, I SAY AZUMA AND OJI DID GREAT WORK TODAY!
I'M HAPPY TO SHOOT SOME PRAISE YOUR WAY!
YAY!
MEAN-ING...
...YOU THINK TAMAKOMA-2 HAS A DECENT SHOT OF ENDING UP IN AT LEAST SECOND PLACE?!
LOOK, IT'S A FOUR-WAY BATTLE WITH A BUNCH OF FIGHTERS.
SO PICKING UP FOUR POINTS SHOULD BE NO PROB FOR THEM.
DURING THE LAST FOUR-TEAM BATTLE BETWEEN ELITES...
...THEY WON THE MATCH WITH SIX WHOLE POINTS.
Points
Survival Bonus
Total
Tamakoma-2 4 2 6
Azuma Squad 2 2
Kageura Squad 2 2
Suzunari-1 1 1

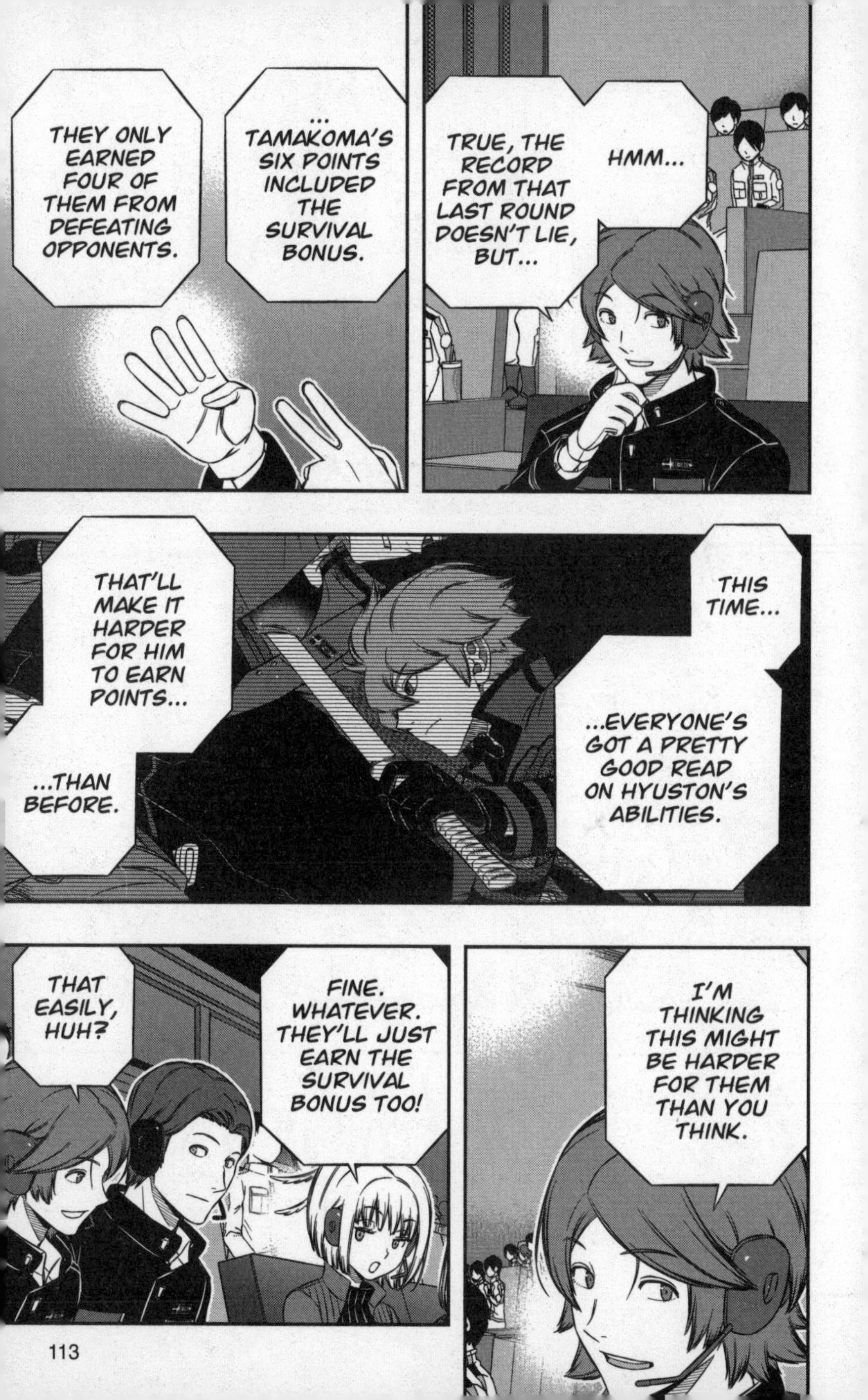
HMM...
TRUE, THE RECORD FROM THAT LAST ROUND DOESN'T LIE, BUT...
... TAMAKOMA'S SIX POINTS INCLUDED THE SURVIVAL BONUS.
THEY ONLY EARNED FOUR OF THEM FROM DEFEATING OPPONENTS.
THIS TIME...
...EVERYONE'S GOT A PRETTY GOOD READ ON HYUSTON'S ABILITIES.
THAT'LL MAKE IT HARDER FOR HIM TO EARN POINTS...
...THAN BEFORE.
I'M THINKING THIS MIGHT BE HARDER FOR THEM THAN YOU THINK.
FINE. WHATEVER. THEY'LL JUST EARN THE SURVIVAL BONUS TOO!
THAT EASILY, HUH?

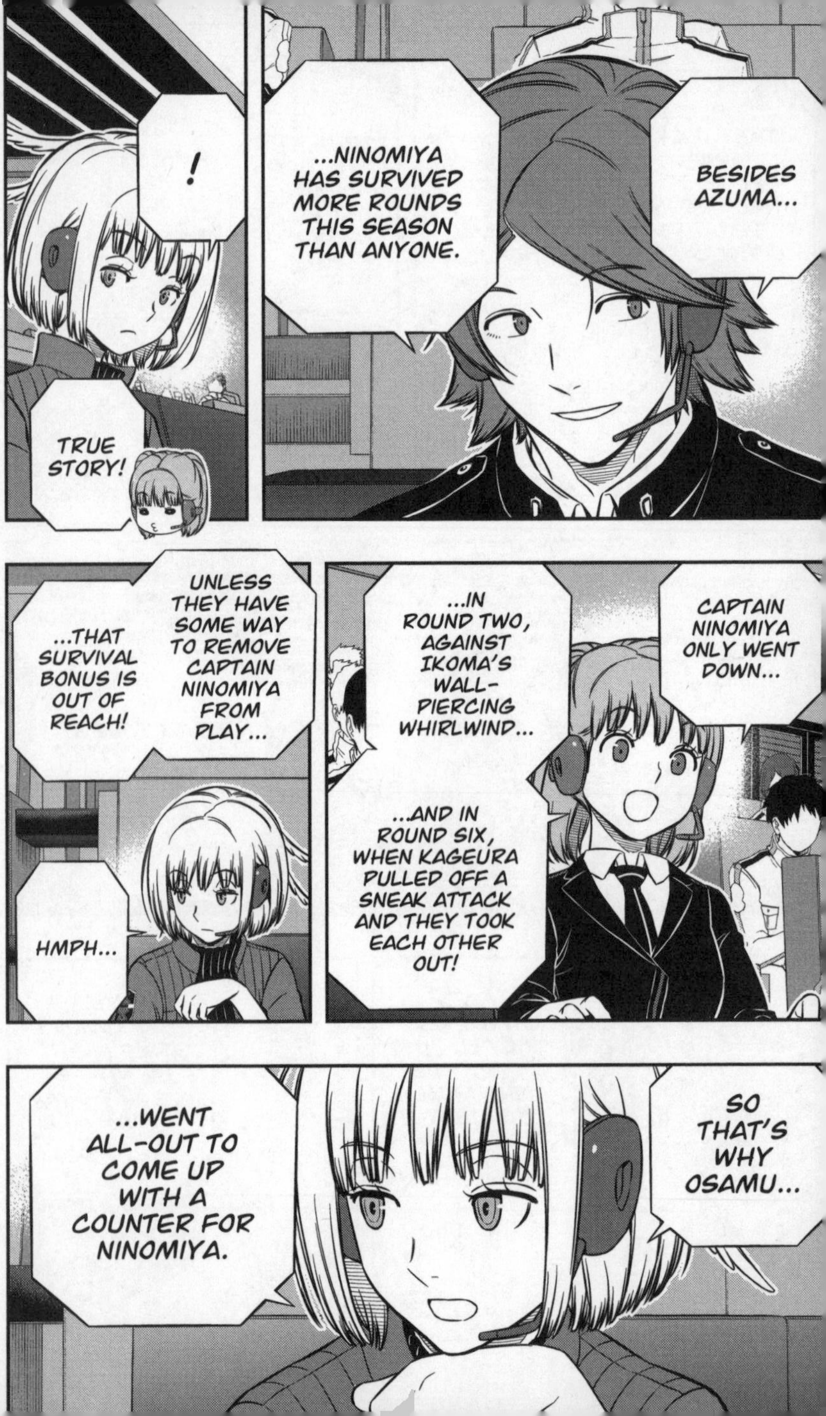
BESIDES AZUMA...
...NINOMIYA HAS SURVIVED MORE ROUNDS THIS SEASON THAN ANYONE.
!
TRUE STORY!
CAPTAIN NINOMIYA ONLY WENT DOWN...
...IN ROUND TWO, AGAINST IKOMA'S WALL-PIERCING WHIRLWIND...
...AND IN ROUND SIX, WHEN KAGEURA PULLED OFF A SNEAK ATTACK AND THEY TOOK EACH OTHER OUT!
UNLESS THEY HAVE SOME WAY TO REMOVE CAPTAIN NINOMIYA FROM PLAY...
...THAT SURVIVAL BONUS IS OUT OF REACH!
HMPH...
SO THAT'S WHY OSAMU...
...WENT ALL-OUT TO COME UP WITH A COUNTER FOR NINOMIYA.

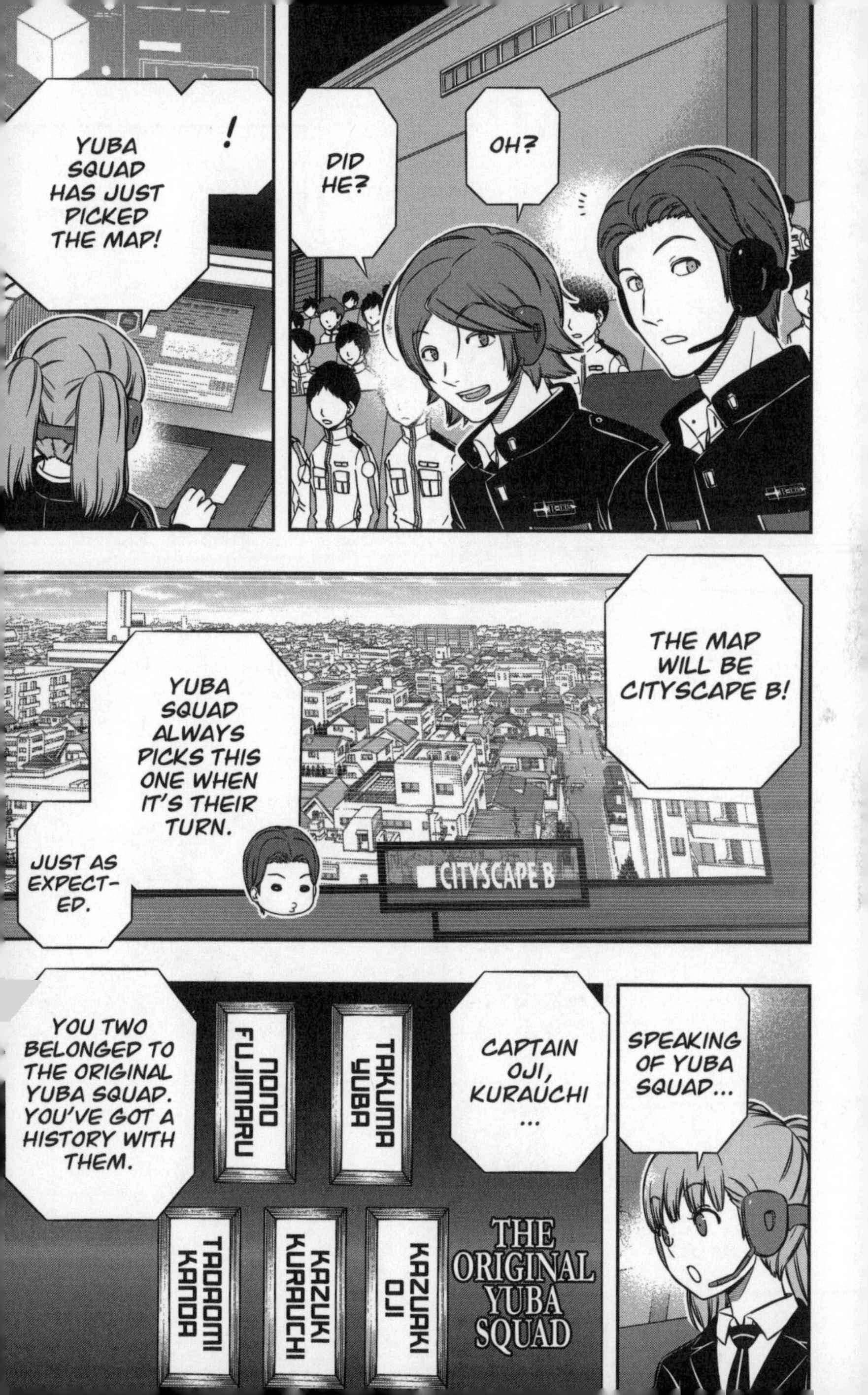
OH?
DID HE?
!
YUBA SQUAD HAS JUST PICKED THE MAP!
THE MAP WILL BE CITYSCAPE B!
CITYSCAPE B
YUBA SQUAD ALWAYS PICKS THIS ONE WHEN IT'S THEIR TURN.
JUST AS EXPECT-ED.
SPEAKING OF YUBA SQUAD...
CAPTAIN OJI, KURAUCHI ...
THE ORIGINAL YUBA SQUAD
TAKUMA YUBA
NONO FUJIMARU
KAZUAKI OJI
KAZUKI KURAUCHI
TADAOMI KANDA
YOU TWO BELONGED TO THE ORIGINAL YUBA SQUAD. YOU'VE GOT A HISTORY WITH THEM.

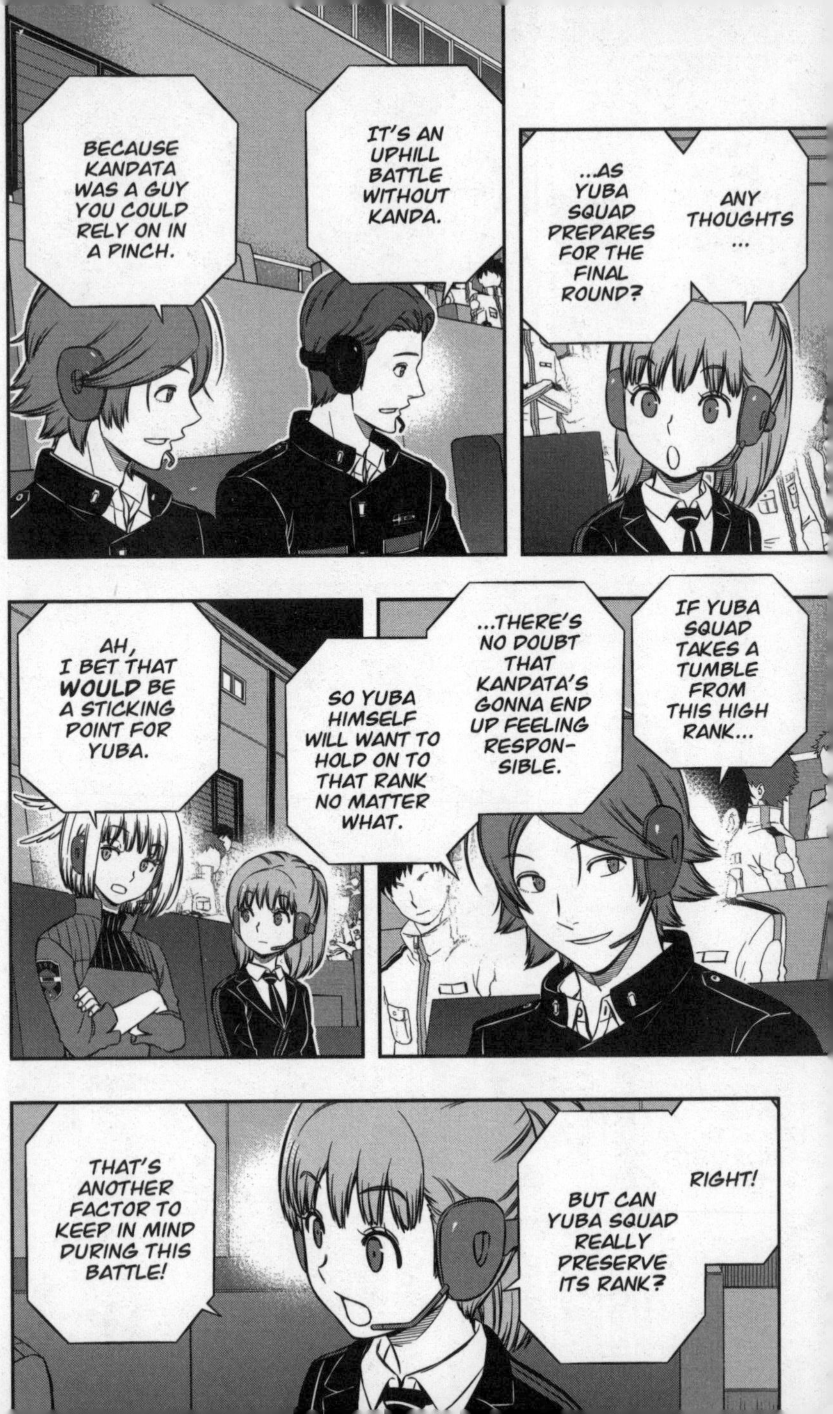
ANY THOUGHTS...
...AS YUBA SQUAD PREPARES FOR THE FINAL ROUND?
IT'S AN UPHILL BATTLE WITHOUT KANDA.
BECAUSE KANDATA WAS A GUY YOU COULD RELY ON IN A PINCH.
IF YUBA SQUAD TAKES A TUMBLE FROM THIS HIGH RANK...
...THERE'S NO DOUBT THAT KANDATA'S GONNA END UP FEELING RESPONSIBLE.
SO YUBA HIMSELF WILL WANT TO HOLD ON TO THAT RANK NO MATTER WHAT.
AH, I BET THAT **WOULD** BE A STICKING POINT FOR YUBA.
RIGHT!
BUT CAN YUBA SQUAD REALLY PRESERVE ITS RANK?
THAT'S ANOTHER FACTOR TO KEEP IN MIND DURING THIS BATTLE!

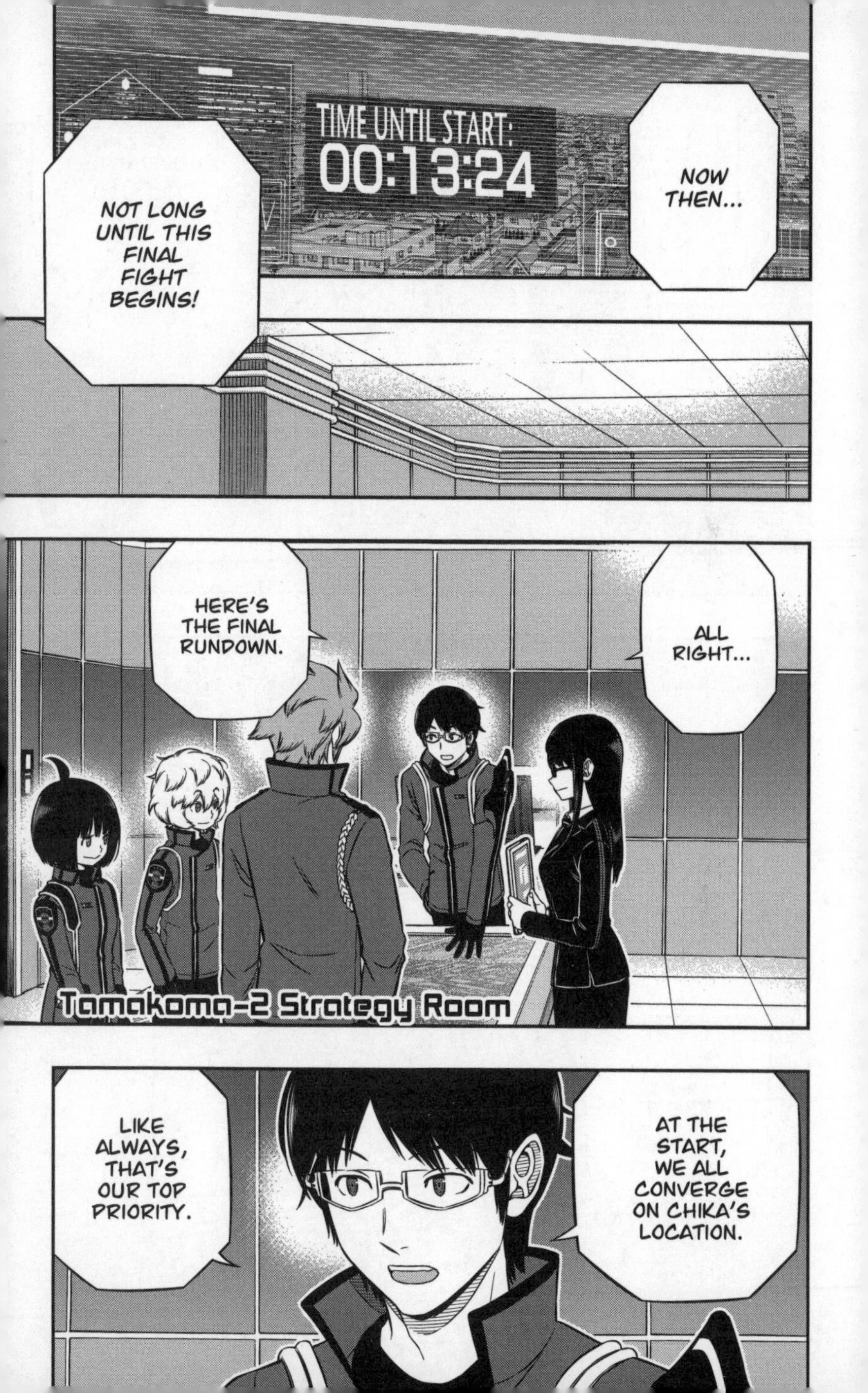
NOW THEN...
TIME UNTIL START:
00:13:24
NOT LONG UNTIL THIS FINAL FIGHT BEGINS!
ALL RIGHT...
HERE'S THE FINAL RUNDOWN.
Tamakoma-2 Strategy Room
AT THE START, WE ALL CONVERGE ON CHIKA'S LOCATION.
LIKE ALWAYS, THAT'S OUR TOP PRIORITY.

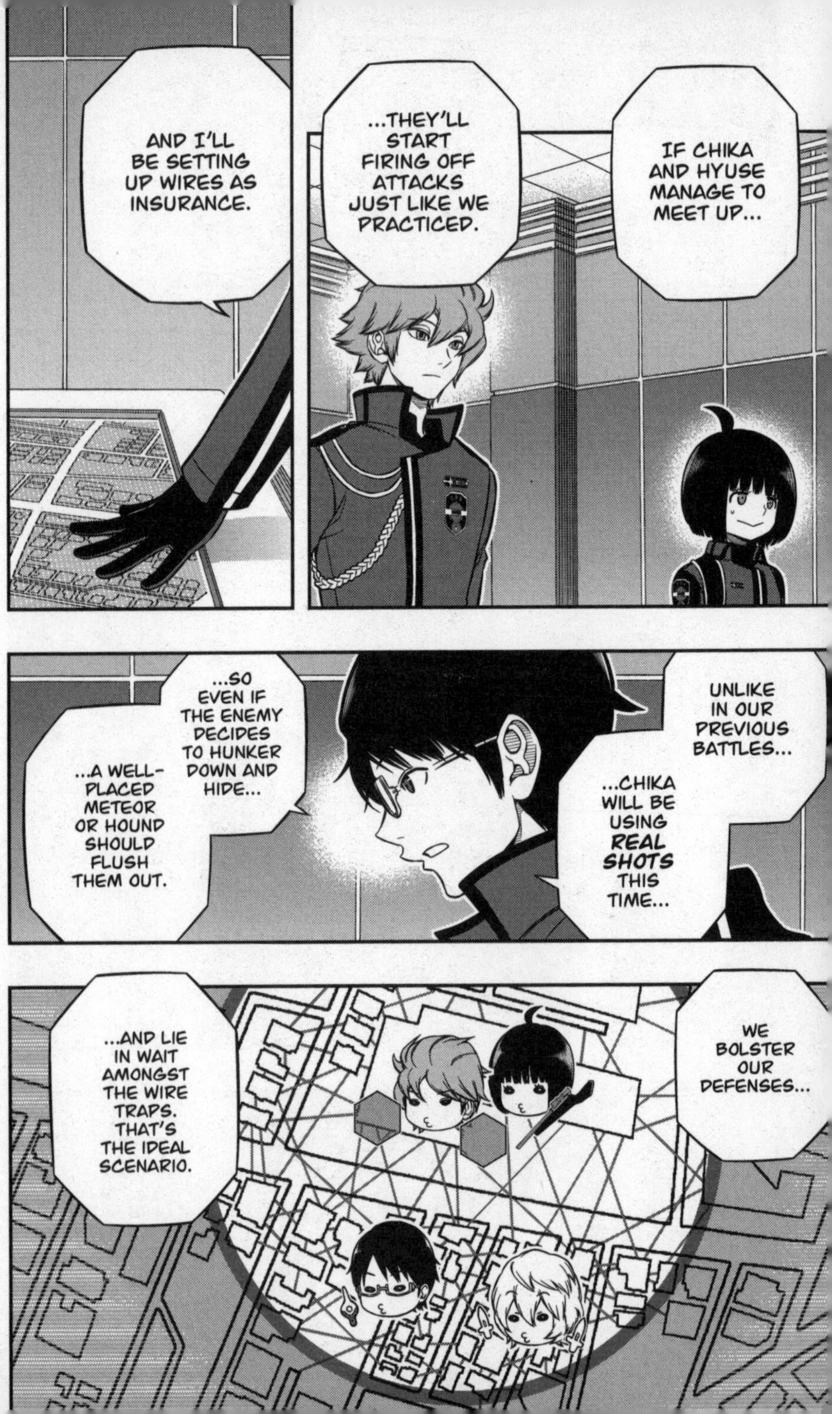
IF CHIKA AND HYUSE MANAGE TO MEET UP...
...THEY'LL START FIRING OFF ATTACKS JUST LIKE WE PRACTICED.
AND I'LL BE SETTING UP WIRES AS INSURANCE.
UNLIKE IN OUR PREVIOUS BATTLES...
...CHIKA WILL BE USING **REAL SHOTS** THIS TIME...
...SO EVEN IF THE ENEMY DECIDES TO HUNKER DOWN AND HIDE...
...A WELL-PLACED METEOR OR HOUND SHOULD FLUSH THEM OUT.
WE BOLSTER OUR DEFENSES...
...AND LIE IN WAIT AMONGST THE WIRE TRAPS. THAT'S THE IDEAL SCENARIO.

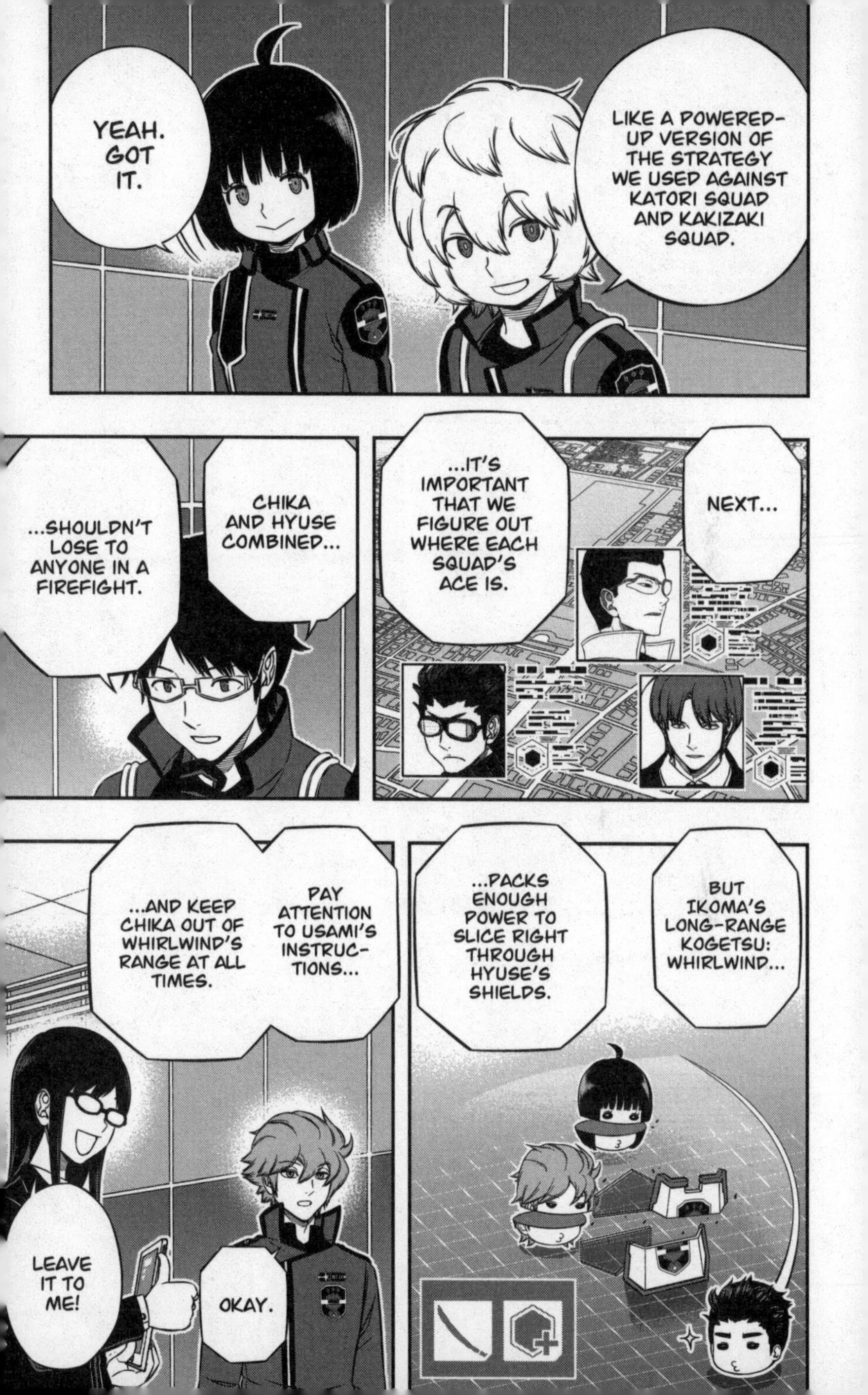
LIKE A POWERED-UP VERSION OF THE STRATEGY WE USED AGAINST KATORI SQUAD AND KAKIZAKI SQUAD.
YEAH. GOT IT.
NEXT...
...IT'S IMPORTANT THAT WE FIGURE OUT WHERE EACH SQUAD'S ACE IS.
CHIKA AND HYUSE COMBINED...
...SHOULDN'T LOSE TO ANYONE IN A FIREFIGHT.
BUT IKOMA'S LONG-RANGE KOGETSU: WHIRLWIND...
...PACKS ENOUGH POWER TO SLICE RIGHT THROUGH HYUSE'S SHIELDS.
PAY ATTENTION TO USAMI'S INSTRUCTIONS...
...AND KEEP CHIKA OUT OF WHIRLWIND'S RANGE AT ALL TIMES.
OKAY.
LEAVE IT TO ME!

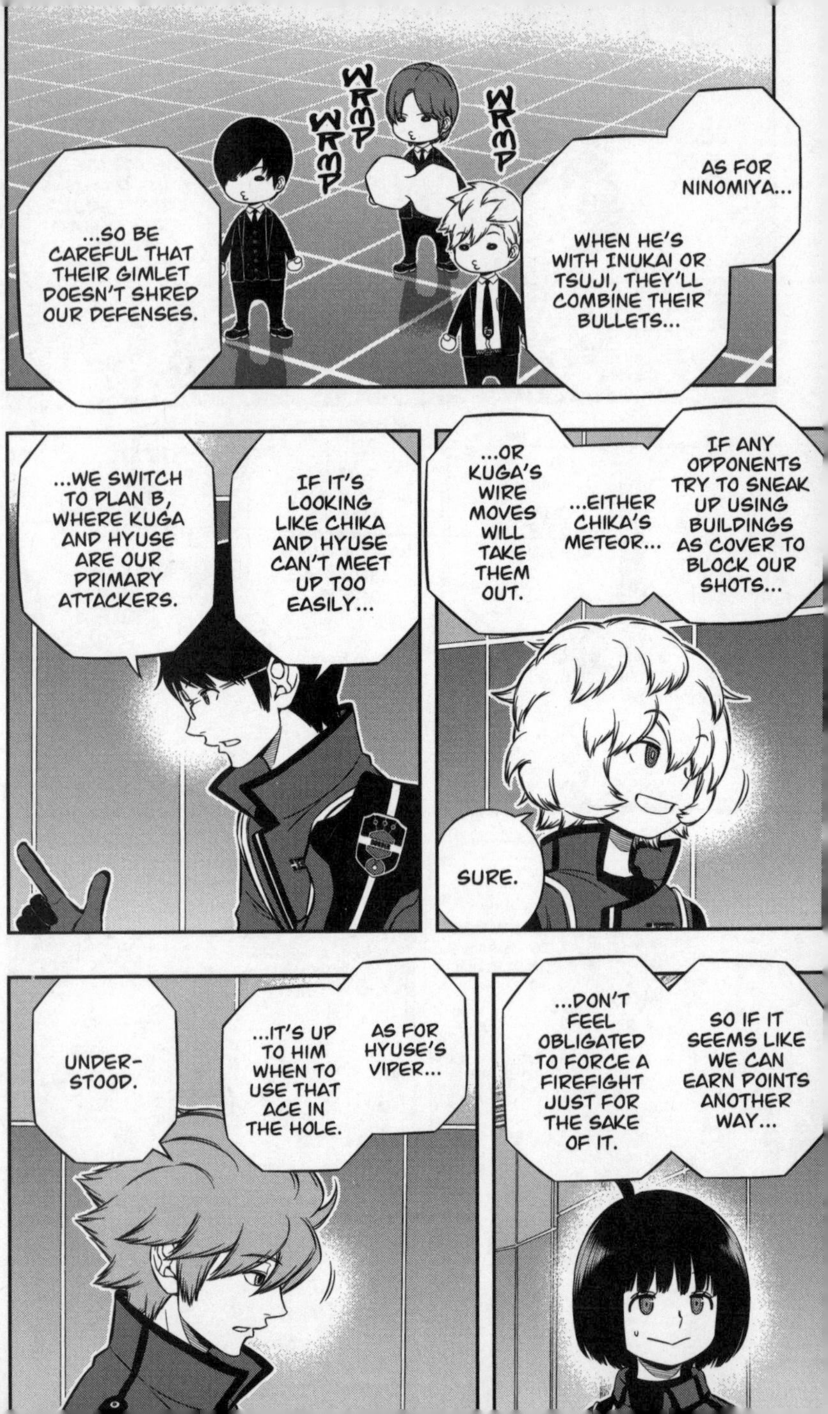
AS FOR NINOMIYA...
WHEN HE'S WITH INUKAI OR TSUJI, THEY'LL COMBINE THEIR BULLETS...
WRMP
WRMP
WRMP
...SO BE CAREFUL THAT THEIR GIMLET DOESN'T SHRED OUR DEFENSES.
IF ANY OPPONENTS TRY TO SNEAK UP USING BUILDINGS AS COVER TO BLOCK OUR SHOTS...
...EITHER CHIKA'S METEOR...
...OR KUGA'S WIRE MOVES WILL TAKE THEM OUT.
SURE.
IF IT'S LOOKING LIKE CHIKA AND HYUSE CAN'T MEET UP TOO EASILY...
...WE SWITCH TO PLAN B, WHERE KUGA AND HYUSE ARE OUR PRIMARY ATTACKERS.
SO IF IT SEEMS LIKE WE CAN EARN POINTS ANOTHER WAY...
...DON'T FEEL OBLIGATED TO FORCE A FIREFIGHT JUST FOR THE SAKE OF IT.
AS FOR HYUSE'S VIPER...
...IT'S UP TO HIM WHEN TO USE THAT ACE IN THE HOLE.
UNDER-STOOD.

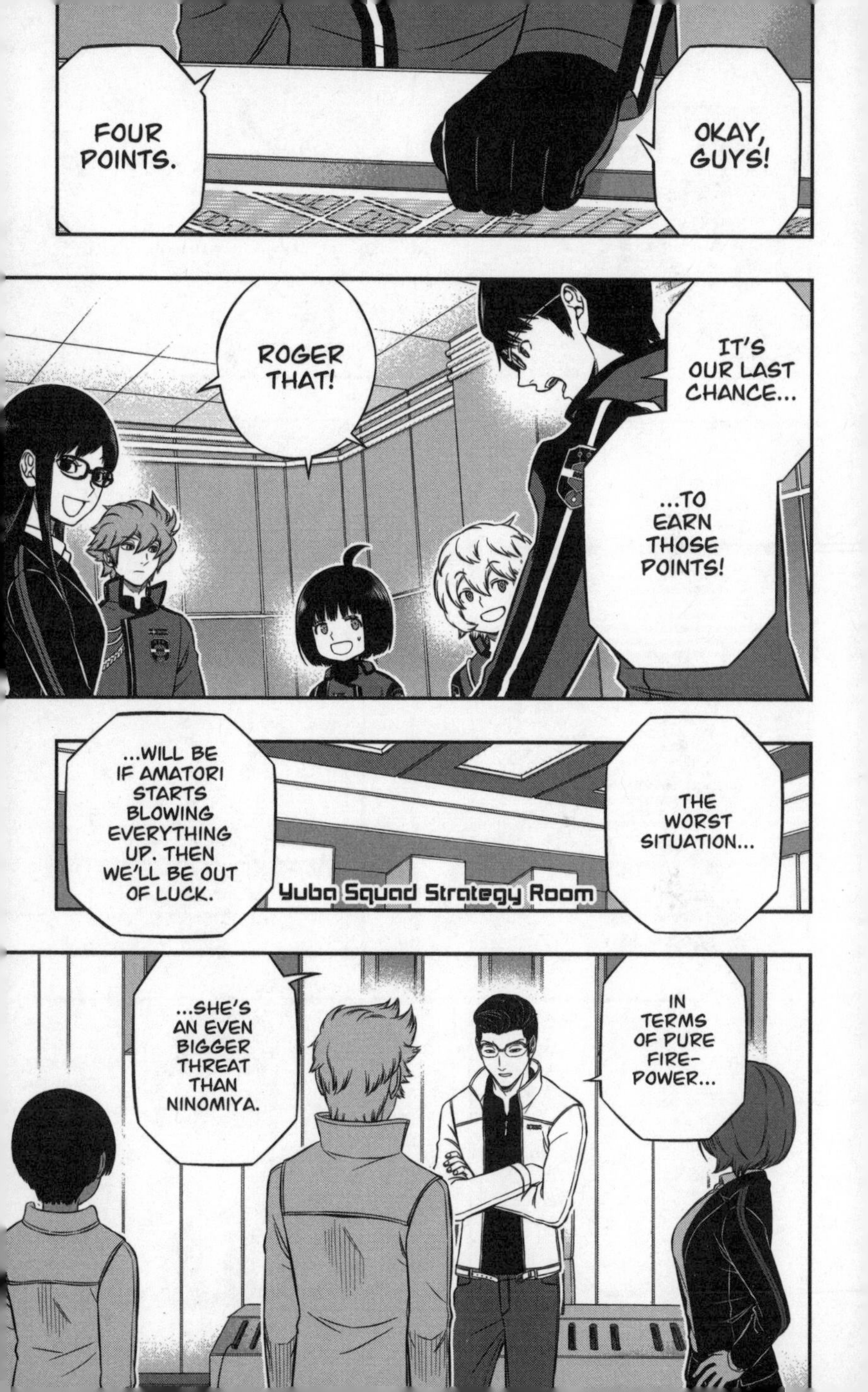
OKAY, GUYS!
FOUR POINTS.
IT'S OUR LAST CHANCE...
...TO EARN THOSE POINTS!
ROGER THAT!
Yuba Squad Strategy Room
THE WORST SITUATION...
...WILL BE IF AMATORI STARTS BLOWING EVERYTHING UP. THEN WE'LL BE OUT OF LUCK.
IN TERMS OF PURE FIRE-POWER...
...SHE'S AN EVEN BIGGER THREAT THAN NINOMIYA.

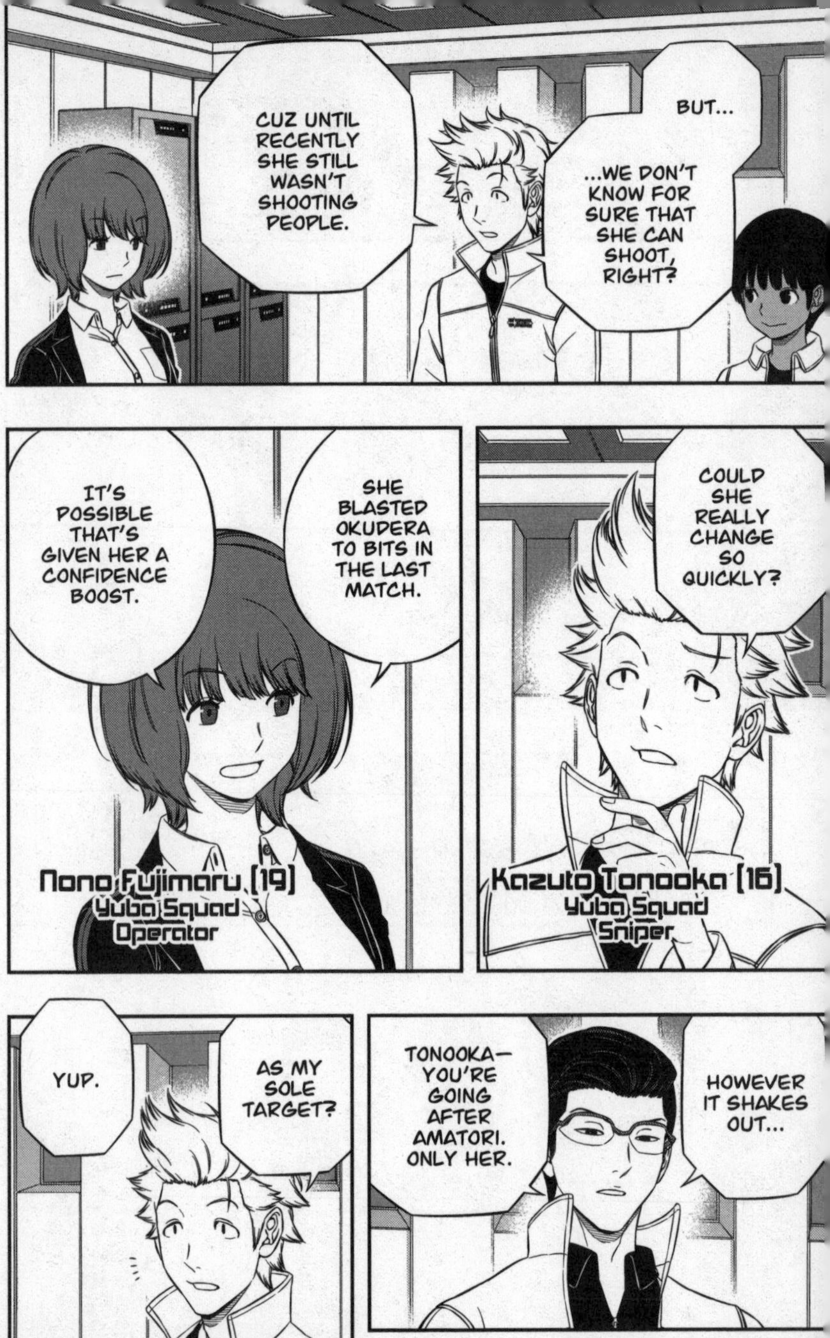
BUT...
...WE DON'T KNOW FOR SURE THAT SHE CAN SHOOT, RIGHT?
CUZ UNTIL RECENTLY SHE STILL WASN'T SHOOTING PEOPLE.
COULD SHE REALLY CHANGE SO QUICKLY?
Kazuto Tonooka [16]
Yuba Squad
Sniper
SHE BLASTED OKUDERA TO BITS IN THE LAST MATCH.
IT'S POSSIBLE THAT'S GIVEN HER A CONFIDENCE BOOST.
Nono Fujimaru [19]
Yuba Squad
Operator
HOWEVER IT SHAKES OUT...
TONOOKA— YOU'RE GOING AFTER AMATORI. ONLY HER.
AS MY SOLE TARGET?
YUP.

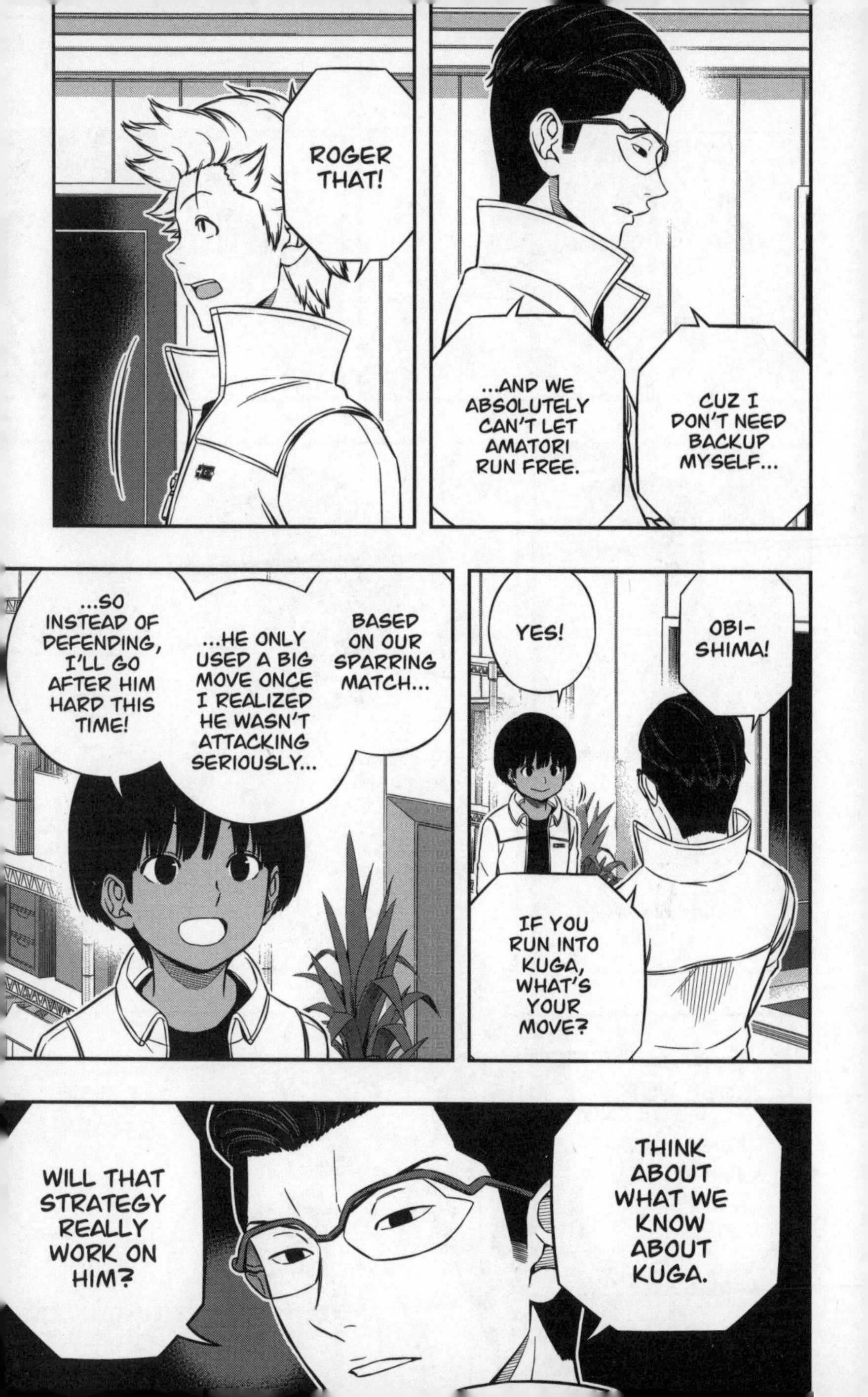
CUZ I DON'T NEED BACKUP MYSELF...
...AND WE ABSOLUTELY CAN'T LET AMATORI RUN FREE.
ROGER THAT!
OBI-SHIMA!
YES!
IF YOU RUN INTO KUGA, WHAT'S YOUR MOVE?
BASED ON OUR SPARRING MATCH...
...HE ONLY USED A BIG MOVE ONCE I REALIZED HE WASN'T ATTACKING SERIOUSLY...
...SO INSTEAD OF DEFENDING, I'LL GO AFTER HIM HARD THIS TIME!
THINK ABOUT WHAT WE KNOW ABOUT KUGA.
WILL THAT STRATEGY REALLY WORK ON HIM?

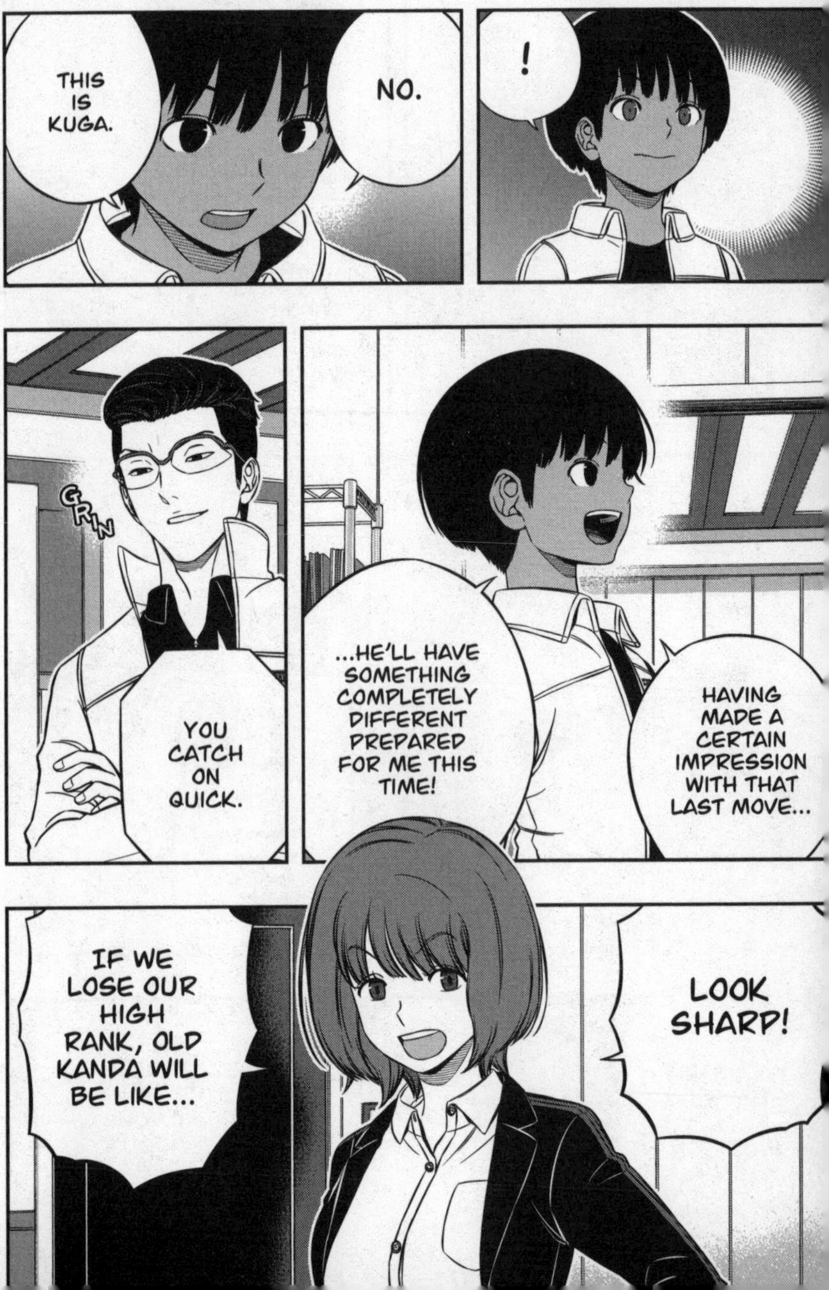
!
NO.
THIS IS KUGA.
HAVING MADE A CERTAIN IMPRESSION WITH THAT LAST MOVE...
...HE'LL HAVE SOMETHING COMPLETELY DIFFERENT PREPARED FOR ME THIS TIME!
GRIN
YOU CATCH ON QUICK.
LOOK SHARP!
IF WE LOSE OUR HIGH RANK, OLD KANDA WILL BE LIKE...

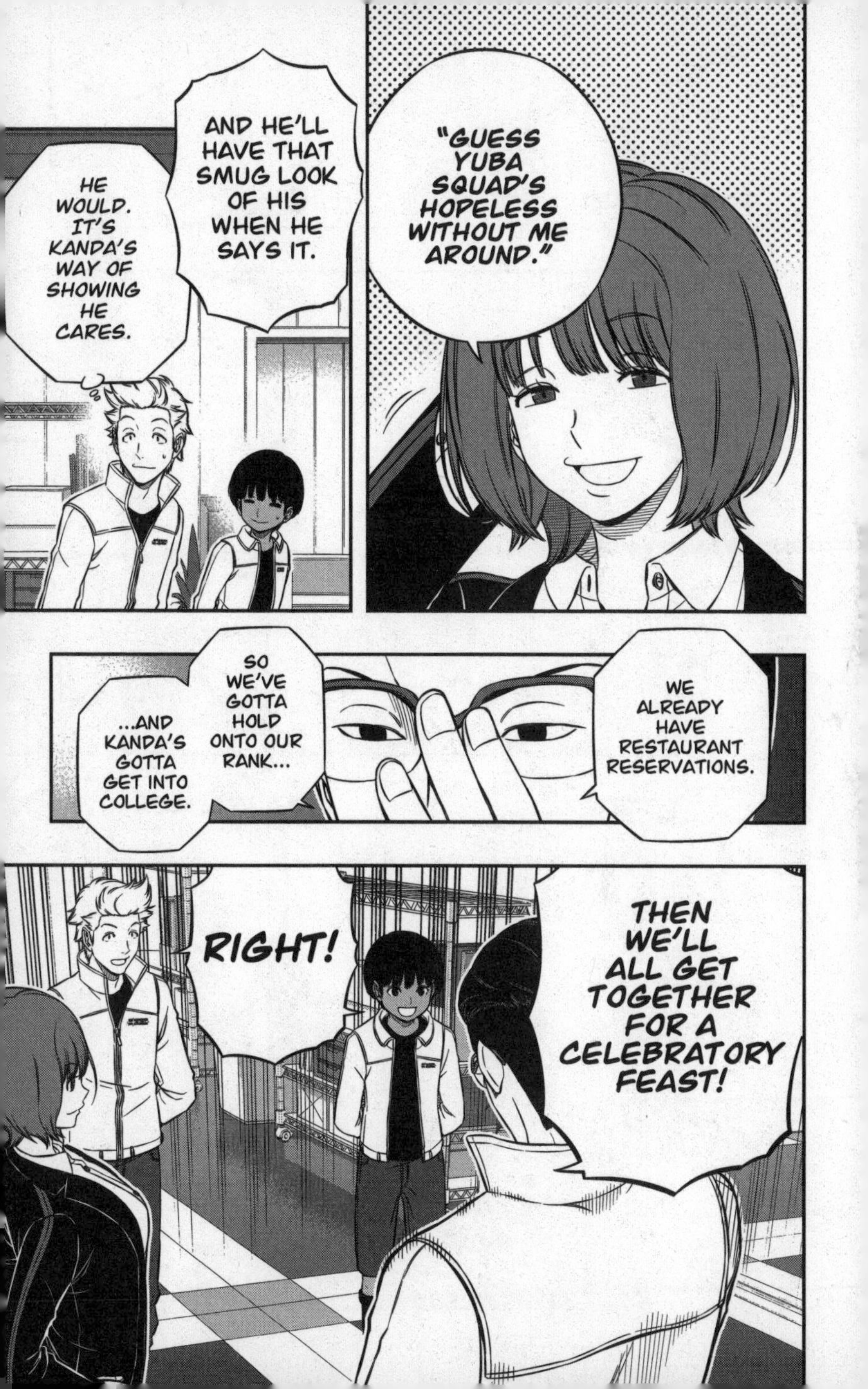
"GUESS YUBA SQUAD'S HOPELESS WITHOUT ME AROUND."
AND HE'LL HAVE THAT SMUG LOOK OF HIS WHEN HE SAYS IT.
HE WOULD. IT'S KANDA'S WAY OF SHOWING HE CARES.
WE ALREADY HAVE RESTAURANT RESERVATIONS.
SO WE'VE GOTTA HOLD ONTO OUR RANK...
...AND KANDA'S GOTTA GET INTO COLLEGE.
THEN WE'LL ALL GET TOGETHER FOR A CELEBRATORY FEAST!
RIGHT!

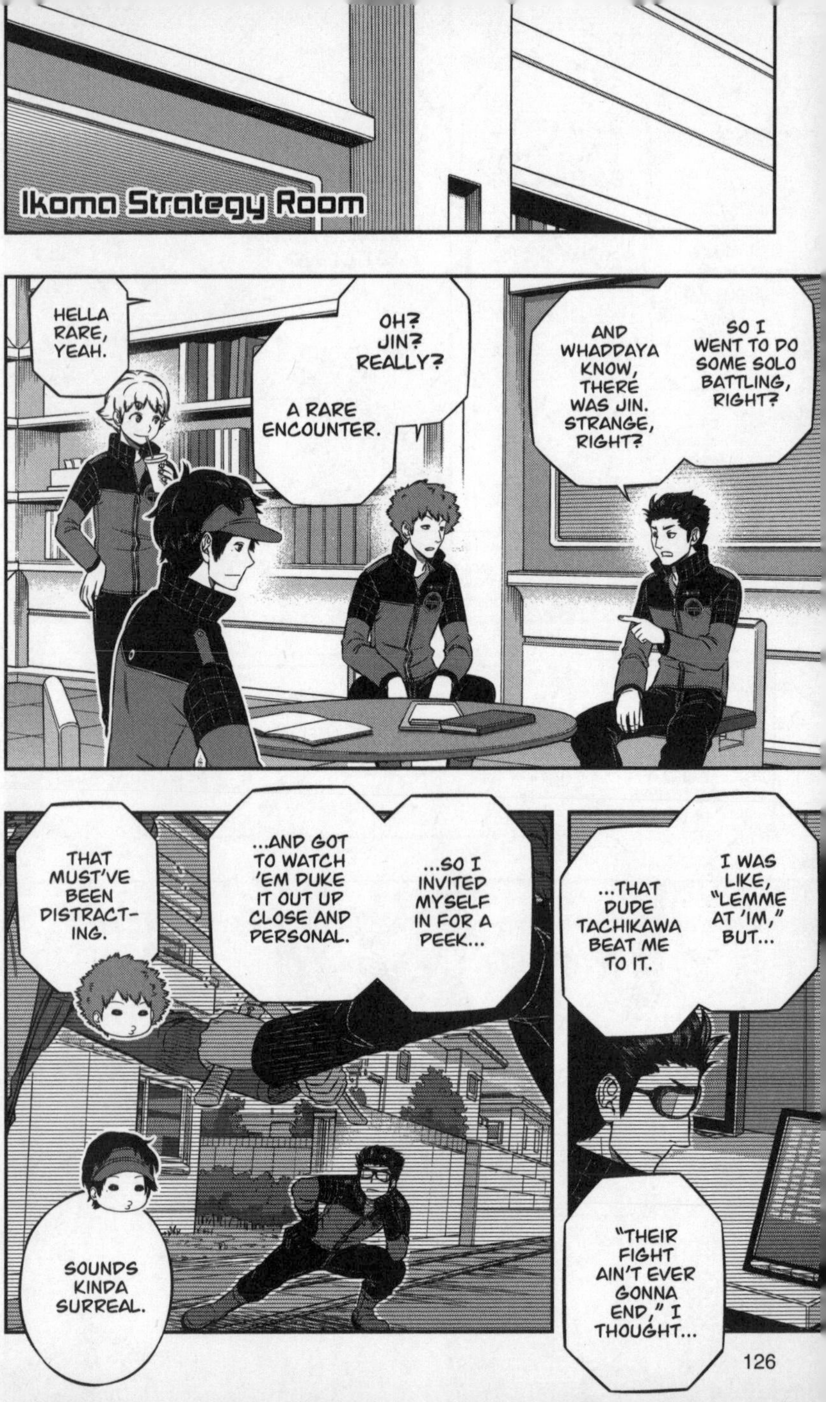
Ikoma Strategy Room
SO I WENT TO DO SOME SOLO BATTLING, RIGHT?
AND WHADDAYA KNOW, THERE WAS JIN. STRANGE, RIGHT?
OH? JIN? REALLY?
A RARE ENCOUNTER.
HELLA RARE, YEAH.
I WAS LIKE, "LEMME AT 'IM," BUT...
...THAT DUDE TACHIKAWA BEAT ME TO IT.
"THEIR FIGHT AIN'T EVER GONNA END," I THOUGHT...
...SO I INVITED MYSELF IN FOR A PEEK...
...AND GOT TO WATCH 'EM DUKE IT OUT UP CLOSE AND PERSONAL.
THAT MUST'VE BEEN DISTRACTING.
SOUNDS KINDA SURREAL.

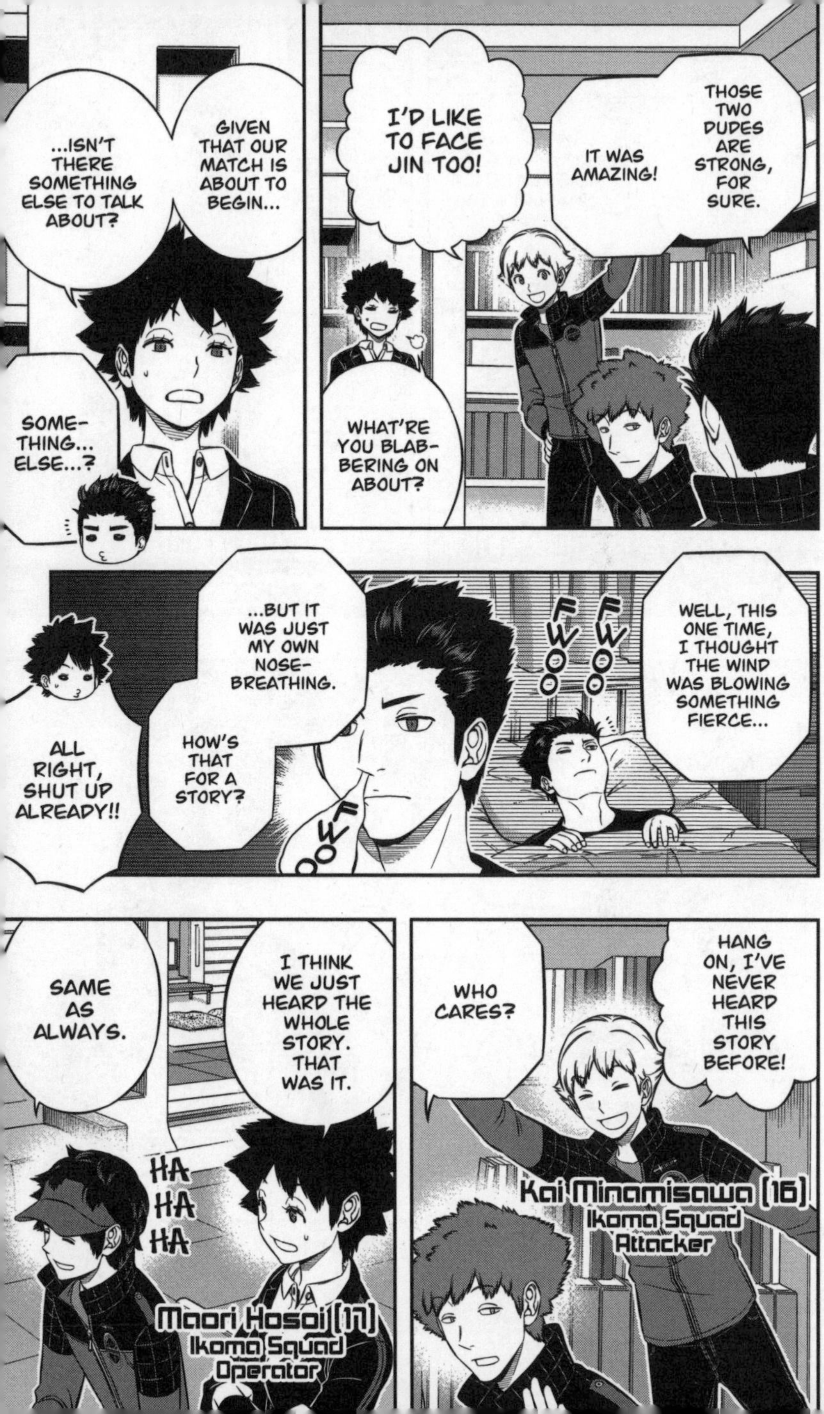
THOSE TWO DUDES ARE STRONG, FOR SURE.
IT WAS AMAZING!
I'D LIKE TO FACE JIN TOO!
WHAT'RE YOU BLABBERING ON ABOUT?
GIVEN THAT OUR MATCH IS ABOUT TO BEGIN...
...ISN'T THERE SOMETHING ELSE TO TALK ABOUT?
SOME-THING... ELSE...?
WELL, THIS ONE TIME, I THOUGHT THE WIND WAS BLOWING SOMETHING FIERCE...
FWOO
FWOO
...BUT IT WAS JUST MY OWN NOSE-BREATHING.
FWOO
HOW'S THAT FOR A STORY?
ALL RIGHT, SHUT UP ALREADY!!
HANG ON, I'VE NEVER HEARD THIS STORY BEFORE!
WHO CARES?
Kai Minamisawa (16)
Ikoma Squad
Attacker
I THINK WE JUST HEARD THE WHOLE STORY. THAT WAS IT.
SAME AS ALWAYS.
HA HA HA
Maori Hosoi (17)
Ikoma Squad
Operator

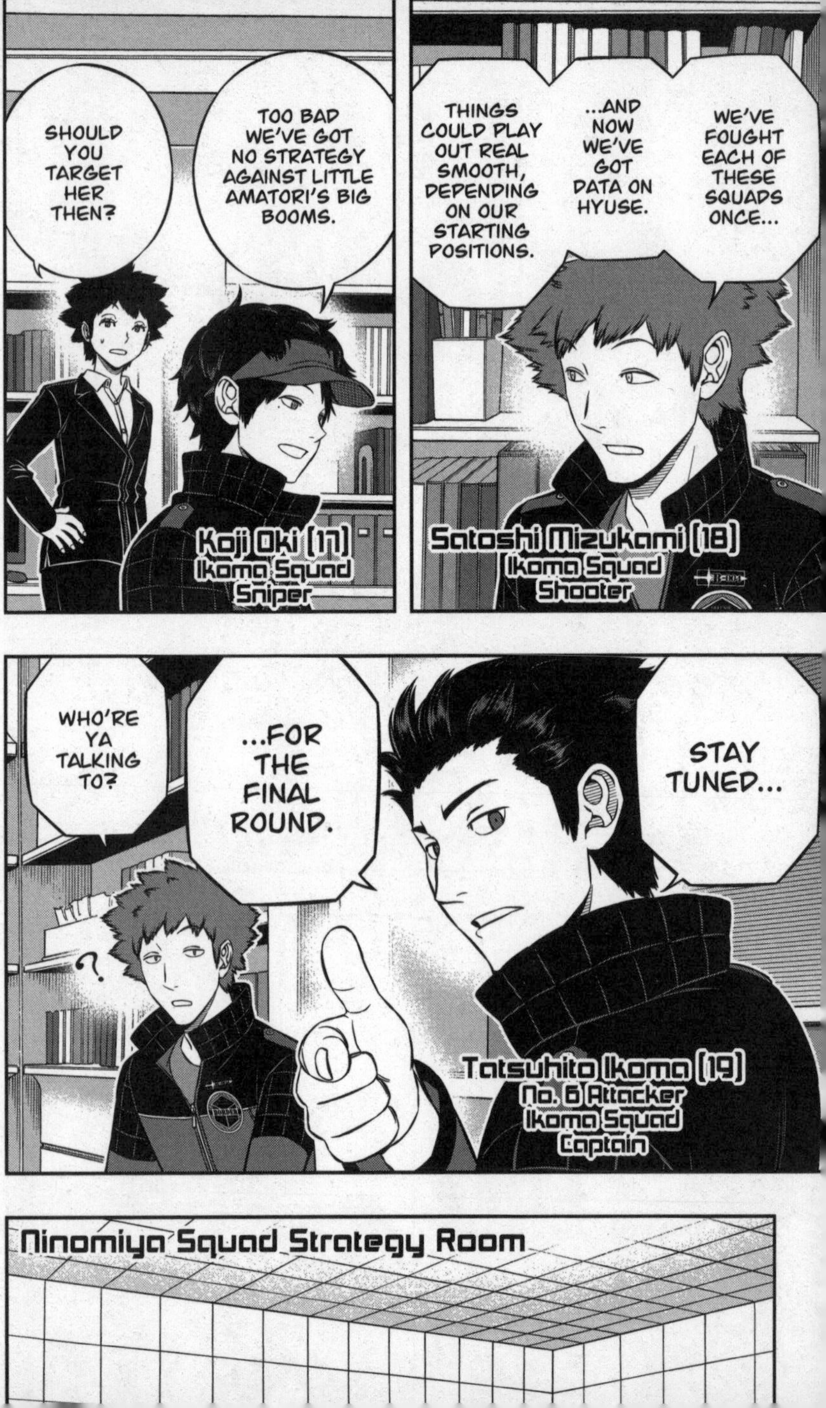
WE'VE FOUGHT EACH OF THESE SQUADS ONCE...
...AND NOW WE'VE GOT DATA ON HYUSE.
THINGS COULD PLAY OUT REAL SMOOTH, DEPENDING ON OUR STARTING POSITIONS.
Satoshi Mizukami (18) Ikoma Squad Shooter
TOO BAD WE'VE GOT NO STRATEGY AGAINST LITTLE AMATORI'S BIG BOOMS.
SHOULD YOU TARGET HER THEN?
Koji Oki (17) Ikoma Squad Sniper
STAY TUNED...
...FOR THE FINAL ROUND.
Tatsuhito Ikoma (19) No. 6 Attacker Ikoma Squad Captain
WHO'RE YA TALKING TO?
?
Ninomiya Squad Strategy Room

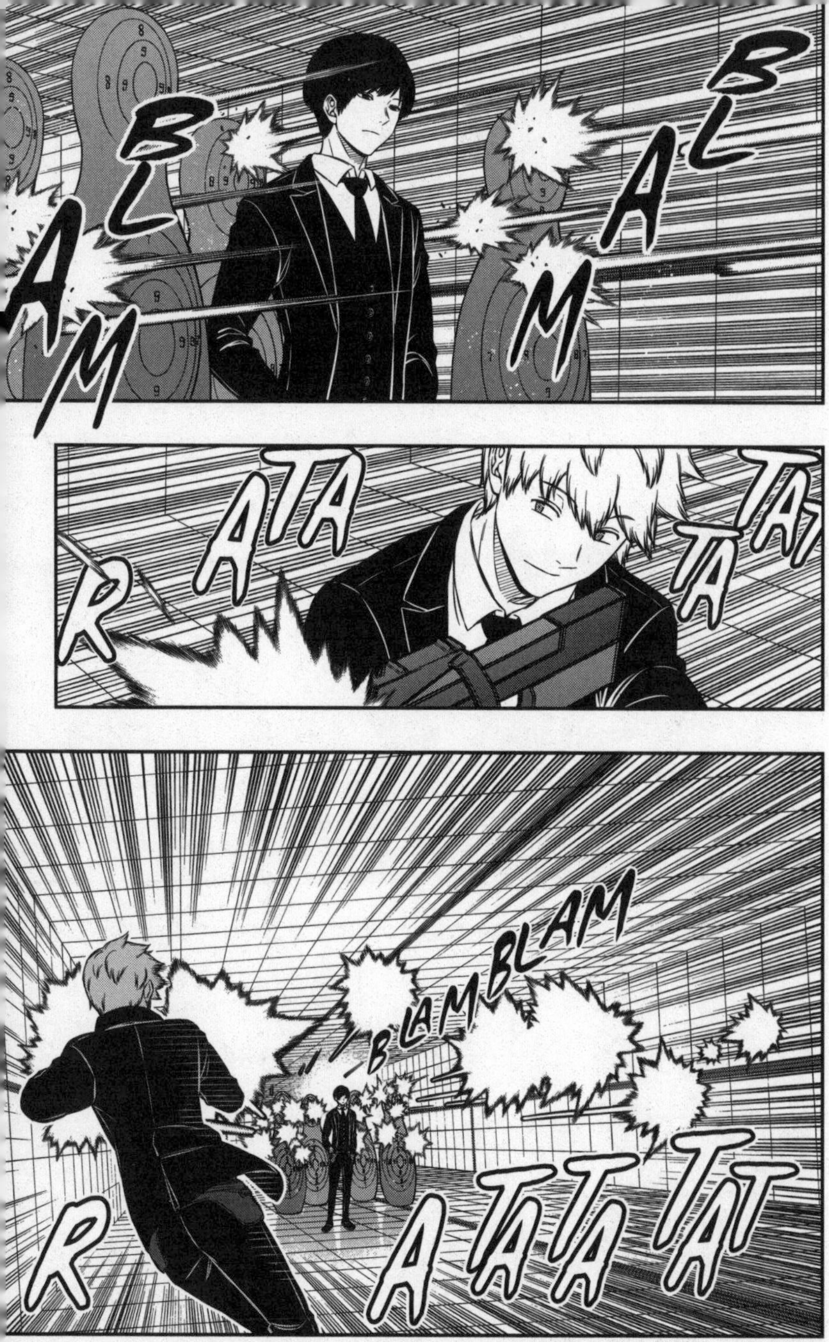
BLAM
BLAM
RATATA
BLAM BLAM
RATATATATAT

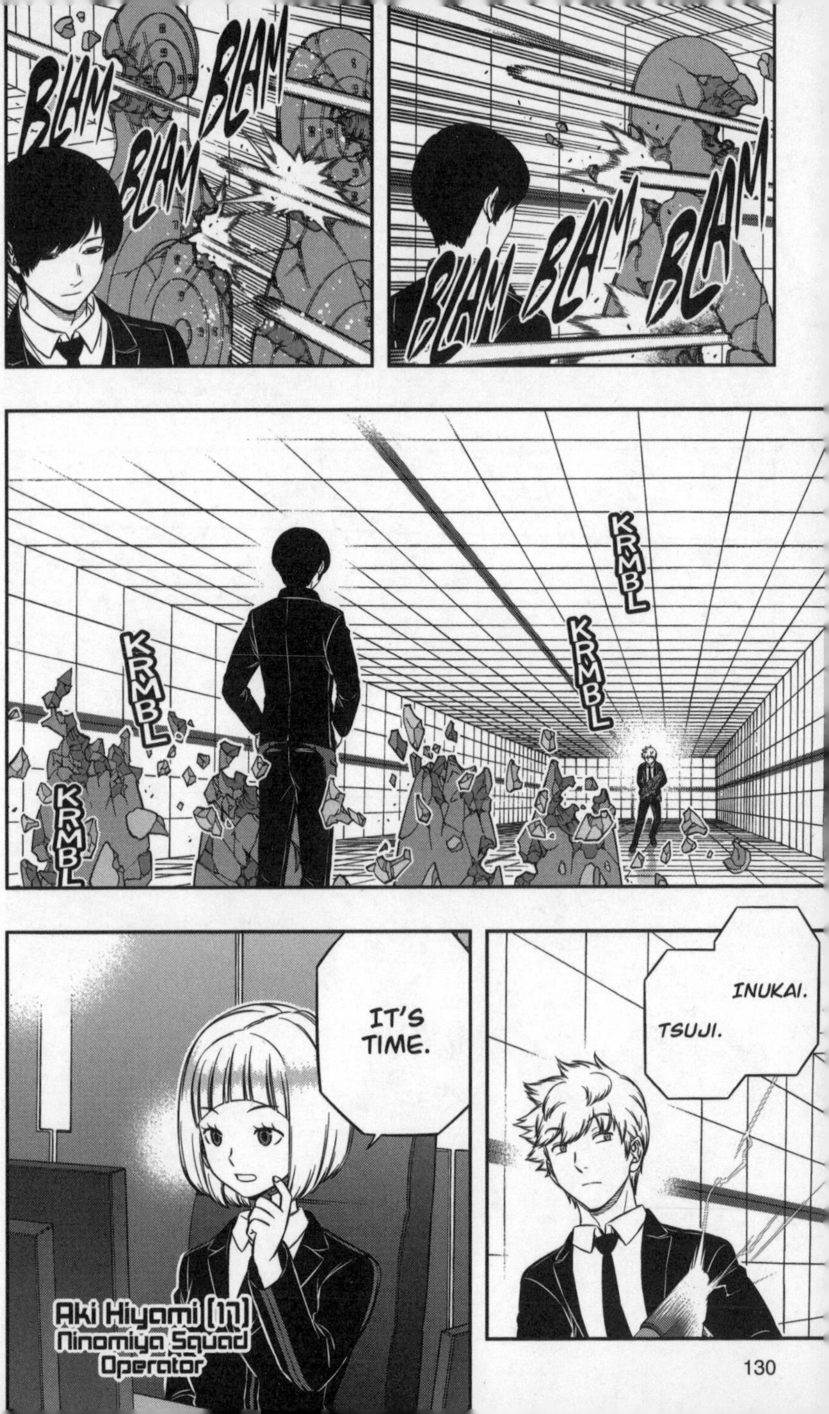
BLAM
BLAM
BLAM
BLAM
BLAM
BLAM
KRMBL
KRMBL
KRMBL
KRMBL
INUKAI.
TSUJI.
IT'S TIME.
Aki Hiyami (17)
Ninomiya Squad
Operator

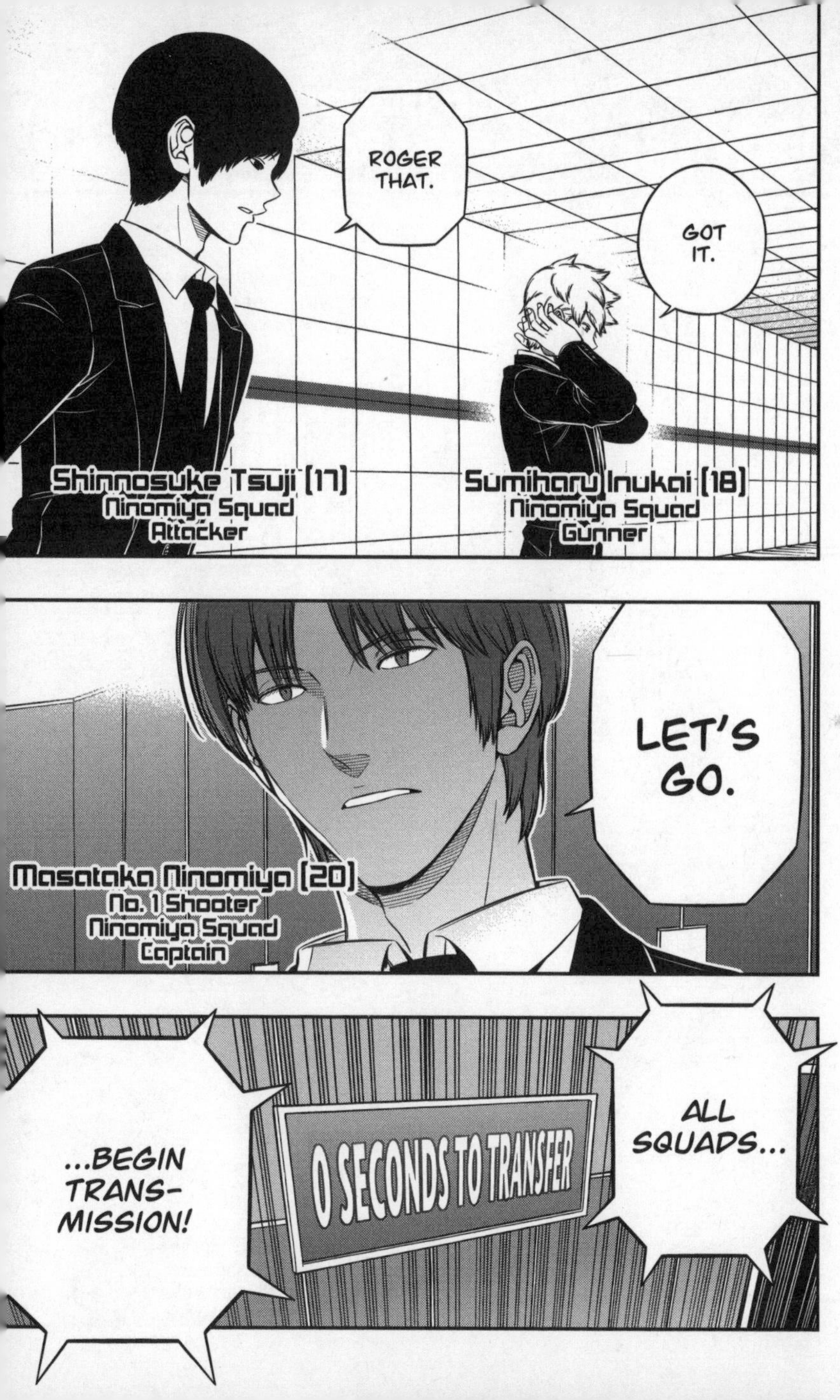
GOT IT.
ROGER THAT.
Sumiharu Inukai (18)
Ninomiya Squad
Gunner
Shinnosuke Tsuji (17)
Ninomiya Squad
Attacker
LET'S GO.
Masataka Ninomiya (20)
No. 1 Shooter
Ninomiya Squad
Captain
ALL SQUADS...
0 SECONDS TO TRANSFER
...BEGIN TRANS-MISSION!

[redacted]
Strategy Room

Yuba put away the chair and bail-out mat that Kanda used to use. They'll need more of those if they get new members.

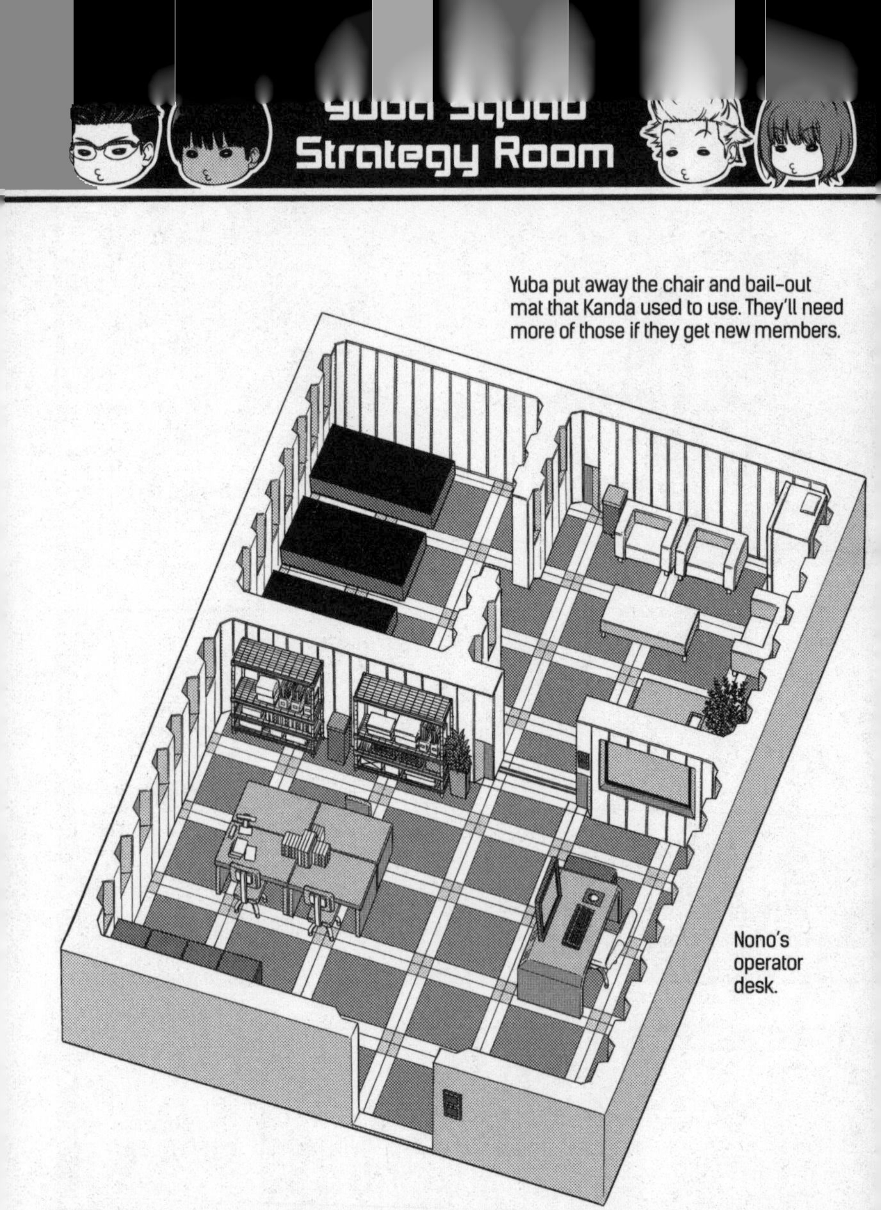

Nono's operator desk.

Not only does the Yuba Squad room lack personal effects—Yuba himself doesn't even have a chair. For some reason, he prefers to stand. Bizarre. Perhaps that's why squad meetings tend to be short. The other three are plotting to order a chair for Yuba, but he's stubbornly vowed to stay standing until they make it to A-rank. Bizarre.

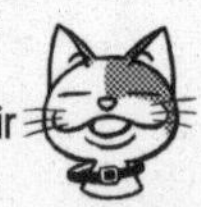

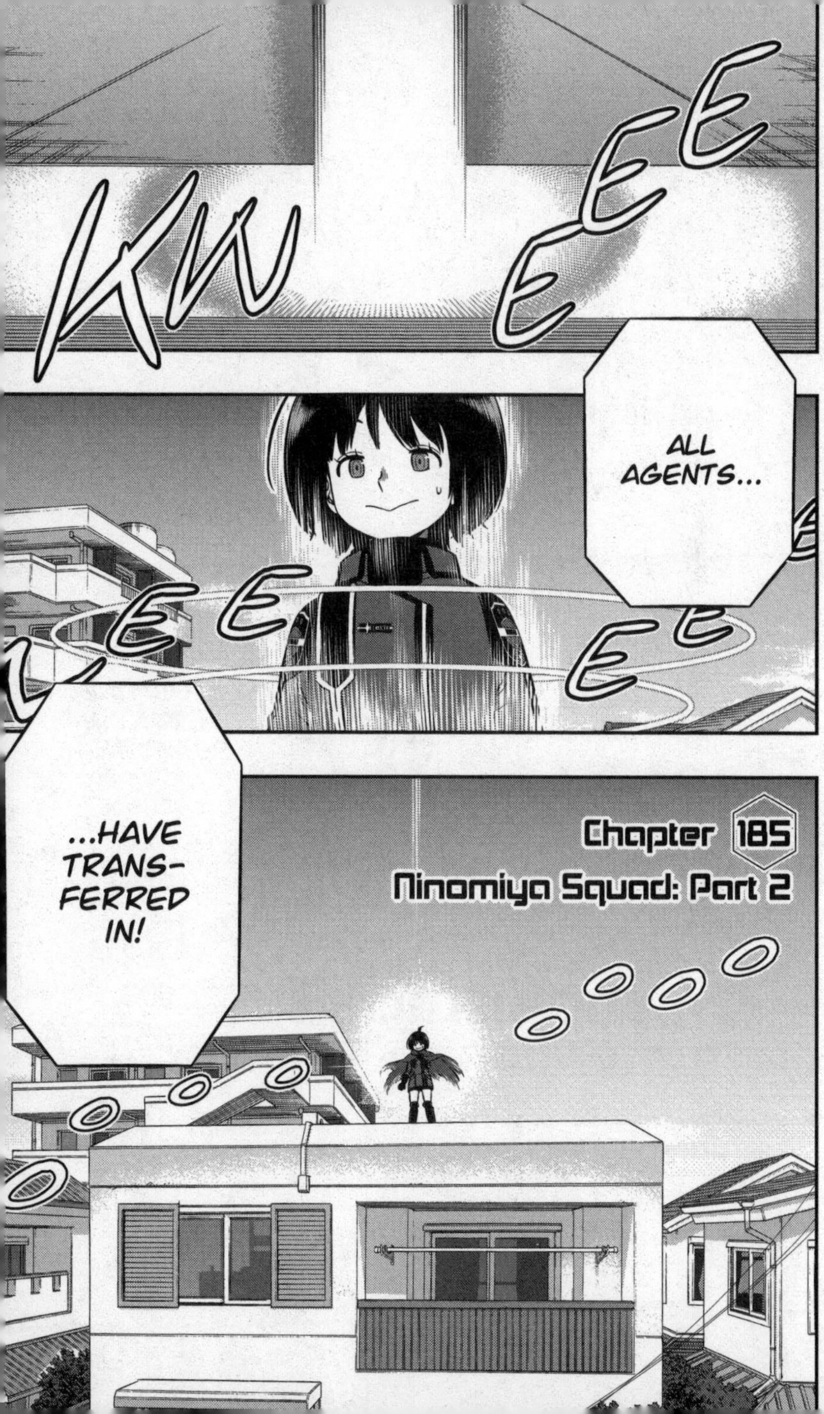
KWEEEE
ALL AGENTS...
EEEEE
...HAVE TRANS-FERRED IN!
Chapter 185
Ninomiya Squad: Part 2
OOOOOOOOO

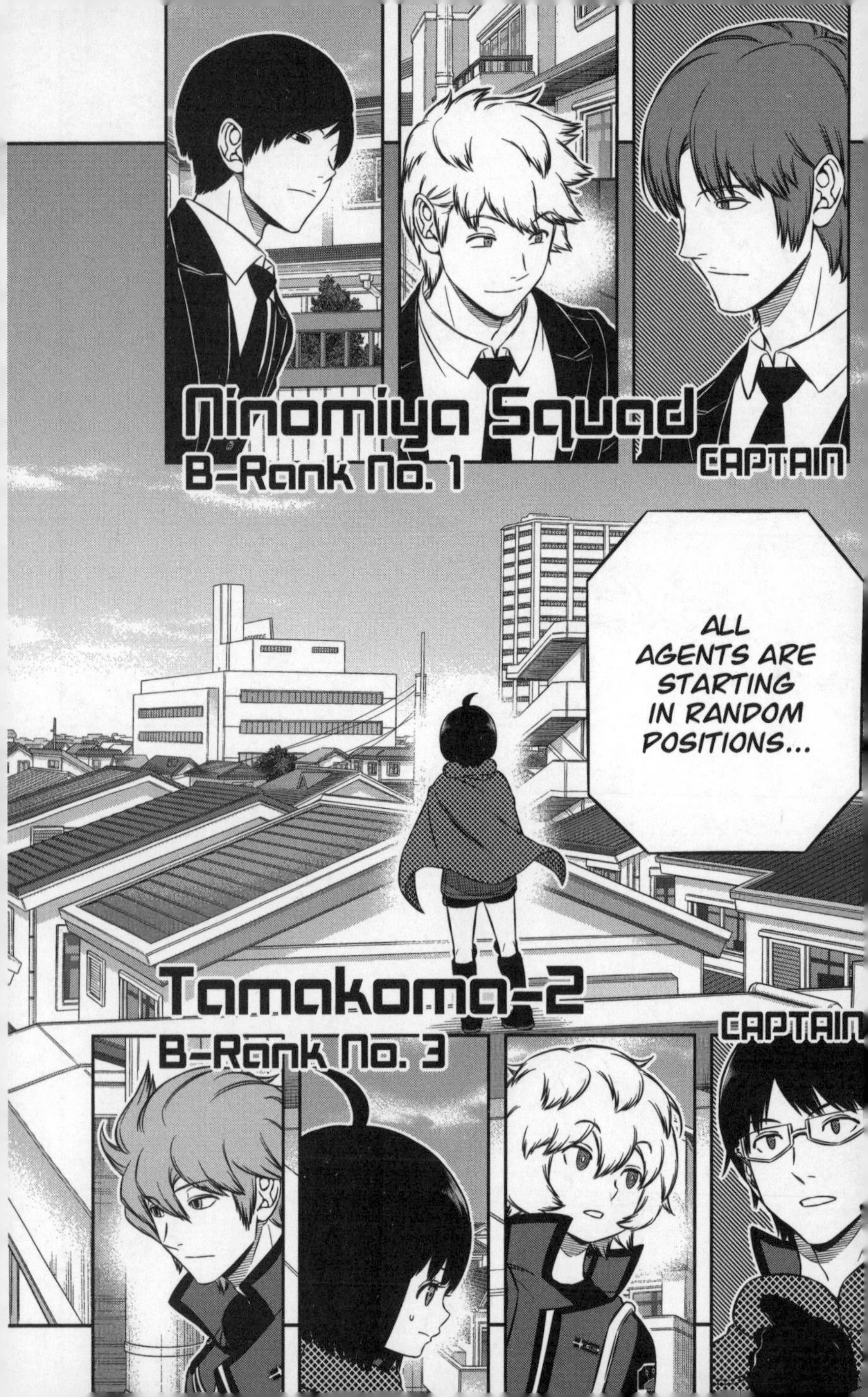
Ninomiya Squad
B-Rank No. 1
CAPTAIN
ALL AGENTS ARE STARTING IN RANDOM POSITIONS...
Tamakoma-2
B-Rank No. 3
CAPTAIN

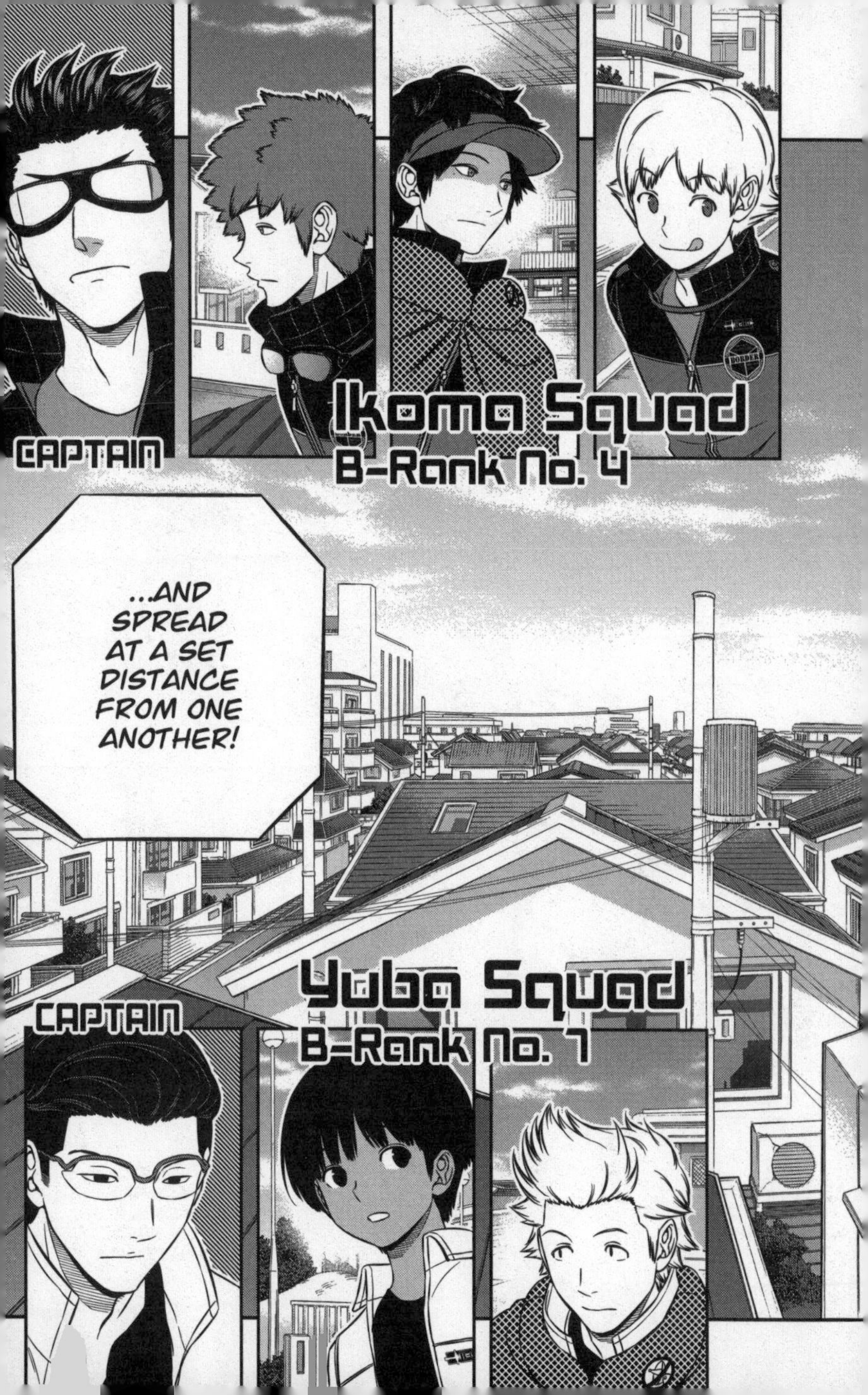
Ikoma Squad
B-Rank No. 4
CAPTAIN
...AND SPREAD AT A SET DISTANCE FROM ONE ANOTHER!
Yuba Squad
B-Rank No. 7
CAPTAIN

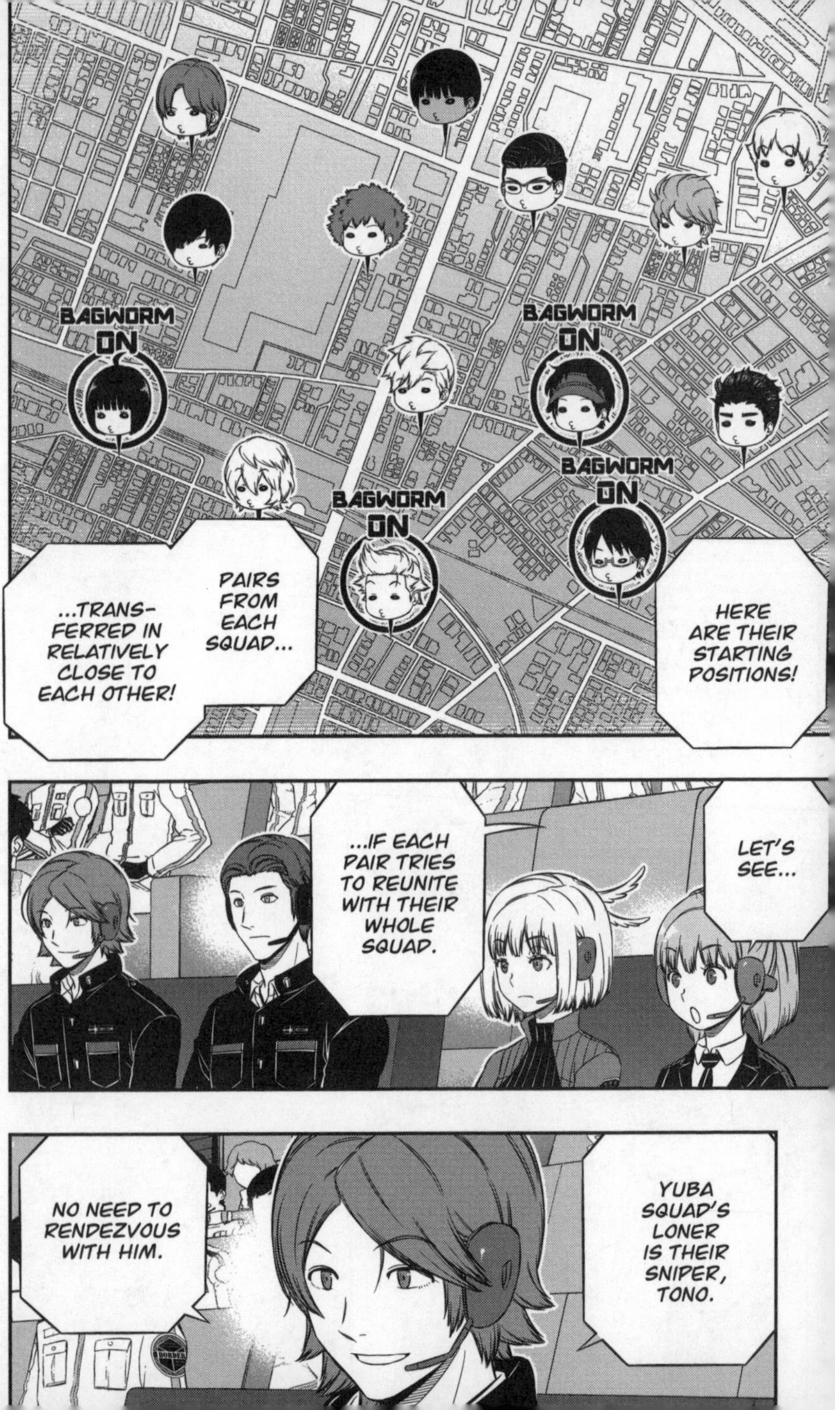
BAGWORM ON
BAGWORM ON
BAGWORM ON
BAGWORM ON
HERE ARE THEIR STARTING POSITIONS!
PAIRS FROM EACH SQUAD...
...TRANSFERRED IN RELATIVELY CLOSE TO EACH OTHER!
LET'S SEE...
...IF EACH PAIR TRIES TO REUNITE WITH THEIR WHOLE SQUAD.
YUBA SQUAD'S LONER IS THEIR SNIPER, TONO.
NO NEED TO RENDEZVOUS WITH HIM.

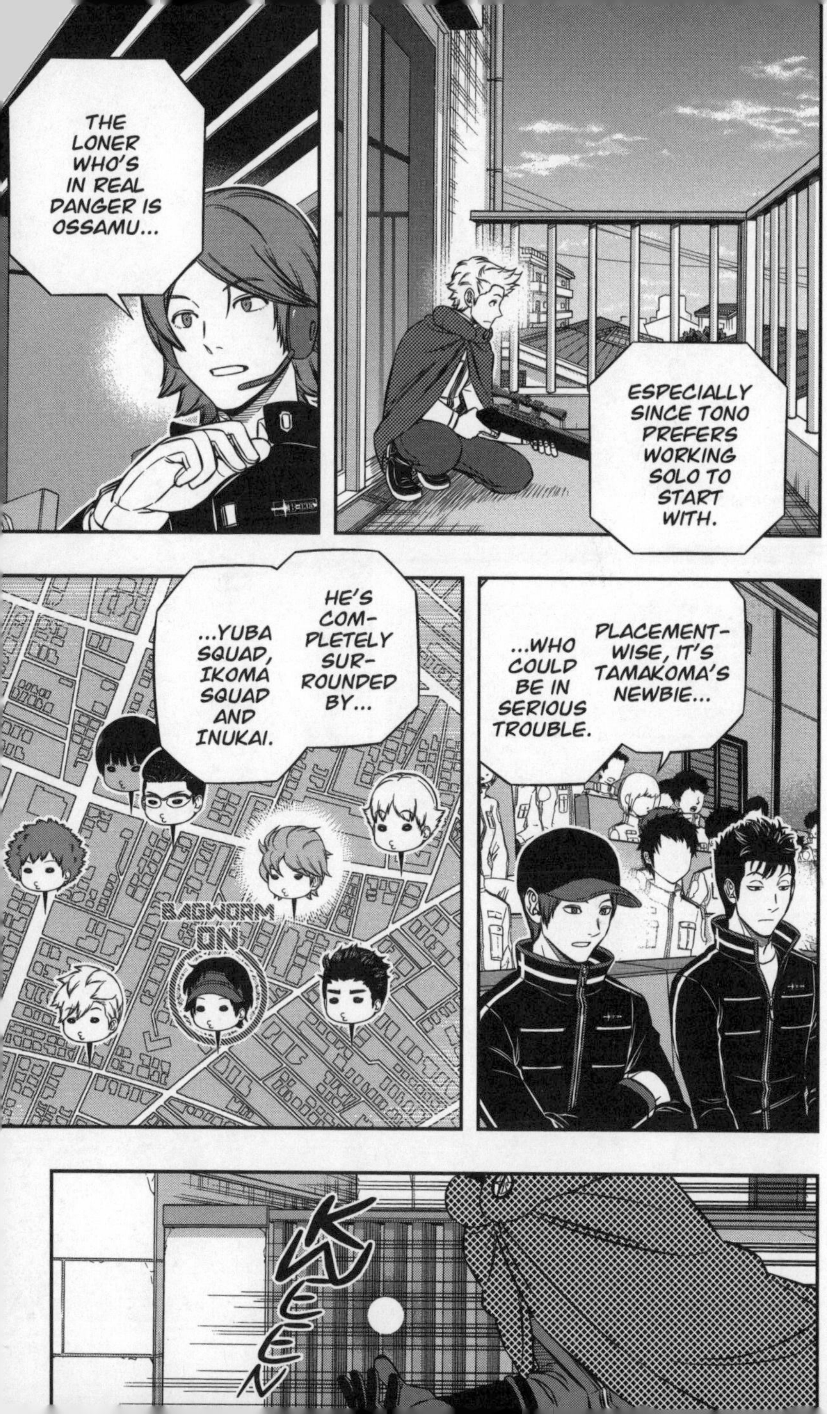
ESPECIALLY SINCE TONO PREFERS WORKING SOLO TO START WITH.
THE LONER WHO'S IN REAL DANGER IS OSSAMU...
PLACEMENT-WISE, IT'S TAMAKOMA'S NEWBIE...
...WHO COULD BE IN SERIOUS TROUBLE.
HE'S COMPLETELY SURROUNDED BY...
...YUBA SQUAD, IKOMA SQUAD AND INUKAI.
BAGWORM ON
KWEEEN

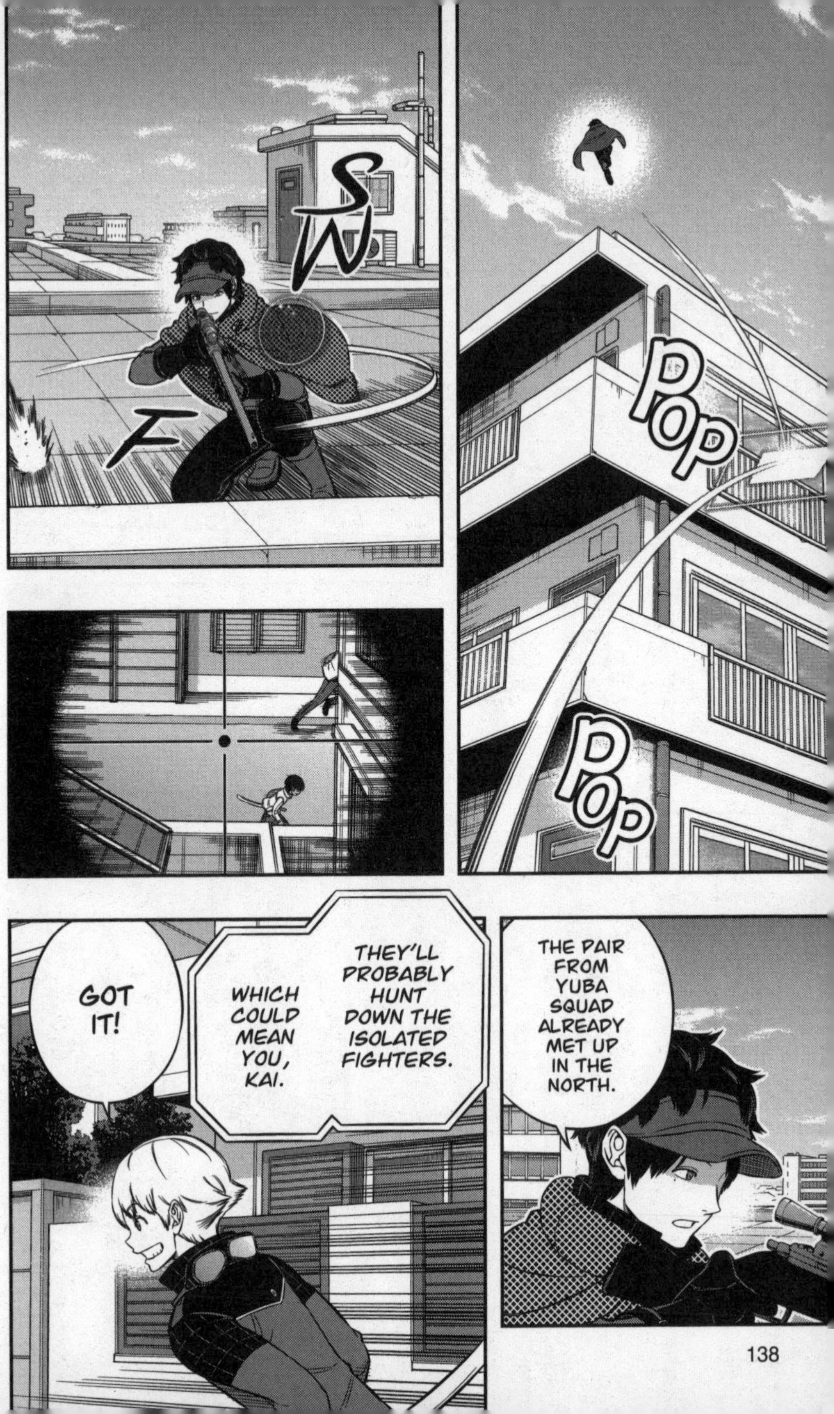
POP
POP
SW
F
THE PAIR FROM YUBA SQUAD ALREADY MET UP IN THE NORTH.
THEY'LL PROBABLY HUNT DOWN THE ISOLATED FIGHTERS.
WHICH COULD MEAN YOU, KAI.
GOT IT!

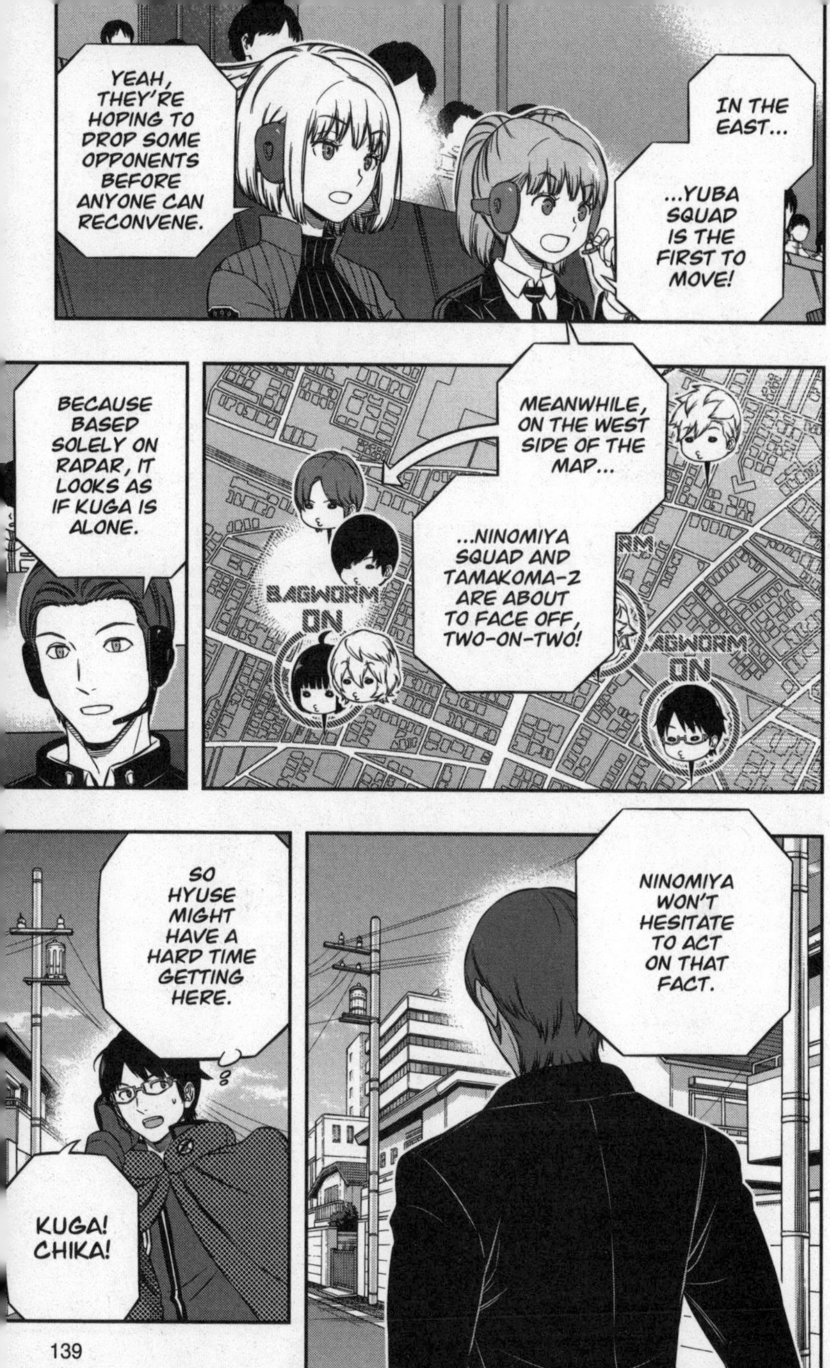
IN THE EAST...
...YUBA SQUAD IS THE FIRST TO MOVE!
YEAH, THEY'RE HOPING TO DROP SOME OPPONENTS BEFORE ANYONE CAN RECONVENE.
MEANWHILE, ON THE WEST SIDE OF THE MAP...
...NINOMIYA SQUAD AND TAMAKOMA-2 ARE ABOUT TO FACE OFF, TWO-ON-TWO!
BAGWORM ON
BAGWORM ON
BECAUSE BASED SOLELY ON RADAR, IT LOOKS AS IF KUGA IS ALONE.
NINOMIYA WON'T HESITATE TO ACT ON THAT FACT.
SO HYUSE MIGHT HAVE A HARD TIME GETTING HERE.
KUGA! CHIKA!

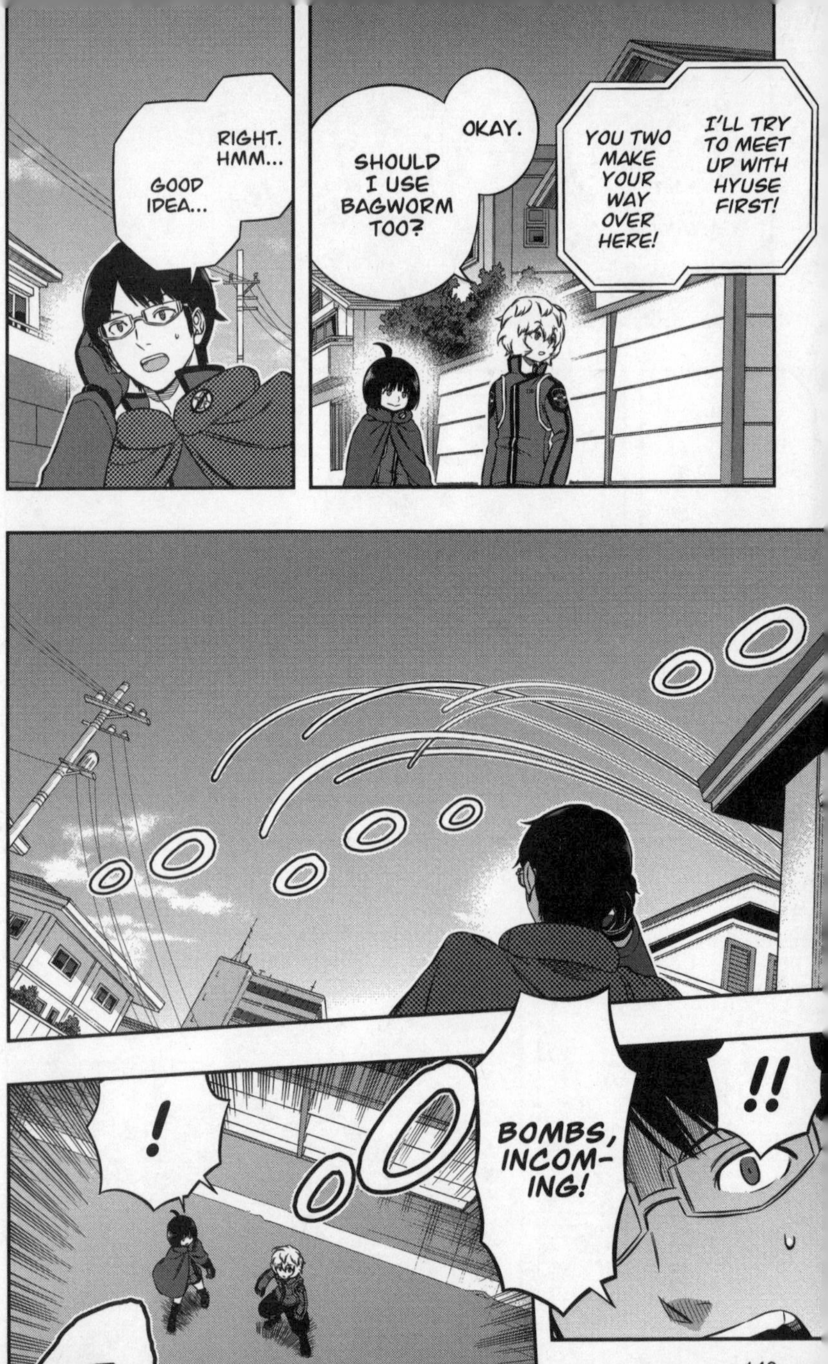
I'LL TRY TO MEET UP WITH HYUSE FIRST!
YOU TWO MAKE YOUR WAY OVER HERE!
OKAY.
SHOULD I USE BAGWORM TOO?
RIGHT. HMM...
GOOD IDEA...
!!
BOMBS, INCOMING!
!

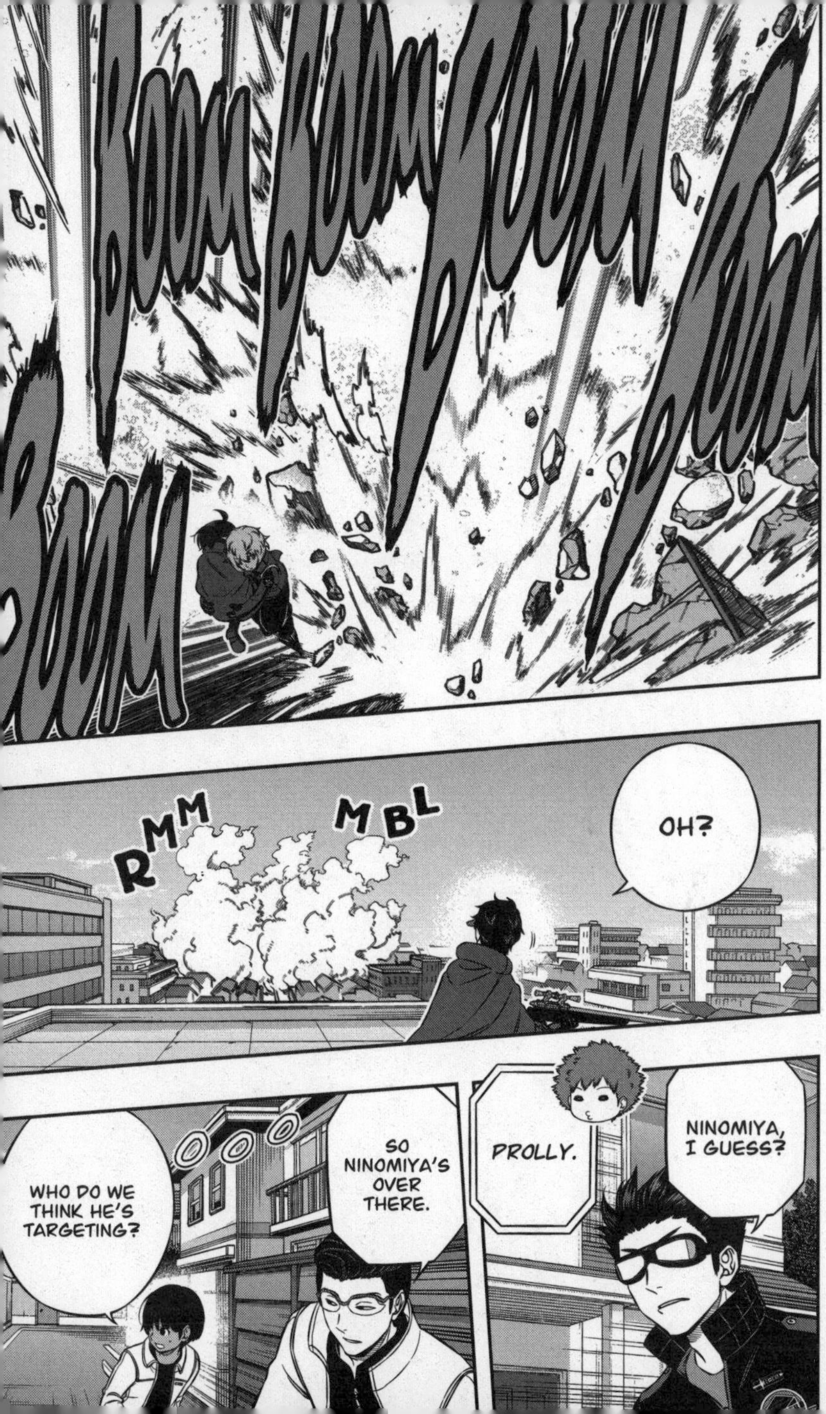
BOOM BOOM BOOM
BAM
BAM
OH?
RMMMBL
NINOMIYA, I GUESS?
PROLLY.
SO NINOMIYA'S OVER THERE.
WHO DO WE THINK HE'S TARGETING?

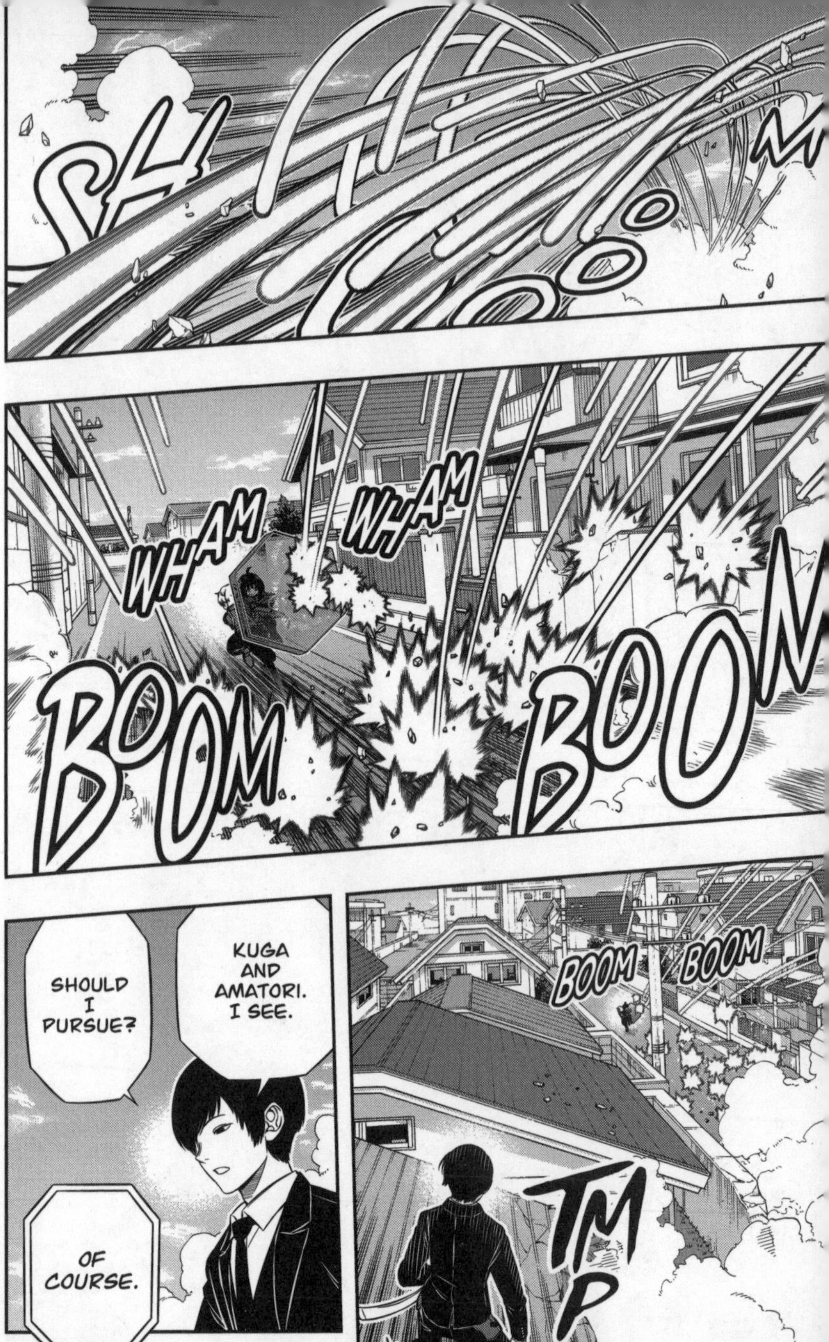
WHAM
WHAM
BOOM
BOOM
BOOM
BOOM
TMP
KUGA AND AMATORI. I SEE.
SHOULD I PURSUE?
OF COURSE.

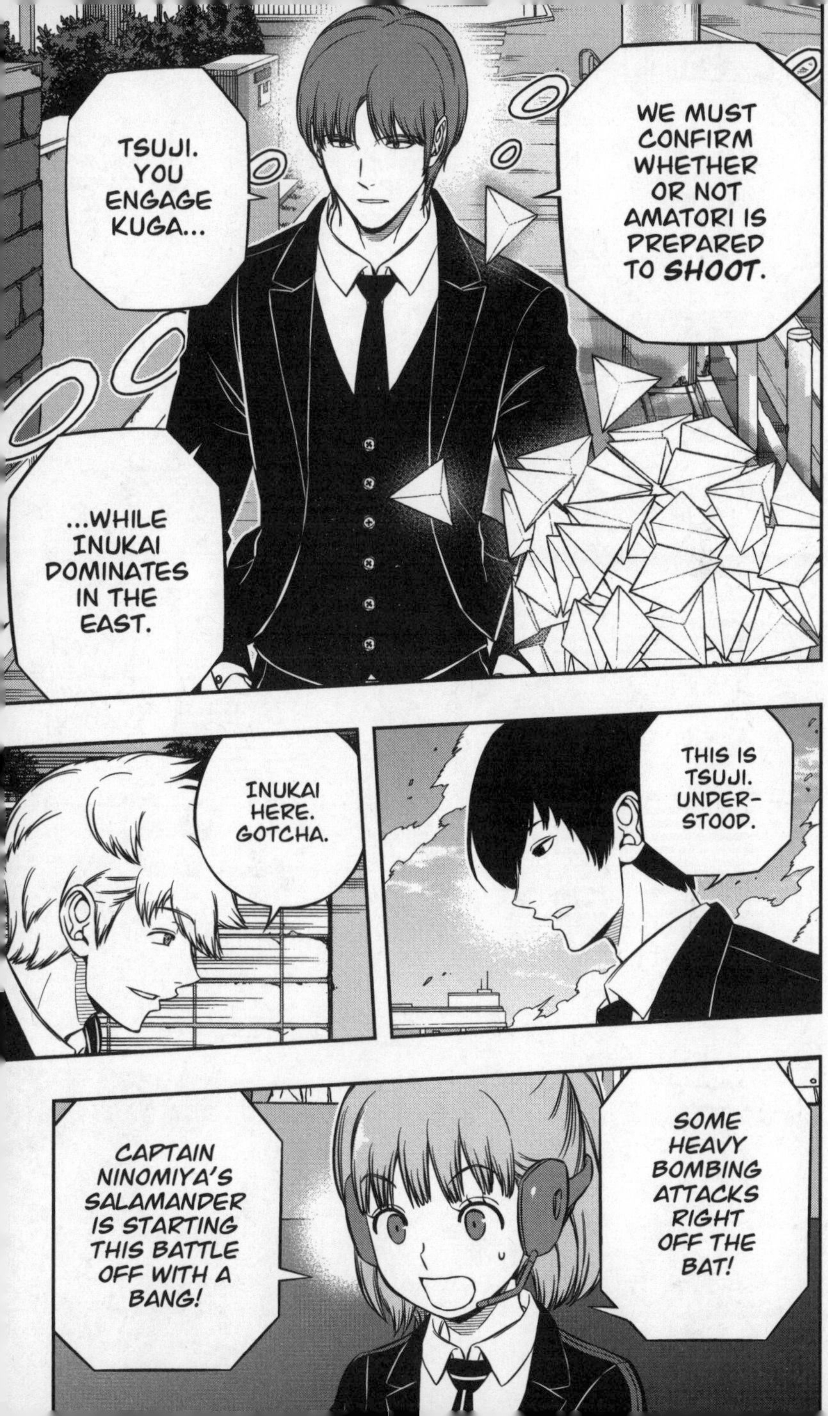
WE MUST CONFIRM WHETHER OR NOT AMATORI IS PREPARED TO **SHOOT**.
TSUJI. YOU ENGAGE KUGA...
...WHILE INUKAI DOMINATES IN THE EAST.
THIS IS TSUJI. UNDER-STOOD.
INUKAI HERE. GOTCHA.
SOME HEAVY BOMBING ATTACKS RIGHT OFF THE BAT!
CAPTAIN NINOMIYA'S SALAMANDER IS STARTING THIS BATTLE OFF WITH A BANG!

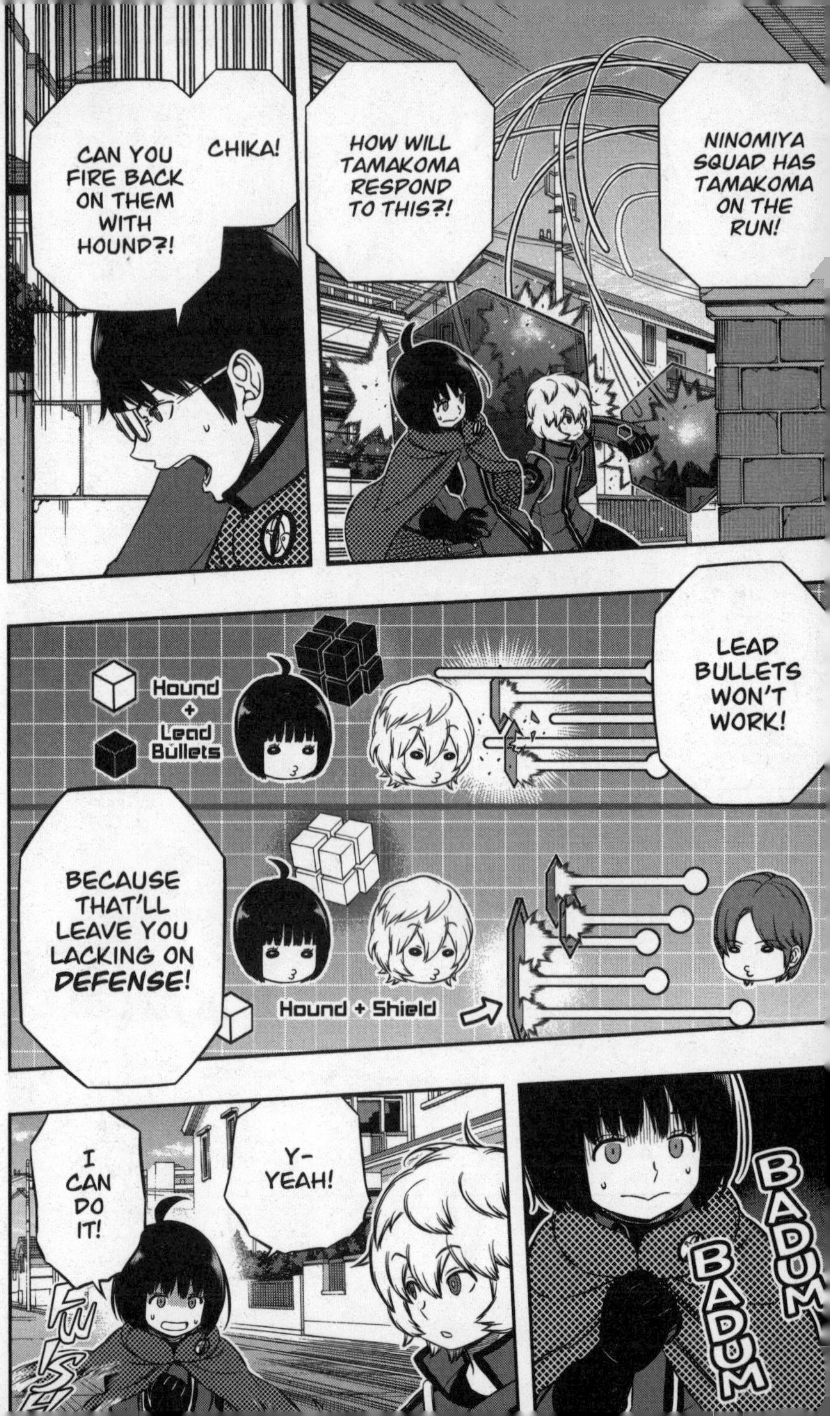
NINOMIYA SQUAD HAS TAMAKOMA ON THE RUN!
HOW WILL TAMAKOMA RESPOND TO THIS?!
CHIKA!
CAN YOU FIRE BACK ON THEM WITH HOUND?!
LEAD BULLETS WON'T WORK!
Hound + Lead Bullets
BECAUSE THAT'LL LEAVE YOU LACKING ON DEFENSE!
Hound + Shield
BADUM
BADUM
Y-YEAH!
I CAN DO IT!

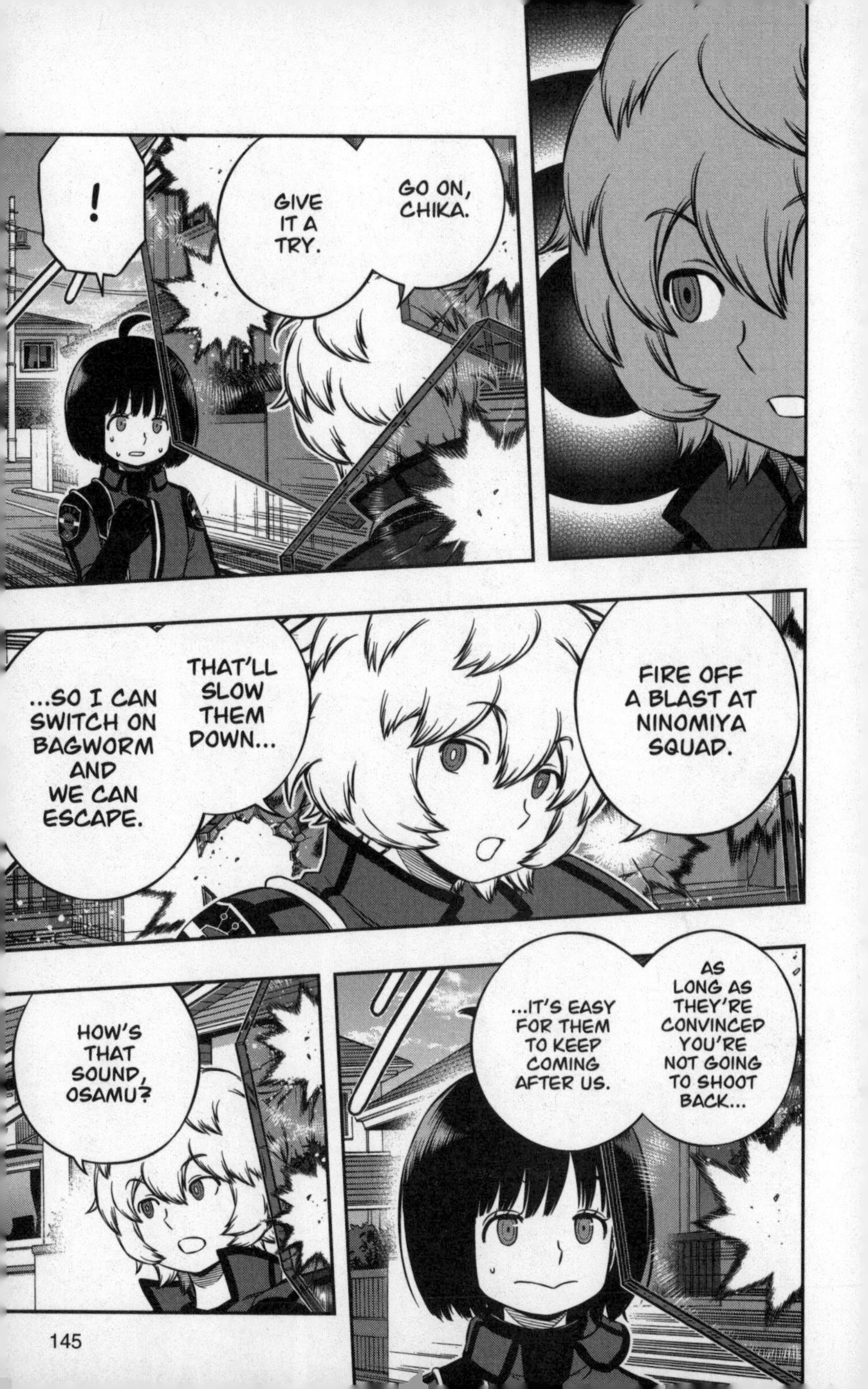
GO ON, CHIKA.
GIVE IT A TRY.
!
FIRE OFF A BLAST AT NINOMIYA SQUAD.
THAT'LL SLOW THEM DOWN...
...SO I CAN SWITCH ON BAGWORM AND WE CAN ESCAPE.
AS LONG AS THEY'RE CONVINCED YOU'RE NOT GOING TO SHOOT BACK...
...IT'S EASY FOR THEM TO KEEP COMING AFTER US.
HOW'S THAT SOUND, OSAMU?

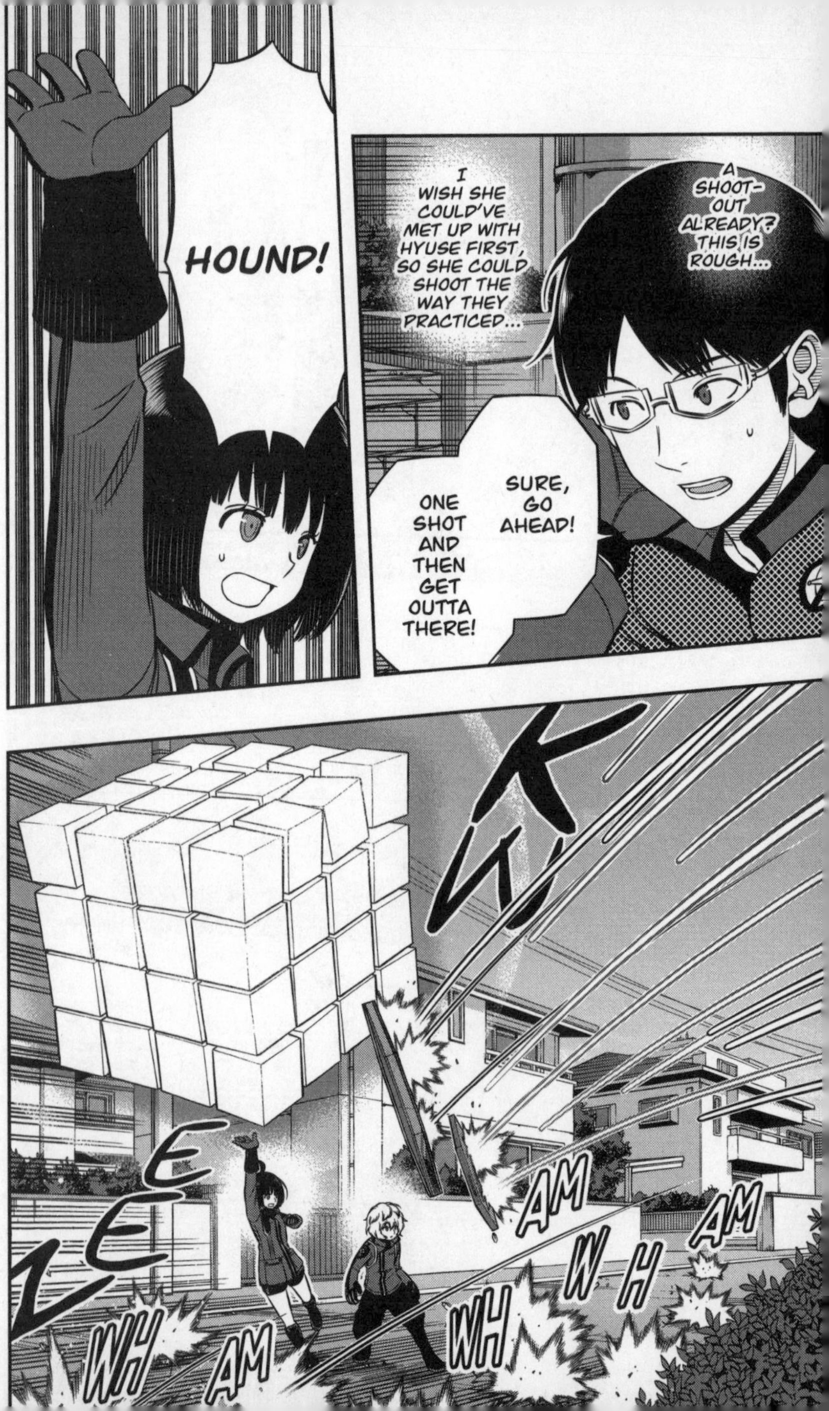
A SHOOT-OUT ALREADY? THIS IS ROUGH...
I WISH SHE COULD'VE MET UP WITH HYUSE FIRST, SO SHE COULD SHOOT THE WAY THEY PRACTICED...
SURE, GO AHEAD!
ONE SHOT AND THEN GET OUTTA THERE!
HOUND!

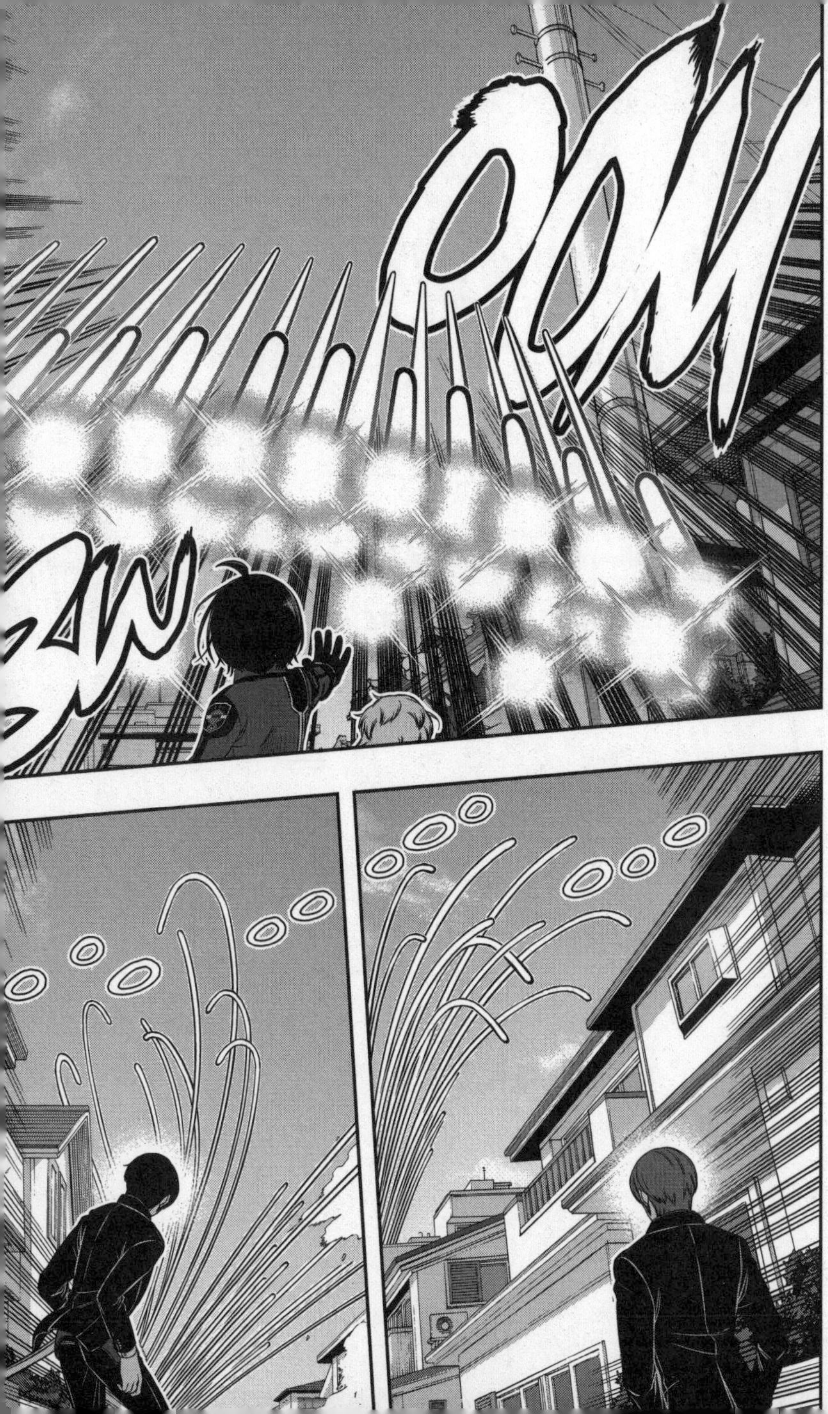
OOM

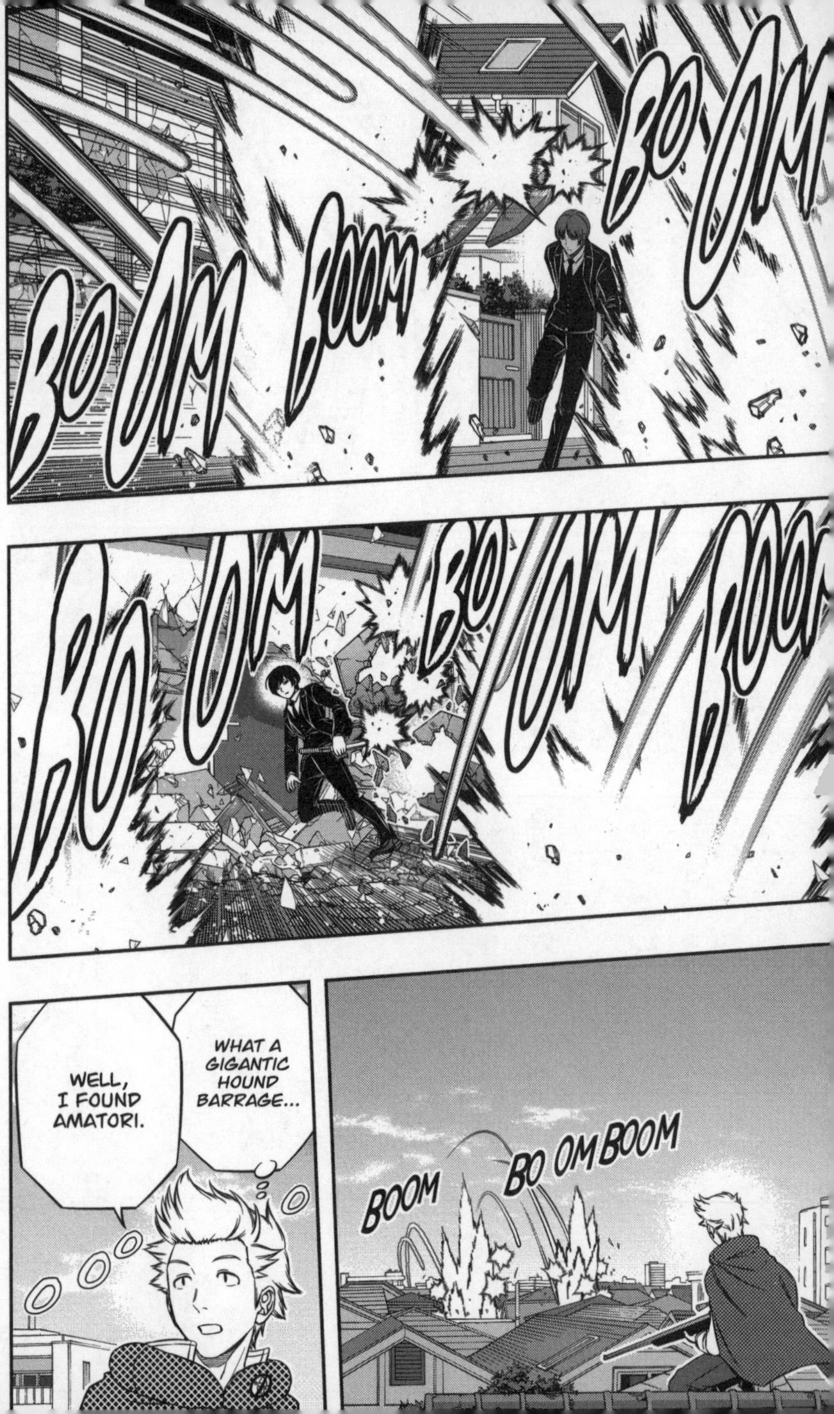
BOOM
BOOM
BOOM
BOOM
BOOM
BOOM
BO OM BOOM
BOOM
WHAT A GIGANTIC HOUND BARRAGE...
WELL, I FOUND AMATORI.

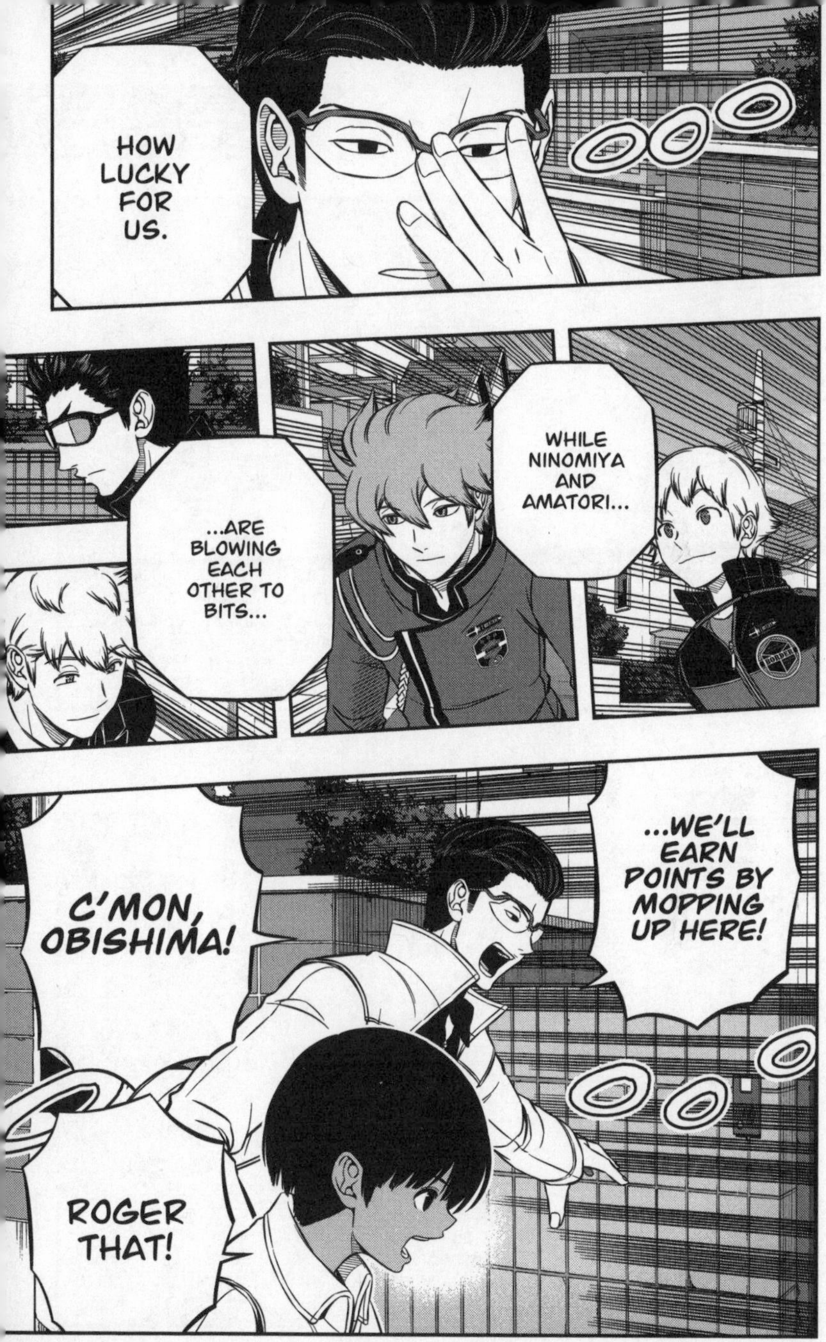
HOW LUCKY FOR US.
WHILE NINOMIYA AND AMATORI...
...ARE BLOWING EACH OTHER TO BITS...
...WE'LL EARN POINTS BY MOPPING UP HERE!
C'MON, OBISHIMA!
ROGER THAT!

Once Again: The Schools of Mikado City (Part 3)

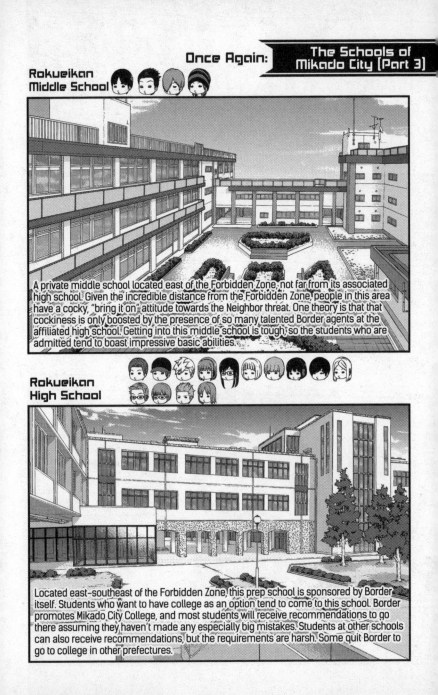

Rokueikan Middle School

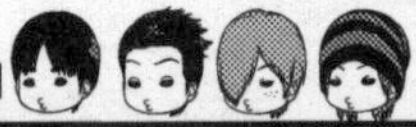

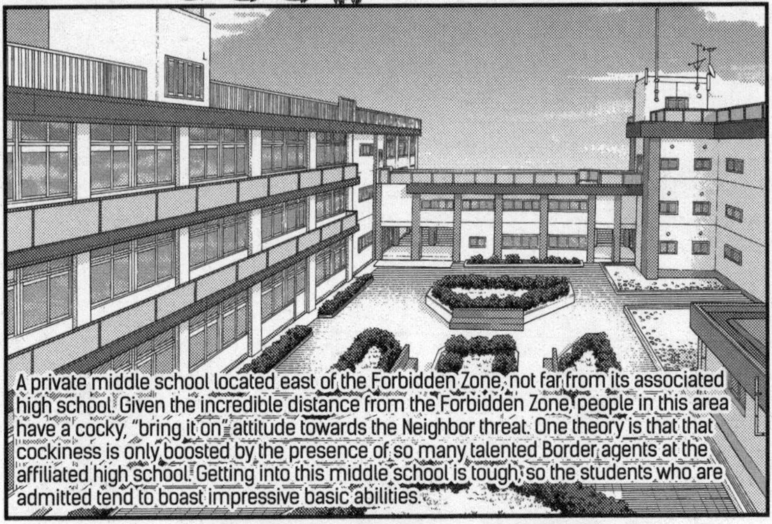
A private middle school located east of the Forbidden Zone, not far from its associated high school. Given the incredible distance from the Forbidden Zone, people in this area have a cocky, "bring it on" attitude towards the Neighbor threat. One theory is that that cockiness is only boosted by the presence of so many talented Border agents at the affiliated high school. Getting into this middle school is tough, so the students who are admitted tend to boast impressive basic abilities.

Rokueikan High School

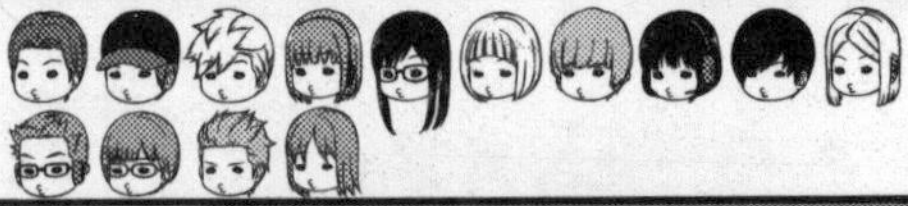

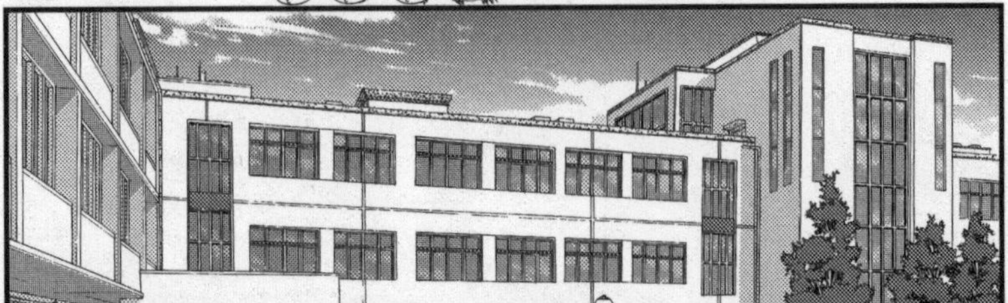
Located east-southeast of the Forbidden Zone, this prep school is sponsored by Border itself. Students who want to have college as an option tend to come to this school. Border promotes Mikado City College, and most students will receive recommendations to go there assuming they haven't made any especially big mistakes. Students at other schools can also receive recommendations, but the requirements are harsh. Some quit Border to go to college in other prefectures.

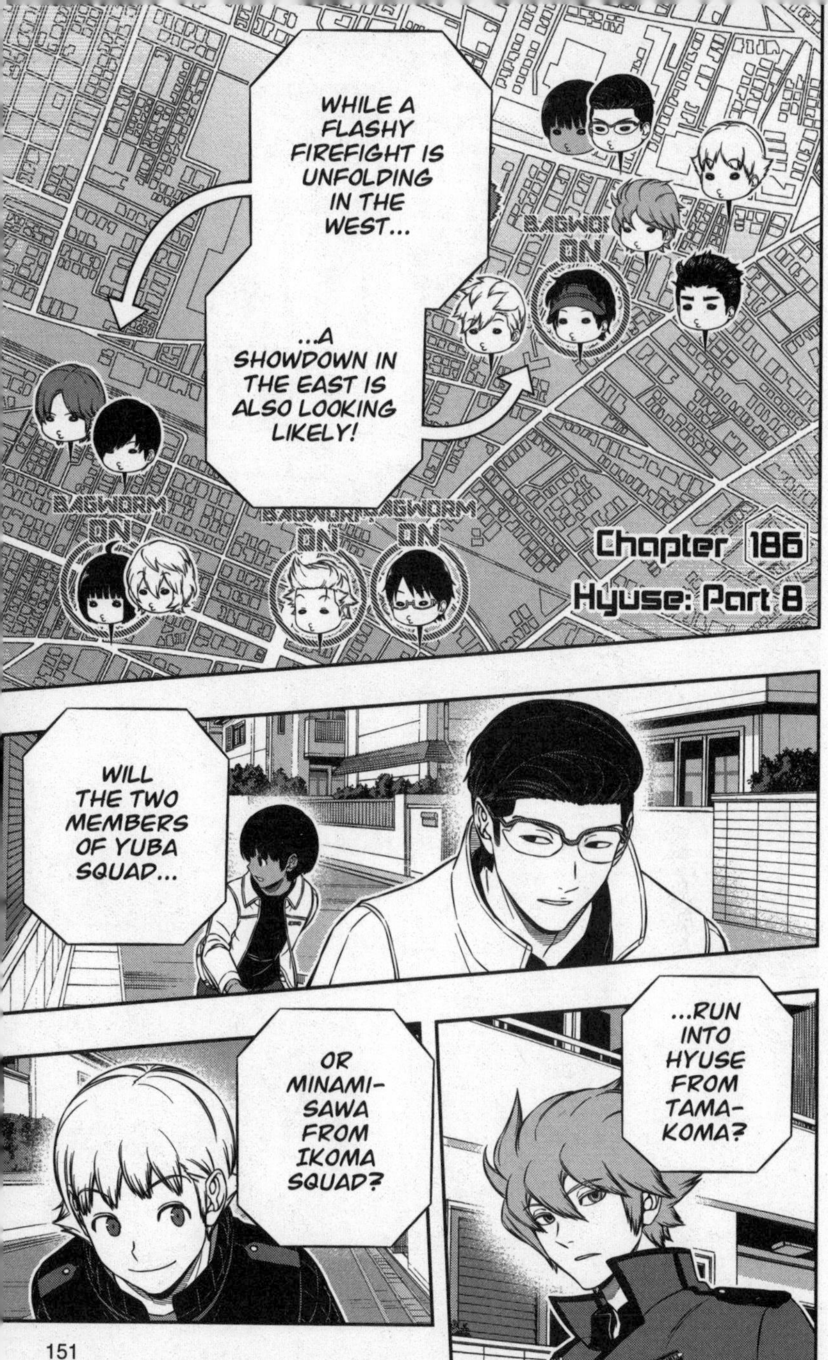
Chapter 186
Hyuse: Part 8
WHILE A FLASHY FIREFIGHT IS UNFOLDING IN THE WEST...
...A SHOWDOWN IN THE EAST IS ALSO LOOKING LIKELY!
BAGWORM ON
BAGWORM ON
BAGWORM ON
BAGWORM ON
WILL THE TWO MEMBERS OF YUBA SQUAD...
...RUN INTO HYUSE FROM TAMA-KOMA?
OR MINAMI-SAWA FROM IKOMA SQUAD?

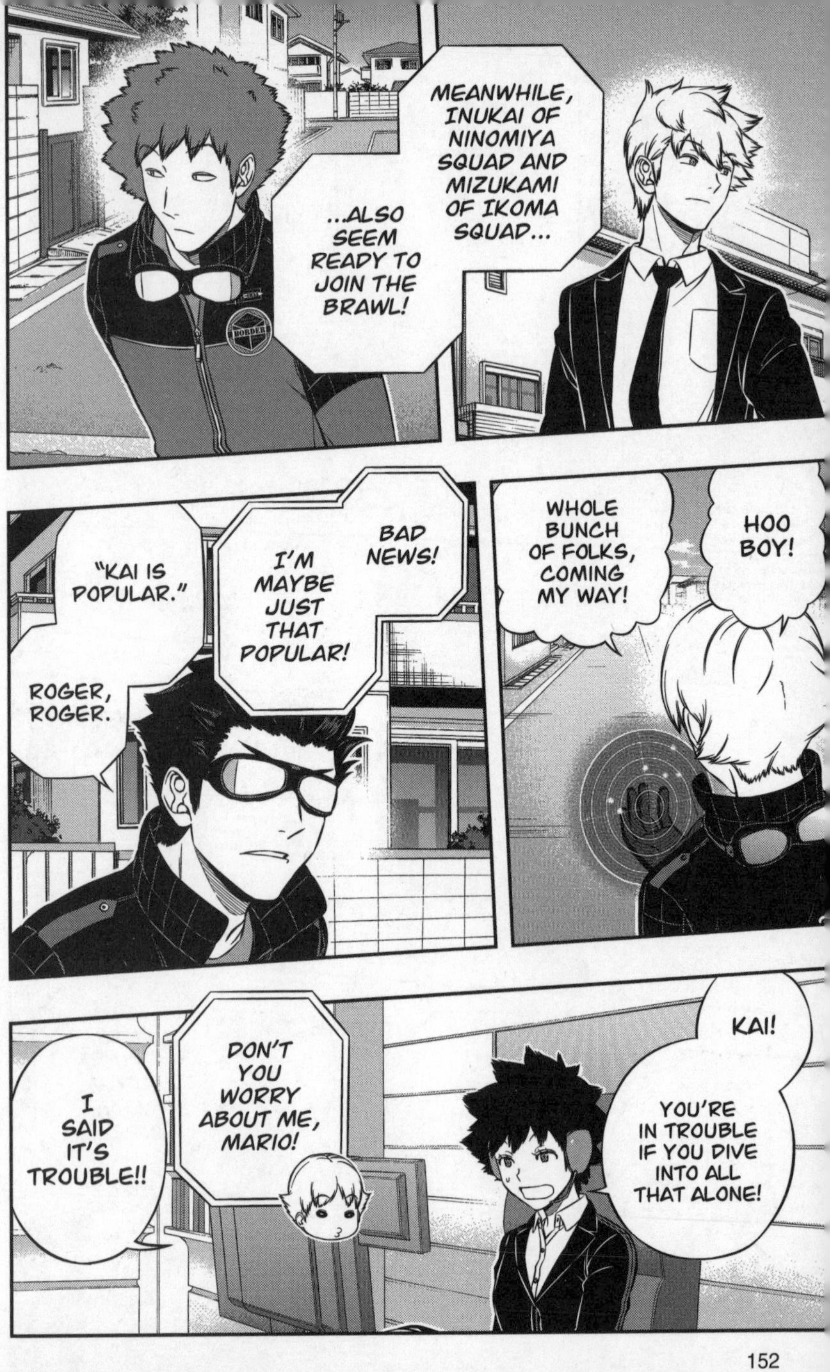
MEANWHILE, INUKAI OF NINOMIYA SQUAD AND MIZUKAMI OF IKOMA SQUAD...
...ALSO SEEM READY TO JOIN THE BRAWL!
HOO BOY!
WHOLE BUNCH OF FOLKS, COMING MY WAY!
BAD NEWS! I'M MAYBE JUST THAT POPULAR!
"KAI IS POPULAR." ROGER, ROGER.
KAI! YOU'RE IN TROUBLE IF YOU DIVE INTO ALL THAT ALONE!
DON'T YOU WORRY ABOUT ME, MARIO!
I SAID IT'S TROUBLE!!

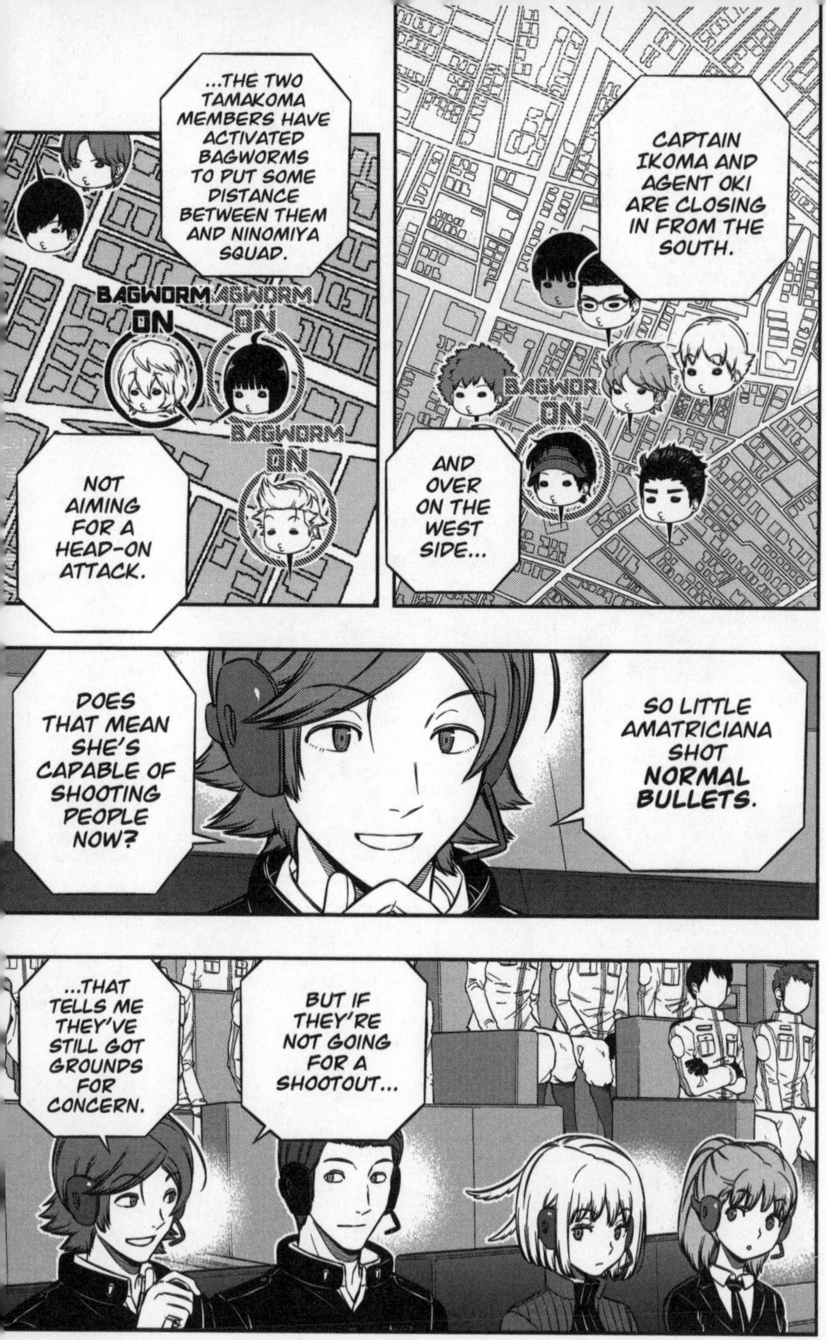
CAPTAIN IKOMA AND AGENT OKI ARE CLOSING IN FROM THE SOUTH.
BAGWOR ON
AND OVER ON THE WEST SIDE...
...THE TWO TAMAKOMA MEMBERS HAVE ACTIVATED BAGWORMS TO PUT SOME DISTANCE BETWEEN THEM AND NINOMIYA SQUAD.
AGWORM ON
BAGWORM ON
BAGWORM ON
NOT AIMING FOR A HEAD-ON ATTACK.
SO LITTLE AMATRICIANA SHOT NORMAL BULLETS.
DOES THAT MEAN SHE'S CAPABLE OF SHOOTING PEOPLE NOW?
BUT IF THEY'RE NOT GOING FOR A SHOOTOUT...
...THAT TELLS ME THEY'VE STILL GOT GROUNDS FOR CONCERN.

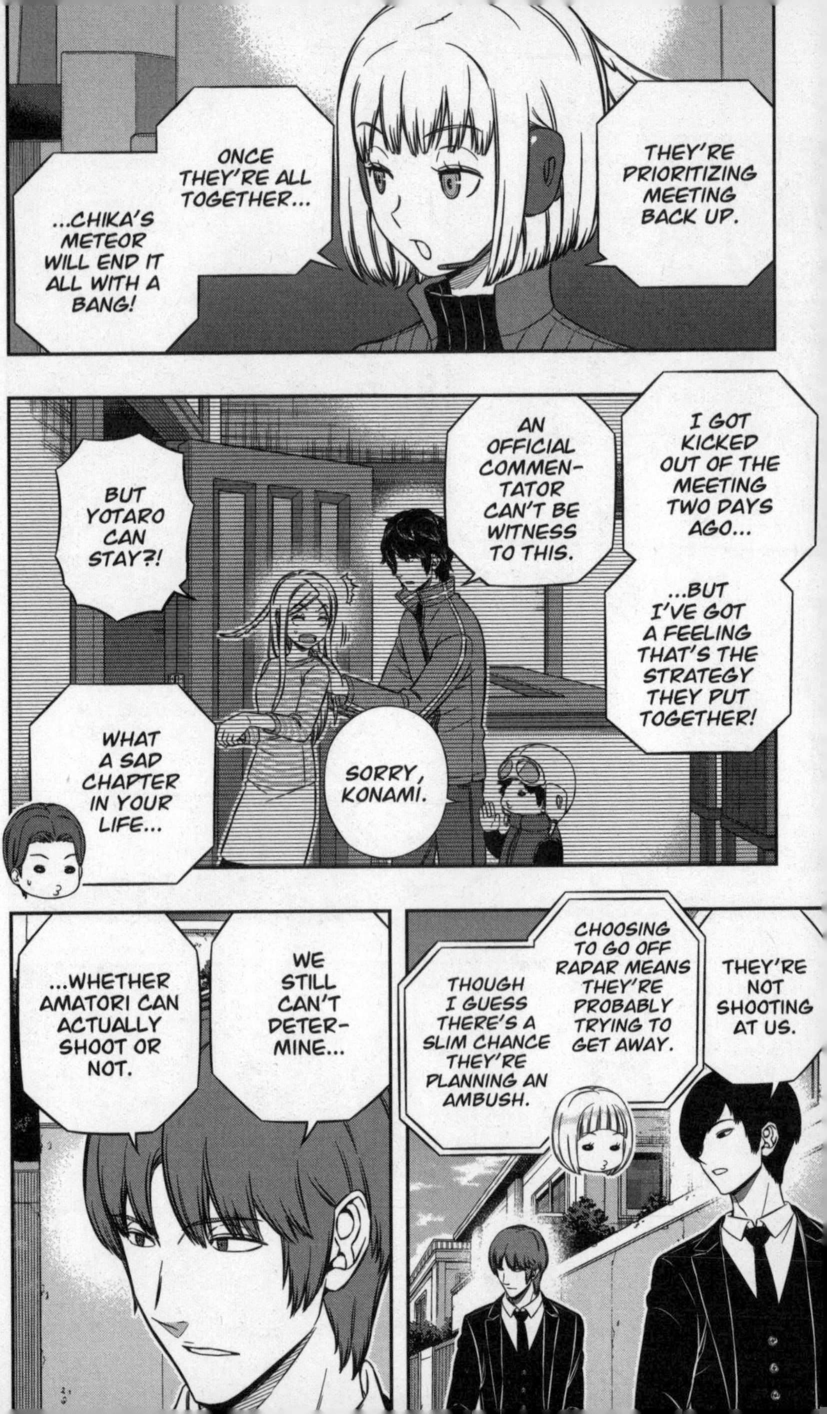
THEY'RE PRIORITIZING MEETING BACK UP.
ONCE THEY'RE ALL TOGETHER...
...CHIKA'S METEOR WILL END IT ALL WITH A BANG!
I GOT KICKED OUT OF THE MEETING TWO DAYS AGO...
...BUT I'VE GOT A FEELING THAT'S THE STRATEGY THEY PUT TOGETHER!
AN OFFICIAL COMMENTATOR CAN'T BE WITNESS TO THIS.
SORRY, KONAMI.
BUT YOTARO CAN STAY?!
WHAT A SAD CHAPTER IN YOUR LIFE...
THEY'RE NOT SHOOTING AT US.
CHOOSING TO GO OFF RADAR MEANS THEY'RE PROBABLY TRYING TO GET AWAY.
THOUGH I GUESS THERE'S A SLIM CHANCE THEY'RE PLANNING AN AMBUSH.
WE STILL CAN'T DETERMINE...
...WHETHER AMATORI CAN ACTUALLY SHOOT OR NOT.

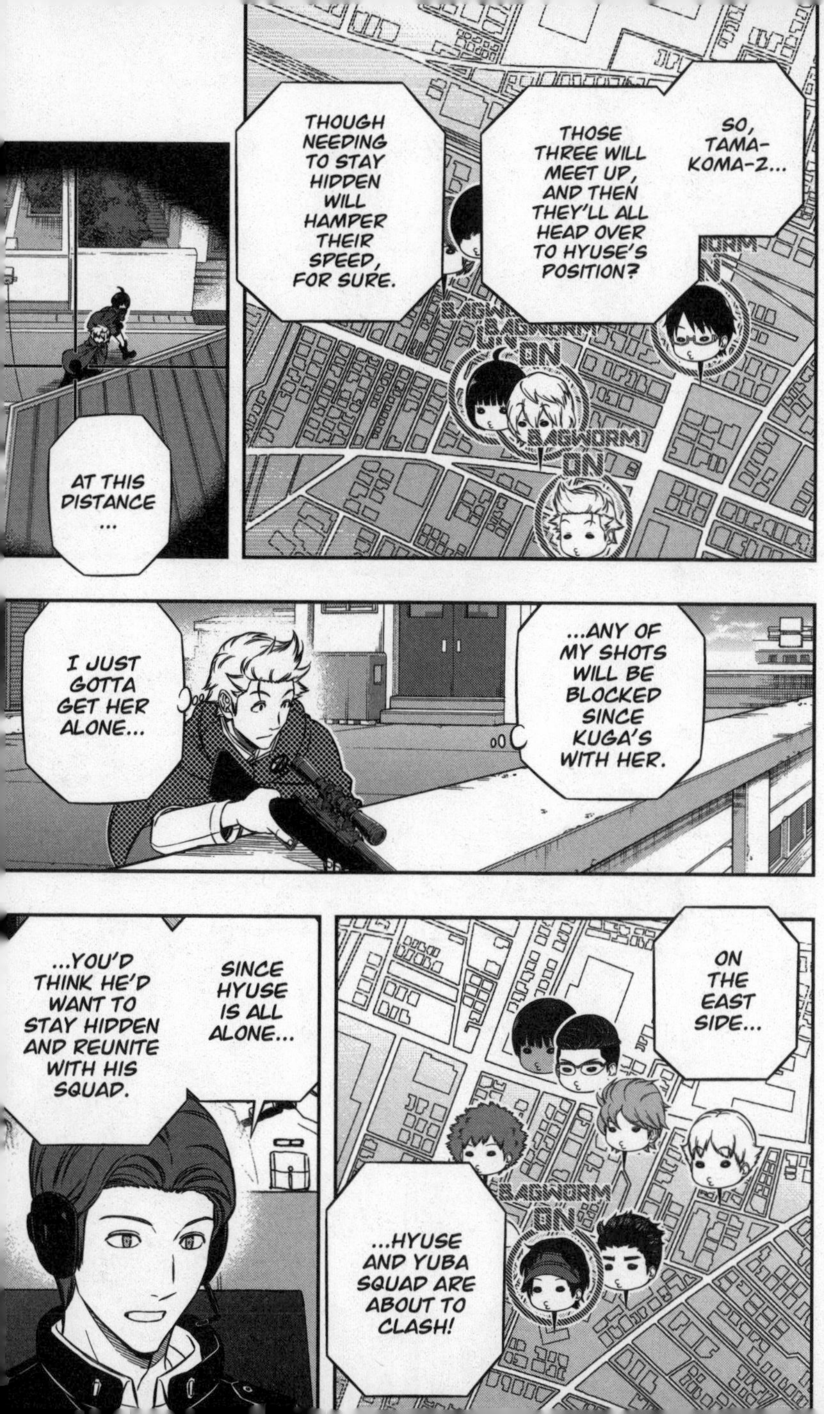
SO, TAMA-KOMA-2...
THOSE THREE WILL MEET UP, AND THEN THEY'LL ALL HEAD OVER TO HYUSE'S POSITION?
THOUGH NEEDING TO STAY HIDDEN WILL HAMPER THEIR SPEED, FOR SURE.
BAGWORM ON
BAGWORM ON
AT THIS DISTANCE...
...ANY OF MY SHOTS WILL BE BLOCKED SINCE KUGA'S WITH HER.
I JUST GOTTA GET HER ALONE...
ON THE EAST SIDE...
...HYUSE AND YUBA SQUAD ARE ABOUT TO CLASH!
BAGWORM ON
SINCE HYUSE IS ALL ALONE...
...YOU'D THINK HE'D WANT TO STAY HIDDEN AND REUNITE WITH HIS SQUAD.

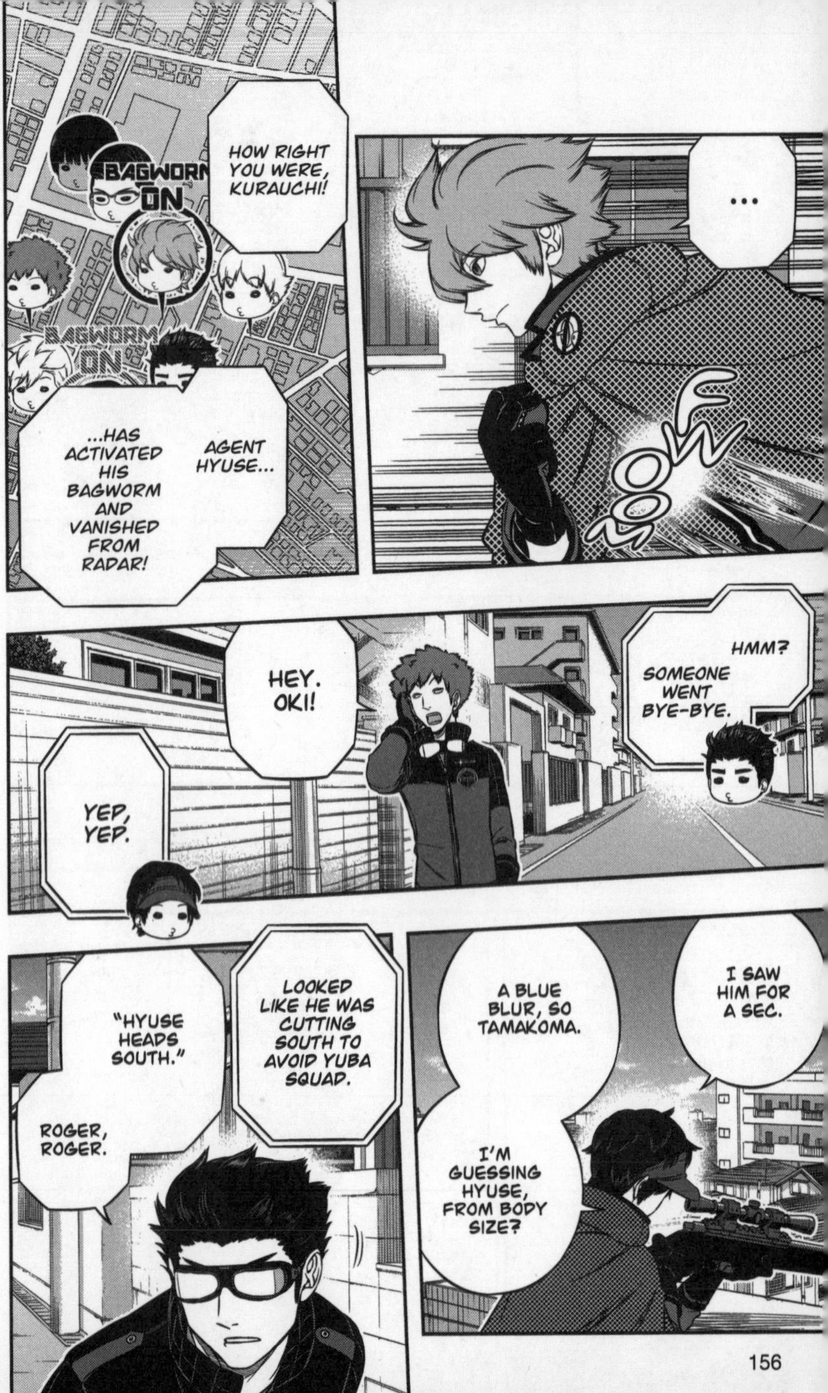
...
FWOOM
HOW RIGHT YOU WERE, KURAUCHI!
BAGWORM ON
BAGWORM ON
AGENT HYUSE...
...HAS ACTIVATED HIS BAGWORM AND VANISHED FROM RADAR!
HMM?
SOMEONE WENT BYE-BYE.
HEY. OKI!
YEP, YEP.
I SAW HIM FOR A SEC.
A BLUE BLUR, SO TAMAKOMA.
I'M GUESSING HYUSE, FROM BODY SIZE?
LOOKED LIKE HE WAS CUTTING SOUTH TO AVOID YUBA SQUAD.
"HYUSE HEADS SOUTH."
ROGER, ROGER.

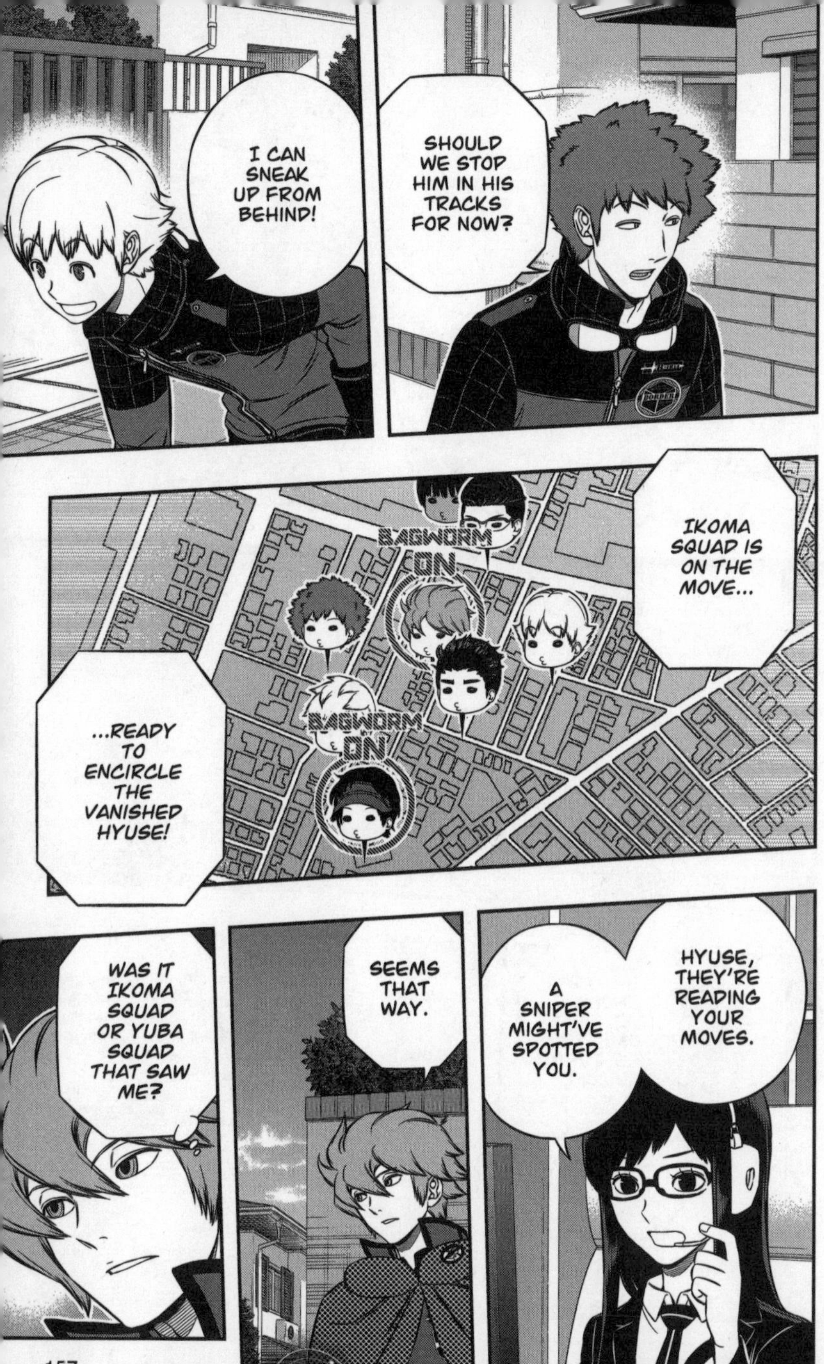
SHOULD WE STOP HIM IN HIS TRACKS FOR NOW?
I CAN SNEAK UP FROM BEHIND!
IKOMA SQUAD IS ON THE MOVE...
BAGWORM ON
BAGWORM ON
...READY TO ENCIRCLE THE VANISHED HYUSE!
HYUSE, THEY'RE READING YOUR MOVES.
A SNIPER MIGHT'VE SPOTTED YOU.
SEEMS THAT WAY.
WAS IT IKOMA SQUAD OR YUBA SQUAD THAT SAW ME?

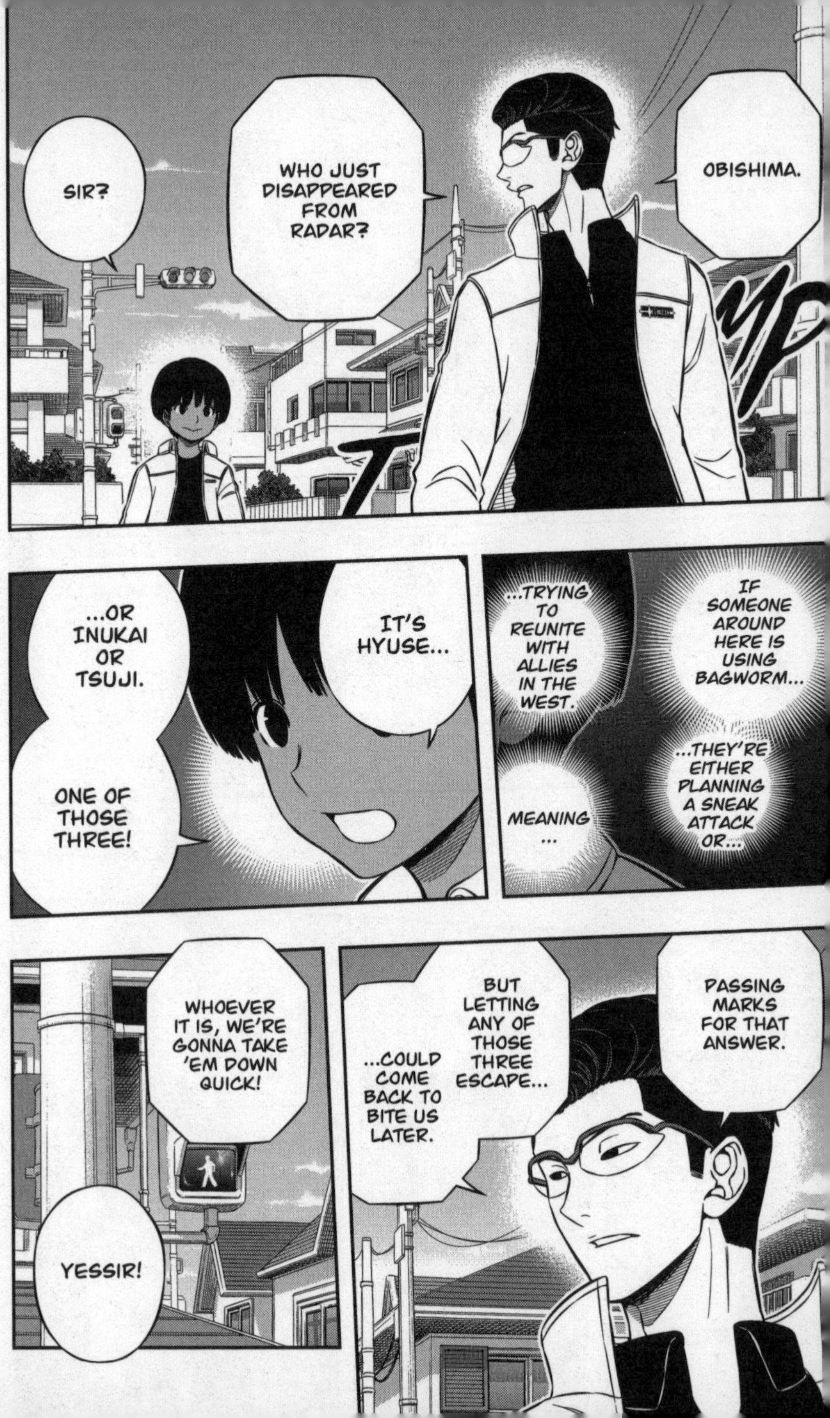
OBISHIMA.
WHO JUST DISAPPEARED FROM RADAR?
SIR?
IF SOMEONE AROUND HERE IS USING BAGWORM...
...THEY'RE EITHER PLANNING A SNEAK ATTACK OR...
...TRYING TO REUNITE WITH ALLIES IN THE WEST.
MEANING...
IT'S HYUSE...
...OR INUKAI OR TSUJI.
ONE OF THOSE THREE!
PASSING MARKS FOR THAT ANSWER.
BUT LETTING ANY OF THOSE THREE ESCAPE...
...COULD COME BACK TO BITE US LATER.
WHOEVER IT IS, WE'RE GONNA TAKE 'EM DOWN QUICK!
YESSIR!

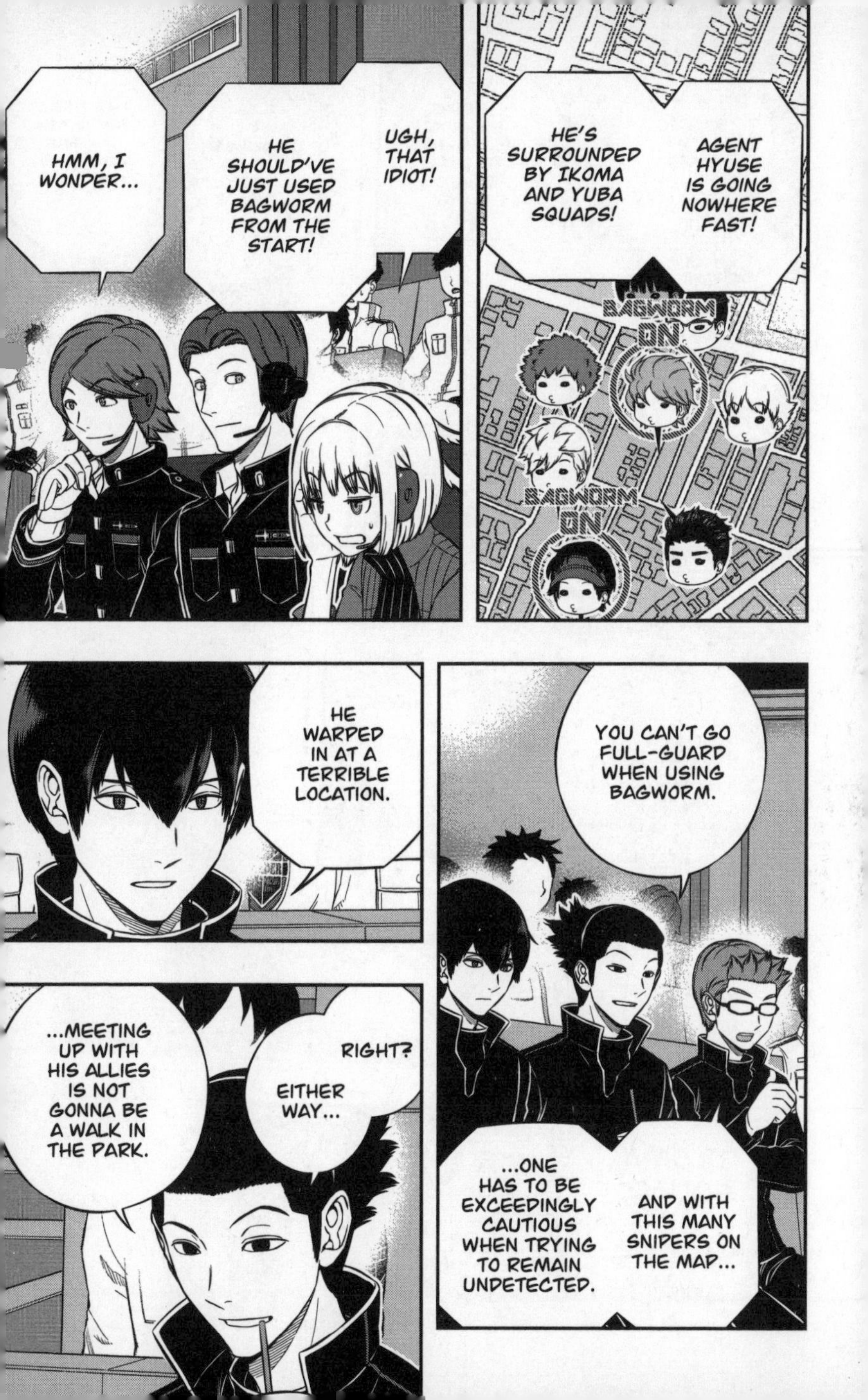
AGENT HYUSE IS GOING NOWHERE FAST!
HE'S SURROUNDED BY IKOMA AND YUBA SQUADS!
BAGWORM ON
BAGWORM ON
UGH, THAT IDIOT!
HE SHOULD'VE JUST USED BAGWORM FROM THE START!
HMM, I WONDER...
YOU CAN'T GO FULL-GUARD WHEN USING BAGWORM.
AND WITH THIS MANY SNIPERS ON THE MAP...
...ONE HAS TO BE EXCEEDINGLY CAUTIOUS WHEN TRYING TO REMAIN UNDETECTED.
HE WARPED IN AT A TERRIBLE LOCATION.
RIGHT?
EITHER WAY...
...MEETING UP WITH HIS ALLIES IS NOT GONNA BE A WALK IN THE PARK.

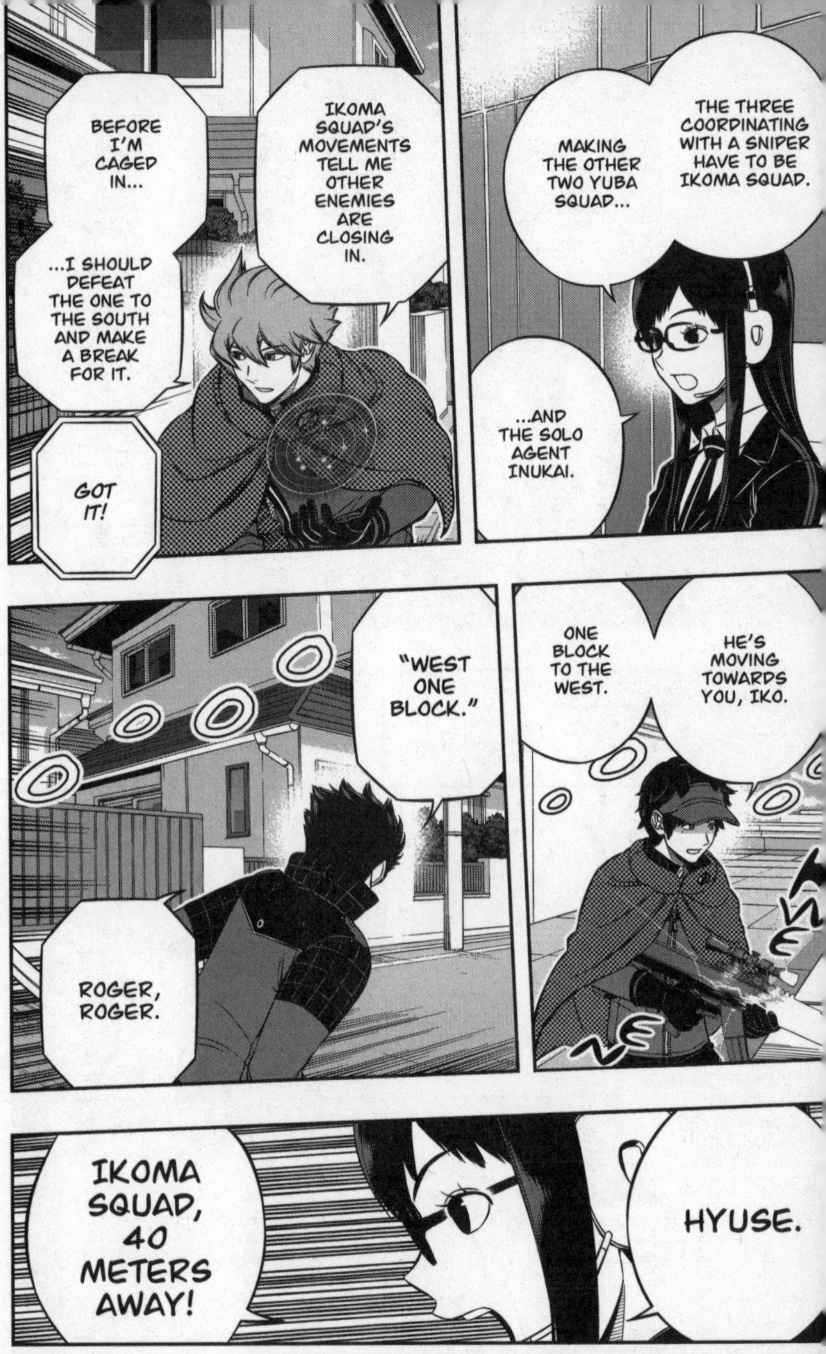
THE THREE COORDINATING WITH A SNIPER HAVE TO BE IKOMA SQUAD.
MAKING THE OTHER TWO YUBA SQUAD...
...AND THE SOLO AGENT INUKAI.
IKOMA SQUAD'S MOVEMENTS TELL ME OTHER ENEMIES ARE CLOSING IN.
BEFORE I'M CAGED IN...
...I SHOULD DEFEAT THE ONE TO THE SOUTH AND MAKE A BREAK FOR IT.
GOT IT!
HE'S MOVING TOWARDS YOU, IKO.
ONE BLOCK TO THE WEST.
"WEST ONE BLOCK."
ROGER, ROGER.
HYUSE.
IKOMA SQUAD, 40 METERS AWAY!

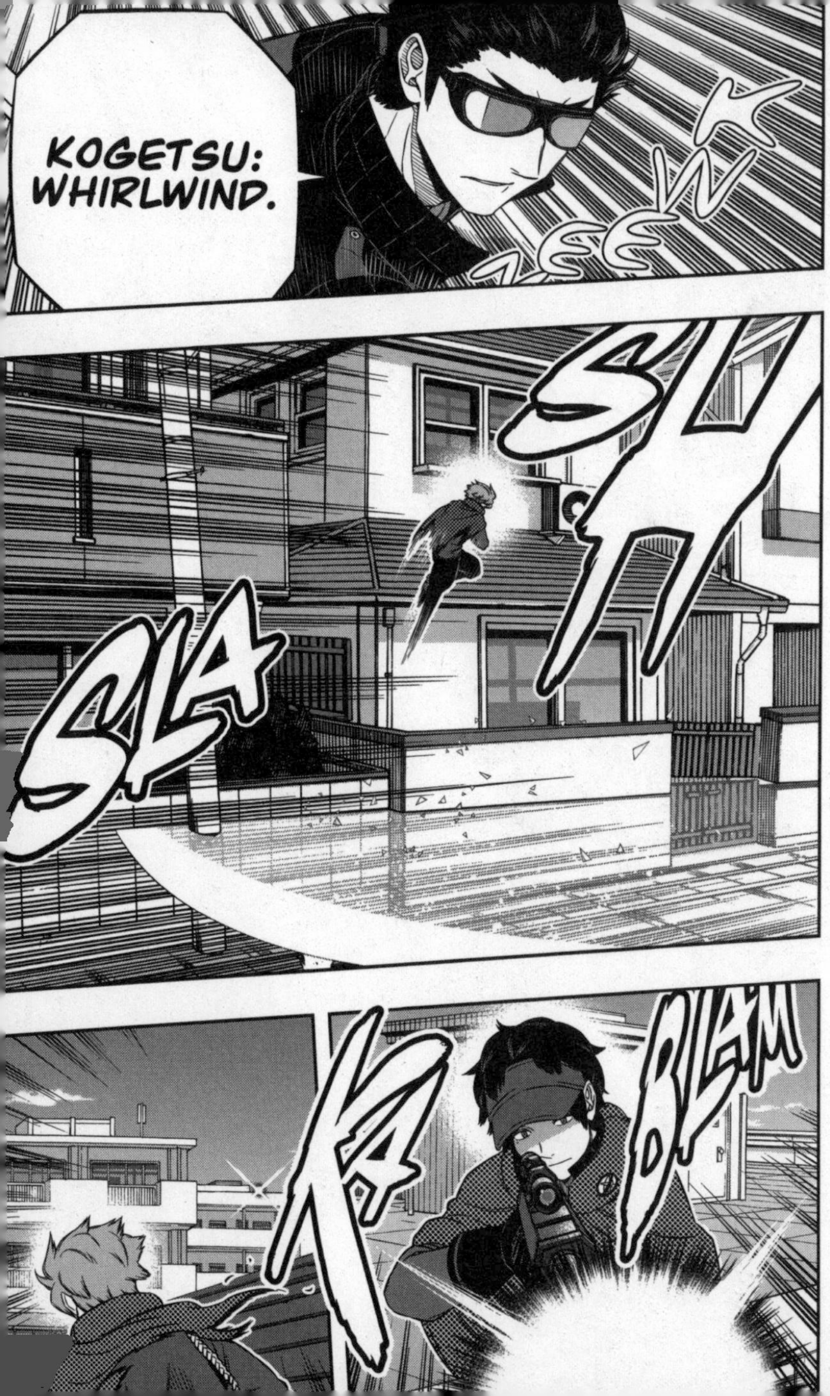
KOGETSU: WHIRLWIND.
SLA
SH
KA
BLAM

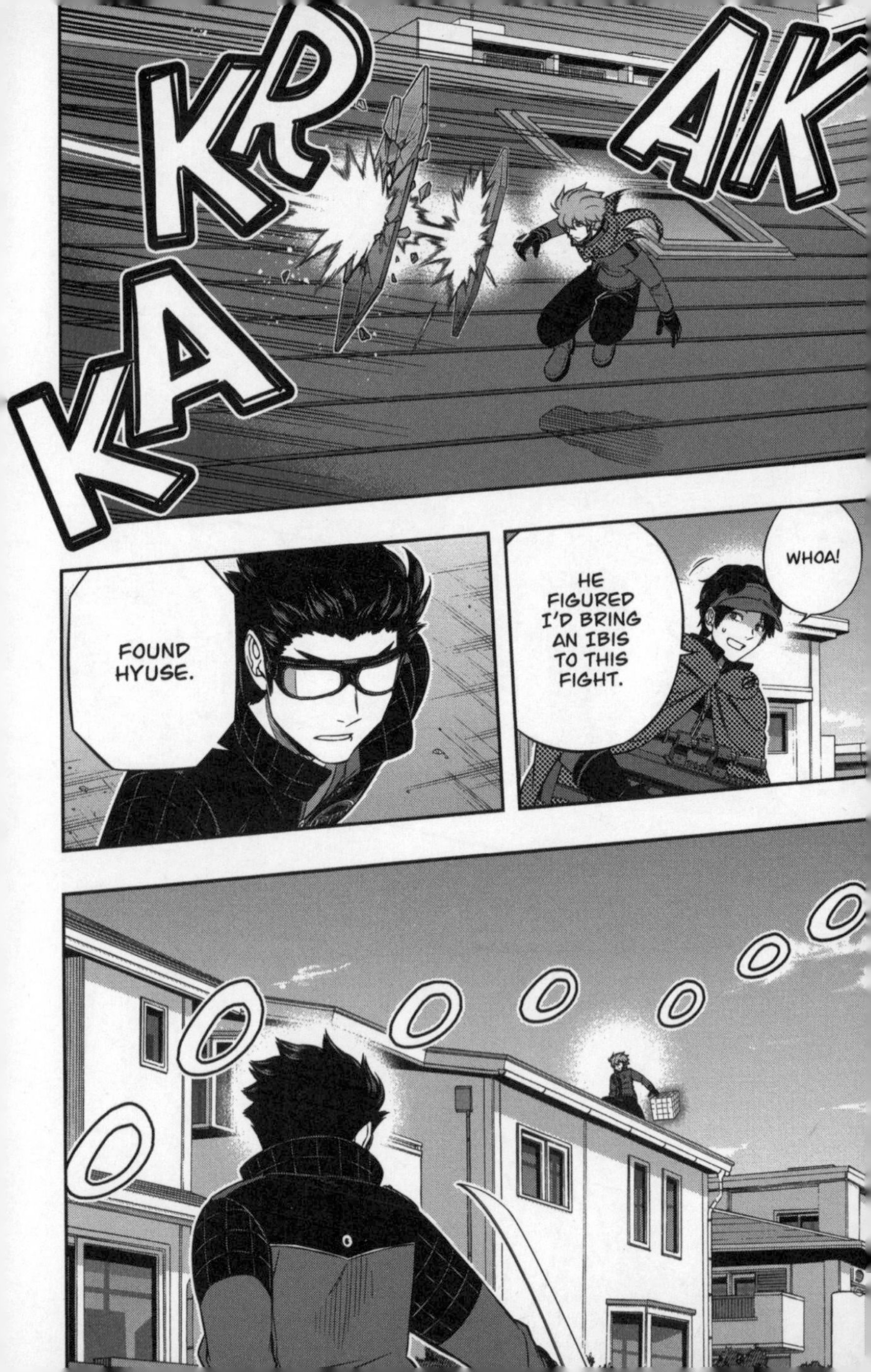
KAKRAK
WHOA!
HE FIGURED I'D BRING AN IBIS TO THIS FIGHT.
FOUND HYUSE.

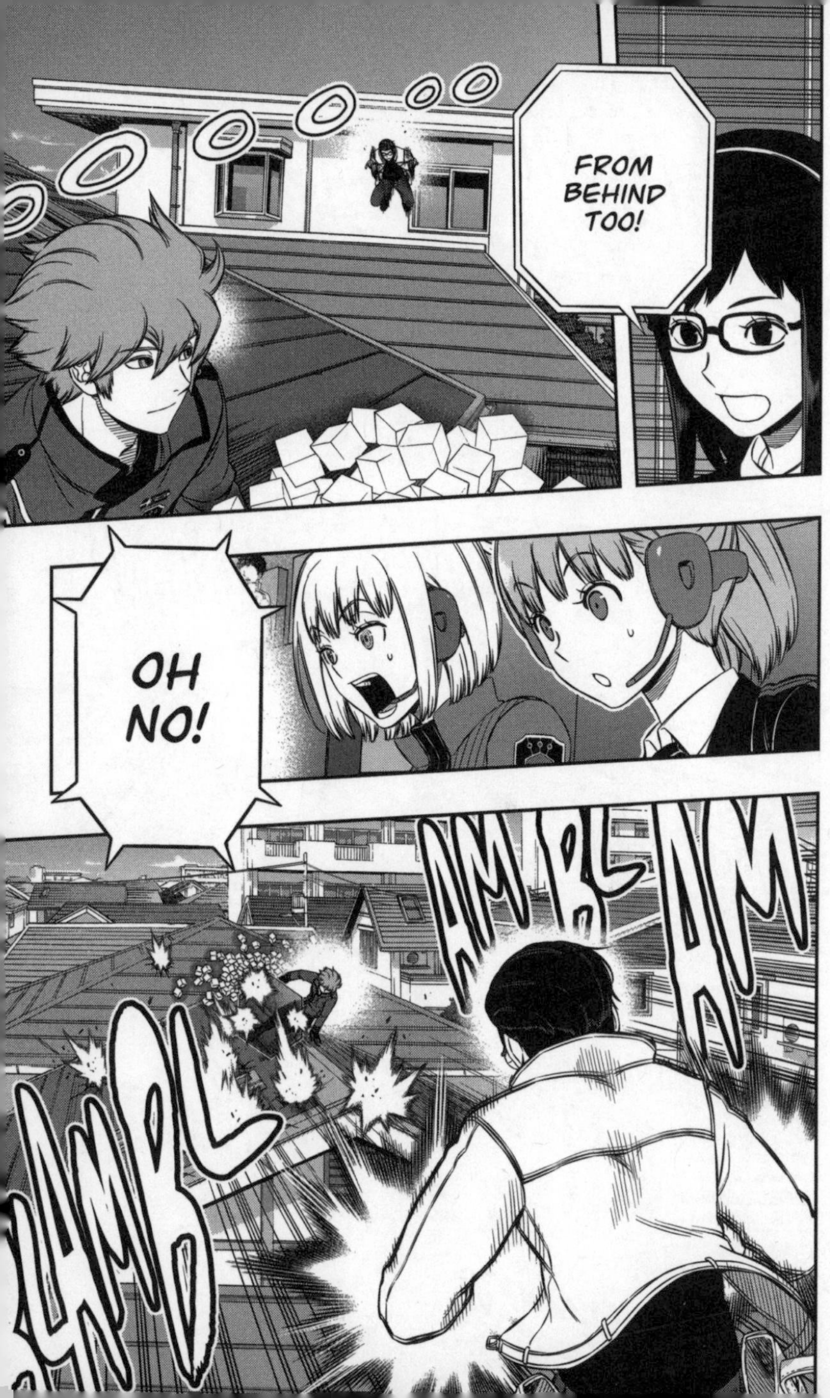
FROM BEHIND TOO!
OH NO!

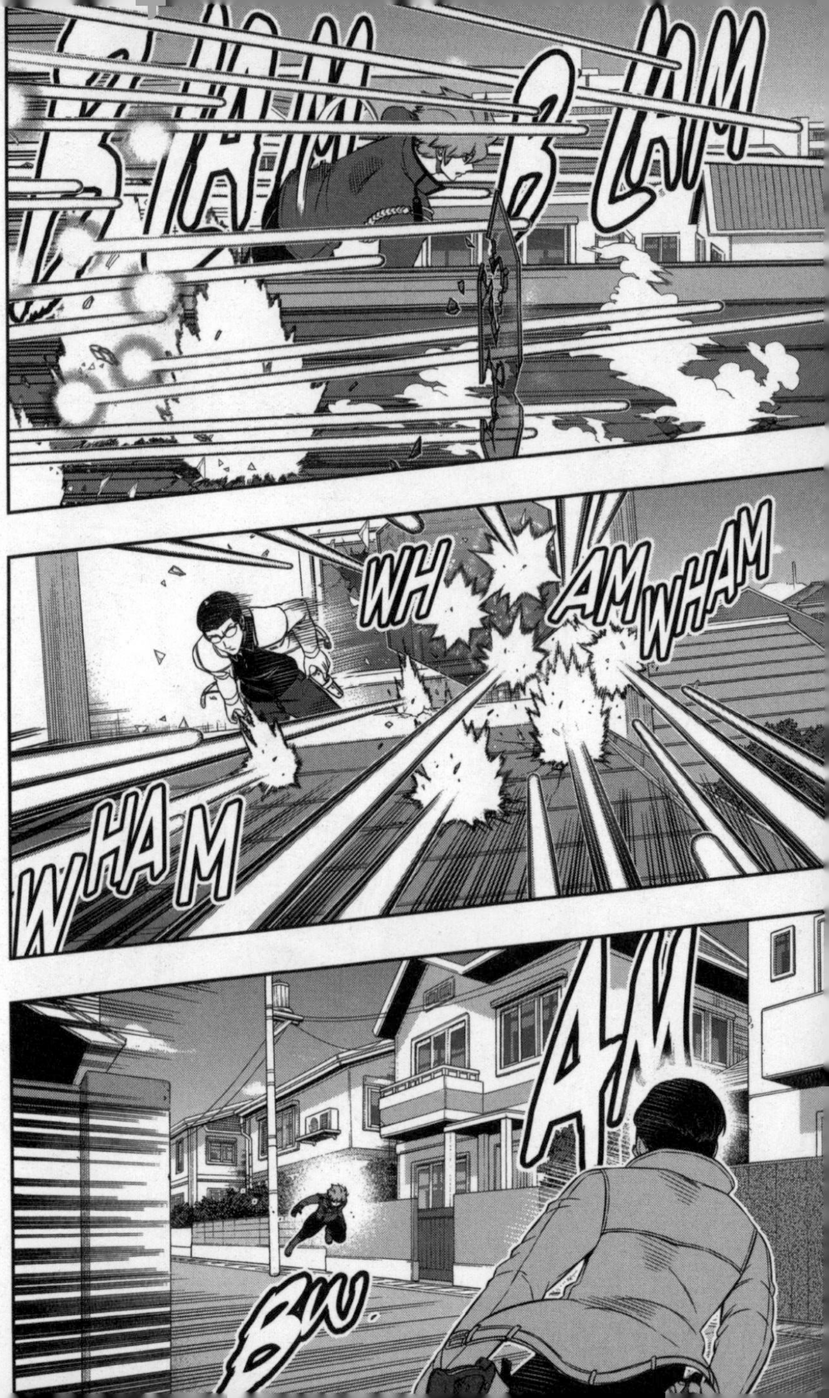
BLAM
BLAM
WHAM
WHAM
WHAM
AM
BA.

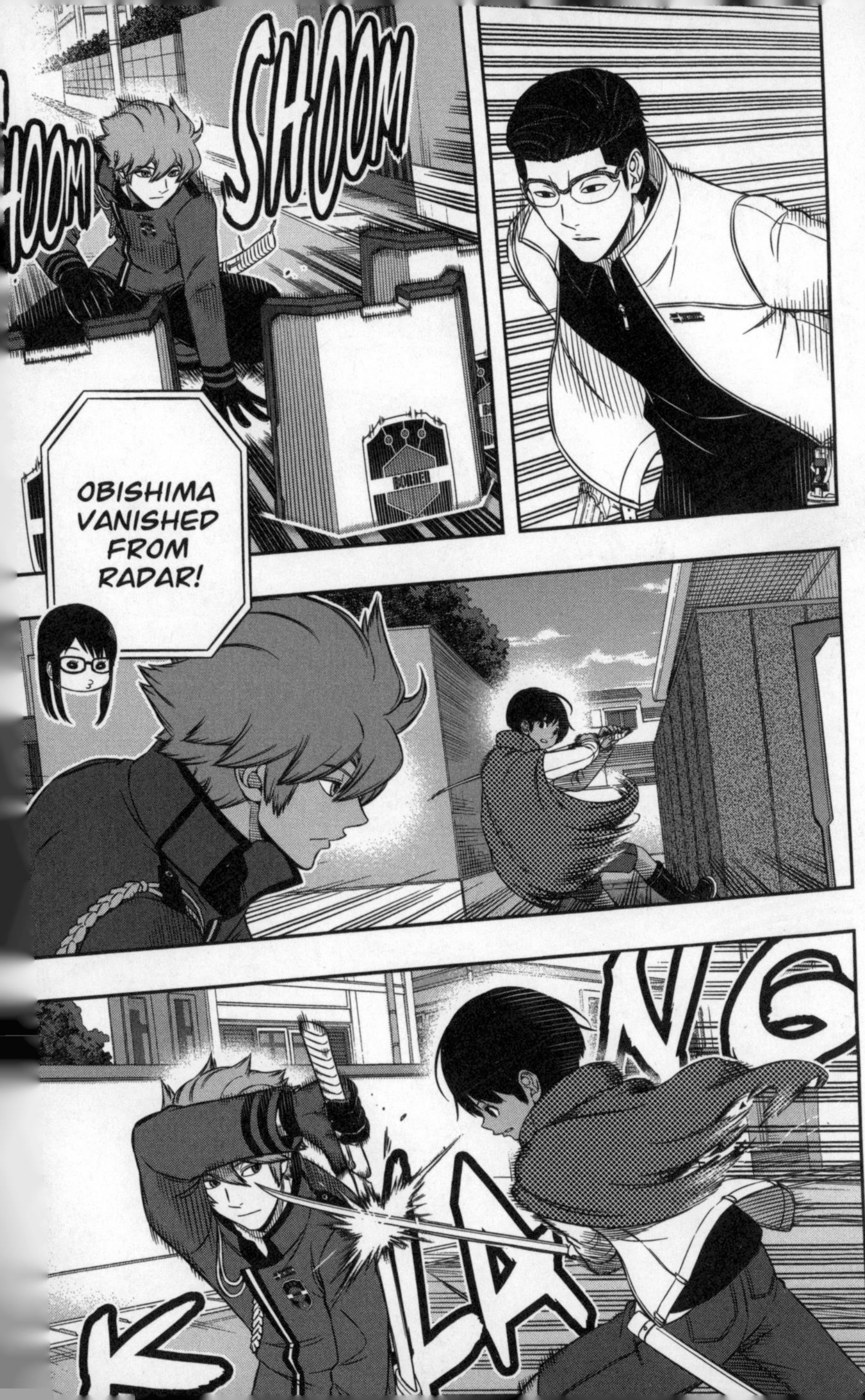
SHOOM
HOOM
OBISHIMA VANISHED FROM RADAR!
KLANG

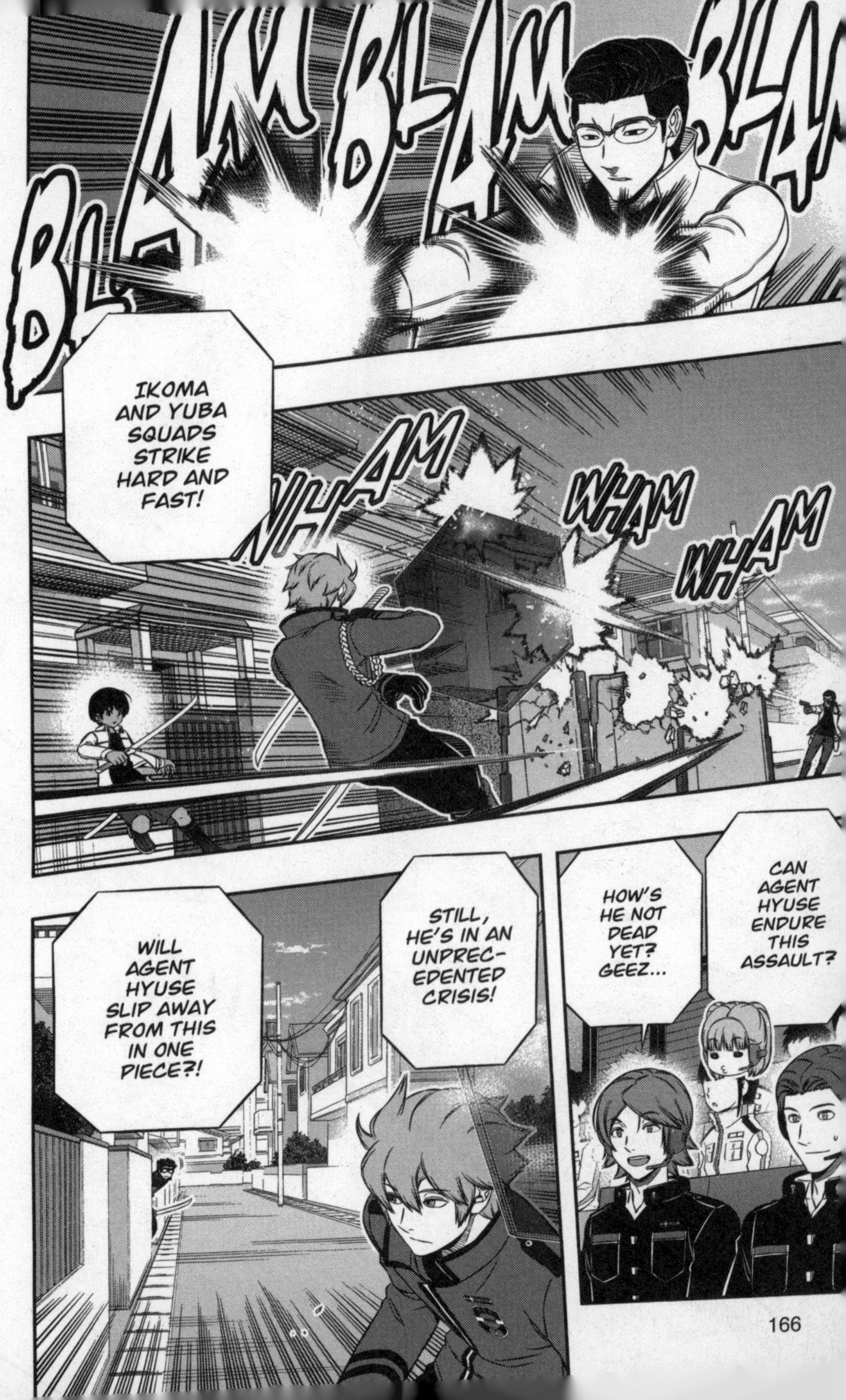
BLAM BLAM
IKOMA AND YUBA SQUADS STRIKE HARD AND FAST!
WHAM
WHAM
WHAM
CAN AGENT HYUSE ENDURE THIS ASSAULT?
HOW'S HE NOT DEAD YET? GEEZ...
STILL, HE'S IN AN UNPREC-EDENTED CRISIS!
WILL AGENT HYUSE SLIP AWAY FROM THIS IN ONE PIECE?!

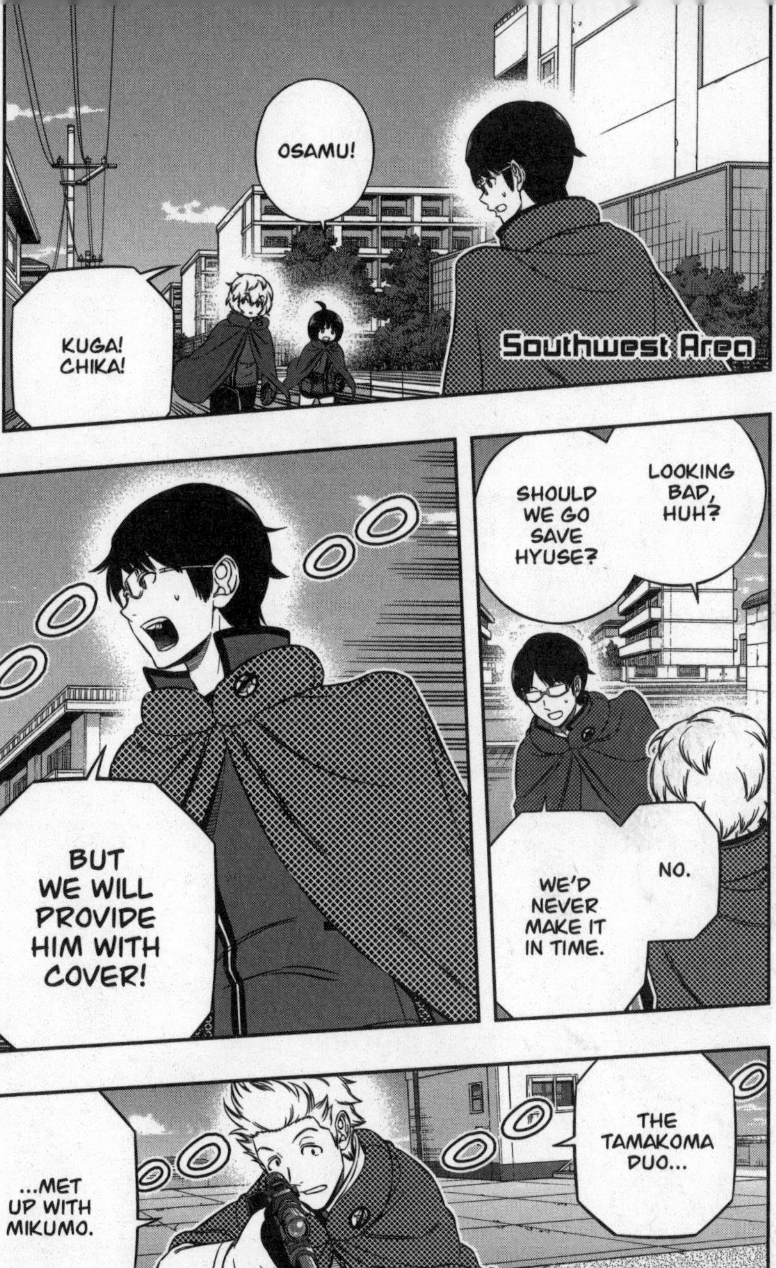
Southwest Area
OSAMU!
KUGA! CHIKA!
LOOKING BAD, HUH?
SHOULD WE GO SAVE HYUSE?
NO.
WE'D NEVER MAKE IT IN TIME.
BUT WE WILL PROVIDE HIM WITH COVER!
THE TAMAKOMA DUO...
...MET UP WITH MIKUMO.

Even More:

The Schools of Mikado City (Part 4)

Seirin Girls' Academy (Middle + High School)

A girls' school located far to the west of the Forbidden Zone, past Tamakoma Branch. It looks old-fashioned on the outside, but inside, it's all high-tech. Given the distance from the forbidden zone, most students here think of the Neighbor problem as being no skin off their noses. They treat classmates affiliated with Border as hometown heroes and celebrities.

Mikado City Public High School 01

A Border-affiliated school located west-southwest of the Forbidden Zone. Students can still graduate even if they take tons of time off for missions and training. Since most classes have at least a few agents in them, Border affiliates aren't seen as anything special. Many students here were victims of past Neighbor attacks, so they're excused from school fees in accordance with how much they've suffered.

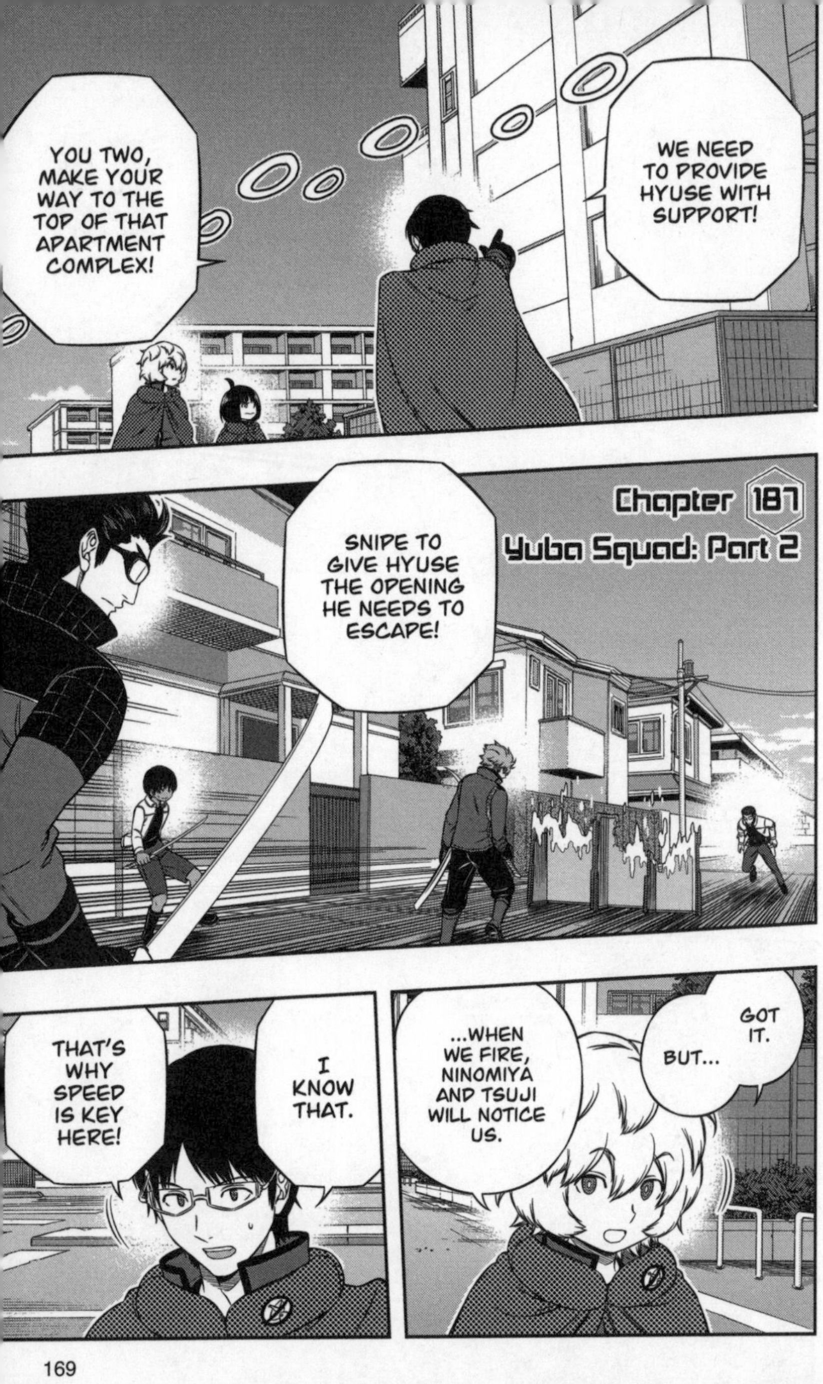
WE NEED TO PROVIDE HYUSE WITH SUPPORT!
YOU TWO, MAKE YOUR WAY TO THE TOP OF THAT APARTMENT COMPLEX!
Chapter 187
Yuba Squad: Part 2
SNIPE TO GIVE HYUSE THE OPENING HE NEEDS TO ESCAPE!
GOT IT.
BUT...
...WHEN WE FIRE, NINOMIYA AND TSUJI WILL NOTICE US.
I KNOW THAT.
THAT'S WHY SPEED IS KEY HERE!

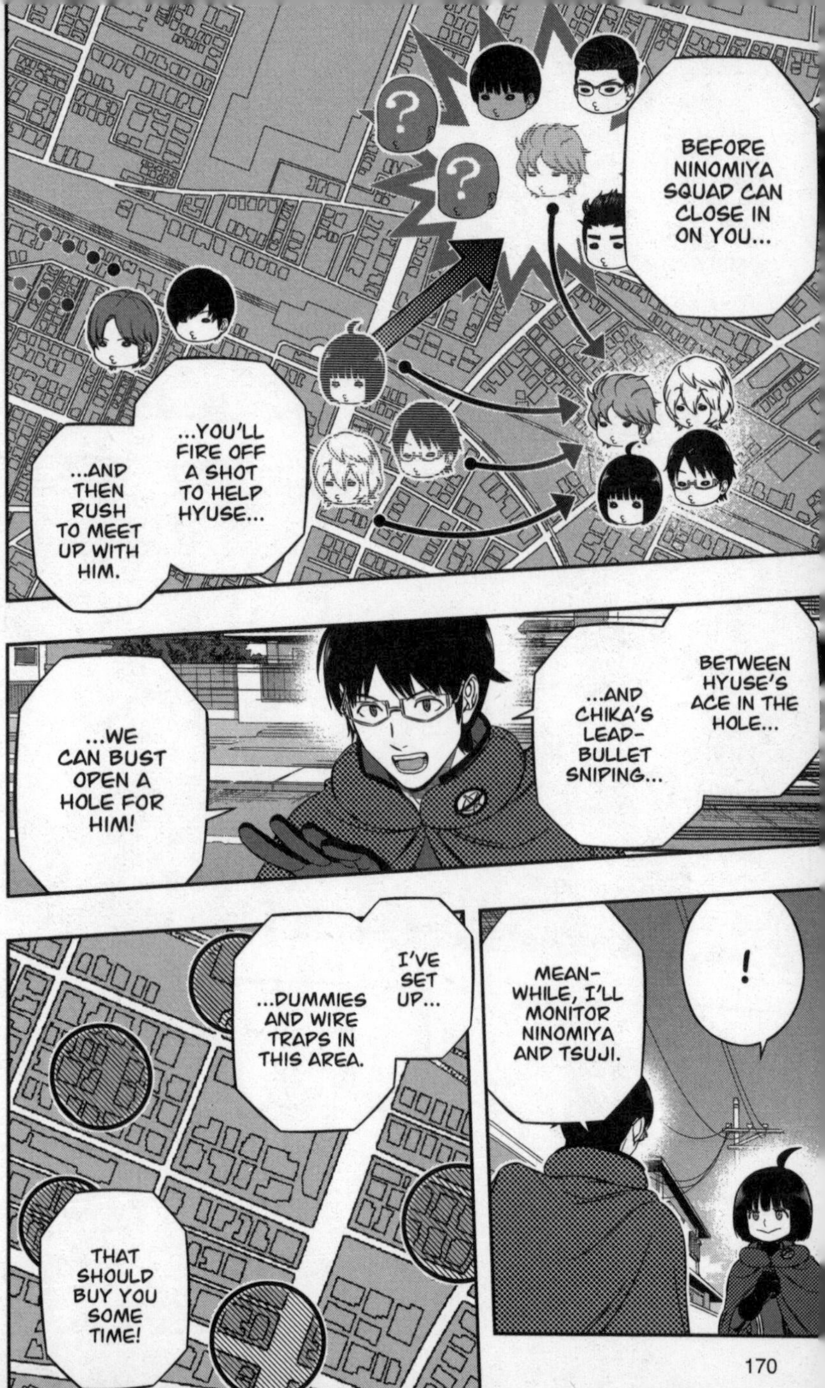
BEFORE NINOMIYA SQUAD CAN CLOSE IN ON YOU...
...YOU'LL FIRE OFF A SHOT TO HELP HYUSE...
...AND THEN RUSH TO MEET UP WITH HIM.
BETWEEN HYUSE'S ACE IN THE HOLE...
...AND CHIKA'S LEAD-BULLET SNIPING...
...WE CAN BUST OPEN A HOLE FOR HIM!
!
MEAN-WHILE, I'LL MONITOR NINOMIYA AND TSUJI.
I'VE SET UP...
...DUMMIES AND WIRE TRAPS IN THIS AREA.
THAT SHOULD BUY YOU SOME TIME!

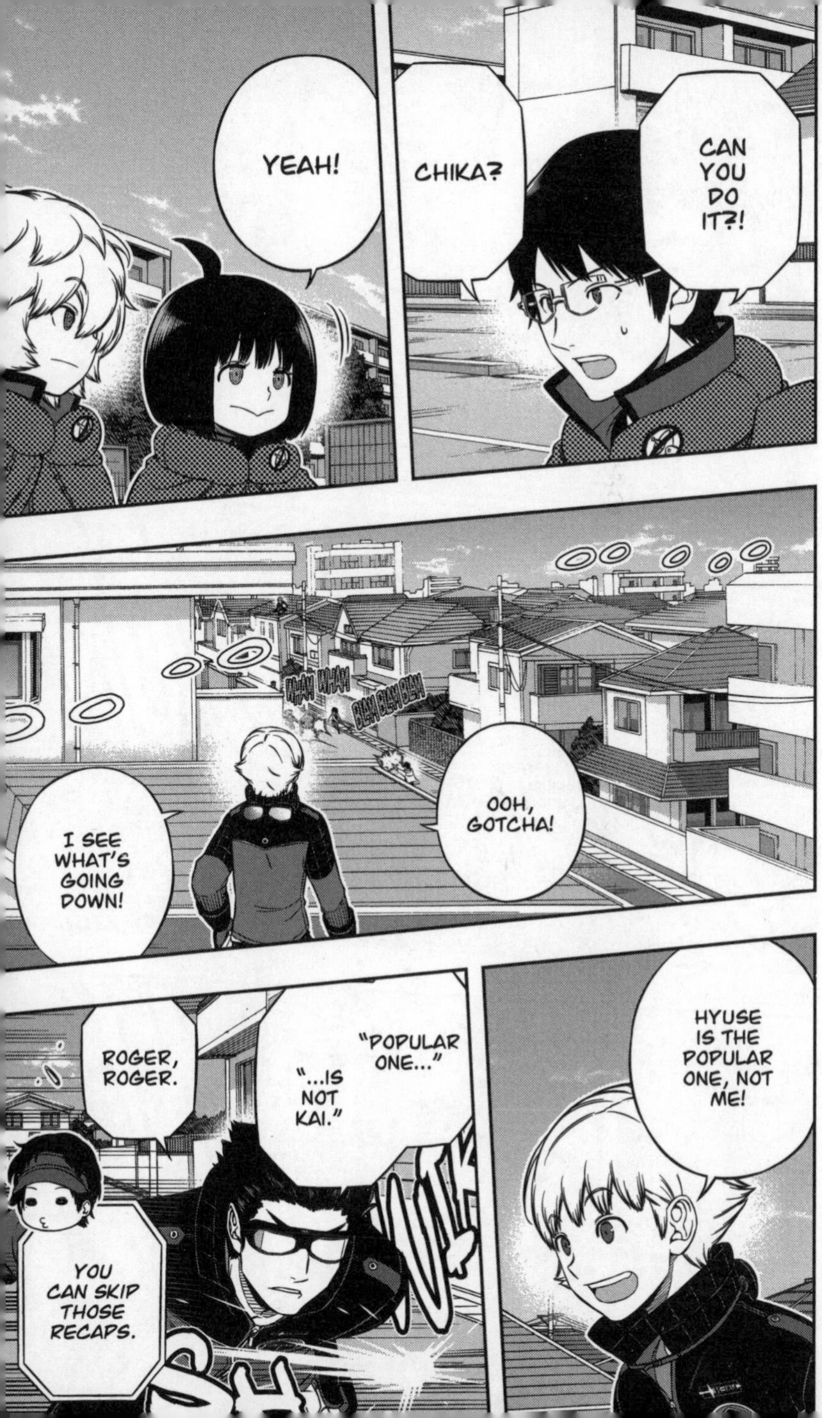
CAN YOU DO IT?!
CHIKA?
YEAH!
OOH, GOTCHA!
BLAH BLAH BLAH
WHAM WHAM
I SEE WHAT'S GOING DOWN!
HYUSE IS THE POPULAR ONE, NOT ME!
"POPULAR ONE..."
"...IS NOT KAI."
ROGER, ROGER.
YOU CAN SKIP THOSE RECAPS.

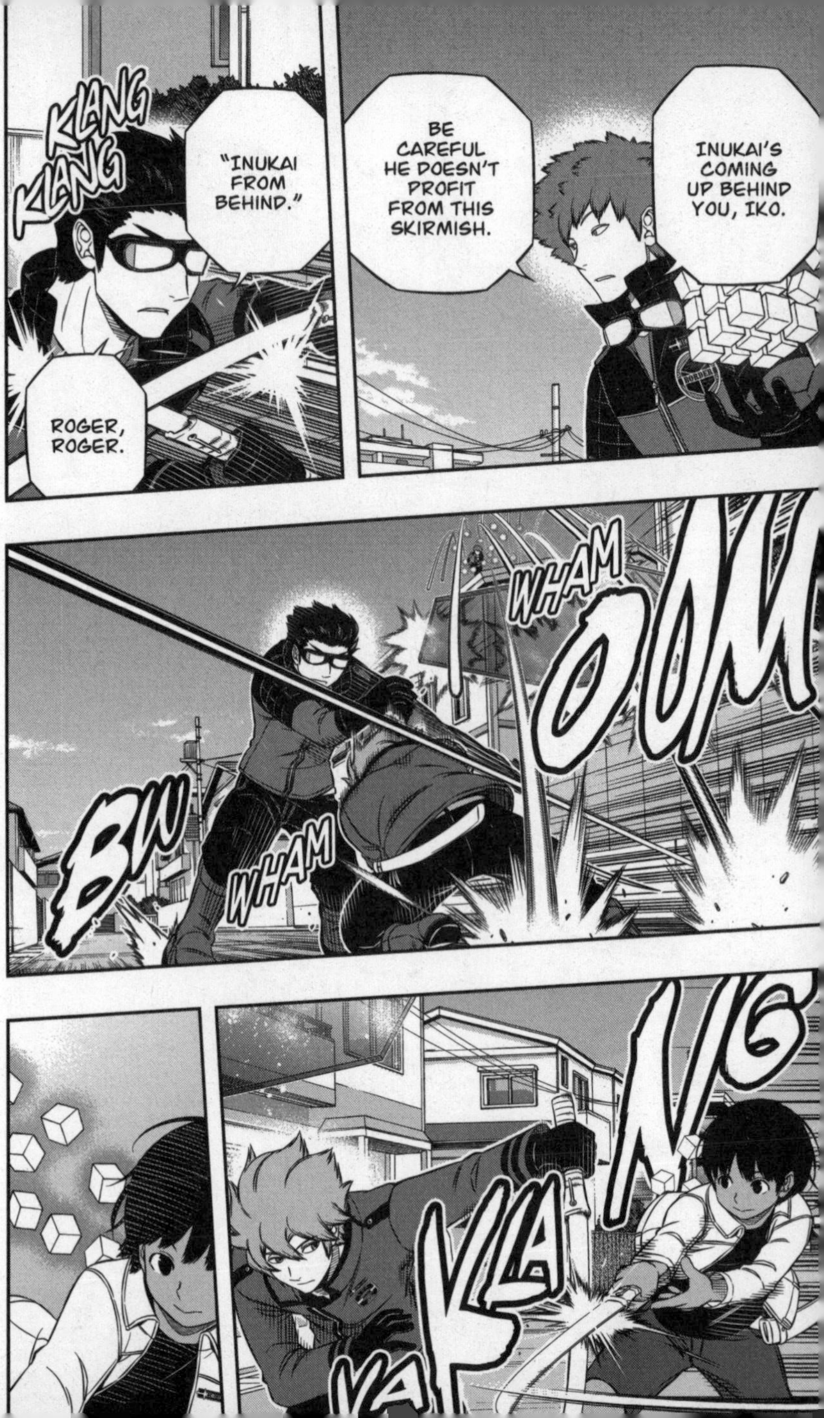
INUKAI'S COMING UP BEHIND YOU, IKO.
BE CAREFUL HE DOESN'T PROFIT FROM THIS SKIRMISH.
KLANG KLANG
"INUKAI FROM BEHIND."
ROGER, ROGER.
WHAM
OOM
BW
WHAM
NG
KLA

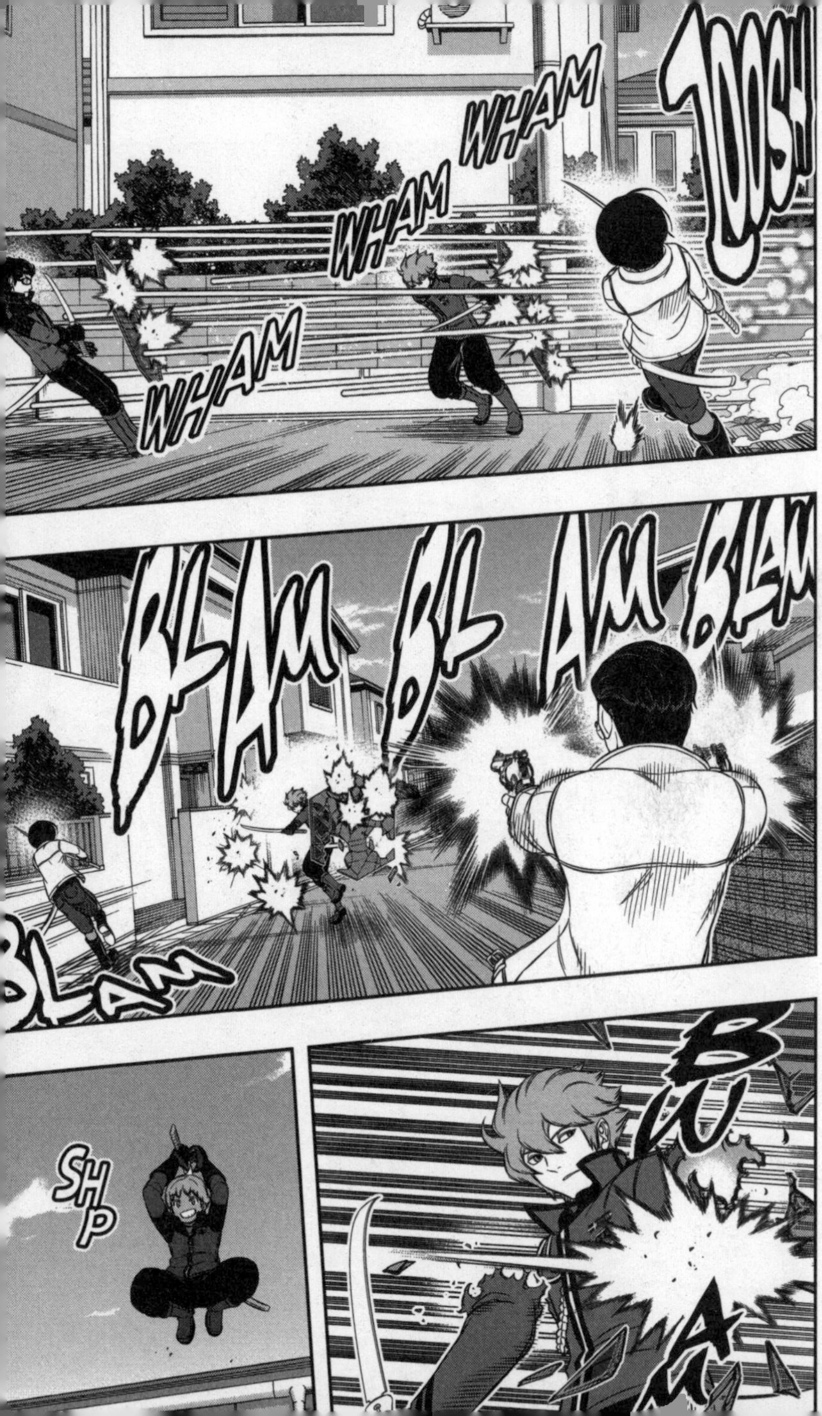
ZOOSH
WHAM
WHAM
WHAM
WHAM
BLAM
BLAM
BLAM
BLAM
BWA
SHP

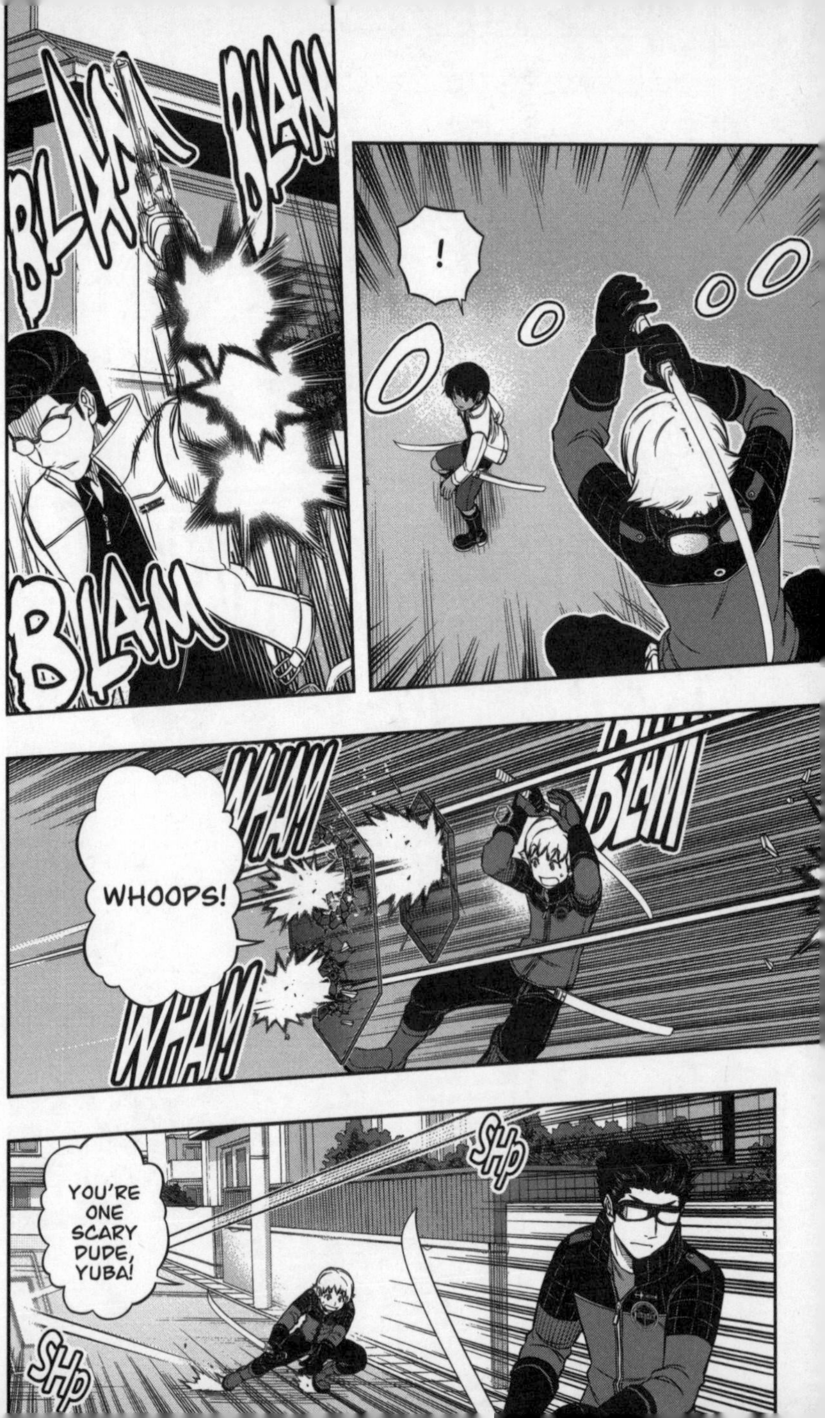
!
BLAM
BLAM
BLAM
BLAM
WHAM
WHOOPS!
WHAM
SHP
YOU'RE ONE SCARY DUDE, YUBA!
SHP

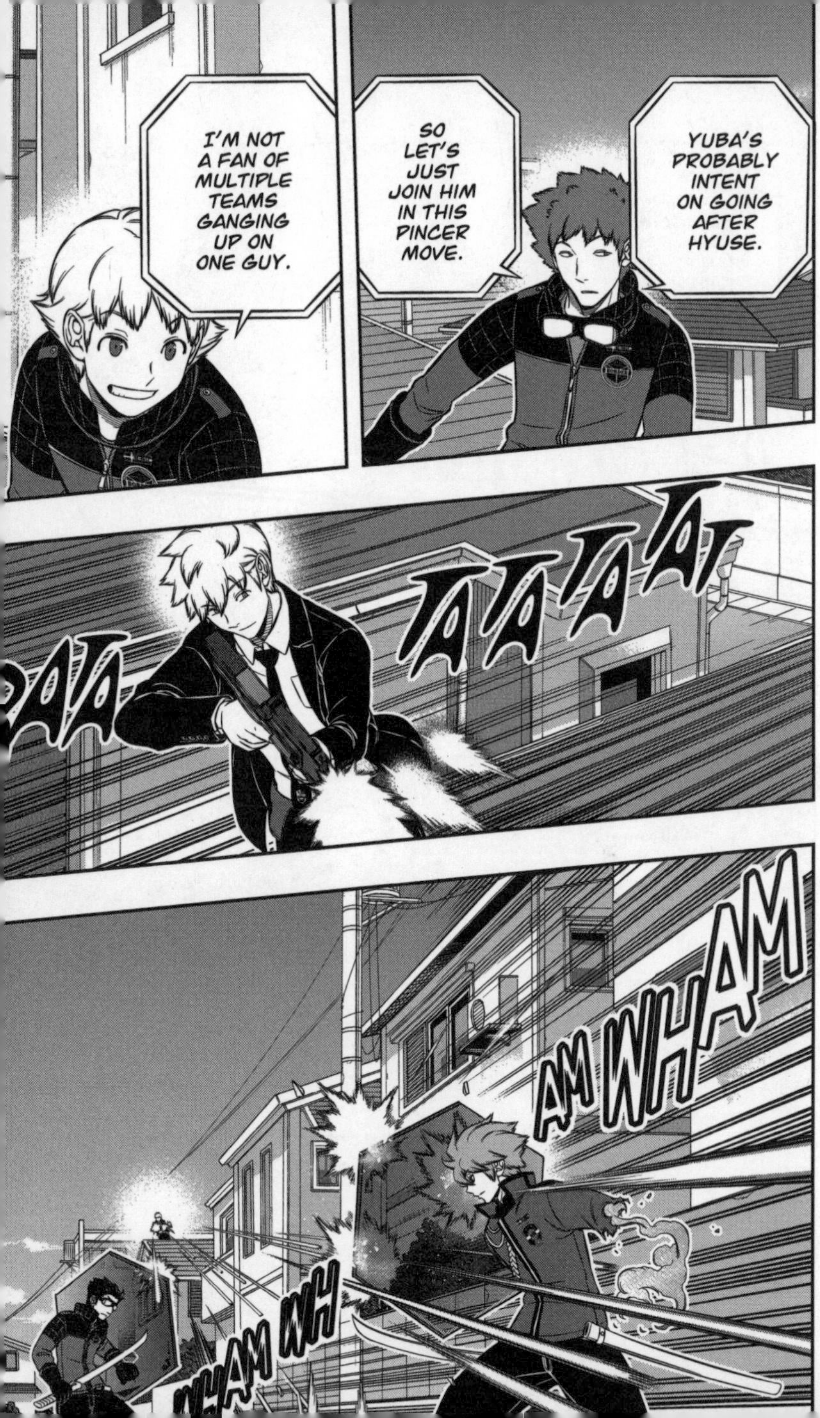

YUBA'S PROBABLY INTENT ON GOING AFTER HYUSE.
SO LET'S JUST JOIN HIM IN THIS PINCER MOVE.
I'M NOT A FAN OF MULTIPLE TEAMS GANGING UP ON ONE GUY.
TATATAT
AM WHAM
WHAM WH

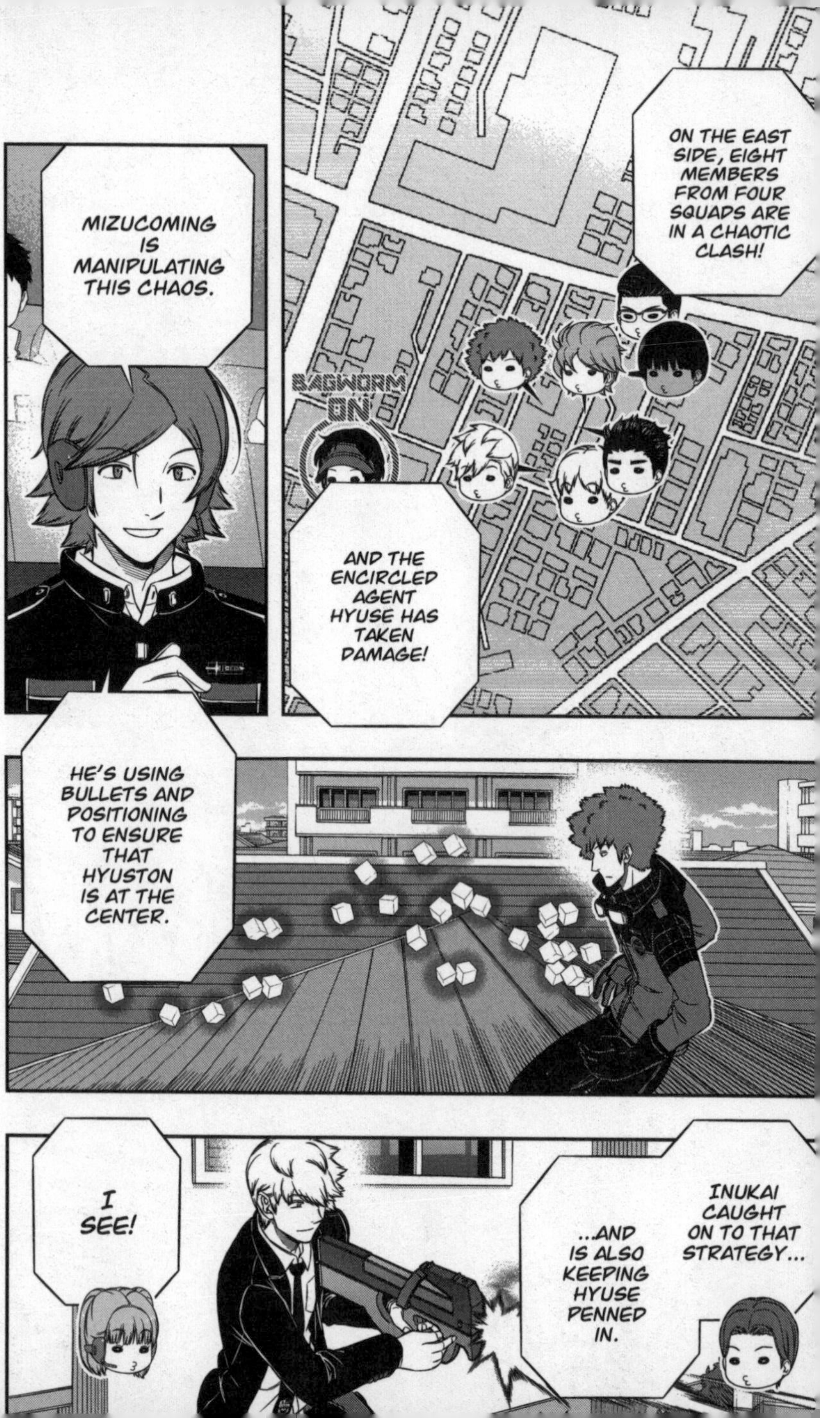
ON THE EAST SIDE, EIGHT MEMBERS FROM FOUR SQUADS ARE IN A CHAOTIC CLASH!
BAGWORM ON
AND THE ENCIRCLED AGENT HYUSE HAS TAKEN DAMAGE!
MIZUCOMING IS MANIPULATING THIS CHAOS.
HE'S USING BULLETS AND POSITIONING TO ENSURE THAT HYUSTON IS AT THE CENTER.
INUKAI CAUGHT ON TO THAT STRATEGY...
...AND IS ALSO KEEPING HYUSE PENNED IN.
I SEE!

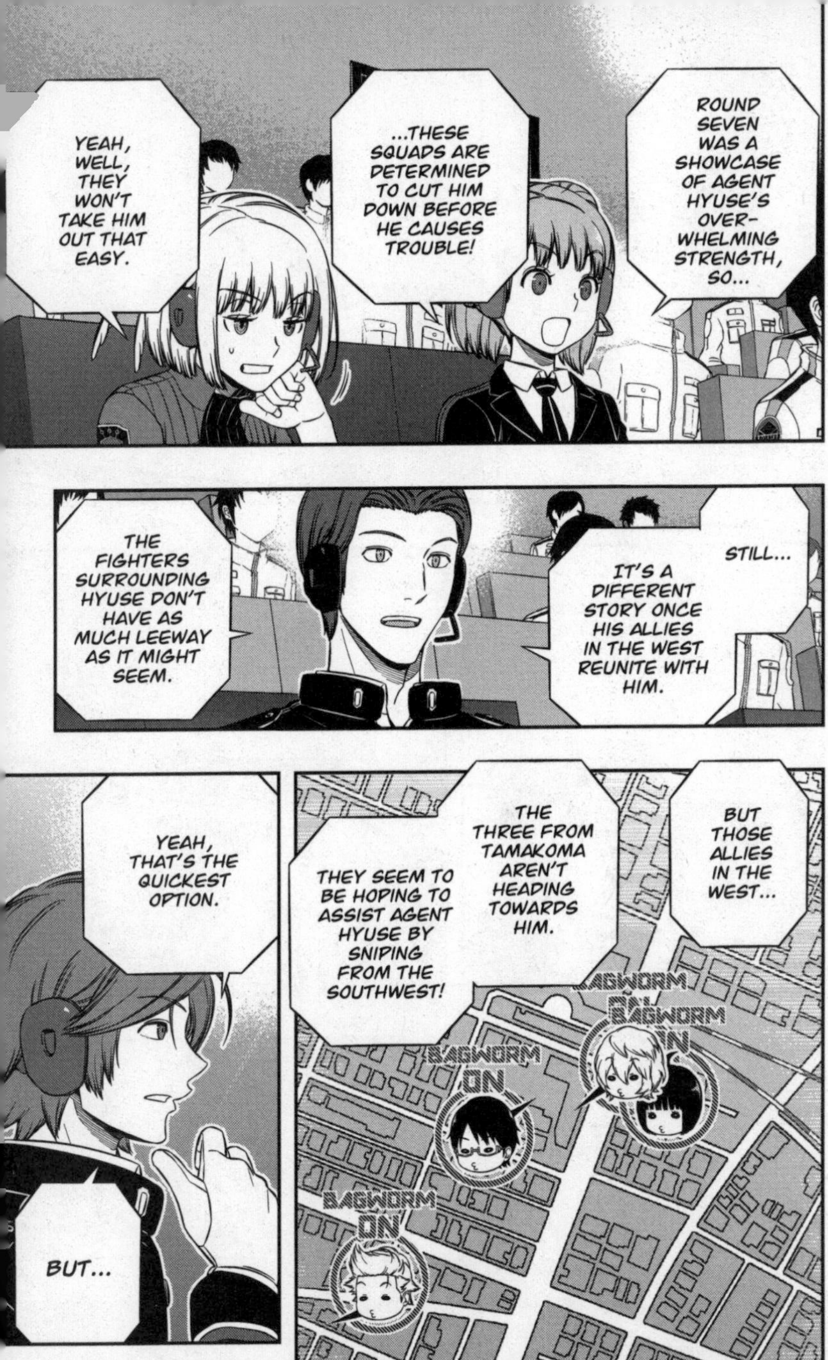
ROUND SEVEN WAS A SHOWCASE OF AGENT HYUSE'S OVER-WHELMING STRENGTH, SO...
...THESE SQUADS ARE DETERMINED TO CUT HIM DOWN BEFORE HE CAUSES TROUBLE!
YEAH, WELL, THEY WON'T TAKE HIM OUT THAT EASY.
STILL...
IT'S A DIFFERENT STORY ONCE HIS ALLIES IN THE WEST REUNITE WITH HIM.
THE FIGHTERS SURROUNDING HYUSE DON'T HAVE AS MUCH LEEWAY AS IT MIGHT SEEM.
BUT THOSE ALLIES IN THE WEST...
THE THREE FROM TAMAKOMA AREN'T HEADING TOWARDS HIM.
THEY SEEM TO BE HOPING TO ASSIST AGENT HYUSE BY SNIPING FROM THE SOUTHWEST!
BAGWORM ON
BAGWORM ON
BAGWORM ON
BAGWORM ON
YEAH, THAT'S THE QUICKEST OPTION.
BUT...

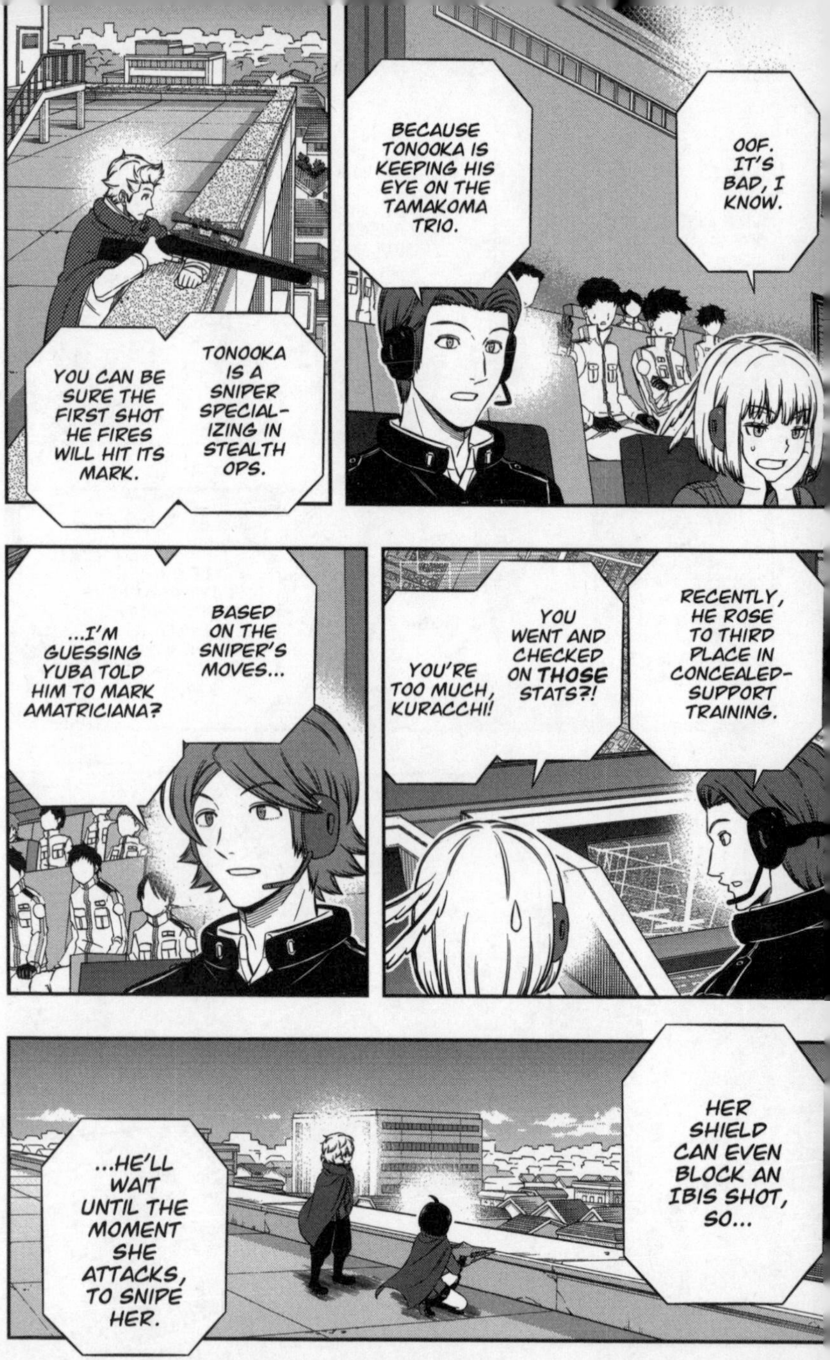
OOF. IT'S BAD, I KNOW.
BECAUSE TONOOKA IS KEEPING HIS EYE ON THE TAMAKOMA TRIO.
TONOOKA IS A SNIPER SPECIALIZING IN STEALTH OPS.
YOU CAN BE SURE THE FIRST SHOT HE FIRES WILL HIT ITS MARK.
RECENTLY, HE ROSE TO THIRD PLACE IN CONCEALED-SUPPORT TRAINING.
YOU WENT AND CHECKED ON THOSE STATS?!
YOU'RE TOO MUCH, KURACCHI!
BASED ON THE SNIPER'S MOVES...
...I'M GUESSING YUBA TOLD HIM TO MARK AMATRICIANA?
HER SHIELD CAN EVEN BLOCK AN IBIS SHOT, SO...
...HE'LL WAIT UNTIL THE MOMENT SHE ATTACKS, TO SNIPE HER.

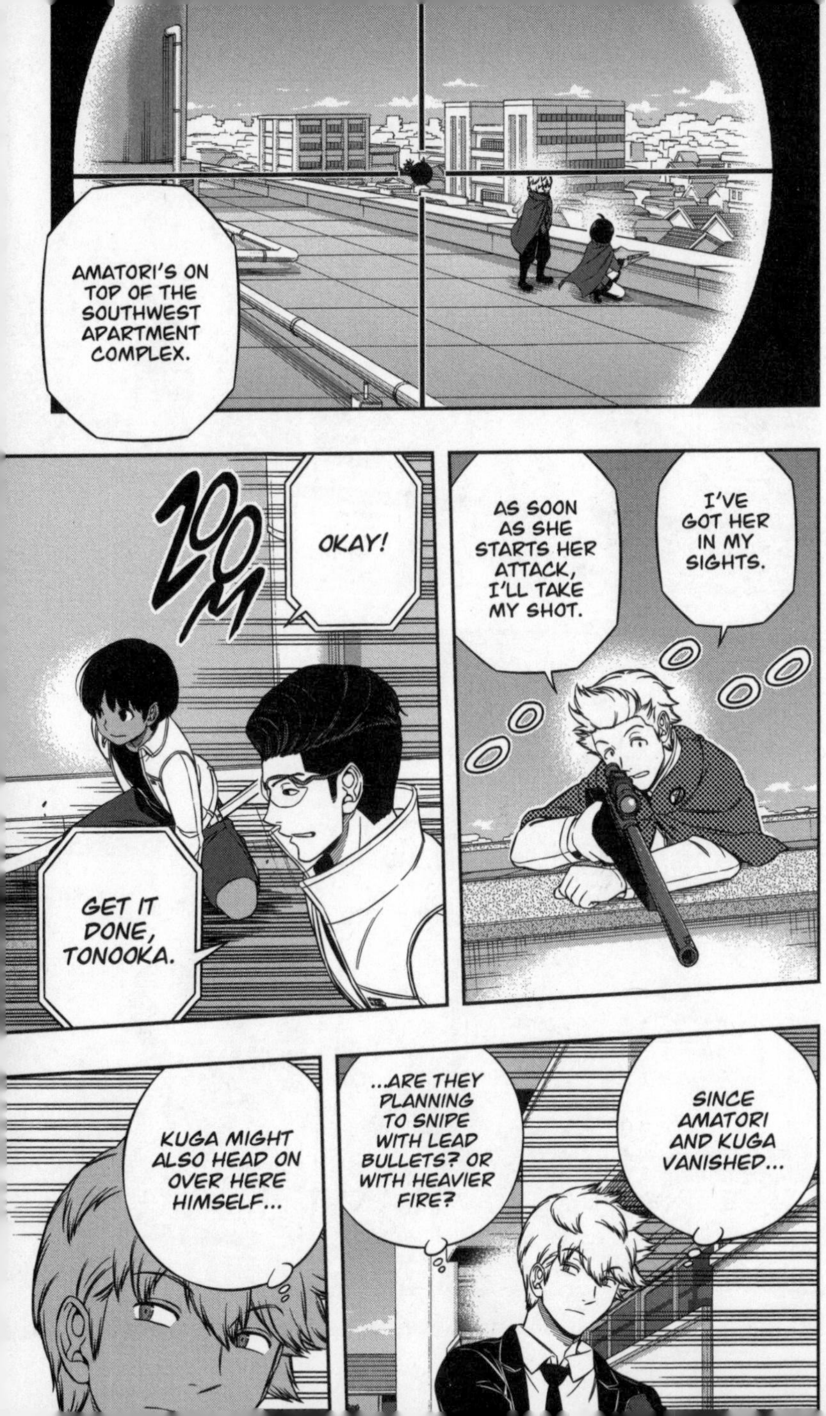
AMATORI'S ON TOP OF THE SOUTHWEST APARTMENT COMPLEX.
I'VE GOT HER IN MY SIGHTS.
AS SOON AS SHE STARTS HER ATTACK, I'LL TAKE MY SHOT.
ZOOM
OKAY!
GET IT DONE, TONOOKA.
SINCE AMATORI AND KUGA VANISHED...
...ARE THEY PLANNING TO SNIPE WITH LEAD BULLETS? OR WITH HEAVIER FIRE?
KUGA MIGHT ALSO HEAD ON OVER HERE HIMSELF...

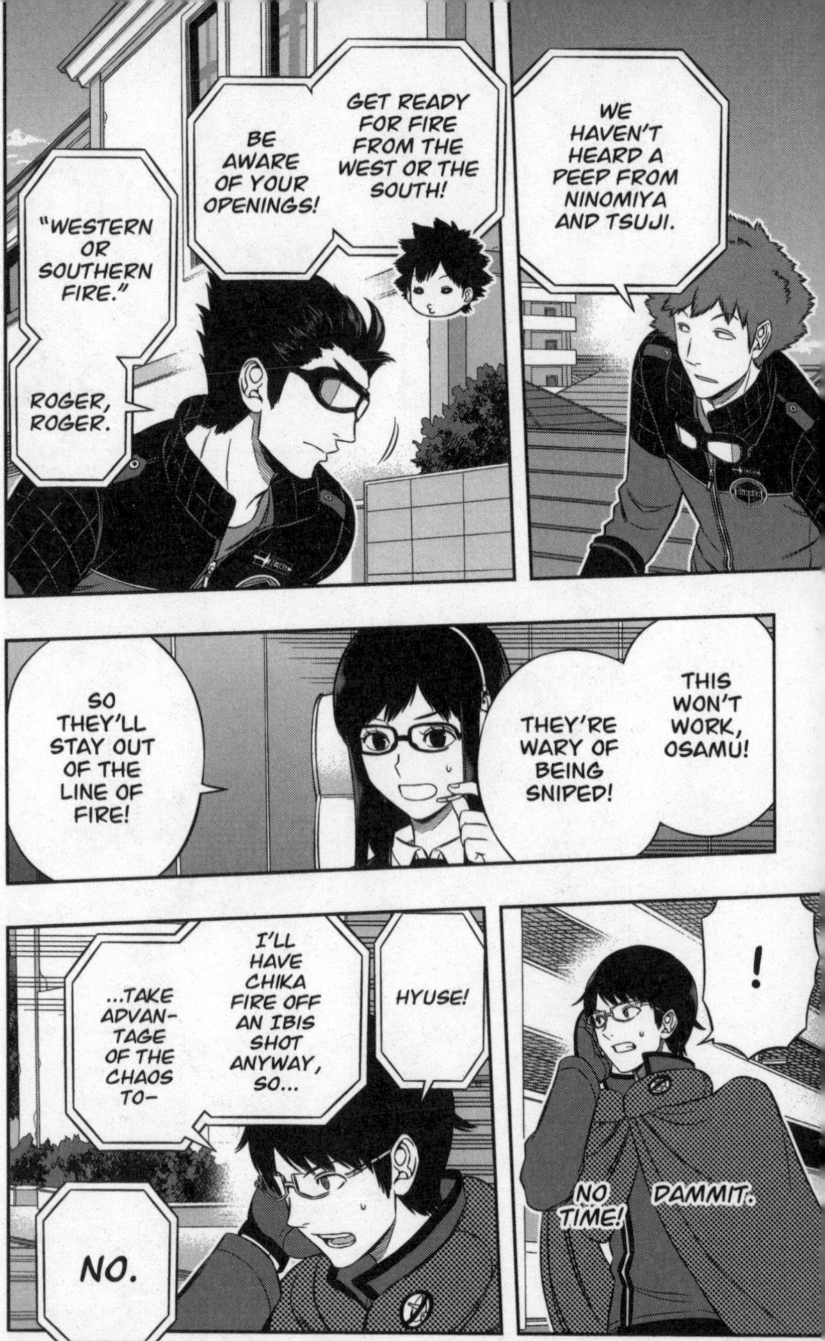
WE HAVEN'T HEARD A PEEP FROM NINOMIYA AND TSUJI.
GET READY FOR FIRE FROM THE WEST OR THE SOUTH!
BE AWARE OF YOUR OPENINGS!
"WESTERN OR SOUTHERN FIRE."
ROGER, ROGER.
THIS WON'T WORK, OSAMU!
THEY'RE WARY OF BEING SNIPED!
SO THEY'LL STAY OUT OF THE LINE OF FIRE!
!
DAMMIT.
NO TIME!
HYUSE!
I'LL HAVE CHIKA FIRE OFF AN IBIS SHOT ANYWAY, SO...
...TAKE ADVAN-TAGE OF THE CHAOS TO-
NO.

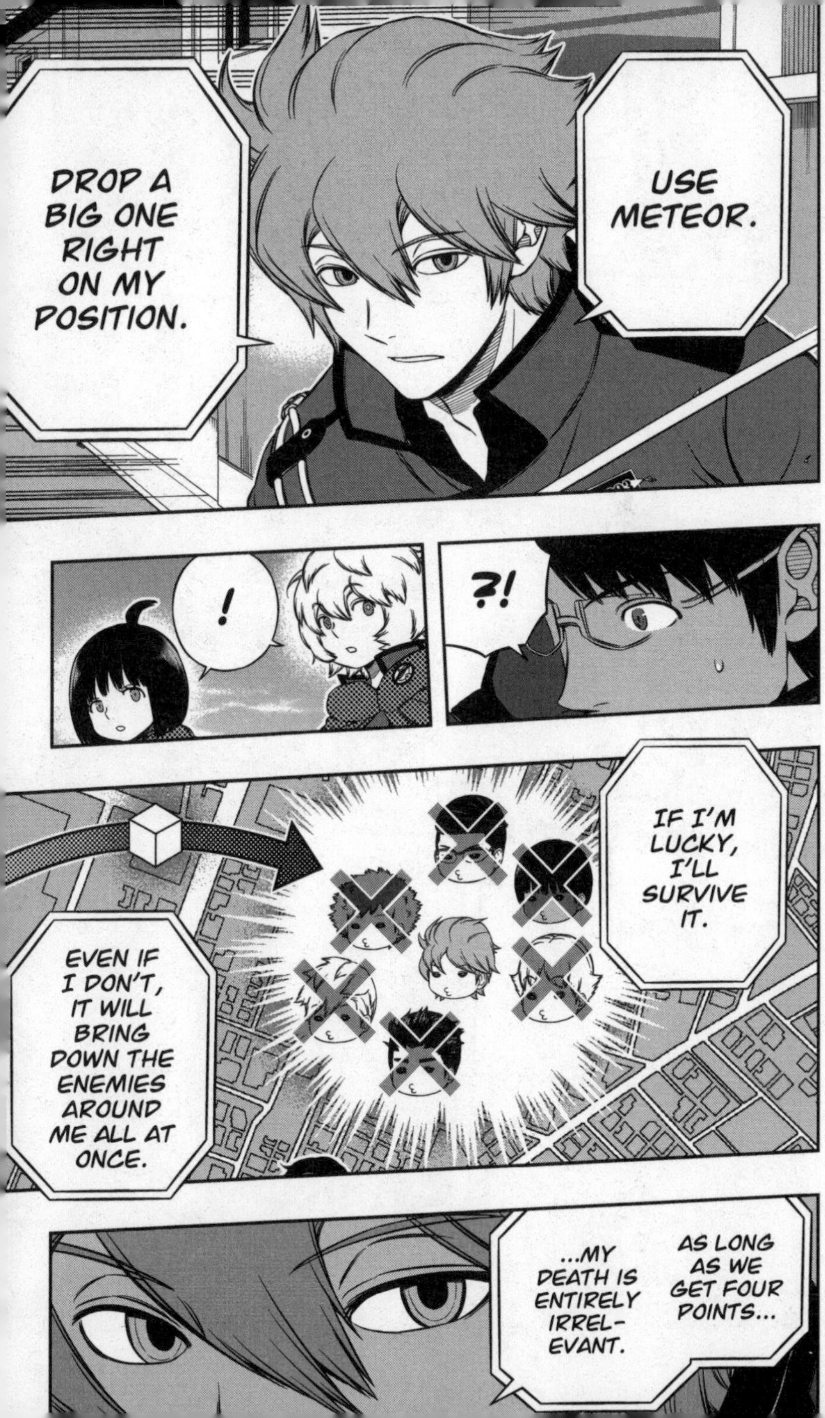
USE METEOR.
DROP A BIG ONE RIGHT ON MY POSITION.
?!
!
IF I'M LUCKY, I'LL SURVIVE IT.
EVEN IF I DON'T, IT WILL BRING DOWN THE ENEMIES AROUND ME ALL AT ONCE.
AS LONG AS WE GET FOUR POINTS...
...MY DEATH IS ENTIRELY IRREL- EVANT.

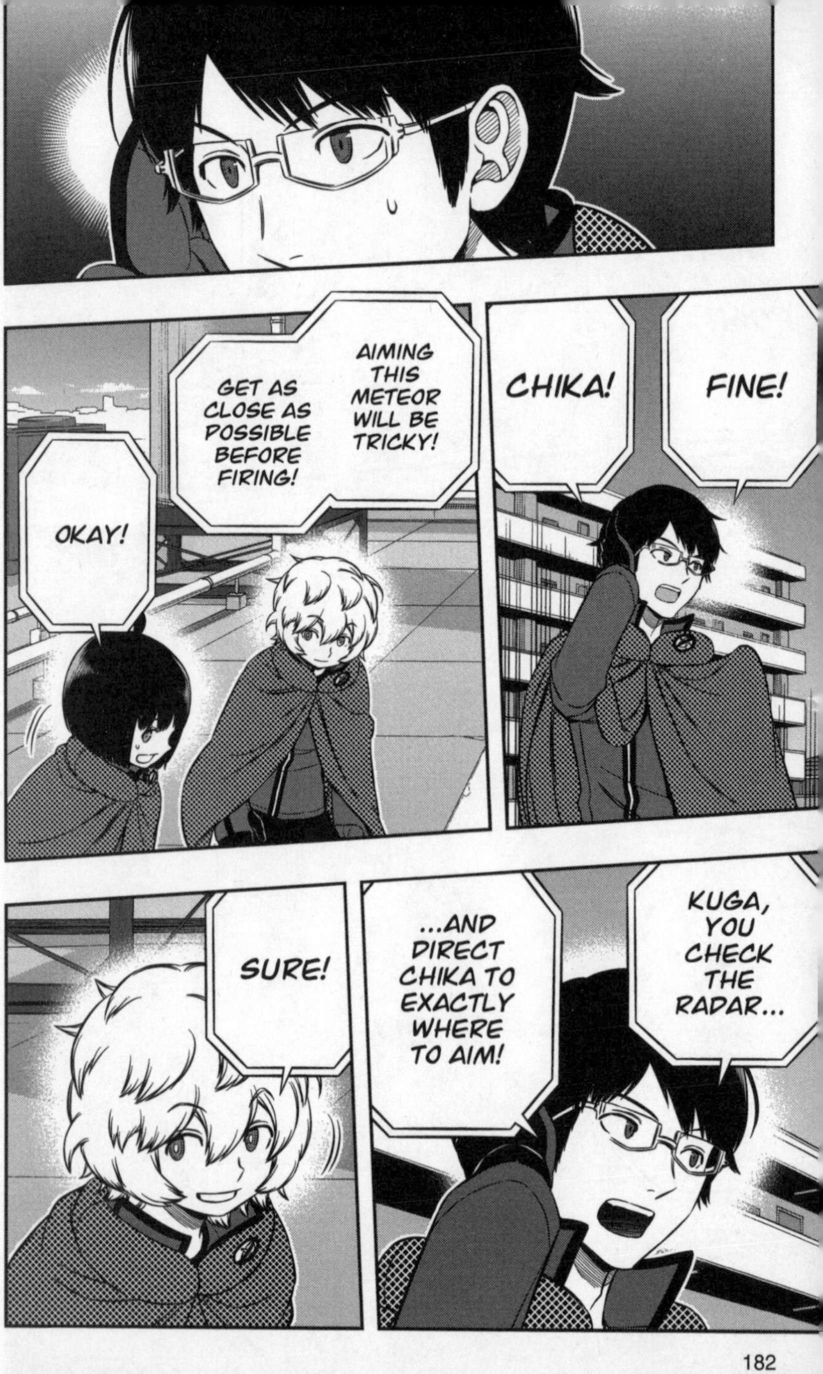
FINE!
CHIKA!
AIMING THIS METEOR WILL BE TRICKY!
GET AS CLOSE AS POSSIBLE BEFORE FIRING!
OKAY!
KUGA, YOU CHECK THE RADAR...
...AND DIRECT CHIKA TO EXACTLY WHERE TO AIM!
SURE!

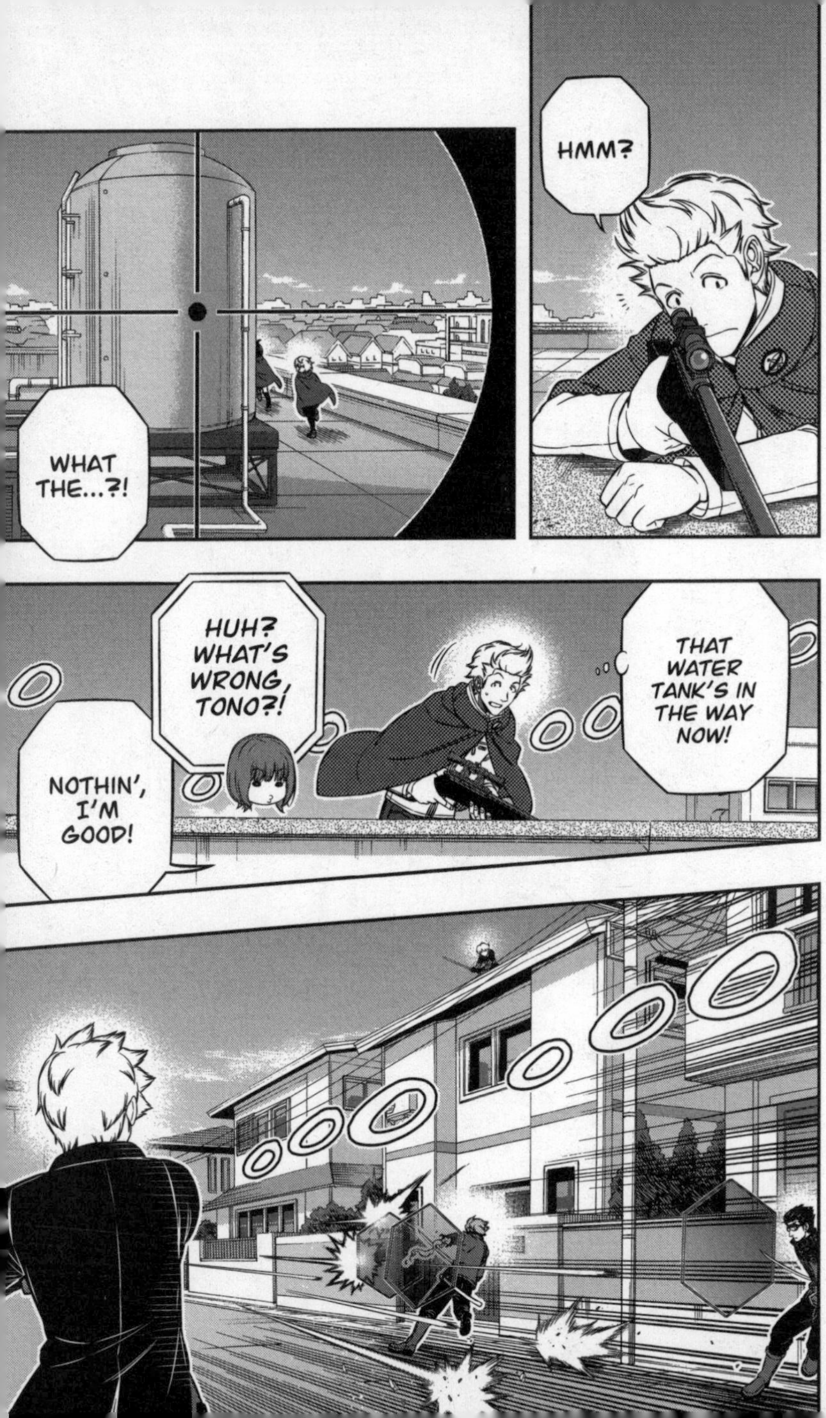
HMM?
WHAT THE...?!
THAT WATER TANK'S IN THE WAY NOW!
HUH? WHAT'S WRONG, TONO?!
NOTHIN', I'M GOOD!

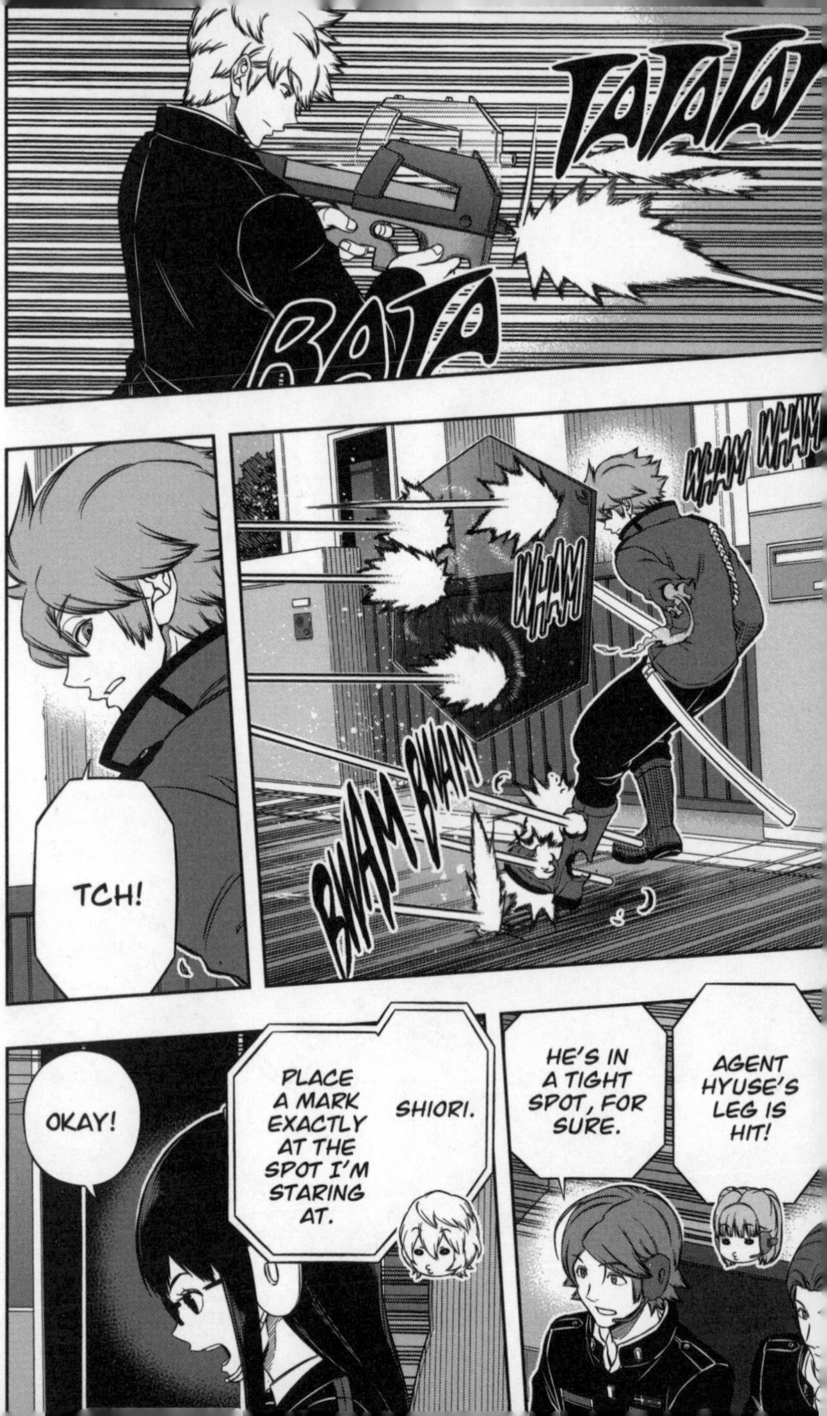
TATATA
BATA
WHAM WHAM
WHAM
BWAM BWAM
TCH!
AGENT HYUSE'S LEG IS HIT!
HE'S IN A TIGHT SPOT, FOR SURE.
SHIORI.
PLACE A MARK EXACTLY AT THE SPOT I'M STARING AT.
OKAY!

TARGET
TARGET LOCKED!
METEOR!
KA-BOOM...

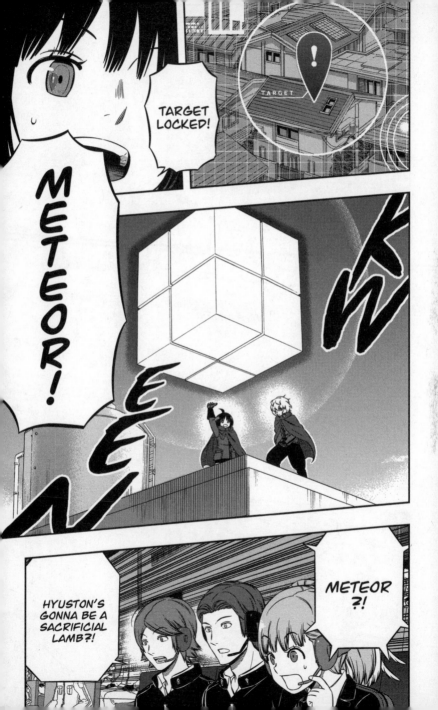

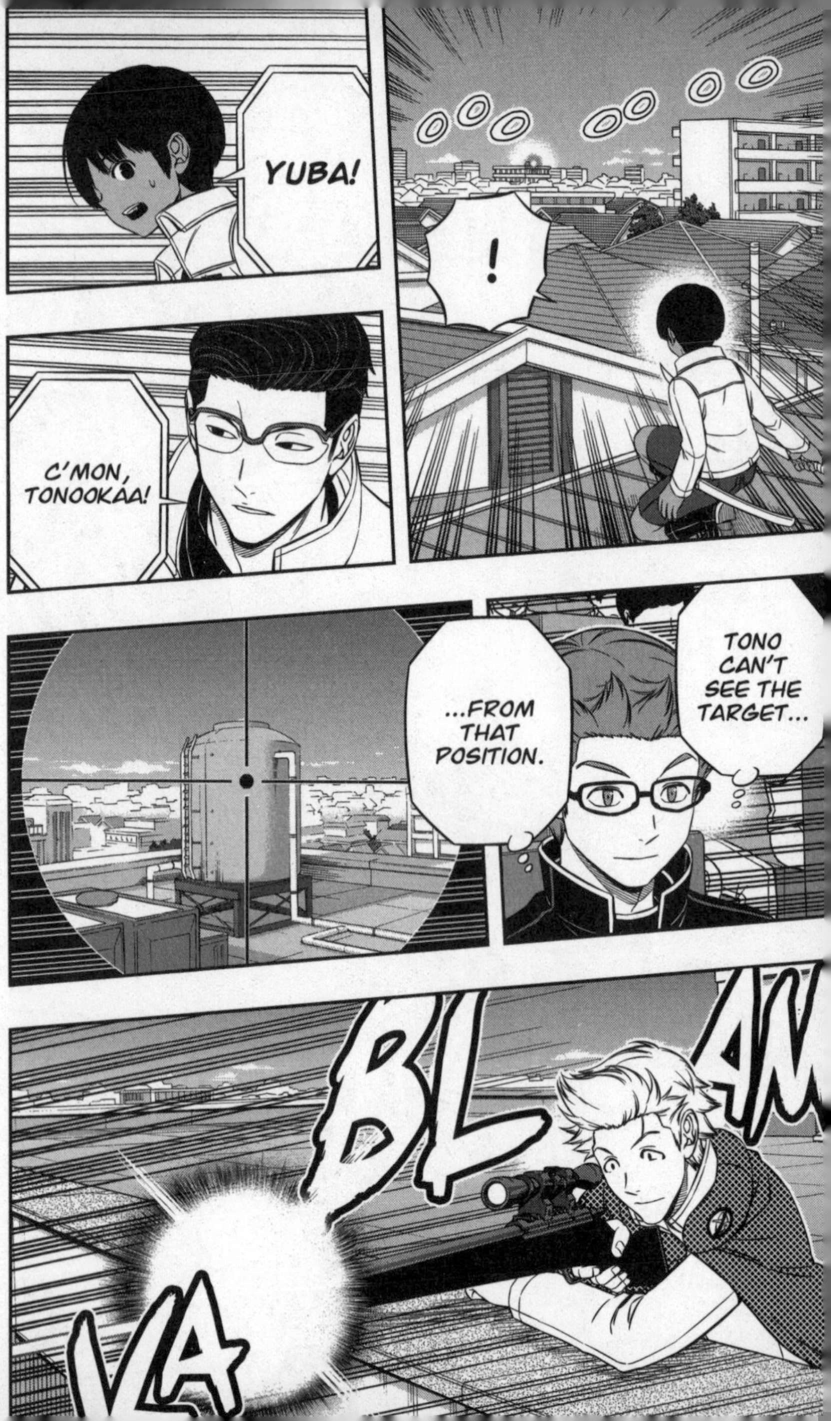
!
YUBA!
C'MON, TONOOKAA!
TONO CAN'T SEE THE TARGET...
...FROM THAT POSITION.
BLAM
VA

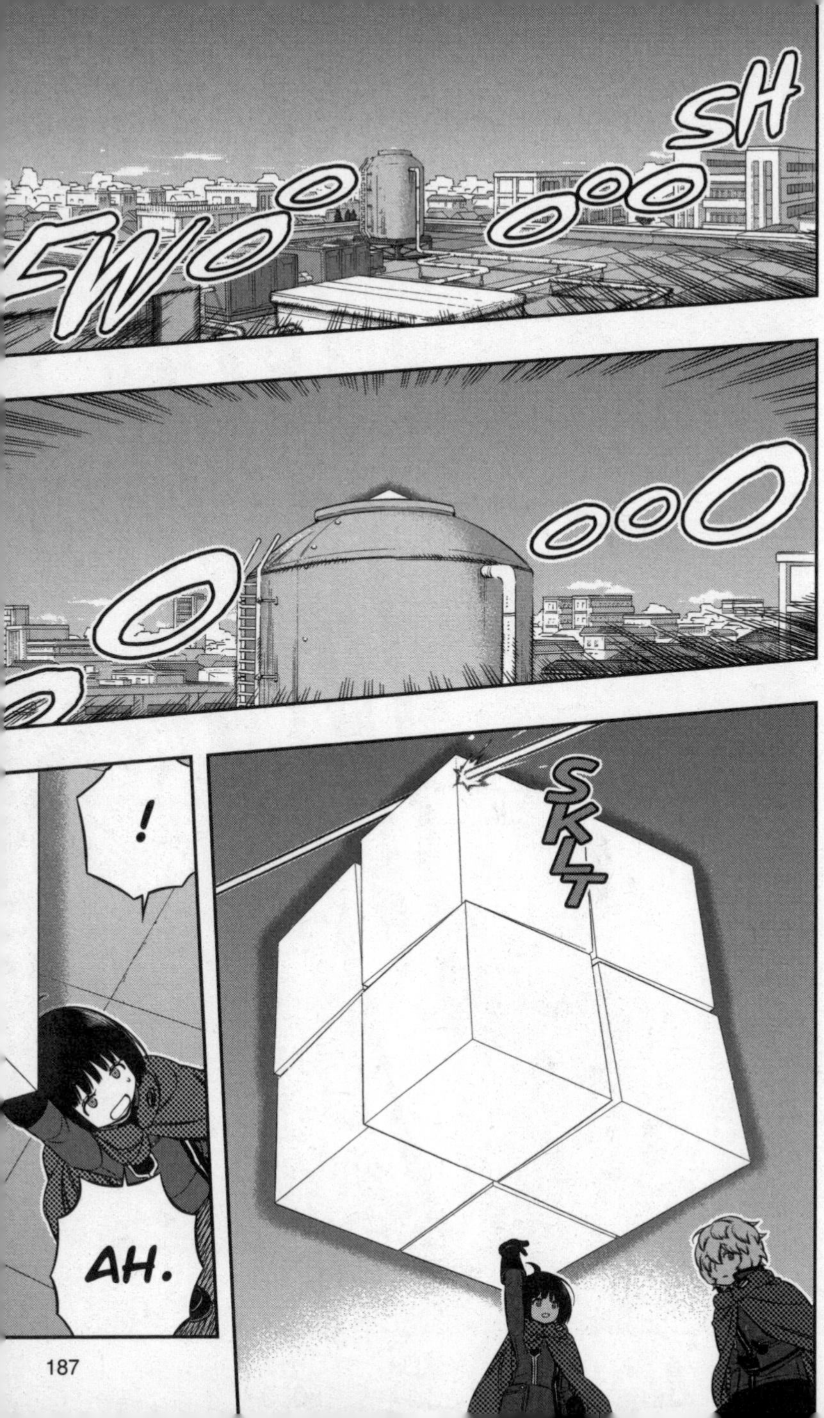
FWOOOOOSH
OOOOO
SKLT
!
AH.

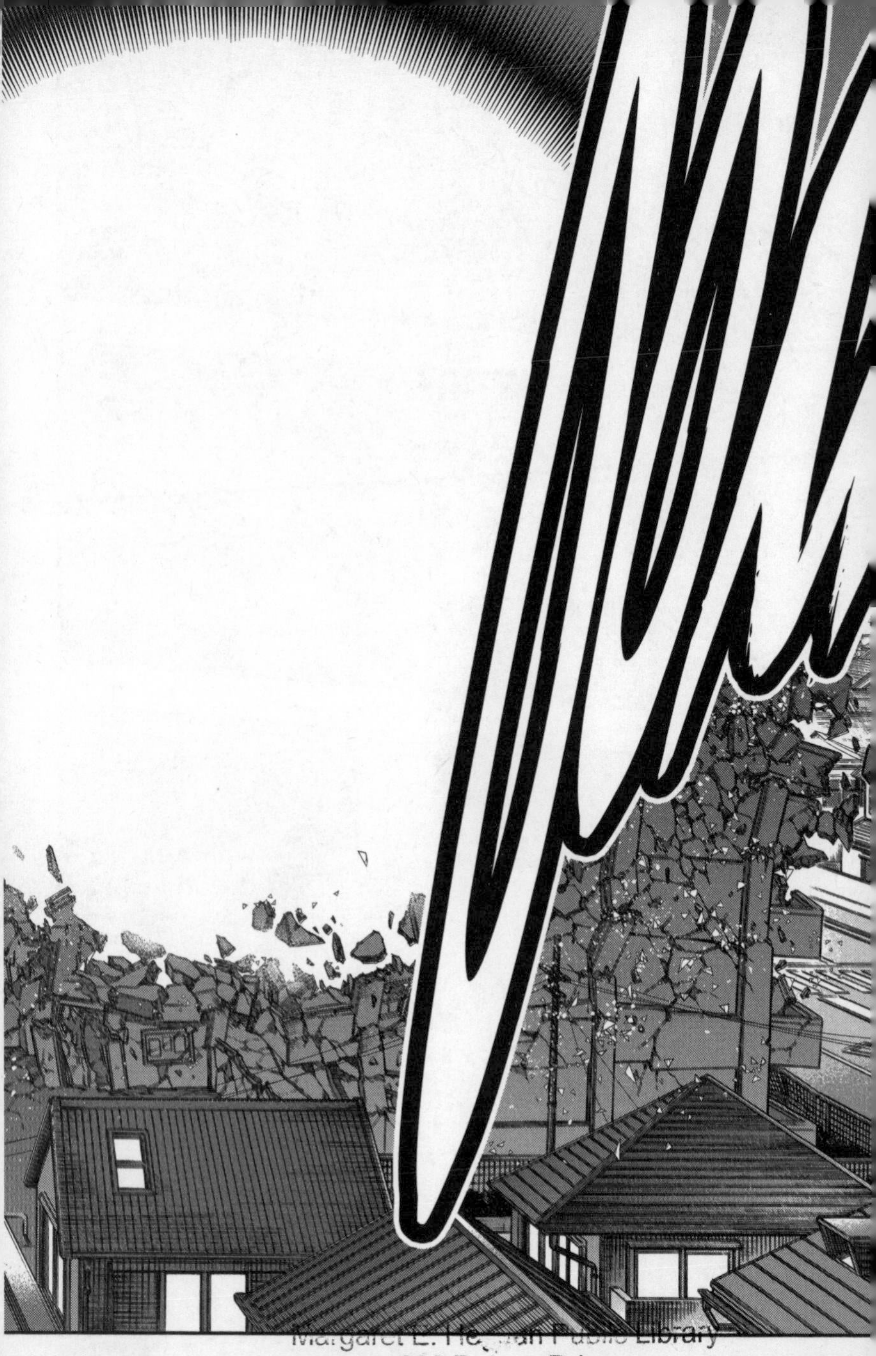

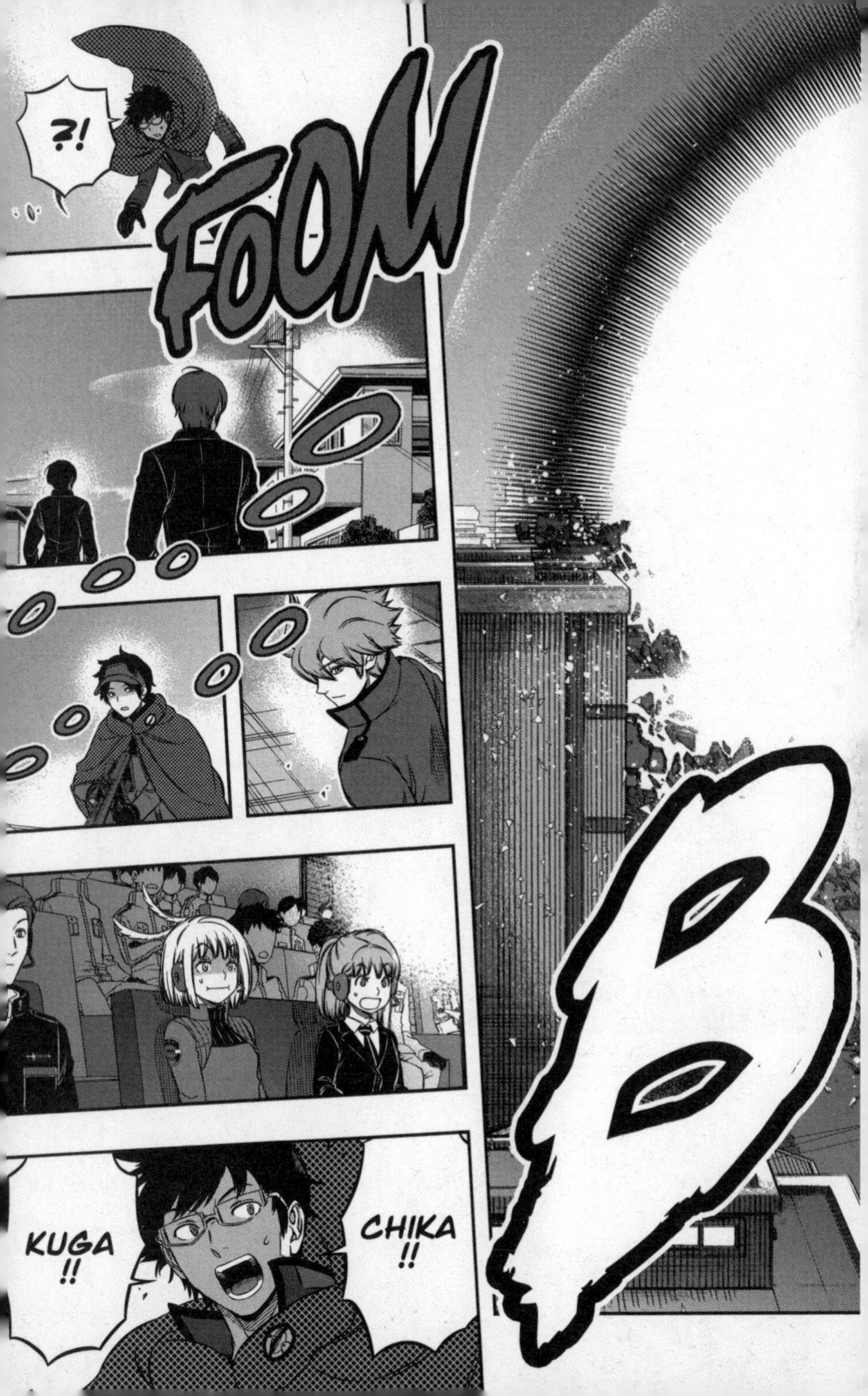
B
?!
FOOM
CHIKA !!
KUGA !!

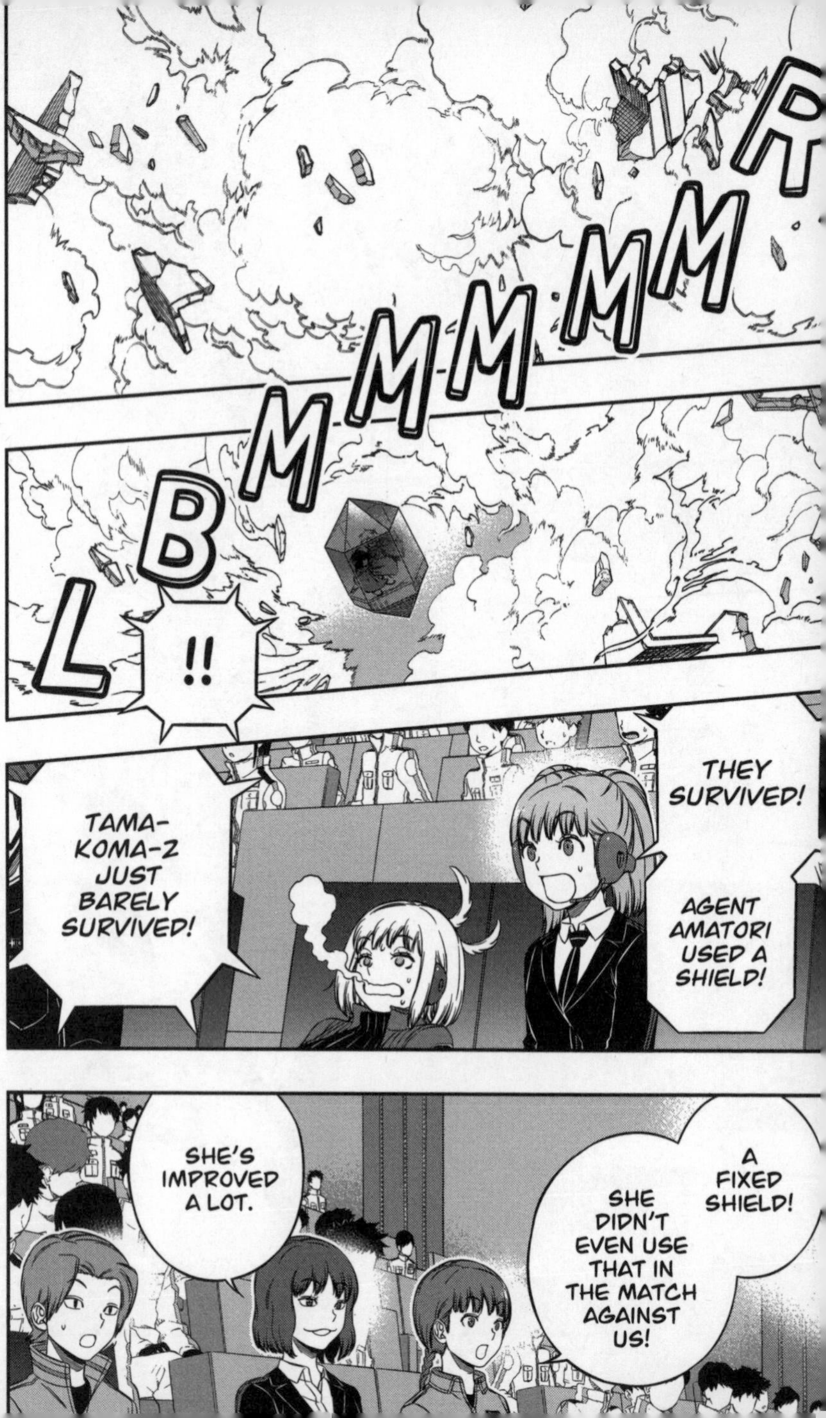
LBMMMMMR
!!
THEY SURVIVED!
AGENT AMATORI USED A SHIELD!
TAMA-KOMA-2 JUST BARELY SURVIVED!
A FIXED SHIELD!
SHE DIDN'T EVEN USE THAT IN THE MATCH AGAINST US!
SHE'S IMPROVED A LOT.

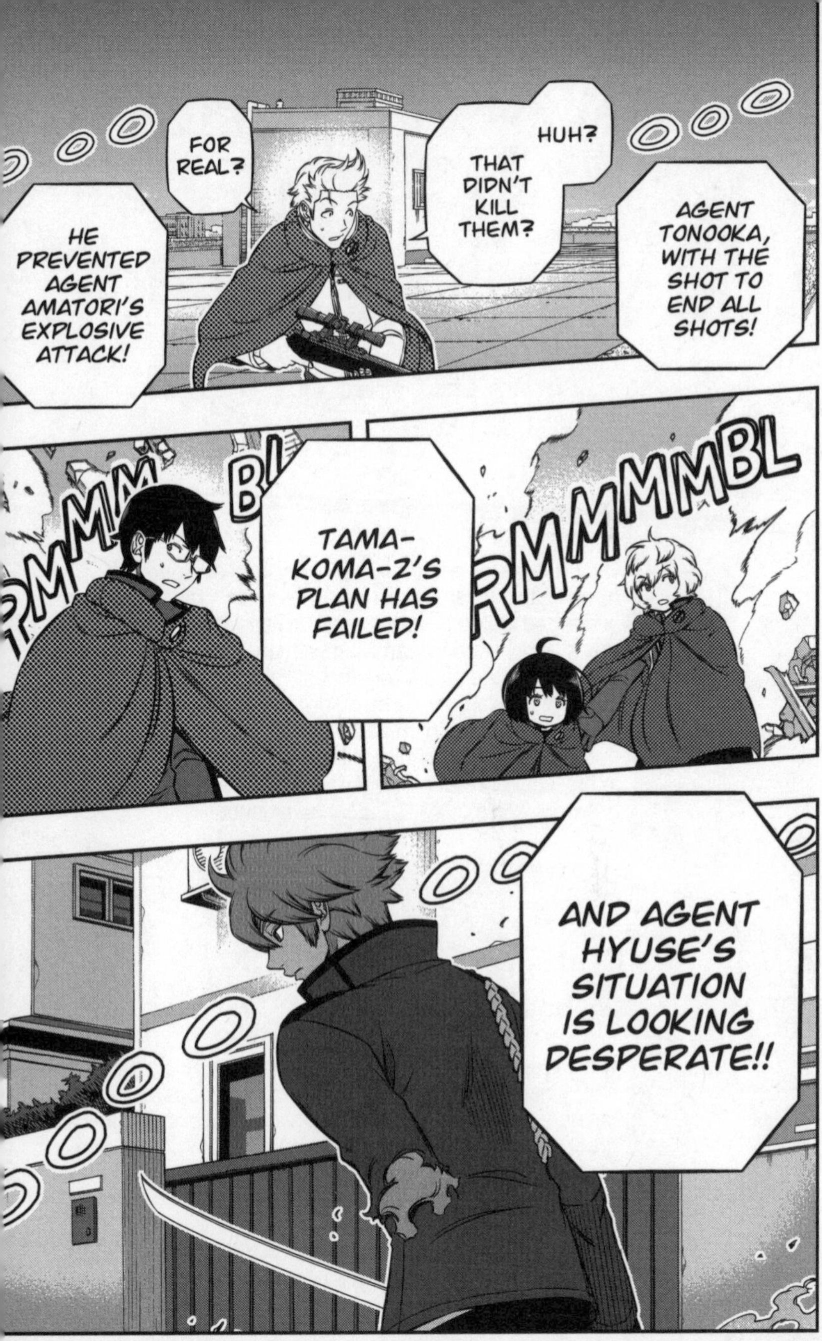
AGENT TONOOKA, WITH THE SHOT TO END ALL SHOTS!
HUH?
THAT DIDN'T KILL THEM?
FOR REAL?
HE PREVENTED AGENT AMATORI'S EXPLOSIVE ATTACK!
RMMMMMBL
TAMA-KOMA-2'S PLAN HAS FAILED!
AND AGENT HYUSE'S SITUATION IS LOOKING DESPERATE!!

WORLD TRIGGER

Bonus Character Pages

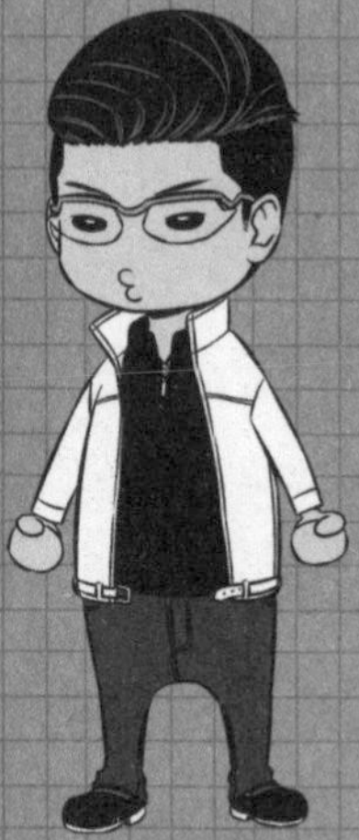

Yuba

Aaaaah!

The dual-pistol-wielding tough guy who decided that bizarre glasses are cool. He comes from a fancy prep school, as would be expected from someone with glasses that sharp. I actually came up with this dangerous manly man before the series began, but Yuba's appearance was delayed until after volume 20 out of fear that he would overpower the main characters, or that he would utterly destroy the world building. Like an older brother, he reins in his fellow 19-year-olds (i.e. Jin,, Iko, Arashiyama) and prevents Zaki's death-by-gag-exhaustion.

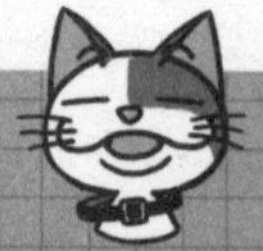

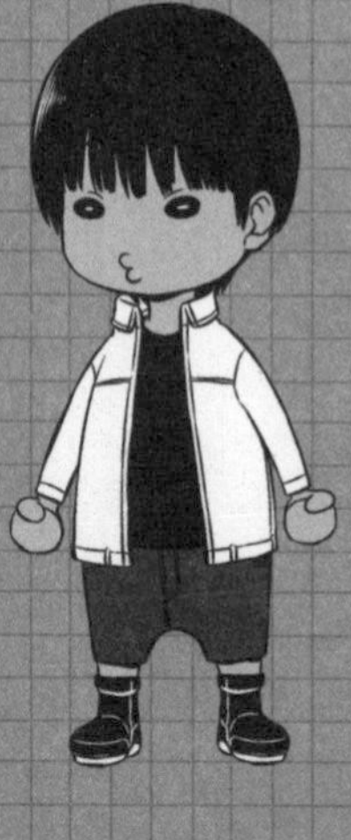

Obishima

Her brothers' names are Aoi and Midori

This tomboyish all-rounder was mistaken for a boy by the staff when she was drafted. Her family has been mikan farmers for four generations, since the days of her great-great-grandfather. Her tan comes from helping out on the family farm. Rumor has it that at school, Obishima is either in the baseball club, tennis club, soccer club or track-and-field club, and until somebody observes closely enough to get confirmation, it's as if she simultaneously exists in all four states of being. So please assume she's in whichever club you prefer.

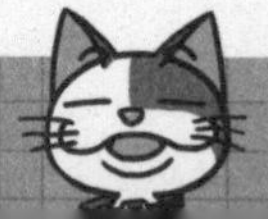

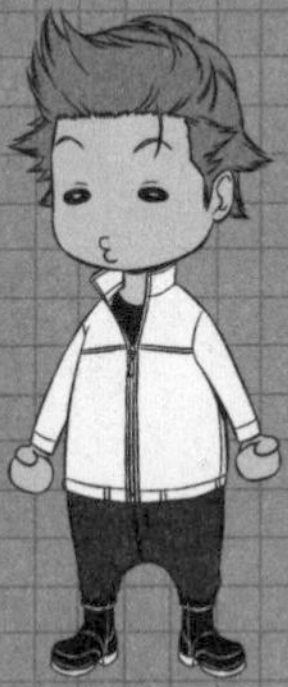

TONO

Full-Bodied Thud

This sniper is like mellow *katsuo-dashi* broth that balances out his more intensely flavored squad mates. Despite being a lone wolf who loves his alone time, Tono's got great communication skills, is naturally a good listener and conversationalist. He used to commute to HQ from home during middle school, but once he reached high school, he started living in a room at HQ by himself. Tono is highly valued as a conversation partner by his fellow boarders.

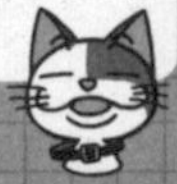

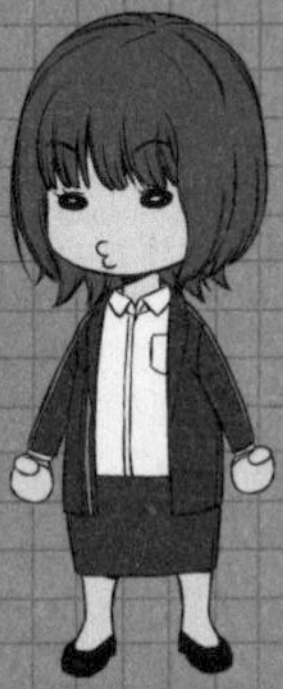

Nono

Mom is Nene, little sis is Nana

An athletic operator who's got the strong skills needed to manage her squad. Nono went to high school with Haya from Oji Squad, and the two girls are friends. She wasn't very popular in school due to her bluntness. Nono has the biggest bust size of any current character in the series, though I am not capable of bringing that size to life. In the end, it took a brand new technological transformation tool to give her rough sketches the necessary boost. An I-cup born of geometry.

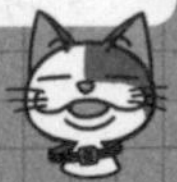

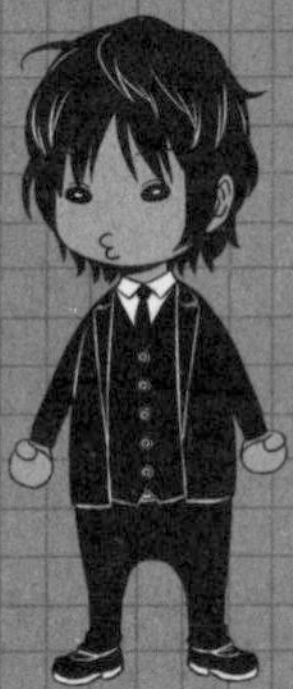

Ninomaru

Ultra-Rare Limited-Time Character

A synthesized monster with astounding special abilities who managed to increase the number of popularity poll votes by 16 percent all on his own. I introduced him without much thought, so now maybe he'll never show up again. Thanks to a mischievous, devilish scheme by the editor at *Jump SQ*, a bonus collectible headshot of Ninomaru was included in the magazine. Since I was in high spirits, he had done that particular illustration without even being asked. *Jump SQ* is pure hell.

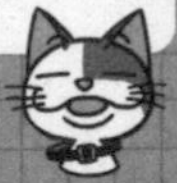

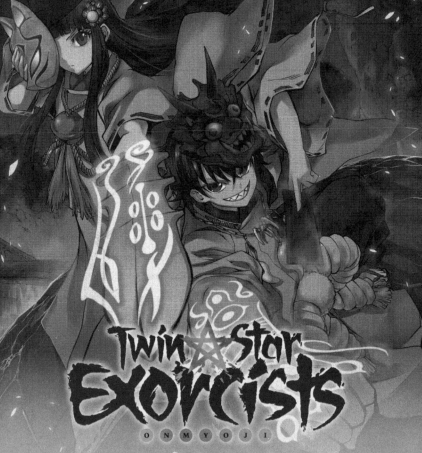